OTHER SIDE OF PARADISE

OTHER SIDE OF

PARADISE

KENNY PANDEY

VAJRA
BOOKS

Published and Distributed 2017 by

Vajra Books

Jyatha, Thamel, P.O. Box 21779, Kathmandu, Nepal

Tel.: 977-1-4220562, Fax: 977-1-4246536

e-mail: bidur_la@mos.com.np

www.vajrabooks.com.np

Other Side of Paradise

ISBN 978-9937-623-79-7

Printed in Nepal

DEDICATION

This book is dedicated to my loving mother Tommy Pandey, and very compassionate family members Bina Pandey, Dr. Ruby Pandey, Dr. Manju Pandey, Reena P. Chhetry, Robin Pandey, Apil Pandey, Himal Chhetry, Reva Pandey, Sophia Pandey, Vivit Chhetry, Adrian Pandey, Roman Chhetry, Mason Pandey and Jay Raj Singh.

Also, founder of INTERNATIONAL NEPALI COMMUNITY group that has nearly 10K members now, I dedicate the book to the COMMUNITY for its encouragement and affection, and to the entire underprivileged hard-working common people of America and Nepal.

ACKNOWLEDGEMENTS

First and foremost, I would like to express my gratitude to Pramod Sharma, who made arduous efforts in reading every word, line and chapter so that my writing and character formation would improve.

For technical support, my sincere gratefulness goes to Alexander Darino and Prem Singh for their hard work in formatting the manuscript in an attractive manner.

To Karen Armstrong, Mahesh Paudyal and Marie Williams, I extend my thankfulness for editing the manuscript in an energetic and passionate manner. Similarly, I am thankful to Gretchen Wills for coordinating the process from its very inception until the final product was launched with humane touch.

CHAPTER ONE

March 1985

Pemba had enormous love and respect for the mountains. He treated them as living creatures and as holy entities. For him, the mountains provided spiritual solace, inspiring faith and lessons of devotion in life. He was a simple, God-fearing and emotional person. He carried responsibility and affectionate feelings toward his mother and two sisters. His only goal was to provide higher education to his sisters and a comfortable life to his mother. Since he was the only son in the family, all the upbringing, daily domestic expenses, and maintenance of the family property fell directly on his shoulders. He was not satisfied with his current profession, but it made him a happy person, as he kept himself close with the mountains most of the time and supported his family's lifestyle. He had a vision to be a rich and happy person on earth. But at the moment, he did not like risk his life.

About six months earlier, an Australian woman fell in love with him during a trek. She asked him to move to Australia and marry her. She was blunt, aggressive, and determined. Pemba had hard times handling that delicate situation and refusing the proposal. Now he realized, maybe he made a mistake. In fact, Pemba had conflicting emotions that he might not understand a woman from another culture, and the relation might not last, due mainly to such cultural difference.

Pemba remembered Tsering, his close friend, who married a Japanese girl who had fallen in love with him during a trek, and later moved to Japan. After five years of their marriage, they got a baby girl. But they divorced immediately after. In life, Pemba did not want failure. He always thought, marriage should and must be for lifetime. Moreover, he did not like to live in foreign countries away from his family for a long time at the moment.

Pemba understood the struggle his parents undertook for his upbringing and education was untellable. He was grateful to his father's sacrifices and his efforts in managing the current property. He also admired Sir Hillary, who contributed knowledge and gave some financial support in building the house in Phaplu. Further, his mother's selfless love and care in making him a complete man were on the top of his eternal acknowledgments.

Although Pemba had a vision, he was a pragmatic person and did not like to have false dreams. During his college days, he accumulated vast knowledge of arts, culture and history of the world. He had a keen interest in local and world politics. He studied Marxism and Leninism besides the Western capitalist ideology. He neither liked the communist philosophy nor the Western capitalistic worldview. He preferred a pattern similar to Kibbutz Community in Israel, which he thought was more suitable for a happy and simple society. The origin of Kibbutz was a combination of socialism and Zionism and depended on agriculture. Since Nepal was primarily an agricultural society, Pemba thought that the Israeli Kibbutz model to develop a community and to turn it into a utopian society might be useful.

In political science, Pemba had studied the biographies of almost all the prominent leaders, beginning from Lenin to Chow-En-Lai, Nasser, Sukarno, Abraham Lincoln, Kennedy, and Jawaharlal Nehru. Every biography inspired him in a way, but Gandhi's miraculous non-violent movement to force the British out of India was a brilliant achievement.

Since Pemba followed the Buddhist path, he preferred a non-violent approach to life. He believed a solution to all political conflicts in the world lay in this approach. He was a conservative Buddhist, but in life, when he came out from his place every morning to go to work, he committed himself, "God, give me the power; if I am not able to help anyone today, let me not harm anybody." This was the kind of mantra he recited every day. Perhaps he realized this was not a recognized religion, but he cherished it.

During his golden days in the college, he slept hardly five hours a night. He spent his time reading poems of Wordsworth, Byron, Shelly, Keats, and Eliot, and fictions of Gorky, Tolstoy, and Chekov. *The Old Man and the Sea* and *To Kill a Mockingbird* were great influences on him. He especially liked James Hilton's *Lost Horizon*, a novel about the fictional, utopian, mystic and harmonious valley called Lamasery in Tibet. He read Tagore's *Gitanjali*, read the teachings of Confucius, *Bhagavad Gita*, the *New Testament*, the inscription of *Torah*, the *Koran*. Once, he even became a monk for a month, and lived in Kapan Monastery, Kathmandu. He was perhaps comparing his religion with world religion, trying to confirm if the real peace—inner happiness he meant—and the sense of achievement he had found from Buddhist religion were really superior. But he truly respected all the religions of the world, as they taught more or less the same thing, though delivered in different but unique manner and style of grace.

Pemba had a very strong build; he had broad shoulders, a round Mongolian face and dark, black eyes. He was always clean-shaven. A sharp weather–bitten face but quick smiles charmed his personality.

Pemba knew a beautiful Sherpa girl from his village with whom he went to Phaplu School together, and had a crush. He had not seen her for the past two years after college; he had no idea where she went. The other day, he heard through the grapevine that she went to Australia for her higher study. Well, he thought, perhaps by now, she has had a new boyfriend. She was two years younger to him and must have forgotten him. All these thoughts came to Pemba's memory; they just rewound like the pages of a book he had read during his college days.

Pemba was almost thirty-five—tall, almost six-foot, five nine, to be precise—and educated, from a Sherpa's perspective. He had a diploma from Sir Edmund Hillary School in Phaplu and was a graduate from Tribhuwan University in Microeconomics. He'd tried to get a suitable job in his field of study but could not find anything other than a teacher at one of the high schools in Kathmandu. After two years of teaching, he was fed up and returned to the village to take care of his mother and two sisters.

Pemba Sherpa was born in Phaplu in the northeastern part of Nepal, a mountainous place, and their house was at a walking distance from the Phaplu airstrip. In fact, after landing and coming out of the airport, this was the first white-wash stone-barricade house that looked like a European cottage. No one could ignore it. The house had a distinguished character and was noticeable to all passengers coming out of the Phaplu airport. Tourists considered the good-looking cottage a hotel, and some approached it to ask for accommodation as well. The house was built by Pasang Pemba's father sometime in 1965. It was said that while the house was being built, Sir Edmond Hillary gave some financial and technical help, and the house bore a unique New Zealand architecture and style. Unfortunately, Pasang passed away in early 1982. Pemba was thirty-two and was still in college, about to graduate. After Pemba's father's death, a trust of the Sherpas helped Pemba to get through his educational expenses and also supported his mother's domestic daily expenses for some time. Pemba's mother, Dolma, did hard work. She also had to sell a prime piece of land next to Wednesday marketplace down in Salleri Bazaar. Pemba's sisters—Tashi, twelve, and Nima, nine— still went to Hillary's school. Pemba had assured them that he would provide good education, and hoped to send them to some good college in future for higher education.

After he had handled a teaching job in Kathmandu for two years, Pemba's mother wanted to call him back home. But after working as a guide for a trekking company for over fourteen months, Pemba had an offer from Mountain Travel to work as a trekking coordinator and also to work in the office under the manager Dawa Sherpa, who was a family friend. He accepted the job, and after convincing his mother and sisters, he came back to Kathmandu. Dawa helped him get a suitable place to live in—close to the Mountain Travel office in Maharajgunj.

Pemba received a letter from his mother informing him that everything was fine in the family. His younger sister was sick, maybe due to cold; she had fever as well. She could not go to school for two days. Everything else was fine, except the sad news that one of his relatives, an old man of eighty-five, died of phenomena. They had enough grain and other food supplies for the winter. The letter further informed him that Sir Edmund Hillary had come to school last Tuesday.

All such news of normalcy was there in the letter. His mother could not write and read, but she took her nephew's help to send him the letter. Anyway, he got the news from his mother regularly, though the letter took a month since she posted to reach Pemba. Most of the time, the mother chose hand-delivery though People travelling between Kathmandu and the village.

Pemba's lifestyle in Kathmandu was simple and mostly eventless. He went to office in the morning and returned to his place in the evening. He cooked for himself, and sometimes, when he was exhausted, he went to a restaurant for dinner. This mostly happened during the weekends.

Now and then, Dawa took Pemba to the Boudha area, and they enjoyed *chhyang*, a typical beer made of rice, popular among the Sherpa and Gurung Community.

Once, a strange event took place. A matured hermit came to the place where the two were having *chhyang*. The man was tall with a bright face, sharp, penetrating eyes, and long and graceful white beard. He sat next to Pemba and requested him to offer a shot of *chhyang* to him too.

Surprised at this request, Pemba asked him, "I never saw a pious person like you drink *chhyang* before. But it will be my pleasure to order a shot for you."

"My child! I have just renounced the world and have chosen solitude. But my desires are like any other human being's." The old man continued, "Experiences in life are essential. It is a process of growing, and I also want to be a partly normal person sometimes."

While the man was talking, Dawa, Pemba, and two of their friends, Ang and Tsering looked on his face constantly. There was a kind of hypnotism in the way he talked. His personality as a whole bore an aura of attraction.

A boy of filthy looks brought a pint *chhyang* for the old man. He did not immediately touch it, however.

The old man fished out some tiny objects from his bag and distributed each one to Pemba's group. He said, "Let me give you small gifts; hope you will like them."

They were all handed a small Buddha made of blue jade; it was so beautiful that everyone accepted it with pleasure.

Accepting the gift, Pemba completely fell on the man's feet and thanked him. The moment he raised his head, the pious man had disappeared. The *chhyang* that was there a moment ago, too was nowhere to be seen.

For some time, nobody spoke; they just exchanged meaningful glances among themselves. The silence prevailed. Dawa paid the bill, and they left the restaurant with feelings of amazement.

Pemba carried that small jade Buddha in a golden locket on his neck all the time. He never parted with that precious gift. He believed, it was a good-luck charm for him. Once, in dream, he walked with Buddha as his follower and went from house to house to collect alms for their meals. When he woke up, he felt enormous strength mounting on him, and a different kind of peace and blissful feeling running throughout his body and mind. He believed in the existence of a powerful force that controls and operates the universe.

Buddha had a central position in Pemba's life. He analyzed his whole life's progress; by all means, he concluded that he was blessed. He remembered an incident that took place when he was once traveling to Pokhara by bus. Someone, without his knowledge, took away his wallet from his back pocket. The conductor came to ask for fare. But the wallet was missing. Pemba felt embarrassed, as the conductor was making all sorts of lousy comments on him. An old man with a dirty face full with beard, clad in haggard clothes, paid the fare for Pemba too. Pemba had not seen the old man before; when he approached to thank him for the help, suddenly, he vanished in front of his eyes. He didn't have time even to express his gratitude. Pemba really felt uneasy, but was pleasantly surprised. He told this incident to Dawa and to no one else, thinking that people might not believe such a ridiculous but divine story. Dawa believed him and said, "Such things happen in life."

When he was fifteen, Pemba once carried his neighbor's two-year-old sick child through over six miles to a clinic and brought her back. The whole village went talking about that incident for a long time. He had no idea how he got the energy, strength, and confidence for such an act. Only God knows.

The Phaplu School had a nice, clean, large cafeteria. The School provided free lunch to all its students. It had dieticians from New Zealand, who supervised the lunch menu and provided a balanced diet with carbohydrates, green vegetables, meat, and sweets. The grocery supplier was contracted by Pemba's father, who also cooked and supervised the food. Most of the time, between classes and during lunchtime, Pemba ate and learned different methods of cooking through his father in the kitchen. People said, he had magic in his hands, and everyone appreciated his father's cooking. Pemba also wanted to learn cooking techniques from his father. His mother's cooking never stimulated Pemba.

During his final year in the school, Pemba learned a great deal about cooking; he almost adopted his father's style and technique and turned into a good cook. This education had given him confidence to cook Western taste, which later became an asset during his treks.

After cooking almost three years for the Mountain Travel, Pemba earned reputation as an excellent cook from many trekkers from the USA, Australia and Europe, but the Japanese group brought their own cook from Japan. They were very conservative and insisted on Japanese food all the time. Pemba had not learned how to prepare Japanese food, though he was fond of sushi, tempura, and okinomiyaki. Consumption of this kind of food, he had heard, kept one healthy and prolonged life expectancy. The food platter presentation was highly attractive in a multicolored array balanced diet, and pleased everyone's eyes and taste.

As an employee of the Mountain Travel, Pemba had multiple tasks. He worked as an office assistant, guided the trekking group, and prepared food. Accordingly, his salary was handsome. Pemba had a good life in Kathmandu, and his family lived happily in Phaplu. He had no complaints with the travel management. He had an excellent relationship with Dawa, Robert, Colonel Bradley, and all other employees. He really appreciated the initiative of Dawa and Robert to keep his name and picture in the company brochure. He earned lots of compliments and heavy gratuities in foreign currency from the trekkers at the end of the trek during the farewell dinner. The amount was heavy, and normally, more than expected.

Pemba's coworkers were jealous of such an exuberant amount he received. But they didn't realize that Pemba wore many hats during the trek, along with his pre and post-management job.

At one point of time, a group of porters complained to the management that all the gratuities should be put in a common coffer, and everyone should divide it equally. Colonel Bradley had explained in a meeting that Pemba's contribution was much more than that of a porter as he worked as a cook, a guide and a member of the administration simultaneously, and was responsible for the successful operation of the expedition. The trekkers provided the amount directly to him; so he was entitled to that money. After that meeting, no one raised any question again, but jealousy continued to exist between Pemba and some of the porters. In reality, Pemba had outstanding compassion toward others. This was a quality everyone that came in contact with Pemba admired and loved.

Although, Pemba looked strong and his style of talking sometimes was commanding, he was in fact soft and delicate, and held no animosity toward anybody, either in the office or in his village. He tried to keep balance and make everyone happy. He thought he had softness in personality through his mother, and a commanding style of communication, perhaps inherited from his father. Humans could not escape the core genes of their parents; they necessarily inherit some of their traits.

Pemba remembered one very pleasant incident that took place when he was in the seventh grade at Phaplu School. While playing on the school grounds, he found some ancient Tibetan gold coins, marbles, and a gold ring embossed with a magnificent statue of Buddha. He looked around, but there was no one; the things were lying in an isolated place, hidden under a stone on the southern part of the school ground. He thought the gold coins and Buddha ring were antiques and might fetch a large value. He was happy, and while sleeping, he kept the stuffs under his pillow.

That night, he dreamed that he was sitting with a number of pupils, wearing saffron dress, and the Buddha was under a large tree, giving a sermon and saying, "If you find anything that does not belong to you, you must return it to the owner. That would provide you peace, and you would be rewarded with a significant gift, which would help you to achieve nirvana in your life."

Immediately after the dream, he woke up and made up his mind: he would return those coins, marbles, and ring to the school that very day.

Prior to his class, Pemba dropped by the school office and returned those valuables to a teacher. The teacher was extremely happy with his honesty, and thanked him. A few hours later, the headmaster of the school came to his class and asked Pemba to stand next to him.

"My dear students," he said, "I would like to share an exemplary event with you today. Pemba came to our office this morning and handed over these coins, marbles, and this Buddha gold ring. If they belong to any of you, please come to our office and place your claim. We encourage this kind of sincerity from all the students at our school; please give a round of applause to Pemba."

The headmaster took Pemba to all the classes and repeated more or less the same version everywhere. Pemba was made a big hero and considered the most honest person in the school. During the school anniversary, the headmaster gave him a nice, impressive certificate, which his mother hung in his bedroom wall.

Pemba had a vision to travel across the world, starting from Lumbini—birthplace of the Buddha—to Bodhgaya in India, and then to see His Holiness Dalai Lama in Dharamshala. After the religious trip, he wanted to go to the Taj Mahal, and then travel to Australia to see the famous opera house, to Los Angeles for Hollywood, to Grand Canyon for the spectacular view, and then travel further to Niagara Falls on the East Coast, stroll in the shadow of Big Ben in London, shout from the top of the Eiffel Tower, observe the Sistine Chapel in Rome, see the Peeing Boy in Belgium and matadors in Spain, cruise the canal in Amsterdam, witness the Archipelago of Greece, and scale Kilimanjaro in Africa and Mount Fuji in Japan. Now it was just a dream for Pemba; one day, maybe he could turn it into reality. Who knows!

About two years ago in the month of March in 1983, Mountain Travel sponsored a rafting program in River Trisuli. There were about twenty agents specialized in adventure travel from the States, who came to participate in the rafting educational tour. Dawa and Pemba had the responsibilities given by the management. Colonel Bradley wanted to make this educational trip a grand success.

During the rafting session, everything was going smoothly. Suddenly, a raft occupied by five people—incidentally all from Boulder, Colorado—drifted toward a large stone and smashed into it, full force. Everyone dropped out of the boat and fell in the river. It happened in that area, where the force and speed of the river were unusually high. Pemba, who was ahead of the raft saw it, and without thinking, dived into the river. It was a miracle, but he was able to take all five of them out one by one to safety. The event was simply an act of God; the whole rescue process was captured by a person from the group in his video camera.

When Colonel Robert saw the footage in the office the next day, he could not believe his eyes. It was a rare act of heroism from Pemba. The footage was sent to the Department of Tourism, and they had an elaborate press conference in which they accorded a grand felicitation to Pemba at the national level. Moreover, Colonel Bradley presented him a ten thousand-rupee check for his daring episode. Besides, all five people from Boulder, Colorado sent him a cashier check worth five-thousand dollars.

Money did not matter much; the friendship Pemba had made with those five people he rescued was a treasure for him. Jack, out of that boat group, had become quite close to him. Their friendship turned into an outstanding relationship. Jack, who owned a rafting company, wanted Pemba to go with him to Colorado and work for him as a rafting technician. Jack had even promised to arrange all immigration papers for him. But Pemba turned down his offer politely.

Since the capsizing and rescue incident, their friendship had grown closer. Pemba received Christmas cards and letters from Jack at least two times a year; he never forgot to mention the invitation for a visit to Colorado at Pemba's convenience.

Pemba did not have many things to offer to his friends. He did not have many friends, but the few friends he had were very close and intimate. During his school days, he had a close friend Kalden from his own village. They liked each other and spent all their spare time going moving around in the village together. They also did combined study, either at Pemba's or Kalden's house, even sleeping overnight during test time. They shared each other's kitchens, and both the families treated them as their own members.

Once when Kalden's father was leading a trek in Mustang, his mother got sick, and they took her to a nearby hospital in Phaplu. The doctor suggested that she needed an immediate surgery of her appendix; otherwise, her life would be in danger. Unfortunately, Kalden's family did not have money to meet the operation expenses. On Kalden's request, Pemba asked his father to manage the cash. Kalden would never forget the compassion shown by Pemba and his family. After nearly six months, Kalden's father paid the money back to Pemba's father.

Pemba always went beyond his responsibilities to help his friends. Once, while he was in the college, a friend from his village did not receive money from his home on time. Pemba paid the tuition fees when that boy was about to be expelled from the school.

Somehow, Pemba did not want to see his friends in peril. He tried to pitch in whenever he could afford, and provided some support. Most of his friends considered him a compassionate, generous, and extremely helpful person.

Pemba's philosophy in life was to live and let others live. He felt human life span was limited to a hundred years, and the earth had existed for millions of years; so understanding life and the universe was highly complicated. The punishment and rewards in life were given on the basis of your deeds during your lifetime. If you were a good person, your life would be comfortable, happy, and without problems; and on other hand, if your deeds had not been good, you would have all the trouble and misfortune during your lifespan. Consequently, life would be miserable and one would be far from bliss. Pemba had full faith in this, and he wanted to devote all kinds of positive assistance to others as much as possible. He knew he could not be another Buddha, but he could be a significant human being at least.

Pemba remembered the situation in which Diana was thrust some time back. Diana suddenly got sick in the hotel on the next day after her arrival in Kathmandu. Prior to the trek, she had to be admitted to the hospital as soon as possible as per the advice of the doctor arranged by the hotel. It was an odd hour, around 1:00 a.m. in the morning. Colonel Bradley had phoned Pemba as Dawa was on a trip to Thailand to print the office brochure. Otherwise, normally, Dawa handled such situations. Pemba went to Shanta Bhawan Hospital on his motorbike. Both Colonel Bradley and Robert were waiting for him in the hospital lobby.

"Pemba, Diana is being treated by a British doctor, and her condition is slightly better now," Robert said. "If only you could spend the night here and look after her…," he added in a tone of request.

"Of course, Robert, I will be here and look after her along with the nurse."

"Please call us in the morning, and keep us informed."

"Sure," Pemba assured them.

In the morning, around nine, a team of doctors came to Diana's room with an X-ray plate and some diagnostic reports of blood and urine. In the meantime, Colonel Bradley and Robert came to the hospital and went to see the chief physician for consultation. They came out at around ten and informed Pemba, "Diana's situation is critical. She needs an immediate operation, but hospitals in Nepal are not equipped with the proper instruments; so they need to take her to a hospital in Delhi."

Robert asked Pemba, "Can you go with her to Delhi as an attendant?"

Pemba replied without hesitation, "I can."

They arranged a flight leaving at one-thirty in the afternoon for Delhi. In the meantime, the US Embassy in Kathmandu had arranged a last-minute operation in Delhi at Safderjung Hospital through the US Embassy in Delhi. All arrangements were fixed, and the hospital was sending an ambulance to the airport to pick up Diana.

They arrived in Delhi at two forty-five and reached the hospital at three-thirty. A medical team was waiting for them at the hospital, and they rushed Diana to the operation room straightaway.

After two hours, as Pemba was waiting outside the operation room, a doctor came out and informed him that everything went well with Diana, and her condition was normal.

No one knew, but Pemba really prayed hard and used all his power and inner strength for Diana's recovery. After the good news, no one but Pemba seemed really happy. As per the doctors' advice, Dina would need at least two days' bed rest. During those two days, Pemba took good care of her and provided all sorts of comfort. Diana had never experienced so much closeness; she had never received this degree of unselfish services of Pemba which she did in the last two days. Even her son might not be able to do what Pemba had done for her.

On the third day, Diana moved to Claridge Hotel from the hospital. Her husband and daughter reached from Seattle. Pemba—after meeting Diana's husband Mark, who was an executive at Boeing, and daughter Margaret—left the Claridge Hotel and went to a friend's house in Karol Bagh. It was an extremely emotional parting with Diana.

Angden, one of Pemba's friends, ran an antique shop in Connaught Place and had been living in Delhi for the past six years. They had a great reunion. After Pemba spent a night with Angden's family, he left Delhi the next day.

After nearly two months, Pemba received a registered mail from Seattle. When he opened it, he saw a cashier check worth three thousand dollars and a long letter from Diana with an invitation to come to Seattle. Pemba had never expected it.

Pemba was also given a promotion immediately after his return from Delhi. In fact, he had not hoped for such unexpected rewards; he was simply making casual and normal human efforts.

Pemba had done numerous favors for his friends and had accomplished commendable achievements in the course of his duties at work. But above all, his priority was his family. He loved them all closely and deeply. Besides his parents, he loved both of his sisters, and always tried to be close with them whenever possible. His reunion with them during their new year in Kathmandu about three years back when he was teaching at a school was remarkable. His family visited from Phaplu and stayed with him in a one-room apartment they rented. They had difficulties accommodating the entire family together, but they had developed an unforgettable bond among themselves. He was happy to take them to the zoo and Swoyambhu Buddhist stupa on the top of the mountain; the view from above the city was spectacular. He remembered how a small monkey followed his sisters, and they were very scared.

They visited Kapan Monastery, where all of them had a wonderful time and prayed along with the chief Lama, who gave them a warm blessing. Pemba noticed his parents' faces lightened with joy when the chief Lama blessed them. From the Monastery, they went to Boudha area where Pemba bought gifts for his sisters and parents. They had a Tibetan meal, which was delicious and enjoyable. Pemba told his sisters and parents about the early morning bus trip to Lumbini and Pokhara. They left Pemba's apartment early for the bus stop; everyone was excited for the trip. The bus left on time.

"How long will it take to reach Lumbini?" his father asked.

"About eleven hours. We will stay a night in Bhairahawa and go to Lumbini next morning." Pemba knew there were no good places to stay in Lumbini.

"Have you been there earlier?" Pemba's father was curious.

"Yes, twice."

"Did you feel peaceful there?"

"Of course. It was enchanting," Pemba expressed.

"Brother, did you see the actual place of Lord Buddha's birth?" his younger sister questioned.

"Yes. There's a balcony around it. Everyone should have a close look. There is also a pond where the Buddha's mother took bath."

Dolma's face glittered and expressed divine happiness.

Pemba had enjoyed the company of his family in the bus and felt greater happiness in providing all the information as an enlightened guide. The bus was picking up speed. In the midst of noises in the mountains, no one talked for a long time. Everyone was engaged, watching the fantastic mountain sceneries, serpentine roads, and blue river flowing deep in the distance.

"You may have lunch; will be here for an hour," the conductor announced to the passengers.

All the passengers, including Pemba's family, came out of the bus. The lunch-counter looked clean and attractive with tall pine trees in the background, and a water tap flowing on one side continuously. The water had a deep white color that was inviting, and the passengers formed a queue to taste the water. After drinking some water and washing their hands and feet, they slowly walked into the restaurant. There were two kinds of food: vegetarian and non-vegetarian. Pemba's family chose non-vegetarian food for everyone. The meals were delicious and tasty. Pemba liked the food which had rice, lentil, goat meat and cauliflower in the course, but it tasted flat; he requested green hot chilies and enjoyed it afterwards.

After nearly an hour, the bus left the restaurant. Now the road seemed smoother. So, the bus speed up. Normally, after food, the passengers in the bus relax and look as though they are intoxicated. Almost everyone starts dozing. Pemba saw, his family was also half asleep; he did not like to disturb them. He had his own thoughts and feelings. He was happy that he had convinced his parents to leave their place for a few weeks. Normally, their home was their comfort zone, and they did not like to leave. He'd had hard time convincing his father; his mother wanted the trip, though. Pemba was happy to see his family enjoying the trip; the younger sister was still very young, and she might not remember after some time.

The bus reached Bhairahawa toward the evening. Pemba, who was familiar with a lodge, took his family to it, and they spent the night there. They enjoyed the meals inside the cabin as everyone was tired after a long bus journey, but was excited at the fact that they would be in Lumbini the following morning. They went to sleep early in excitement. Pemba thought he was doing a humble duty toward his family for managing this religious trip. He thanked God for providing him this opportunity.

They arrived at Lumbini after a quick breakfast. It was a huge area, and in the middle was a large milky-white stupa alluring the visitors. Far away, a drum was penetrating the melancholy and peaceful atmosphere. The sound of a Japanese monk praying echoed in the region.

Although the reconstruction of Lumbini area had started at the request of the United Nations Secretary-General U Thant from Burma, about twenty years back, people were still working to finish various projects. Pemba's family walked slowly to all the important areas, including the Maya Devi shrine, the birthplace of Buddha, and they spent sufficient time in the pond area next to Asoka's pillar. Pemba noticed that his mother had become very sentimental watching all the places; she had tears in her eyes and blissful emotions shimmering on her face.

They stayed in the garden almost the entire day and all the family members enjoyed every single moment of the trip.

"Pemba, we thought of coming here a long time ago, but you know, we could not get away as there were no flight," Pasang said, as if he were thanking his son for bringing them to this pious place.

"I know it was hard, but now we have planes at our doorstep."

"I understand. Sonam is building a hotel close to our house in Phaplu."

"Yes, a French partner is investing all the money," Pemba confirmed.

Pemba and Pasang were walking ahead. Pemba's mother and sisters followed them. Soon were got out of the camp area. The Japanese monk's drum prayer was still echoing in the vicinity. Golden paint emanated from the parting sun, making the entire atmosphere extremely peaceful, added by the chirping of birds from the nearby *peepal* tree close to a pond, making their departure quite memorable. Pemba felt he left behind a piece of his soul in the garden.

The next morning, they left for Pokhara by bus. The moment they reached Pokhara Valley, the sceneries were fantastic, alluring enough to attract a crowd of people from far and near. The mountain's reflection on the lake was especially spectacular. The lush green vegetation surrounding the other sides of the lake produced an incredible impact on everyone's intellect.

Pemba thought Wordsworth and Shelly could have made this place immortal long before with their inspirational poems, had they ever been here. This place could have been exposed to the world so that by now, it could have been preserved as one of the most beautiful places on earth, and the spot might have had significant value on the tourism map of the world.

"This place is more beautiful than I had imagined," Pasang commented.

Nobody spoke, as if everyone was in agreement.

"We will go to Sarangkot tomorrow morning. We will have a majestic view of Pokhara Valley from the top," Pemba announced to his family.

In Pokhara, an uncle of Pemba from a distant relation ran a hotel on a leased property. The family was planning to go to that hotel named Mount Fishtail. From the bus stop, they rented a taxi and without problem reached the lodge. The lodge was next to the airport, carrying a commanding view of the airport in the south and toward the north, the famous Fishtail Mountain looked close, as though you could touch it with your hand straightaway.

The first day of their arrival, they traveled to all the major spots of Pokhara—the Gupteshwar Cave, Davis Fall, and a monastery atop a mountain—and had a delicious dinner to their fill at a famous Thakali restaurant where Pemba had come previously too, during his college excursion.

The early morning trip before sunrise to Sarangkot was outstanding. They had the most magnificent view of Pokhara Valley.

After that breathtaking scene, they hiked to the top of the mountain, where a restaurant was so popular that even a simple meal turned into gourmet cuisine entirely because of the water of that mountain. That day was not an exception; everyone, even the tourists, liked the ethnic food served there so much. Besides the exceptional food, the scene from the top of the mountain was awesome. People liked to linger in the restaurant for a long time, but darkness was engulfing the area slowly. So everyone hurried to return to Pokhara.

In spite of Pemba's family's desire to stay a few more days in the most beautiful place on earth, Lhosar was getting closer. Pemba's mother needed to make lots of preparations for the festival. So they decided to leave next morning for Kathmandu and then fly to Phaplu.

Pemba, after this remarkable trip, felt that he had completed one obligation to his family. He got satisfaction and thanked the Almighty for the occasion; he also felt he'd done one of the prime responsibilities in life as a senior and only son. In fact, most of the parents expect some kind of obligation from their son when he stands ably on his own feet and can afford such expenses with time and money.

Pemba knew the whole village would be talking about this trip. His parents would be happy, and their reputation in their social circle would elevate.

After they arrived in Kathmandu, Pemba's family left on the third day, as they had to wait for the seats confirmation on the plane. At the airport, prior to the flight's departure, Pasang embraced and told Pemba quietly in the ear, "Son, you made us proud."

After his family left, Pemba's attention was drawn to the opening of his school, next week. After a short break, he once again became busy, as classes resumed. He needed to prepare lessons and then a test paper for the quarterly examination, followed by paper grading and test results. He would be extremely busy until the school closes for a week for Lhosar.

***

CHAPTER TWO

September 1985

Thirty-eight hundred Wilshire Boulevard in Los Angeles was popular, and was associated with a renowned as the corporate address of defense lawyer's Adam Smith, recognized as the second top defense lawyer in the country. Smith was a tall personality with azure, shrewd and sharp eyes, a chiseled nose, high cheekbones, a round face with grizzly fur, lower face concealed with a beard, and gold-rimmed sparkling white glasses. For a man, the beard can be as much a personal statement as a pair of shoes or a lipstick shade for a woman. Adam's whole magnificent personality was reflected in his beard: a distinguished identity.

At the end of a case, normally it was a tradition that both the lawyers—plaintiff's and defendant's—commented on the judgment. During TV coverage, Adam's comments would always be fascinating and dramatic— a hot topic for national tabloids.

Besides his shrewd eyes, his charming personality was a matter of interest in gossip columns in some of the national magazines.

Linda Barton, after her graduation from UCLA, accepted the job of secretary to Adam Smith. One of the main reasons was Adam's soft-spoken manner and magnetic expressions that prevailed all the time on his charming face.

The office suite was large and spacious. The small room attached to Smith's office was occupied by Linda, and the room allowed a panoramic view of the road outside between Wilshire Corners and Hollywood Boulevard. The Intersection could be seen vividly, and at a distance, part of Beverly Hill Hotel could be glimpsed from one side of the room, though it looked so tiny from this distance. This property with a prestigious name was an icon in itself.

Monday morning, on her way to the office, Linda was stuck in the usual traffic. It was already seven twenty-five, and she was about ten miles away from the office. She'd left home early in consideration of the nasty traffic, so that she could get to the office a bit earlier to prepare Smith's daily routine and appointments. She had all the concerned files to compile and make ready for the court for all the partners.

She liked to reach the office at least an hour earlier than Smith, which was around eight forty-five on weekdays if he was in town. Traffic was moving slowly but steadily, and Linda hoped she would be in the office by at least close to eight. She looked at the digital clock on the dashboard; it was now seven twenty-nine. Linda knew, Smith was never late to the office because he used his Bell Helicopter, which landed on the terrace of the building at eight forty on weekdays, and usually, after hopping in the short elevator for the thirty-fifth floor, he was in the chamber by eight forty-five sharp.

Linda's attention went back to the traffic again. She was almost at the exit and, after that, would shortly be on Wilshire Boulevard. It would only take a short drive to 3800's underground garage and the thirty-fifth floor. Linda sighed in relief and breathed deeply. It was almost seven fifty-five. She reached the garage and found a proper parking spot close to the elevator. She approached the elevator and at eight, reached the office and then finally her room.

Linda's routine was no different that day. She had been following it for five years. But before she got to the usual routine, she had a pressing desire for a cup of coffee from the break room.

"Hi Linda, how was your weekend?" She heard the voice of Kathy from behind on the way to break room.

"Oh, Kathy, it was great but short, as usual, you know what I mean."

Kathy nodded in approval. "How is your long-awaited vacation coming?"

The question brought a fresh breath of air on Linda's face; it suddenly glowed with happiness and childlike delight. "Oh, yeah, October; it's just around the corner. I need to prepare so many things in advance for that trekking to Mount Everest area." Linda finished her sentence and then added immediately, "I've received part of the itinerary and will have the final one by the end of this week."

"Paul never stops talking about it," Kathy added, "He likes it so much even after six years, he mentions it frequently."

"I am looking forward to it. Thanks, Kathy!"

Both left the break room with a coffee mug each in their hands.

Kathy, an attorney and a partner of the firm, had come earlier, and Linda walked a short distance to her room on the right side of Kathy's office.

Paul was also an attorney and associate in the firm as a partner. It was Paul who'd motivated Linda to go for a trek to Nepal. She was involved with a Buddhist sanctuary in West Los Angeles, a short distance from her home—a small but cozy place for meditation and learning the Buddhist way of life. The Dalai Lama had visited there about three years back, and his speech had left a lasting impression about the Buddhist religion and their way of life. Linda had been profoundly impressed with the Dalai Lama, and she found their way of life so peaceful, out of the world, compared to the crime going on in East Los Angeles. She thought it was needed badly to combat the violent American gun culture.

In fact, she might stop pursuing further study in law and get a master's and PhD in Buddhist religion and culture. She'd already discussed that path with one of the professors of Eastern religions at UCLA and obtained the necessary information; but first things first, she needed to finish her master's—which could be done within two years and needed thirty credit hours. Then she would pursue higher education, a PhD in a subject of her liking and perhaps take up a teaching job after that. She was already fed up with law, and after Nepal, she would leave Smith and Associates and go for full-time study at UCLA perhaps next fall—a tempting thought at the moment. She snapped out of her thought process and tried to concentrate on the present, which was more important for her.

"Linda, what are my appointments for today?" Smith's voice echoed through the intercom.

"I will be there shortly with the list," Linda responded.

"Thanks, dear."

Linda printed out a copy of the day's schedule and went to Smith's office.

"Good morning." Linda never addressed Smith as 'Sir'. He despised the word and had instructed her not to use it for him.

"Oh, very good morning! How are you? Sorry to make you rush. I may have to fly to the East Coast today for a preliminary hearing with one of our clients. Linda, dear, is it possible to squeeze all my appointments before lunch?"

Linda glanced closely at the appointments after 1:00 p.m. There were only two follow-ups. She could possibly shift them to Wednesday, but she needed to inform the clients. Tuesday—normally a conference on every first week of the month—Smith spent the entire day discussing existing cases with his partners and all other offices in the Midwest, South, and East Coast to follow up on their progress.

"Yes, Mr. Smith, I could postpone Mrs. Carter and Mr. Fredrick for Wednesday but need to inform them. When will you be back in town?"

"If I get a red-eyes flight on Tuesday night, I will be here Wednesday afternoon for work. Does that solve the problem?"

"That could work perfect," Linda assured Smith.

"Will you please reconfirm with John that they will have the hearing set up for 9:00 a.m. tomorrow?"

"Sure, Mr. Smith."

Linda left and went to her office to call John to New York. The next moment, Linda heard John's secretary, Marsha's, voice.

"Yes, Linda, how are you? What can I do for you, honey?"

"Marsha, I am fine here; how is the weather like today?"

"Not bad, sunny but with a touch of Canadian cold wave."

"Marsha, please do me a favor. Mr. Smith wants to reconfirm the preliminary hearing of that famous Chester case. Can you confirm if it will be tomorrow? If so, he will visit New York tonight."

"Linda, may I put you on hold for a second?"

"Sure, go ahead, Marsha," Linda confirmed.

There was a short hum on the line.

"Sorry for the hold, Linda. Yes, John confirmed it is for tomorrow at nine."

"I appreciate your help, Marsha; I'll talk to you soon. Mr. Smith, John confirmed it is for tomorrow at nine," Linda passed on the message.

"Great, Linda. Thanks."

Now Linda needed to call the travel agent and make travel plans for Smith with flights, limo, and hotel—the Doubletree in Times Square. It was done within fifteen minutes. Linda received a faxed confirmation for the ticket and hotel. She dropped the documents in front of Smith, who glanced at them and inquired, "Linda, what time is the flight?"

"Two thirty, and as usual, with Delta." Linda continued, "Limo's confirmed, and hotel's okay at Tree."

When Linda was about to leave the room, he said, "Linda, would you please call my wife and tell her about my New York trip today?"

"Sure, Mr. Smith."

Smith left the office at around twelve-thirty for the airport. Normally, the office atmosphere changed after Smith's departure. Linda felt a sort of calmness prevail in her mind like the peace and serenity that comes after the end of a hurricane. She also felt a sort of desire to eat something delicious. She'd brought some salad with fresh cucumbers, carrots, and lettuce from home.

Somehow, Linda felt she'd developed a tendency of not eating meat in her meals. But a vegetarian diet could be difficult to support her lifestyle, which had developed since her birth.

Her family, which hailed from Ohio, was fond of red meat; so every meal had a heavy portion. Perhaps as the Dalai Lama said, if Linda could remember correctly, meat made one's nature violent and may prevent core happiness. Linda realized, in her every meal, the meat portion was slashing gradually, knowingly or unknowingly. The way it was going suggested, she might turn a complete vegetarian one day, quite soon.

Linda was on her way to the break room. Paul was following her.

"Hi, Linda! Has Smith left for the airport?"

"I forgot to ask him about a case."

"Yes, he did."

"By the way, how is your trip shaping up?"

"It's getting there, and I am really excited, Paul."

"Make sure you acclimatize yourself at least four days prior to the trek by staying in Kathmandu and the Namche area," Paul cautioned Linda.

"Yes, the Mountain Travel in Frisco has taken care of that." Linda continued, "Paul, do you feel I am physically fit for this hefty trip?"

Linda, your age, stamina, and energy satisfy me; did you have a physical recently? I suggest a thorough physical check-up before your departure."

"Yes, indeed, I had a complete physical last quarter and am due again at the end of September."

"Linda, stop worrying so much; everything will be fine. After your trip, your body and mind will transform to a whole new level. You will find yourself a changed person in a much better way." Paul continued passionately, "The kind of food, hospitality, natural serenity will work the magic on you, and you will have more time to evaluate yourself in a new atmosphere—being away from cars, traffic, phone, TV, radio, and all modern gadgets. The trip will take you to the strange but aromatic world that will entice and make you intoxicated ...Really, Linda, I mean it." Paul expressed his feelings as if he was talking to himself.

"Paul, I really appreciate you sharing that with me. I will treasure your feelings and try to share those experiences . . . Maybe I will also become a saint after the trip, who knows?"

With that, Paul left the office and Linda remembered her salad and entered the break room. The room was less crowded. Only a few tables were occupied, and everyone was eating lunch quietly. This was the way Linda preferred.

The rest of the day passed without any interesting event. Linda left the office around five-thirty and reached home. There were a few messages on the phone. The first one was from her mother and the second from Lama Dorje Pasang of the monastery. Her mother requested a call back, and Pasang informed her about a coming event on Friday evening. A Lama, close to the Dalai Lama, was visiting from Dharamshala, India, and was delivering a short speech on Buddha's teachings.

Linda went to the washroom to freshen herself up and, after changing to a comfortable light dress, put on soft music and relaxed in the Lay-Z-Boy chair.

She had no intention of calling her mother. The mother cared so much about Linda's life and always pressed her on marriage and finding a suitable Christian man. Linda was in no hurry to settle at this time. She wanted to be free, learn more about the world and all kinds of religion. She had a different opinion on religion. She believed religion should be given as an option a little later in life. Normally, people adopt the religion they are born into. She feels, when the individuals are mature enough, they should be given a choice of religion. For her, religion was meant to give happiness and peace of mind. She felt, a monastery had this kind of environment, which the churches lacked. Her mother would not understand this inner quest and strange desire. Moreover, she had not found a person whom she might consider as her husband.

She'd had a boyfriend during her college days as a student of law. He was kind of nice and had a unique personality, but his smoking and drinking habits were annoying.

After leaving the college, Linda's current lifestyle did not support a boyfriend. The other reason Linda would not like to settle as a married woman was that she did not approve of the epidemic of divorce that was growing in society. She wanted to have a steady family and a really peaceful way of life. Linda sometimes felt, she needed to learn cooking, as she hated to spend time in the kitchen unnecessarily, and she knew one of the ways to win a man's heart was through his stomach. Her mother always mentioned the importance of kitchen life for a woman, which Linda took as old-fashioned.

Tuesdays were a little hectic in the office, but today, Smith was not in town; the scheduled meetings, conferences, and liaison with other offices would be under John Cunningham—the senior partner after Smith. Linda needed to dig all the important summary case files currently at the court throughout the country and keep them in the conference room next to John's desk. She'd compiled the files, took them in the file trolley, and kept them in the conference room; now she needed to prepare and send the meeting notice to all the secretaries. After ninety minutes of lunch recess, it would continue till four in the afternoon.

Linda took to the fax machine and sent faxes to all concerned offices about the meeting today and advised them to prepare their queries and other concerns in the conference agenda. She knew Adam had a vision that by the year 2000, he wanted to establish offices in almost all the big cities in the United States—including towns that had a population of over ten million. Linda heard Adam saying on many occasions in the meetings and conferences that he wanted to provide legal services to most Americans on the grassroots level. He emphasized that legal defense services should not be within the reach of only a pocketful of people who had money. Rather, it should be an option for poor people as well. Through franchises, keeping overhead cost much lower, he wanted to be able to elaborate and provide legal services to most Americans. He had a vision that everyone should be able to pay monthly installment for the services they availed. Mr. Smith wanted to avoid the "money pit"—a thing that was gaining roots in the American political system.

This idea of a franchised legal system was liked by many lawyers, and most of the well-known judges and people in the legal profession completely backed Mr. Smith. This was one of the prominent reasons Mr. Smith was highly respected in the legal profession. Clients all over Los Angeles and the entire country preferred Mr. Smith to handle his or her case.

John Cunningham worked as senior vice-president in the firm and was entirely responsible for developing the program and keeping close observation of its progress. As far as Linda knew, the project was going smoothly, and by the beginning of the year 2000, it would be implemented in New York, Atlanta, Boston, Chicago, Detroit, Cleveland, Dallas, Los Angeles, Seattle, Minneapolis, and Phoenix. After June, it would cover the rest of the country including the small cities. Linda, besides working as Mr. Smith's personal assistant, would also assist the human resource manager to recruit and position personnel in all the respective offices. Linda didn't want to think about the added responsibilities and the enormous time she might have to devote to the process.

"Linda, I am missing the Steve Swift file of Chicago. Could you please try to locate it? Their conference call will be next." John's voice came through the intercom.

"Sure, John, I will look into it and bring it to you as soon as possible."

"Thanks, Linda."

After two minutes, the file was on its way to the conference room and Linda dropped the file next to John's table. She made a sign to John, who nodded his head; both of them remained silent. Linda returned to her room immediately. She didn't know how that file had not been included in the bunch she gave earlier. She thought she was becoming absent-minded, her emotion and vision diverting more toward the coming trip. She needed to control her mind and not allow diversions, at least when at the office.

The conference room was empty as all the partners left for a ninety-minute lunch recess. Linda, after a quick glimpse around the room, also headed toward the break room.

Linda noticed that Sarah, Pauline, and Brenda, as usual, were talking at one of the corner table. When she approached, the conversation suddenly ended, and everybody had sarcastic smiles on their faces.

"Hi, Linda. Please come and join us," Brenda extended an invitation.

Linda realized these legal assistants of partners must be involved in the usual office politics and backbiting. Linda, wanted to avoid the unnecessary gossip and negative talks about the office as much as possible.

She said, "Thanks, Brenda. I will sit at the other table." She turned down the request politely, took her lunch box from the refrigerator, and occupied the seat next to Daniel.

"Hope you don't mind."

"Not at all, Linda, my pleasure."

Daniel was a good-looking, pleasing person—African-American with smooth skin, a large face, and small eyes. He'd gotten his legal degree from Yale, had been with the firm for the last seven years, and was a promising, dynamic assistant to partner Doug McPherson.

Daniel was a rising star in the firm and could be a partner once he completed his master's degree. Smith had particular interest in his progress.

Linda had a normal and regular chitchat with Daniel, finished the lunch, and after thanking him for his company, left for her room. She heard the phone ring from outside the room, went inside, and grabbed the phone.

"Linda, may I help you?" It did not surprise Linda that her mother was on the line.

"Yes, I am fine. Mother, I am kind of busy now; may I call you this evening?"

Linda knew her mother would engage her in a long conversation, and she wanted to avoid it during office hours.

"Don't forget; I called you the other day and you did not return my call."

"I know, Mother. I will definitely call you this evening." She concluded the conversation briefly in a business-like fashion.

Linda hung up the phone. She knew exactly what her mother's sermon would be: she would not stop bitching about the trip to Nepal and advise her to cancel the trip to that dangerous part of the remote world.

Linda kept herself busy with regular office work. She did not realize it was almost four.

"Linda," John echoed on the intercom, "we are almost done for the day. Please collect your files; we will wrap up in the next ten minutes."

"Thanks, John, I appreciate it. I'll be there in ten minutes."

Linda, after storing her files in the office and cleaning her desk, left for the conference room, collected the files scattered all over the table, and locked them in her file cabinet. When Linda left her room, the offices were almost empty. The cleaning lady was vacuuming the rug in the far corner. Linda nodded toward her, said, "Good night, Maria," and left for the elevator.

While going to her car, Linda remembered, she needed to go to the market for groceries. The grocery store, named Fresh Depot, was on the way home, and she had to stop for some essentials and a fresh cut of flowers for her visit to a Buddhist monastery.

After her grocery shopping and hectic drive from the office, she finally reached her home.

After a quick shower, she prepared a cocktail of gin and tonic with a twist of lemon on the glass. Then, she sat down in front of the TV. Midwest News reported a flight crash after its takeoff from Milwaukee, Wisconsin. It was discussing the catastrophic 8.1 earthquake in Mexico that had killed ten thousand people, injured thirty thousand, and left ninety-eight thousand people homeless. For business news, Steve Jobs from Apple Computer resigned in order to found NEXT. The general news never excited Linda. She cared for the unemployment, house prices, and other related matters that directly impacted her daily life. The current unemployment rate was 7.5 percent.

Reagan, an actor elected President, might do something dramatic to reduce the high unemployment rate. Gas prices had risen five cents recently and was now $1.20 per gallon. Crime rate was rising in East Los Angeles as usual. The law enforcement authorities seemed to be losing their battle with gangs from Mexico, other South American countries, Korean and Vietnamese violent gangs, and high school dropout youth extremist groups.

Although Linda lived in the northwest and the crime rate in that part of Los Angeles was nonexistent, she was scared that, sometime in the future, it might spread to other areas as well. She valued the gift of life from God and felt it should not be a gang victim any day. She had a vision of utopia where everyone should live happily and without any violence. She remembered the Dalai Lama preaching about life, and about living happily in the midst of misery. Normally, suffering is created through jealousy, anger, hatred, and pride; these negative factors corrupt the mind. In order to overcome these negative forces, one needs to develop a source of compassion. Linda felt the phenomenon of compassion was slowly vanishing from the American way of life. The Dalai Lama talked about nirvana—that was the highest achievement in Buddhism—which led to the end of suffering and rebirth. The enlightened ones achieved wisdom of emptiness. In the state of nirvana, one could exist and not exist at the same time. Linda had a hard times understanding the core meaning of nirvana—the reason she would like to study and research Buddhism for her PhD. She found this religion quite fascinating, exhilarating, and practical.

She was in deep thought when the phone rang.

"Yes, Mom, I was just about to call you," Linda explained once she heard her mother's voice. "I am fine, Mother. How are Dad and Samantha?" Samantha was her younger sister of middle-school age.

"They are fine Linda. Since you don't believe what I tell you, please have a talk with your dad. Her mother passed the phone to her dad.

"Hi, sweetheart, how are you?" her father asked. "My dear, I just read the news in the *Los Angeles Times*—a hiker is missing in Nepal."

She explained, "Dad, there are twelve people in our group. Five are from Los Angeles, three from Colorado, two from Frisco, and two from Oregon—and all middle-aged professionals." Linda tried to defend, "Besides, Dad, five are ladies and soon, Mountain Travel is organizing a get-together in its office with an object to know each other before departure."

"That sounds good, Linda. You are mature enough to understand life, and I am sure you will make the right decision for your welfare."

"Of course, Dad. I am twenty-eight. But explain to Mom; she worries too much."

"Okay, I will, but talk with her as well. Here she is."

"Linda, our job is to warn you about travel in that part of the world." Her mom was now on the line.

"Yes, Mom, I do understand."

"People were talking about cholera and other mosquito-borne diseases; have you taken the necessary vaccinations?"

"Yes, Mom, I have. It was taken care of by Mountain Travel, and they have all the information. Besides, they are pioneers in this kind of journey to Nepal. They have been organizing this kind of trip since 1965 successfully."

Linda felt she needed to finish this conversation as she was getting hungry for dinner. "Mom, I need to make a sandwich; I came hungry from office."

"Okay, Linda. Take care of yourself and try to be safe wherever you are."

It was a sort of blessing combined with preaching from her mom as usual. After the phone call, Linda hurried to the kitchen quickly to fix a sandwich with a piece of boiled chicken, some tomatoes, lettuce, cucumber, carrots, and things in between.

She did not feel like watching TV anymore. Instead, she took a book *How I Became a Buddhist* by Kusala that was lying on the top of her nightstand, and went to bed.

In her dream, someone pulled her from the earth. In fact, she was sitting in her backyard when an angel shaped like a butterfly with multiple colors on her wings reached her hand and flew up. Linda did not believe how light she turned out to be, as she floated toward a cluster of stars in the night. Everything was so calm, and serenity prevailed everywhere. She soared up and up. Normally, she was scared of heights, but as she was moving slowly up, it did not scare her at all. Up there, she saw a bright but pleasing light; it was intense but did not hurt her eyes.

They crossed the bright light and entered through a patch of cloud to a land. She couldn't believe her eyes. It was a magnificent sight, an artistic view of with blue grass one the meadow decked by a stream, a dark tall mountain and a ridge, a large green ground, where children were playing in a swing and adults were sitting not too distant from the swings, were talking softly, laughing, and enjoying the fruits in the basket, which was in the middle of their circle.

The grass they were sitting on produced the effect of a soft velvet. No one was wearing shoes. Everyone looked young and fresh, like the fruits kept in their circle. Linda, with the angel, softly landed on the grass close to a bunch of sitting people. Her angel again held her hand and took her to the group of people, introducing herself as Linda from California. No one asked her any question; they just welcomed her and asked her to sit with them. Linda accepted their invitation and a conversation with them.

The conversation was totally different from usual. No one was looking at her dress and figure as is usually done in a party down on the earth. She didn't see people backbiting, talking critically about the looks of a lady, here dresses, makeup, breakups, new and old boyfriends, etc. It was nothing like that; rather, they were talking about the angels, God, happiness, peace and tranquility. Nobody talked about food, appointments, commuting, parties, work, bosses, employers, or workers. All they talked was about nature, animals, and plants.

Linda had never seen a landscape so beautiful and attractive.

The meadow was green and soft, and the color was pleasing to her eyes. The flowers had so many colors, and were manicured in such a way that they looked like a painting. The multicolor roses, daffodils, orchids, tulips, pink carnations, and blue hydrangeas were abundant and vibrant. Although Linda was sitting next to a group of people, her mind was wandering to the green lush ridge; and through a mountain, the waterfalls of a deep-white stream cascaded about thirty feet down to the ground. The sound of waterfalls was running like soft music in the background. There were abundant colorful peacocks, baby deer, and numerous multicolored butterflies adding to the intoxication in the sound, creating a mysterious aura all around. Someone in the group was watching Linda closely.

"Linda, let me show you some of the flowers that you may not have seen down on earth. Would you be interested to see?"

Linda said, "Of course. May I ask you your name, if you don't mind?"

"Not at all, Linda. My name is Sophia, and you may call me Sofy."

Sofy held Linda's hand and politely dragged her to the little wild part of the garden.

"Linda, I do not know where to begin; every name may sound peculiar to you." Sofy smiled to herself. "Look, Linda, this one is called jade vine, which, you can see, is blue in color and hangs from the trees." Sofy went on, "This one is chocolate cartoon, this one is Koki's — bright red color. This one is called yellow-and-purple lady slippers, and this one is middle mist." Sofy went on, "These flowers cannot be sustained on earth; as you know, the climate there changes constantly. It is not like here, which remains constant all the time." Sofy added, "All gods decided to bring these extinguished flowers from the Earth and preserve them here until they will be sent back sometime in the future."

Linda had never seen these peculiar and amazing plants surrounding the area. She diverted her attention to the people around. Not very far, close to another beautifully landscaped meadow, she saw a small group, and she could not believe her eyes. She was amazed to see figures that looked like Jesus, Buddha, Shiva, and Nanak talking together softly and smiling at each other. She could not hear the talk they were having but could infer, it was on some issues of mutual interest. Everyone seemed quite interested in the subject, and nodded their heads in approval with subtle smiles.

Linda could not believe the peculiar group who personified pious religious figures that represented almost all of mankind sitting together. She thought, *if all these gods can sit together, discuss, and like each other, why are we people on earth fighting to prove religious supremacy?*

Linda experienced celestial and spiritual feelings. Her body felt lighter and drifting toward the tall, shinning, and dark green trees. Linda could see numerous trees on her left side assembled like a parade bursting with many colors—red, green, blue, yellow, and white. It was planted in such a way that the sizes of the trees were symmetrical and proportionate. The trees were planted in a circle, and the pond was made of the water coming from the waterfall and accumulating in the pond. The trees' reflection on the pond gave an amazing impression, and it produced remarkable atmosphere. Linda also saw some trees with shining, dark green leaves and felt that the dew was just about to drop from the tree branches lavishly laden with more than thirty different kinds of tempting, ready-to-be-eaten fruits. One tree had peaches on one branch and on another branch apricot, mango, and so on. Linda had never seen a tree with varieties of fruits; it was just astonishing.

In fact, she saw so many flowers, plants, trees—things she had never seen in her life before. She needed to tell her friend Sarah, the botanist, all about this experience when she would see her next. She looked at her purse for her small camera to take pictures, but she could not find it. She realized, even her feet were without shoes. She looked at herself and realized she was not just wearing a dress, but something like a toga, which covered her upper and lower body in a decent manner and was perfectly fit and comfortable. She'd never seen this outfit in her closet before and did not understand how she was wearing it now.

Linda, a little further on her left, saw a setting like a park, with children playing in it. But she did not hear loud noises from them. Rather, occasionally, a burst of quiet giggling constantly emanated from them, and they seemed to be enjoying the company of each other, playing together in harmony. Linda was not in any sort of hurry for marriage and children. She wanted to establish the career of her choice before she settled for marriage, but when she saw these lovely and adorable children, a desire to have a child like one of those kids suddenly cropped up in her mind.

"Hi, Linda! I understand, you want to become a Buddhist, don't you?" the Buddha figure asked her. She had not even seen the personality approaching her. She'd been lost in her thoughts.

Linda got up politely, bowed her head slightly and said, "Yes, Lord, I am trying to understand your religious doctrine."

"Please do not address me as Lord. I am a simple and ordinary person like you; call me Gautama." The voice was delightful and charming. "Look, Linda, all religions are the same and lead to one path, no matter which one you choose."

Gautama further said, "It is not hard to understand any religion. Try to understand the portion you find easy, and do not even try to understand a thing which you feel is hard. Religion should be simple enough even for simpleminded people like you and me to understand."

A sharp noise came from afar. Linda thought, it was one of the birds making a peculiar noise. But when she fully awoke, she realized that it was her phone ringing. Linda picked up the phone reluctantly.

"Hey, Linda, are you all right?"

Kathy was on the other side. When she looked at the wall clock, it was already nine-thirty.

"Kathy, I am sorry. Somehow I missed the alarm and overslept. Please tell Smith I will be there in an hour."

Kathy consoled her, "Never mind, Linda. We're all late once in a while. You are not an exception. See you later."

Kathy hung up the phone. Linda did not waste time and finished her morning chores quickly. In no time, she was on her way to the office.

Linda approached her desk, the office in full motion. She felt a little awkward coming to the office so late. She noticed Smith in the next room with one of the clients, deep in conversation. Linda took out papers and some files from the drawer, which she needed to complete that day, and kept herself busy.

At around twelve-thirty, Smith called her. "Linda, what happened to you this morning?"

"Sorry, Mr. Smith. Somehow I did not hear the alarm and overslept."

"It's all right, Linda. Everyone does once in a while. I am going to lunch with Andrew," he said. Andrew was the client he was with. "We'll be back around two-thirty. We need to discuss his case further," Mr. Smith added. With that, Smith cut the line off.

Linda did not feel like having lunch; she wasn't hungry. She was thinking about the amazing dream until she woke up. It was quite real and close to life. She would need to discuss the dream with the Lama this evening in the monastery. She decided to walk to the break room. As she was about to leave the office, she heard her phone ringing and went to pick it up.

"Linda." Lisa from Mountain Travel, which handled her trip, was on the line.

"Yes, Lisa."

"Oh, Linda, how are you?"

"Fine, Lisa."

"I had called you this morning too; there was no reply."

"I was late coming to the office."

"Anyway, I got you now. Linda, our office is having a get-together for the group leaving in October for Nepal. It will be at two in the afternoon next Saturday. Your round-trip ticket will be waiting in the Los Angeles airport at the Delta counter, and you will be returning home from here at seven. How does it sound, Linda?"

"It sounds great."

"Robert, who coordinates all treks in Nepal, is also here and will be answering your questions."

"Really? I am excited to meet all the travelers and Robert, Lisa. I will be there."

Thanking her, Lisa hung up her phone. Linda made a note on her calendar for the Mountain Travel meeting.

"Hi, Linda. You made it in." Kathy poked her head through Linda's door.

"Thank God, Kathy, I appreciate your phone call. Otherwise, I don't know how long I might have kept sleeping. Wait, Kathy, I will join you in the break room." Linda followed Kathy.

"Linda, Andrew called this morning at nine, and the operator passed me the call since you were not here. Something came up with his case and he wanted to see Smith this morning." Linda nodded. "I went to your file drawer, got his file, and confirmed the appointment with Smith for nine-thirty."

"That is great, Kathy. I owe you something."

Kathy reported to Linda what had happened; she was not expecting a favor from Linda. "If you feel that way, bring a small gift from your exciting trip to Nepal. Are you happy now?"

"I will keep that in mind."

Linda and Kathy reached the break room and occupied a small table next to the window. It was a beautiful morning, and Hollywood Hill was clearly visible from the window.

"Linda, did you hear *Wall Street Journal* and *New York Times* journalists are coming next week to the office to interview Mr. Smith regarding his franchising ventures?" Kathy asked.

"I did not know. Perhaps Smith was going to tell me soon."

"Is not it a great idea?"

"I feel it is historical, Kathy." Linda added her feelings.

In the meantime, Linda remembered her salad box from the previous day, excused herself, and brought the box to rejoin Kathy. There was no conversation between them.

After some time, Kathy said, "Bye now, Linda," and left.

Linda was by herself, still thinking about the dream, but at the same time, she was happy that she was going to meet her fellow travelers in Frisco next week. Linda thought, she should tell her parents about the people she met there so that her parents would be at ease. Maybe she could get some phone numbers and pass them on to her mother so that she could talk with them personally and be more convinced about the trip.

The monastery event was at seven. Linda came home, took a quick shower, fixed her sandwich, took the flower bunch from the refrigerator, and got into the car. It was almost six forty-five; she should be at the congregation on time.

The monastery was decorated with lots of flowers, white and yellow scarves and banners hanging from the ceiling. A large sitting statue of Buddha was in the middle, and fragrance of incense floated prodigal in the air. The atmosphere seemed very religious; about fifty people were sitting on the exotic and soft Tibetan rugs. Linda was guided to an area occupied by ladies on the left side of the room. The room was cozy, and aromatic; soft light prevailed all over, creating a celestial atmosphere. It seemed people were waiting for the program to begin. In the meantime, Dorje Pasang came in front of the crowd, and after greetings, introduced his senior, Lama Sonam—a close associate of the Dalai Lama who'd come from Dharamshala to enlighten on the Buddha's teaching in a simple and elegant manner. After the presentation, an hour's time had been allocated discussion session. After the discussion, a light vegetable snack would be served, and the program would come to an end.

Lama Sonam began to speak in a soft, pleasant, and extremely mild tone that lasted for about forty-five minutes. Time went quite fast. The audience, who felt as if they just woke up from a sweet dream, were surprised when the presentation came to a sudden end.

"How do you separate Buddha's religion from the rest of the religions? Will Buddha's religion take you to heaven?" Joseph, a man Linda had seen many times in the congregation in the past, but had not had a conversation with, posed a discussion question.

The Lama thought for a few seconds and began, "Every religion or culture has its distinguishing characteristics. All faiths and religions are good for mankind. Basically, they teach us the same things. Human ethics are similar in all religions. All faiths, although they have contradictory philosophies and doctrines, possess the ability to produce fine human beings. All religions give reasons to appreciate and respect all forms of spiritual pursuit that make human beings better and help create happier and more peaceful world."

Sonam paused for a brief moment.

"The Buddhist faith emphasizes on developing and upholding inner values—such as compassion and wisdom, inner strength, love and gentleness. These are more valuable for us than fame, wealth, and success. We believe in reincarnation; birth and death are inevitable parts of human existence. I believe, through meditation, the Buddhist faith unfolds your realities about birth and teaches easy ways to face death when it comes for you, and prepares you for it. Although there is no guarantee, everyone's death will be smooth and painless, as every faith promises, one becomes a part of God after death. Our faith shows you the method or practice to attain nirvana that will end reincarnation, and this is the supreme and highest achievement one can reach." After the answer, Sonam looked around for more questions.

In the meantime, Dorje Pasang said, "Do we have any more questions for the Lama?" No one had a question anymore.

"Excellent. I really appreciate you all coming this evening and sharing with the respected Lama," Dorje Pasang said. He added further, "For your information, His Holiness Dalai Lama is planning a visit Denver in February next year to attend an international conference. We do not know at this time if he is coming to California as well. We will let you know as soon as we know of his plans. Now please share some snacks and soft drinks served in the next room. Once again, thanks for coming to this event today."

With that note of thanks, people got up slowly and walked to the other room for snacks.

Linda located Lama Sonam and approached him. She waited for a while as a few people were talking with him. When the people left, Linda approached him.

"Hi, my name is Linda."

"Linda, I saw you last time when His Holiness Dalai Lama was here," Sonam said.

"Oh, yes, I was here. I enjoyed it a lot. May I ask you a question—not exactly a question, rather, an interpretation of my dream last night?"

"What kind of dream, Linda?"

"It was a wonderful dream. I was in heaven, meeting all the gods, including Buddha. Buddha talked with me and said the same thing as you did, that all religions are the same and they should be simple enough to be understood by everyone."

"Well, the dream's explanation is simple—you are attracted to our religion and have a deep inclination to go for it," Sonam explained.

"I guess so. And I am also traveling to Nepal for a trek next month."

"That is wonderful! The trip will bring you closer to the religion, and you will experience the culture of that part of the world. It will give you insights into how people there live peacefully and happily with limited resources. If you have time, Linda, you should visit Dharamshala in India. I will do my best to arrange a meeting with His Holiness Dalai Lama, and I will be with you also."

"That sounds great. I will do my best to be in Dharmashala. I will be in Delhi for the flight to Nepal. How far is Dharamshala from Delhi?"

"Not too far," Sonam's reply was quick.

"Since I am with a group, I will talk to my travel agents and see if they can adjust. I would love to visit."

"Please get my address and phone number from Dorje before you leave," Sonam suggested.

"Thanks, I really appreciate it." Linda further added, "Thanks for your time."

***

CHAPTER THREE

October 1985

A national press reception was set up in the office that day for the media. Reporters from the *New York Times, Wall Street Journal*, local TV channels, and a number of radio talk shows were coming to the office at eleven. Linda was extremely busy with preparations, making sitting arrangements, setting audio-visual equipment, setting the meeting agenda, and supervising arrangements of lunch for the invitees and guests.

Adam Smith looked unusually smart and handsome in a white shirt, striped red-black tie, and gray trousers with a navy blazer. On the left side of the blazer was a shining round pin that showed he belonged to a lawyer's association. It also showed an icon of prestigious national special award Mr. Smith had won as a mark of honor. It matched his special demeanor that morning.

Slowly, the large conference hall was coming to life with press reporters, TV journalists, radio hosts, and a nightline anchor of a popular TV show.

John Cunningham opened the show, addressed the dignitaries, and thanked them warmly for the opportunity to enlighten the public on the unique and pioneering "Law Franchisee" venture, proposed by Mr. Smith in order to reach the average Americans throughout the nation.

When the floor opened for the journalists, the first question was from Neil Palmer of the *Wall Street Journal*: "Mr. Smith, as we understand, you plan to provide defensive law services to poor people in the country. What are you going to do if they cannot afford to pay at all?"

"Thanks, Mr. Palmer most people have asked me that question. We will allot ten percent of funds from our net profit to take care of such situations." Mr. Smith added, "My objective is to see that each and every person who deserves our service should not be deprived."

The next question was from Lawrence Wilson of the *New York Times*: "Is it true that you are also allocating ten percent from your profit to hungry children in our society?"

"Indeed." Smith's eyes sparkled. "I see hunger in the land of plenty as a sad, growing phenomenon, and our corporation will allot ten percent of its net profit to that effect."

Sam Miller, a local TV personality, said, "This seems a very ambitious project, Mr. Smith. When do you feel it will be in operation?"

"Of course, this is a unique and aggressive project. That is why I have allowed almost fifteen years to complete it." It seemed Smith had that answer ready.

Sam said, "That is good, but what if someone copies your idea and adopts this project earlier than you propose?"

"Good thinking, Mr. Miller. We thought about that issue; it is registered as our intellectual property and by all means, we will do our best to launch the project earlier than the targeted year."

In the meantime, prominent Los Angeles radio talk show host Patrick Davis raised his hand.

"Yes, Mr. Davis."

"Mr. Smith, with due respect, it seems you are going to deprive many normal lawyers around the country of their regular income. Do you have any critics of this plan?"

"Of course, not everyone likes this project, but more are for it than against."

"What will be your answer to those critics?" Patrick continued.

"Again, Mr. Davis, I respect everyone's freedom of speech as provided by our Constitution and will personally deal with them one at a time and to their satisfaction."

"Mr. Smith." George Harris, a prominent night TV talk show host, stood up. Smith nodded. "Do you have enough professional manpower to establish the service throughout the nation?"

"You know, Mr. Harris, we American have the highest lawyer ratio in terms of population, and we anticipate the ratio to increase rapidly in future. Furthermore, we plan to attract and hire young, energetic, and talented new lawyers so that we will be able to keep our overhead expenses lower. It will not be an issue to establish law firms."

Smith saw a hand go up in the air. "Yes, Judy Olson!" he said. Olson was an investigative journalist from the *Los Angeles Times*.

"The issue of hiring female employees at equal pay is a burning topic of discussion now. How will you see these issues? And, have you given them any priority under your corporate structure?"

"It is indeed a great issue, Miss Olson. We hire female lawyers as much as possible. At the moment about thirty-five percent of our employees are females. Their pay, decided according to their skills and qualifications, is also no less than that of their male counterparts. By 2000, we plan to hire an equal ratio of female employees, and they will all have equal pay."

It seemed, the questions finally dried out. Paul came to the middle of the podium and thanked all the guests and invitees for the outstanding opportunity for publicity in local and national media. He especially thanked the out-of-town guests for coming from New York and other parts of the country and requested they stay for lunch.

For lunch, Linda ordered from a local famous bistro to cater. They prepared sandwiches with roasted beef, cheese, BLT, and dressed with mayonnaise. It looked fresh, tempting, and smelled great. All guests seemed to enjoy the food. Around three in the afternoon, the guests and office employees were done with their lunching.

Linda needed to wrap up with the other helpers from the office so that everything would look clean.

The next day, in the major local and national newspapers, TV, and popular weekly national magazines, coverage was elaborate. Most of them appreciated Mr. Smith's efforts on the law franchisee project. They covered child hunger, female employees' equal pay, and assistance to poor people who deserved their services but were not able to pay.

It was about eleven-thirty in the morning. Linda was working on the press coverage summary that needed to be complied for Mr. Smith's perusal.

Linda noticed the incoming call-light blink. She hoped it was not her mother at this time of the day.

"Linda," a receptionist's voice was on the line, "I am Marsha, the personal secretary for the White House. The President wants to talk with Mr. Smith."

"Yes, Madam," Linda responded promptly.

"Just a minute, please."

"Mr. Smith, the President wants to talk with you."

"Sure, Linda. Put me through."

Linda quickly transferred the call. Linda knew President Reagan was familiar with Smith; Smith had handled a case for Reagan's relative about four years back and had won the case. He had visited their office a couple of times, so he was a known personality—although Smith, a liberal, was a registered Democrat. But in their friendship, party affiliation was not an issue.

Linda noticed, they talked for about ten minutes, and she had no clue what their conversation was about. Perhaps, sometime in the future, Mr. Smith would share the matter with Linda if it was not of a confidential nature.

Linda came to the office a little later after lunch; she needed to run some essential errands to purchase some of her intimate dresses.

When she came back, there was a note from Smith to see him as soon as possible. Linda, without wasting time, went to Smith, who was on the phone and signaled Linda to sit down. She waited for about five minutes, and Smith wrapped up his phone call.

"Linda, please make travel plans to Washington. I will be leaving Tuesday and coming back on Thursday afternoon; put me in the Intercontinental close to the White House. I will need limos on both ends. Please keep this trip confidential. I will talk to you after coming back." Smith finished his instructions in a business-like manner.

Linda completed her assignment and reported it to Mr. Smith personally. She had a hunch he would be offered a political assignment, but she kept everything to herself.

Fridays were casual days at the office. The office atmosphere was also extremely relaxed. Linda was in tight jeans that matched her five-eight figure perfectly and a pink top with heavy embroidery on the upper area. The loose style brought out her inner beauty, just fresh and simple. Her crystal blue eyes, white, smooth complexion, and golden blonde hair espoused an attractive look. Everyone, even the ladies, seemed to envy her outstanding beauty. Her beauty, combined with her soft, sweet, polite manner, was the topic of discussion among bachelors in the office.

Linda noticed the piercing eyes of her coworkers today, directed toward her. She felt a compulsion to look at herself in the mirror and see if anything was obviously wrong with her outfit. She went to the restroom, gave a quick, critical view of her outfit, and didn't notice anything wrong. She threw another critical look again. She could not herself ignore her attractive look exposed by this casual outfit. She added a thin layer of pink lipstick and softly managed her hair with a large hairbrush before stepping out of the restroom.

There, she saw Kathy who was approaching her.

"Hi, Linda! Oh my, you look extremely attractive in this casual outfit. Have any special plans for this evening or weekend?"

"Not exactly, Kathy. You know I've never liked crowds, loud noises, and disco filled with rowdy people and heavy smoke. I always try to keep little distance from that atmosphere. I will go to the botanical gardens on Saturday." Linda expressed her feelings.

Kathy came a little closer to Linda and whispered, "Linda, may I ask you a personal question?" Linda did not speak, she just nodded in approval.

"Do you have a boyfriend?"

"No. My tiring commute, long office hours, and weekends filled with shopping, laundry, and other personal chores do not leave me much time to search for boyfriends."

"Well, Linda, you are so smart and attractive. I'm sure you will find someone soon. Anyway, have a great weekend," Kathy said, and left Linda alone.

Linda returned home a little earlier than usual; as Smith had also left the office early, there wasn't much to do.

On her foyer, she noticed that some of the flowers were not fresh, and needed water soon. She would manage to water them this weekend. Her body and mind were unusually tired on Fridays. She took a pillow, hit the sofa, and lay down.

Linda did not realize she'd slept the entire evening and woke up at eight-thirty. She was hungry. She opened the freezer, took out some leftover food, and placed it in the microwave. She tried it, but was tasteless. So, she had some apple juice, and picked up a book titled *Tiger for Breakfast* about Nepal. It was a book she had in mind for a long time but somehow had not been able to manage time to read, although she read a fascinating book by Hai Suyin, titled *Mountain Is Young*, which she had liked very much.

Tiger for Breakfast, an astounding book by Michael Peissel published in 1966 provided descriptive illustrations of primitive Nepal. This was one of the early books that attracted a number of visitors from Europe and America. The fascinating illustrations of the mountains, peculiar customs, and traditions of the country with most hospitable and powerful characters of the inhabitants, abundant flora, fauna, birds, and unparalleled beauty of the fabled—forbidden until recently—mystical kingdom. In fact, Nepal had been opened for tourists only in 1953. Early on, visitors came to explore the strange forbidden land, with Shangri-La on their minds. Linda found the book so magical that she almost finished a quarter of it in no time. It was hard to put aside and sleep without reading, but she realized it was almost two in the morning, and she must have some sleep to feel fresh in the morning for her trip to the botanical garden. She had a strange, impulsive desire to go to the botanical garden after last night's powerful dream.

It was almost eleven when Linda woke up. She was not expecting it, but the phone rang. Her father said, "Good morning, Linda, my angel. Did I wake you up? You sound sleepy."

"No, Dad, I am up already." Linda felt certainly annoyed inside at the early call.

"Linda, what is your boss up to? We read and listened to so much about him the other day."

"Yes, it was a press conference on his law service 'franchise project.'"

"You should be proud to work for him. Are you happy there?"

"Of course, Dad, I am."

"So how is your travel preparation going on?"

"Next Saturday, we have a get-together in San Francisco at the travel office for our group."

"Sounds great."

"Yeah, Dad."

"Okay then, I will say bye now. Keep in touch. Your mom is at the church; I have a slight headache, so I'm at home."

"Take care of yourself. I'll call you soon." Linda felt relieved.

After a lazy shower, cereal with red juicy strawberries, an omelet, a piece of toasted bread with apricot jelly, and a small glass of orange juice—a complete weekend breakfast—Linda felt satisfied. She put on a cotton skirt of light blue color dotted with small white flowers, a white top, and white comfy walking shoes. She looked perfect for a nature walk at the botanical garden. She had not forgotten the book she was reading last night, *Tiger for Breakfast*. She took it along with her.

Normally, it was a crowded, popular place during weekends. The parking lot was packed. After securely parking, she exited the car, locked the door, and approached the entrance ticket booth. She waited for a while in line, purchased the ticket, and entered the popular garden. She noticed families with children and elderly people who seemed excited for the visit.

Linda was eager because she'd come to this botanical garden with the hope of comparing it with her dream last night. The garden's weather was slightly warm for this time of the year. The wind was blowing over the green shrubs, over the flowers and trees, and occasionally, she heard the sweet chirping sound of birds from the branches. At a distance, she saw a bunch of roses paraded like a multicolored dress, which she saw in the Pasadena, rose parade, that took place on New Year Day street-flower show last time. It was pleasing to the eyes and mind and produced a kind of magical effect on Linda.

Compared to last night's dream, everything seemed and looked familiar, but Linda noticed it lacked one thing. She tried to remember, thought hard to recall. There was the absence of that spiritual aroma—a feel of floating on the air, that total mental peace and amazing serenity. She wished and pined for the same dream again tonight.

Linda spent about two more hours wandering in that part of the garden where she had never been before. She enjoyed looking at the family with cute, small children holding the hands of their parents and grannies. She also enjoyed watching the varieties of plants, flowers, and strange-looking green shrubs. She was a little tired, and sat in a chair on the eastern side of the pond, looking at the colorful goldfish. She put a coin in the nearby stand and took some fish feed and gave it to the fish. She enjoyed when the fish came in crowds and ate the feed in no time. She thought the fish must be very hungry. Nearby was a chair glowing in the sun, surrounded with tiny but cute plants. Roses of many colors were within reach, and she noticed awesome, colorful butterflies humming around.

Linda approached the chair and sat with the intention to read the book she'd brought along, carrying ahead from the mark she had placed last night. After reading a few pages, she enjoyed the description of the book about the nature, mountain, and mystical description of the inhabitants of Nepal.

She immersed in the book. Suddenly, a butterfly sat on the top of a page. The butterfly was so beautiful she held her body tight and hands steady so that it would be not disturbed and fly away. The butterfly also found a cozy place on the book perhaps, it did not move. After a few minutes, she slightly tried to touch the butterfly; it did not move at all.

She noticed this was the same butterfly with small wings gold and dark blue color that had come in her dream last night, appearing as an angel. She tried to reach and touch it again. The butterfly flew but came back and sat on top of the book. Linda tried to touch it again; again, it flew but came back immediately. After trying several times to reach the butterfly, it continued flying and coming back repeatedly time and again. Linda gave up her temptation to touch the butterfly. She could not believe she felt the butterfly was smiling.

She watched critically this time and saw the angel's shape and gorgeous smile. Finally, the angel flew around Linda's head three times and flew away.

Linda was completely hypnotized by the butterfly that behaved strangely and perhaps tried to convey a message. She became intent on this miraculous gesture of the butterfly and spent some time in meditation.

When she woke up, the sun was slowly moving toward the west. The rays penetrated Linda's body and she felt a pleasant, warm feeling. The sky was still blue with a patch of clouds toward the east; the air was warm and brisk.

Linda had no desire to leave the chair. She'd felt a spiritual and divine power. She intended to be there longer but she saw that the sun was setting. People were slowly walking toward the gate in group, small children running around their mothers and grandmothers. The giggling of children and the pleasant chirping of the birds made the atmosphere subtle and inebriated.

Checking in at the Delta counter without luggage was fast and easy. Linda was at the departure gate at one-thirty, boarded the plane, and left for Frisco. Someone was waiting at the arrival area with her name placard. She identified herself, and the person guided her toward a waiting limo.

The office was on the right side after the Bay Bridge, behind a small sign that simply said, "Mountain Travel." At the entrance door, Lisa was waiting.

"Hi, Linda, welcome to the office." It was a warm welcome, and Lisa hugged her.

Linda gave a quick, critical look inside the office. It was simple, with the look of the eighteenth century— ceiling beams of old and tarnished wood matching the wooden floor, faded paints—resonating with a cranking sound, rough, and rugged style. A huge poster of Mount Everest had been plastered on the center wall. Similarly, a large Fish Tail Mountain poster was on the opposite.

On the right part of the wall there were a lot of pictures of pagoda-style temples. Similarly, on the left wall were numerous beautiful life-size pictures of Mongolian faces of women wearing colorful *chuppas* and traditional striped bright aprons. The furniture—tables, chairs, and sofas—looked old and haggard but provided a simple and graceful look.

It was hard to find an office in museum-like eighteen century appearance in the midst of tall and modern-architecture surrounding buildings in the center of Frisco town. It was hard to trust your eyes once you enter this imaginative fascinating office decorated with such an antique but charming look. It had the characters as described in the book *Tiger for Breakfast*.

In front of Linda, there were three other women and about five men sitting on chairs in what looked like a conference room. In the middle was an eight-millimeter projector loaded with the roll of a film, the screen on the opposite wall. To the left side of the room was a cocktail table decked with varieties of beverage along with paper cups and snacks such as potato chips and nuts. Paper plates and napkins too had been placed neatly. Linda got herself a gin and tonic with a piece of lemon, and sat next to the other three women.

After a while, a gentleman with aristocratic Adonis Amazonian–type rugged face with rough, full beard entered the room. He looked athletic, extrovert, around fifty, and had large hands and feet.

"Hi everyone! My name is Peter, and I am the owner of this outfit. We almost have every one of our October group here except three people, who are held up in Denver due to weather. We may have to reschedule them separately either here or in Nepal." Peter continued, "May I request you for your self-introduction? Let's begin from here."

He indicated the person on his right. Everyone gave their brief introduction.

"We will continue with a promotional documentary from the Nepal Tourism Department, which is about twenty minutes long, followed by a brief description about the trek from our man in Nepal—Robert—who is here to answer some of your questions. We will give you some time to talk among yourselves and learn about each other so that you may feel comfortable on the trip together."

After Peter's brief presentation, the documentary started to roll with magnificent mountain sceneries, floras, and waterfalls, typical villages situated on the lap of the tall mountains, green forests with colorful birds, and people singing and dancing with musical instruments. There was also a dance in a monastery with masks and typical drums, glimpses of temples, and beautiful snowcapped mountains.

The documentary was enchanting, and everyone clapped when it came to an end.

Immediately after the documentary, Robert—thin, blue eyed, sharp of figure, in boots— appeared. "Hello, my name is Robert, and I have been in Nepal for twenty years." A pause. "I am a British citizen, worked with the embassy as a diplomat, and have been a trekking guide with Mountain Travel since 1963."

Robert briefly described the current trekking situation in Nepal in about forty minutes. His use of words and presentation style were polite, sweet, and attractive. Linda could understand Robert most of the time, but some words in his heavy British accent were difficult to understand.

"Thanks for your attention. I would like to answer few of your questions now, if you have any." Robert concluded his presentation.

"Robert, what kind of provisions do you have for rescue from remote part of trekking if someone falls sick or indisposed?" Sam from the Los Angeles area put a question.

"First, we have a screening policy for all trekkers on their health, age, and normal stamina." Robert continued, "Most of the time, we choose the established trails for hiking, so you should not have a hard time. In case you fall sick and are unable to proceed, we have a two-way radio communication, and a military chopper is available on short notice."

Linda raised her hand and put a question to Robert: "Although, I am in good health and my physical results are satisfactory, I am not used to climbing the mountains in the past. Do you feel my current health and normal physical stamina is fit for such a hefty trip?"

"Linda, we have gone through your health report. Considering your age, your stamina will support this trip."

"Excuse me!" Linda saw Susan, an anthropologist from Oregon, raise her hand.

"I saw my itinerary for the trip. We are going and coming out of New Delhi. Is it possible on the way back for me to come via Thailand?"

"I am not much familiar with the ticketing process; I request Peter to answer the question."

Peter said, "Of course, Susan. That is possible, but we have purchased your ticket in bulk and used one across the Atlantic both way. If you want to come across the Pacific, we need to calculate your cost, and the fare may be higher."

Susan wanted to know the fare difference and would make the decision then. Peter would inform Susan prior to departure. Linda also remembered her side trip to Dharamshala and asked a question about the side trip from Delhi.

"Linda, you are allowed to take a side trip and may go to Agra, Varanasi, or other places. The cost will be negligible and will be permitted."

A gentleman from the group—Linda did not remember his name—put a question to Robert.

"Everyone's telling me the importance of acclimatization. Do you feel four days will be sufficient to avoid mountain sickness?"

It seemed Robert was ready for the question.

"Indeed. In some cases, in the past, we have given only three days, and it has worked."

The presentation seemed to be coming to an end.

"On behalf of the company, I thank you for coming to this presentation. I wish you a wonderful trek. Of course, Robert will be there to take care of you most of the time. Now please join us for a cocktail and mingle with fellow trekkers."

Linda approached Susan and Karen, two ladies from Oregon. Susan introduced Karen as an architect to Linda, and herself as an anthropologist. The two were almost of the same age—around fifty—and both had pleasing personalities. They had a normal chat, and everyone wished for the best trip and promised they would have a blast.

Linda exchanged phone numbers with Karen and Susan and said, her mother might call them and talk about the trip as she was a little nervous for her taking this Everest trekking and they may be able to convince her.

***

CHAPTER FOUR

Middle of October 1985

Linda finally received the complete daily itinerary for her three-week trip. The itinerary showed two days in Kathmandu Valley with tour of famous Hindu temples and Buddhist shrines along with a step back in time to the golden age of Nepal's art and architectural history, as well as the richness of its modern daily life.

After exploring the exotic Kathmandu Valley, they would fly to Lukla—a remote mountain town—in order to begin the trek, following an ancient spectacular Sherpa trade route to the famous Namche Bazaar. Beyond Namche, the travelers would experience traditional villages, rhododendron forests, terraced fields, and summer pastures for yak grazing, before moving into the stark landscape of attractive glaciers.

The trek would cover monasteries in the heart of the Sherpa settlement, where one could observe the monks in their daily prayers. They would also hike out onto the Khumbu glacier to visit the iconic Everest basecamp, where all famous climbers—following the steps of Edmund Hillary and Tenzing Norgay Sherpa—had prepared intensely for their first and historic successful summit attempts.

They could also stand at the foot of the Khumbu icefall where all the climbers began their own odyssey.

After spending an astonishing night at Everest basecamp, and after taking a day to hike through the village on the ancient trade route, they would fly to the capital city in for a day's rest. They'd have time to shop for handicrafts and antique items and walk the century-old quarter around the city before a farewell dinner with delicious multicourse meals of Nepal's finest cuisine at an old majestic palace with enormous chandeliers and beautiful marble decorations.

Linda read the trip itinerary a couple of times. The more she read, more did she love it. She recited the summary, word for word, to her parents as well.

Along with the itinerary, she had received a few promotional booklets on Nepal with a small and attractive four-page Mountain Travel brochure showcasing a couple of handsome Sherpa porters who would accompany them on their trip to prepare food and carry supplies.

Linda was taking all kinds of precautions and packing her stuff as per the brochure's instructions, along with a small first-aid kit for her personal use—including some bandages, Tylenol, and muscle-relaxing cream to be used on the legs.

Linda was on her way to the office, her mind occupied with next week's long departure from Los Angeles to Nepal. She was not used to such a long trip. She'd gone to Brazil and Mexico a few years back, but those trips consisted of short flights. She kept a few books in her handbag to read on the plane, as there was nothing else to do to pass the time.

She reached the office. After dropping her bag in her work place, she felt a desire for coffee and visited the break room. Paul was sitting at a corner table and enjoying coffee. He has a newspaper in his hand.

Linda approached him and said, "Good morning, Paul."

Paul lowered the newspaper. With excitement in his voice, he said, "Hi, Linda, it's a pleasure to see you. I'm sure your excitement is building up for your trip. Is it Friday or Saturday you are leaving?"

"I am really excited. We're leaving this Friday."

"Do you have a visa for India?" He added, "I understand you are also visiting India for few days. Has Mountain Travel got an India visa for you?"

"Yes, Paul; they have obtained visas for both the countries," Linda said, satisfying Paul's curiosity.

"Please take a lot of photos. You may need to capture the outstanding moments of your life. I was so excited when I was on the trip last. My rolls finished during the early part of my trip; so I had to borrow a few from George, a fellow traveler."

"I have about twenty of them." Linda seemed to assure herself with the reply.

Paul got up from the table. "Well, Linda, I wish you all the best on the trip, if I do not see you later this week. By the way, if you happen to go to the embassy, please say hello to Estella. I understand she is still the personal assistant to the Ambassador."

Linda took a notepad and noted the name. "It will be my pleasure."

Linda came back to her work place and glanced toward Smith's office through the small glass door; he was not in yet.

Linda needed to prepare the schedule for Mr. Smith for the entire day. She took out the schedule of Smith's appointments. It looked like he had a busy day with a couple of clients coming that morning for the consultation of their cases, and after lunch, he was going to attend a fund-raising program for Democrats at the Hyatt. A few key Democrats were in town for the occasion. Linda considered that Smith might not come back to the office for the rest of the day. Linda needed to remind him about a lawyer's dinner program the following night at the Hilton; he needed to deliver an important speech on his law service progress.

Linda got busy with the paperwork. She did not notice that Smith had already arrived at the office. She saw him with a client later, and when the client left, Smith said, "Linda, could you please come in for a moment?"

"Sure." Linda rushed to his office.

"Let me give you some important papers on Nelson, the client who just left. Please keep them with his file; this new evidence may have a significant effect on his case."

Linda took the papers before reminding him about the fund-raising event at the Hyatt that afternoon and dinner at the Hilton the following day.

Smith thanked her for the reminders and requested Linda to have a seat. Linda seemed curious, as Smith never told her to sit unless something was important.

After Linda settled on the seat, Smith looked straight at Linda's eyes.

"Linda, I know you will be away for a three-week trip. How is Charlene picking up on your work?" Charlene was the replacement for Linda while she was away on the trip.

"She is picking it up well. I am sure you will not feel my absence."

"Linda...," Smith paused for a moment. "There's no one to replace you. When you come back after the trip, I am going to promote you to Executive Secretary with a substantial raise, and I am sure you deserve the promotion. Please keep it secret until you come back." Smith continued, "Furthermore, Linda, you also will be a key person on my project, especially on personnel selection throughout the nation." Without awaiting Linda's reply, Smith further added, "Also, you knew president's offer of the post of Attorney General to me in his administration. I refused. As you may understand, I will not fit with the Republican circle." Linda did not reply; she just nodded her head in a concurring manner.

Smith seemed to conclude, "I wish you a wonderful trip. Be safe and enjoy the trip, Linda."

Linda thanked him and left. She knew Mr. Smith had a soft spot for her. He considers her as a daughter after his own daughter Melina passed away in a car accident two year back. Linda also did not mind he used the word 'dear' for her in the office. Her coworkers were also familiar with their relation.

Linda was in the office. Mr. Smith had already left for the fund-raising event. She needed to brief Charlene with lots of paperwork in the coming days, tell her about the Tuesday first week of month meeting procedures, and make her understand the key clients' files. She had compiled a list for Charlene during the few days left before her trip.

It was almost time to leave for home. Linda kept the papers in the proper places and prepared to leave. She remembered to drop by Sonam's place in the monastery and get Pasang's phone number and address at Dharamshala and also to say good-bye to them. She picked a fresh bunch of flowers for the monastery and on her way home stopped at Sonam's.

Sonam was pleased to see Linda. He handed over the phone number and address of Dharamshala, and advised her of the best ways from Delhi. When Linda came home, the phone rang.

"Hi, Mother, I am just back from work."

"Do you want me to call you back?"

"No, I will call back."

Her mother said, "Okay, dear," and dropped the call.

After Linda had finished her chores and prepared a sandwich with avocado, fresh veggies, and a salad with a large amount of lemonade, she called her mother.

"Hi, Mother, how are you and Dad?"

"Well, we are fine, thanks for asking."

"Mother, did you have time to talk with Susan?"

"Yes, dear. I felt much better after talking to her. Susan, I understand, went on another trip around Annapurna or something like that, sometime back."

"Oh, I did not know that," Linda said.

"Yes, she seems an experienced traveler to that part of world, and she likes it very much." Her mother seemed convinced. "Linda, I felt secure with Susan, and on my request, she assured me she would take care of you as well."

"Yes, Mother, they all are professional and nice people."

"Still, Linda, please take care of yourself, and do not travel alone."

Linda's father came on the line suddenly. "Linda, honey, are you not leaving this Friday?"

"Yes, Dad, I am."

"I understand the flight is tediously long with a brief stopover in Europe."

"It stops at Frankfurt, Germany," Linda said.

"Do you have lots of books to read?"

"I do, Dad."

"Listen, Linda, you are a big girl. Take care of yourself. Do not trust strangers. Stay with your group."

"Of course, Dad. Do not worry. I will come back in one piece," Linda consoled her dad.

"Okay, dear, I will talk to you just before you leave."

"Sure, Dad."

With that conversation, Linda hung up the phone and relaxed deeply on the Lay-Z-Boy chair.

She woke up in the chair just after midnight and moved to her comfortable bed, half-naked. As if she were sleepwalking, she approached her bed. The moment she slept, a strange dream came to her. She was alone on the foot of a tall mountain with green lush trees, and surrounded by mystic white clouds covered with beautiful mist. At a distance, she could see a clear and magical waterfall producing a sensational sound of smooth jazz echoing across the whole area, and it looked like all the birds and small animals were enjoying and dancing with the tune. Linda had never experienced these kinds of feelings in the past. A handsome Mongolian man was grazing yaks in the green pasture. The man was clad in typical Sherpa-like dress which Linda had seen in the Mountain Travel booklet.

The man came close to Linda and spoke with politeness and dignity, "Hi, do not be afraid. My name is Pemba Sherpa. What is your name?"

The total serenity, extreme peacefulness and magic of the atmosphere there, and this dominating personality with a soft, gentle, and deep male voice amazed Linda. She tried not to reply, and her efforts to neglect the man badly failed. She could not believe herself when her subtle, low voice replied, "I am Linda."

There was a pause. Nobody spoke. It seemed, the magical effect had been equally shared by both human beings. They seemed to enjoy looking at each other and appreciated this sudden moment.

"You have a beautiful name. It is just perfect and matches your beauty." Pemba's words echoed off the mountain. "I had never seen a goddess-like person with deep-blue expressive eyes, golden hair, and a human being like you floating in the air." Pemba spoke as if his words were coming from his heart, not from his mouth.

Pemba came closer; his fresh, warm body aroma could be smelled by Linda. She could not get away from him. Pemba held her softly in his arms and kissed her. It was a magical moment. Linda tried but could not detach from him as if she'd been waiting for this moment in her life.

When Linda woke up the next morning, she still felt that kiss from Pemba. She touched her lip; an unusual sensation crept throughout her body. She'd never had this kind of emotion in her life. Although it was just a dream, it seemed so real and touching.

Linda walked towards her dressing table and tried to look at herself in the mirror. Somehow, she found herself exceptionally beautiful this morning; perhaps her beauty had been refined with that kiss in the dream.

Linda took out the brochure from Mountain Travel, and saw the photo of Pemba—a handsome face—with a brief description of him. She had not read the description before, but it tempted her now. Pemba had been with Mountain Travel since 1982, and was an important Sherpa, the grandson of Tenzing Norgay—who'd scaled Everest the first time with Edmund Hillary. Pemba was a key porter, guide, and excellent cook. Since his father was also a cook when Tenzing and Hillary scaled Everest, Pemba's contribution to Mountain Travel was outstanding. On the top of the brief description, Pemba's picture looked the same as Linda had seen in the dream last night.

She gazed at the picture for a long time. The more she looked at the picture, higher was her feeling of being hypnotized by it. Her thoughts, she decided, should be shared with her best friend Amanda, whom she was meeting that night at the Marriot for a good-bye happy hour cocktail before her trip.

Linda left the office at five-fifteen. She reached the Marriott, which was on her way to home, at five-thirty, and she approached the cocktail lounge. As usual, the tables were occupied by the after-office-hour crowd; even the bartender was surrounded with happy hour thirsty people. Linda looked around for Amanda. She was not in yet, so Linda approached a small empty table towards the corner. She would wait for Amanda before ordering a drink. Close to five forty-five, Amanda entered the lounge.

"Sorry, Linda. It's always hard to leave the office on time; something comes on at the last moment," Amanda explained the reason for being late.

Linda knew Amanda was an investigative key journalist at the *Herald* and was always busy. She'd made her name in the national journalist circle when she saved a convicted murderer wrongfully accused of a crime in Texas about two years back. She used to live in Texas then, and had moved to Los Angeles just a year ago. Amanda was articulate, expressive, and well-educated. They'd become good friends just after they met at a small party at one of her friend's places. Linda and Amanda's chemistry matched perfectly, and they shared almost anything—whatever went on in life—general or personal.

Amanda said, "Just wait, Linda. Before we jump to conversation, let me get the cocktail. You want the usual?"

Without awaiting Linda's reply, Amanda went to the crowded counter area. Linda liked Amanda—her informal, easy and spontaneous conversation style, and down-to-earth personality. She had saved Linda from odd and ill-mannered men in the bar a couple of times. She had an unusual talent to handle murky situations.

However, Amanda, as compared to Linda, was not pretty at all. She had a number of scars on her face because of bad pimples. Her nose was sharp and pointed, and one of her eyes had been scratched while she was in army training in Jaffa in Israel, where she had grown up. Her parents were the survivors of Nazi atrocities during the Second World War, and had moved to the USA in the early seventies. Amanda was typically Jewish, conservative and traditional. Although she was around forty-five, because of her energetic style and easy manner of conversation, it made her feel younger than her age.

"My dear, here we go." Amanda returned with two cocktails in her hand.

Linda preferred gin and tonic with a twist of lemon, but Amanda took an unusual kind of Jewish cocktail. Sukkoth—a mint flavored, refreshing, easy drink with the complexity of pomegranates. Amanda added gin, honey, lemon, and orange juice to create a true cocktail—a bold taste that suited her personality.

"Linda, truly, I am going to miss you. Is it for a month?"

"Although the trek is for three weeks, I am also visiting the Dalai Lama's place somewhere in India. So it could take more than a month." Linda was excited to give the trip details to Amanda.

"I envy you. You know I am a conservative Jew, but I really admire and respect the Dalai Lama. Somehow I have a deep liking for Buddhism."

"How is David?" Suddenly, Linda wanted to change the subject.

"He is okay. I am having difficulty adjusting with him as he is not a Kosher," Amanda said.

"So you are going to marry a Jew man then?" Linda snapped back.

"Not really, but I am finding it truly awkward, especially during my Jewish festivals." Amanda's words sounded as if they had come from her heart.

"Amanda, let me suggest that you take your time and make a wise decision; it may last your lifetime."

"I am almost forty-one. I need to make a decision quick."

"Indeed, but a quick decision might land you in the wrong choice."

"Well, thanks, Linda. What about you? Do you have anyone in mind? I know you are damn picky."

Slowly, Linda took something out from a manila envelope. "Amanda, in my dream last night, this man kissed me."

Amanda virtually grabbed the brochure. "Which one?"

There were two pictures of the Sherpas in the brochure. Linda pointed toward Pemba.

"Oh my, exceptionally handsome. I am always attracted toward a Mongolian face. Who is he?"

"A Sherpa porter, a guide, and a cook during the trip." Linda was happy; Amanda liked it.

"Linda, this is getting interesting. Let me go and get another drink."

"Yes, okay, this is the last one for me." Linda never had more than two cocktails when she drove.

Linda always enjoyed Amanda's company. Amanda made her feel happy and energetic in life. Getting refills took a while as the crowd was growing, and the murmur turning louder. The room was getting filled with smoke. Linda never liked smoke, and she had not smoked in her life. She wanted to get away but could not leave Amanda. As she was feeling unhappy with the atmosphere, Amanda approached with same cocktails again.

The cocktail gave relief to Linda, and she felt relax.

"The crowd, I hate," Amanda said, "but I'm enjoying your romantic rendezvous."

"Yes, the crowd mixed with smoke and noise gives me a headache as well."

"Did that divine kiss excite you?"

"Yes, Amanda, it seems so real."

"But, Linda, how do you know he is educated, cultured, and compatible to you? I figure, he is not very educated." Amanda continued, "If he were educated, he would not be in that position."

"I have no idea, Amanda, but I have a soft inclination toward the Buddhists; they cannot be violent. Besides, I am planning to do my PhD in Buddhist religion at UCLA. I am perhaps trying to get close with a Buddhist to have more understanding by knowing them and their religion closely," Linda confessed.

"That should not be a reason for picking your life-partner, Linda."

"I agree, but I have not decided. It was just a dream."

Linda again thought about the dream. Amanda did not speak. She just stared at her, as if she were trying to study Linda's facial expressions. Although she was physically there, Linda was lost in her imaginations. Amanda came close to Linda and shook her shoulder. Linda jerked out from her thoughts and was brought back to reality.

"How are you going to keep me informed, Linda, while on your trip? I would like to know your progress about the trip and what goes on in your personal life."

"Amanda, you know I keep a diary and will let you read it when I come back."

"That sounds interesting; promise you will lend it to me to read," Amanda insisted.

A man had been gazing at them for quite a long time; he seemed half-drunk. He finally approached them. "May I offer a drink to lovely ladies?"

Both said, "No, thanks, we are about to leave."

With that remark, both got up and left the lounge—leaving the drunk, noisy, smoky, crowded atmosphere behind. At the parking area, both hugged for the last time and promised to meet immediately after Linda came back from the trip.

It was Thursday, her last day in office and the day before her departure on the much-anticipated trip. Linda needed to complete numerous tasks at the office. She took her to-do list, and when it was coming toward the end, felt some relief. While she was going over some files, Charlene dropped by the room.

"Linda, sorry to bother you. I have been briefed on this week's Tuesday regional and national conference's agendas and files. What should I do next Tuesday?"

"A very good question, Charlene. In fact, I myself don't know what will happen on Tuesday or what files to handle next. Kathy will be in on the Tuesday month meetings, and she will let you know which files to provide next week. Kathy has been briefed; she will inform you at least two days in advance," Linda explained to Charlene.

When Charlene was about to leave, Linda suddenly remembered and requested she stay for a while. Linda took out a file from the confidential rack and showed it to Charlene, making a remark, "This is an important file of our client Nelson. Smith may ask you to keep it in the confidential rack, and give it to Smith when he will need it sometime next week."

Linda showed her the red-covered file and then put it back in the same confidential rack.

"Charlene, please see me if you have time just before you leave the office today. I may remember if I have anything more to share, and if not it could be a good-bye between us."

"Of course, Linda. I will not leave the office before saying you good-bye."

Just after her conversation with Charlene, the phone rang. "Linda, may I help you?"

"Hi, Linda, this is Lisa. I wish you the best for the trip tomorrow," Lisa from Mountain Travel said. "You and everyone from Los Angeles will be taking the Lufthansa flight. Other travelers will be going to Frankfurt from their places of origin, and all will meet in Germany. The flight will go to Delhi with a stop in Tehran."

"That sounds good. Thanks for all your help."

"Again, good-bye and have a wonderful trip."

Linda thanked her and snapped the line.

Linda was in the office until five forty-five. She wanted to make sure everything was covered in the office before she left. Finally, everything was under control. Satisfied with her wrap-up efforts and briefing Charlene, she said good-bye to everyone in the office. She felt like going to the restroom before going home. After freshening up, she gave a last look of the office, and left.

Maria was in the office, vacuuming the floor. Linda went to her and said, "Good evening, Maria," and left the office.

It was almost seven. Linda reached home tired and exhausted, but deep inside her heart, she felt fresh and blissful that she was leaving the following day. The flight was at nine-thirty in the morning, and she should be at the airport at least by eight-thirty.

She needed to check on her final packing, make sure she had not forgotten anything. She checked her American Expressed traveler's check, counted one more time. Everything was up to her satisfaction; she checked the passport again, checked the visas for Nepal and India. After reviewing all the travel documents, she checked her credit cards also. As per Mountain Travel, Nepal businesses might not accept credit cards, but in India, in big business houses, they might accept them. She took her American Express credit card and kept it in her wallet—the rest, MasterCard and Visa card, she put in the drawer. When she was going to the restroom, the phone rang. As expected, her dad was on the phone.

"Hi, sweetheart, is your preparation going smoothly?"

"Yes, Dad."

"Be careful with your luggage, money, and documents. I mean, your passport."

"Of course, Dad. It's in my handbag."

"Is anyone going from your travel and ticket agency?"

"No, Dad, but their Nepal representative will meet us at Frankfurt."

"That's great. Again, Linda, take care. I need not repeat; you are a grown-up girl now. Wish you a wonderful trip."

After that, her mother came on the line.

"I hope, Linda, you have packed and did not forget important thing."

"Yes, Mom."

"After the trip, how long do you plan to stay in India?"

"Less than a week."

"I understand it is hard to call from Nepal, but please call once from India, okay, dear?"

"I will try."

"There is not much to say, Linda. We wish you the best trip and will let you prepare for tomorrow."

"Thanks, Mom, I will try to keep in touch whenever it is possible."

Linda entered the kitchen, but she wasn't hungry and did not know what to eat. She opened the refrigerator; the salad looked attractive. She made the salad in a big bowl and took out a bottle of Thousand Island salad dressing before settling at her small but cozy kitchen table. She went for two pieces of bread and maybe an omelet with two eggs. She sliced red onion, minced a tomato, and added some cilantro to the omelet. When the omelet was ready, she put it on the small plate and toasted two pieces of bread. When everything was ready, she settled and ate the food.

After dinner, Linda was tempted to take a lazy warm-water bath prior to sleeping. After the bath, she went to lie on the bed. As was her habit, she looked for a book to read so that the sleep would come eventually.

With the book in hand, Linda did not realize when sleep came and embraced her.

The next morning, the alarm went off at seven. Linda got up and finished her morning chores, as she had to leave for airport by at least seven forty-five by taxi so that she would be at the airport before eight thirty.

After her morning chores, she had a light breakfast, put on comfortable Wrangler jeans, a white top, and tennis shoes, and carried a sweater in her hand. She called a cab. The cabman promised to be there in twenty minutes. She dragged the two suitcases and handbag and waited for the cab on the porch. She turned off the main water source outside and checked her house for the last time. She softly touched the beautiful plants inside the house, gave a look just before departure, and waited for the cab. She knew Amanda had a duplicate key so that she could come once a week and water the plants.

She saw the cab approach her home. Upon reaching the doorstep, the driver opened the dickey and placed the luggage inside. Linda sat in the backseat, and the taxi pulled away. The day was beautiful, with bright morning sunlight. The birds on the oak tree were twittering, and the whole atmosphere was pleasant. Perhaps nature had made a perfect day for Linda's departure.

The cab took the south route via 405 Expressway and would exit at Inglewood to the Los Angeles Airport.

The cab arrived at the airport at eight-twenty. Linda collected her baggage from the taxi and proceeded toward the Lufthansa check-in counter.

"Hi, Linda." Lisa was waiting for her arrival.

Hi, Lisa, I'm surprised to see you."

"We normally assist passengers leaving from California. I came last night from Frisco." Lisa continued, "Let me have your ticket and passport. I will expedite your check-in process and also help at immigration. Linda, do you prefer to sit together with our group?"

"Of course yes, if possible."

Lisa, after collecting the documents from Linda, went to the airline's counter and asked her to wait for a few minutes.

Linda was surprised when Lisa came with her documents and explained, "Linda, this is your boarding pass from Los Angeles to Frankfurt. This one is from Frankfurt to Tehran, and after a short stay in Tehran, you will proceed to Delhi. By the way, a boarding pass will be issued to you on arrival in Tehran, and you will be in their transit lounge."

"Lisa, I really appreciate you for the trouble."

"Not at all, Linda, this is part of my job," Lisa informed politely. "Now, let us move to the immigration and security area; I have a special pass."

They made it there without any problems.

"Well, Linda, my best wishes for your fantastic trip." With that remark, Lisa hugged Linda and left.

Linda saw the other group members and went to sit next to Karen and Susan.

"Linda, we will have a wonderful trip." Susan hugged her.

"It's going to be wonderful for the next three weeks."

"Of course, Linda."

"I'm sure you talked with my mother. Didn't you?"

"Yes I did. She was worried about the trip; I have done my best to convince her."

"Did you also go to the Annapurna a few years back?"

"Yes, it was a magnificent trip. The Annapurna trek is much easier than Everest; the climb is not so much," Susan explained to Linda.

Linda realized the departure area for the Lufthansa flight was getting crowded and stuffy. Linda looked at her watch—still half an hour before departure. In the meantime, Linda heard the departure announcement of her flight 642. Everyone got up from their seats and collected their handbags.

"Time to go," Susan announced.

They all formed lines, and their group members were all together. Slowly, they approached the gate area. The Lufthansa ground staff was checking the boarding passes and computer list. The boarding tarmac bay was gradually filling up.

The passengers started moving towards their assigned seats in an orderly fashion. Linda followed Susan and Karen to their seats. Linda glanced at her seat number; it was 31-C, an aisle seat. Linda wished she had a window seat; she could have a bird's eye view of Los Angeles. But it was too late to change the seat now. In row 31, Susan had the window seat, Karen had the middle, and Linda the aisle seat. Everyone sat in their assigned seats. Slowly, the huge 747 aircraft were filled up. The stewardesses were helping those passengers who had a hard time reaching the overhead racks and finding their assigned seats. After a few minutes of commotion, everyone seemed to settle down comfortably.

Linda heard, "This is your captain speaking. I, along with my crew, welcome you on board Lufthansa flight 642 to Frankfurt. I am sure you will have a wonderful flight. After reaching our thirty-one thousand cruising height, our stewardesses will be glad to serve cocktails of your choice followed by lunch. You will experience wonderful treatment and sample German hospitality onboard. We are waiting for our turn on takeoff and waiting for tower instruction for takeoff. In the meantime, enjoy the flight, and be comfortable." With that announcement, the captain disconnected the line.

"Linda, you have never been on a plane of this size before; would like to take my window seat?" Susan asked.

"If it will not be uncomfortable for you, Susan."

"It will be a pleasure. Besides, it will be easy for me to go to the restroom without disturbing you guys."

Linda exchanged the seat and felt happy.

After a few minutes, the captain said again, "Ladies and gentlemen! We are ready for the takeoff. Fasten your seatbelts and relax."

Linda heard a loud engine hum. Then the seat shook heavily. When the aircraft left the ground, smoothness prevailed and the noise reduced dramatically. Linda tried to look on the ground down below, but the aircraft took height and she could only see the clouds that obstructed the ground view. The plane soared upward, breaking patches of clouds here and there. After some time, the captain came on the PA.

"We are almost at thirty thousand feet. Soon we will reach our cruising level and the cabin crew will resume service onboard."

"Did you see anything on the ground?" Karen asked Linda.

"Not really. Patches of clouds obscure the view." Linda clearly had disappointment.

"You will have a better view when we land in Frankfurt," Karen consoled Linda.

It seemed the stewardesses showed up in the cabin just after finishing with the first-class cabin, and they were pushing the big cocktail tray and approaching passengers. Linda diverted her mind toward her book—the one given to her by Amanda. It was a book on Jewish belief and faith, on their religion and culture. It seemed the Jews had all sorts of religious traditions and observations. They had Purim, Passover, Rosh Hashanah, Yom Kippur, Hanukkah and several others—which were mostly observed a strict and traditional manner. Linda had joined some of their observations and had enjoyed them. Amanda's family treated her as one of their family members. Linda was thoroughly engrossed in the book when she heard a polite, nice voice with a heavy German accent, "Madam, would you prefer to drink?"

"Please give me a gin and tonic with a twist of lime." Linda was quick with her order.

"Sure." The hostess handed over her drink.

"Thanks," said Linda, politely.

Karen had a Bloody Mary, and Susan, a dry martini.

Linda had two gins and tonics and, immediately after, a delicious lunch with roasted pork, mashed potatoes, green pies and flavorful sauce, making it tasty and exquisite. There was a small bowl of salad with fresh bread and a cocktail of fresh fruits with a sweet creamy sauce. The entire lunch was elegant and fulfilling. Linda was surprised that they were supplied with metal cutlery. Everything seemed to be perfect along with the smoothness of the flight.

After a coffee, Linda made herself comfortable, closed the window panel, and fell asleep. She woke up to the loud noise of the speakers: "Ladies and gentlemen, we will be landing at Frankfurt Airport in forty-five minutes. Cabin crew, please discontinue cabin services and prepare for landing. We will be descending shortly."

Linda realized she'd slept for over six hours and felt fresh and energetic.

"Linda, you may open the window panel now for a great view of Frankfurt," Karen informed.

She opened the window panel and saw the ground at a distance. The city seemed decorated with lights and looked bright and pleasant. She could see the roads, and in the distance, a train was moving on a track. The roads were occupied by numerous cars, and she could see their red taillights. In a big stadium, what looked like a soccer game was going on. It had been decorated with bright lights, and people were sitting in the circular rows. Linda knew that American football was not so popular in Europe compared to soccer.

"We will be landing in fifteen minutes. Cabin crew, please prepare for the final approach," the captain instructed the crew, and it seemed he too was informing the passengers.

The plane finally landed with a big jerk, and Linda could hear the sound sent forth by the breaking and scraping of the plane tires on the ground. After a few minutes, the plane came to a halt on the tarmac.

"Please check your belongings and carry them with you. The transit passengers, please get off and proceed to the transit lounge. On arrival, you will be given a yellow transit pass. Do not forget to take your belongings and handbags with you. Please check the monitor board for your next departure gate on Lufthansa flights."

In no time, everyone in the group came down and assembled in the transit lounge. Some rushed to the restrooms, and a few settled on the chairs. A few went towards the Duty Free shops. Linda felt she needed to stretch her body and legs and decided to go to the Duty Free areas. She saw a variety of watches, perfumes, handbags and liquors from different countries that were on display there. She did not need to buy anything now; she might perhaps shop a few things on her way back home.

As she was walking around, Linda saw a cinema, a saloon, a bath area, bookshops, and a baby-sitting area where the parents could leave their children and go to see an adult movie or take a bath. The airport seemed to be equipped with all sorts of passengers' needs, either for long or short-transit stay. Linda noticed, she had never seen the amenities that she was finding here. She thought, the European airports were perhaps more advanced than the American airports. She would not need these amenities, as she was there for only two hours, but she would get a newly published book by her favorite writer, Fredrick Forsyth.

Two hours passed, and the Lufthansa flight flashed on the monitor, ready for departure to Delhi. Robert showed up in the transit lounge and requested the group to follow him to the flight. After everyone occupied the seats, the plane slowly started sliding on the runway and took off from the airport into the mist. Linda tried to look out, but the weather was gloomy, and the ground looked gray with cars and numerous roads scattered here and there. Linda at least saw a patch of white snow on the ground.

Linda physically was not so tired, but mentally, she seemed to be exhausted due to the long flight. After a couple of drinks, she seemed relaxed, and immediately after dinner, passed out with a sweet dream of Nepal and Pemba.

On October 29, Mountain Travel had a staff meeting organized by Col. Tom Bradley, the owner. About seven employees were in the meeting, which included Dawa Sherpa, the office manager, and Pemba. The main agenda was to provide an outstanding service to the American group arriving the next day. Dawa was responsible for airport reception, transportation, and check-in at Hotel Yak & Yeti. Pemba would assist Dawa for their briefing and reception at the hotel, supervise the city sightseeing, and procure the trekking permits. Col. Tom Bradley would welcome and brief them at the hotel. Everything seemed to work out in detail, and the office was ready to handle this important group.

***

CHAPTER FIVE

End of October 1985

Robert, the Nepal representative of Mountain Travel, joined the group in Frankfurt. It was a long, tiring journey, but Linda began to refresh when she noticed a dramatic change in the landscapes on the ground: green mountains, rivers flowing through the mountains, and a vivid kind of resemblance to what was described in the book *Tiger for Breakfast*. Linda was excited and asked Robert, who was sitting in the front row of the plane, "How long before we land in Nepal?" One could notice the excitement in Linda's voice.

"Maybe about another half an hour."

"Thanks, Robert."

Linda quietly gazed at the green landscape again. In India, she had seen the landscape mostly dry and gray without the mountains. She was told the mountains in India were mostly in the north and east, but it seemed the flight was coming through the northern-mid part of the country. The climate of India might be drier, except during the monsoon season from June to early September every year. She figured that, Nepal, being within the same range, should have a similar climate. But because of the mountains and rainforest, it might have more rain—the reason why the landscape was greener and more attractive.

"This is your captain speaking. Ladies and gentlemen, we will be landing in Kathmandu Airport within the next ten minutes. We hope you all had a wonderful trip and we'll see you next time."

With that remark, the captain planned to land the flight as it took a sharp left turn. Passengers prepared themselves for the final approach and tied their seat-belts. The stewardesses were busy collecting the remaining empty bottles and trash scattered in front of the seats. The aircraft landed smoothly rolling through green pasture, and came to a complete halt without a few minutes.

Linda saw a tiny airport in a distance. Everyone started walking toward the arrival hall. It looked crowded and congested. Robert came to collect everyone's passports. The immigration procedures seemed time-consuming and slow. After a long wait, everyone finally got through the immigration and customs requirements.

In one corner, Linda saw two tall figures approaching the group. One of the figures was none other than Pemba, who had such a distinguished look. He looked more handsome than in the picture.

He came toward Linda and said, "Good morning, welcome to Nepal," in his husky and pleasant voice that surprised Linda.

He welcomed everyone with soft, silky white scarfs, putting them around everyone's neck like a muffler. Linda accepted the scarf with thanks and a polite gesture.

The tourist bus had about twenty-eight seats. It had a shabby look but a clean interior. The bus left after the group occupied the seats, and moved toward the city and the hotel. Linda noticed in the tiny streets, people were walking on both sides of the street on the footpath. The traffic looked primitive, without the traffic lights a policeman standing on a tall square, directing the flow of traffic with hand signals. It was something new and interesting for Linda, and she watched it with curiosity. The valley seemed clean, and people were walking at a leisurely pace; people on the street seemed relaxed. She closely watched their faces, which were without tension and fatigue. She noticed people on the street had very simple subtle smiles on their faces. She enjoyed the tall green mountains surrounding the valley and felt they were so close she could touch them with her hand. Everything was like the image of Shangri-La. Linda was profoundly attracted to the city, the people, nature, and the overall simple-but-touching way of life.

The bus approached an old red-colored building, and on the door, it had the small neon sign that said, "Yak & Yeti." This must be the Boris Hotel the writer wrote about in *Tiger for Breakfast*, Linda thought.

Linda got down from the bus slowly together with the group and assembled in the hotel lobby, which had a black-and-white marble floor that looked simple, exotic, and attractive.

Dawa requested they go to their rooms and freshen up. After lunch, around 5:00 p.m. in the cocktail lounge, they were expected to meet Col. Tom Bradley for a welcome cocktail and briefing on the trek.

After six hours of relaxation and the nourishing lunch, everyone looked energized, vibrant, and ready for the cocktail mixer hosted by Mountain Travel. The group members assembled in a large hall.

The painted ceiling at a formidable height, and the walls there were of eighteenth-century design; the outstanding chandeliers with colorful bright stones sparkled with amber light. The atmosphere of the hall was enchanting and intoxicating. The table arrangement was sophisticated in style with ivory-colored table covers, and chairs were of dark maroon velvet. Linda also noticed the cocktail bar on the left corner. A little further up in the center, a huge chimney with a large fireplace surrounded by comfortable leather chairs had been placed. Linda just loved the setting and professional decoration of the hall with the touch of an old, sophisticated style.

With Dawa and Pemba, Linda noticed a third man: a tall, tanned and rugged person with a Scottish pipe on his mouth. He was holding a gold-rimmed cane in his right hand, as he walked with slight limp on his left leg. He seemed a retired British army officer with more salt than pepper mixed in his hair.

Dawa, standing at the right corner of the hall, tried to draw their attention with a delicate clap.

"May I have your attention please?" Dawa was trying to draw everyone's attention.

Suddenly, the murmur died out. Everyone diverted their gazes toward Dawa, gathering in a circle.

"It is a pleasure to introduce Colonel Bradley, who is in-charge of Mountain Travel operations in Nepal."

Every one in the group clapped, and Colonel Bradley approached with a smile.

"My greetings and warm welcome to Nepal for the three-week trek to the Everest region. I joined Mountain Travel in 1957, shortly after my retirement. Prior to that, I had an opportunity to participate in one of the hunting trips to Nepal. Since then, I fell in love with mystical mountains, the untouched natural beauty of the country, and on top of everything the impact of simplicity and genuine hospitality of the people here."

Bradley continued, "The tall, snowcapped mountains and magnificent well-preserved forests with abundant, diverse birds and wild flowers will touch everyone's heart. This country, which has just opened for tourism, has something virgin and unique to offer to the world.

"In the early days, we had trekkers mostly from England, Germany, and France. The Americans were slow to join. Now, I see people mostly from California, Colorado, and Washington pouring in.

"During the trek, we have porters to carry our supplies, prepare food for us, erect tents, and help complete our daily walk with ease and safety. You will find the people we come across in some of the remote Sherpa villages interesting, kind, hospitable, and peaceful in nature.

"Normally," Colonel Bradley continued, "we do not recommend participants to join our Everest trek before participate in trekking along some easy tracks like around Annapurna or lower elevation area, but younger generation with high stamina and excellent health are encouraged. Besides, in order to avoid high-altitude sickness, we hold them back for about four days in Kathmandu City and Namche Bazaar.

"In conclusion, we have an excellent team in our management. Robert, who is standing behind me, will be on the trek with you. Now I will be happy to answer a few questions you probably have in mind."

A lady standing in front asked, "Hi, my name is Stella, and I am from Colorado."

"Yes, Stella," Colonel Bradley said.

"As I have heard, now and then, some trekkers disappear while trekking in Nepal. How is it possible, and what are the chances of the same thing happening over again?"

"Well," Bradley was quick to reply, "sometimes, we get such sad news. Those people are basically independent trekkers, who undertake this kind of trek without a guide. They could either have lost their way or may have been attacked by wild animals. People from remote villages are mostly helpful and peaceful; we cannot imagine harm done by them. The Nepal Government also recommends hiring a guide, and permits are normally issued in such cases, but as you know, people are either obstinate, or they do not want to incur the additional expenses. In thirty years of our operation, we have not lost a single person from our group. They are safe, and we take good care of them."

Stan repeated the question which was asked earlier in San Francisco to Robert about a trekker being sick or indispose during the trek.

"Indeed an interesting and pertinent question, Stan," Bradley said. "We had an incident in one of our groups about eight years back. Since Robert was on-site, he will be able to answer you more convincingly than me. Robert, will you explain to Stan how you handled the situation."

"Of course."

Robert came in front and faced the group.

"We carry a two-way radio system during the trek. I phoned Namche tower, which sent a priority request for a rescue chopper from the military, and that came to us within a short time. The chopper took the sick trekker to Kathmandu Airport and transferred to Shanta Bhawan, a mission hospital. After the checkup and stabilization of her condition, she was flown to Delhi for further treatment," Robert gave a brief summary.

"Thanks, Robert. Do we have any more questions?" Bradley looked around, but no one spoke.

After a while, Dawa came up front.

"Mountain Travel welcomes you once again. The cocktail will be served straightaway. Please enjoy the cocktail."

Linda saw the boys in white tunics and tops with black belts and ladies with some kind of black-and-red dress holding the cocktail trays and approaching the guests, offering drinks. The cocktail boys and girls looked smart and pretty.

Linda asked for a gin and tonic when a pretty lady approached her and took a glass from the tray. Susan and Karen joined Linda.

"Hi, Linda, how do you like this hall? Is it not gorgeous? It has a rich look of Victorian style with wall decoration and vintage fiber drapes in the window. I love those chandeliers," Karen remarked, and Linda agreed.

Although Linda was physically occupied with her friends, she was, in fact, looking for a chance to talk with Pemba—who was busy with Dawa. They were sitting in the far right corner table and discussing a paper lying on the table. Linda at least had a deep desire to introduce herself casually. But she preferred to wait for a suitable time.

After the cocktail, the crowd slowly went to the dining hall for dinner. Linda, Karen, and Susan sat together with Stan at a gorgeous table filled with colorful cutlery and crystal glasses and bright silver utensils. Subtle, soft music was floating in the room; everyone in the group, including Linda, felt the enormous sensation of hotel hospitality during the dinner that sent forth an enticing aroma.

After the long, leisurely dinner, Linda's mind and body transcended to a strange but pleasant sensation. She felt unique peace and tranquility run through all her sensations; this was a thing she had never experienced in her life. The cocktail, the soothing taste of the food, and maybe the peaceful manner and extraordinarily pleasing hospitality of the people perhaps contributed to that.

Linda could not remember when she left the exotic dining room with completely satisfying food and atmosphere beyond comprehension. She slept like a baby throughout the night.

She woke up to a melodious bird sound at her window, as if the birds were supporting Linda's state of mind. She did not have to take a long drive to the office, carry the tension of being late, or carry out all the weekdays' tedious routine she followed during the five weekdays in office. She noticed a colorful bird making a twittering sound outside the window and partaking of the celebration of her trip in the land of her dream.

Linda took a look at her itinerary of the day in the city, which described a tour of Bhaktapur City to have a look of its primitive houses, magnificent pagodas, and distinctive arts in the royal squares.

The tourist bus left at nine-fifteen from the hotel, moving east along a road covered with persistent low mist. In the distance was a crystal clear mountain range, which Linda noticed from the left side of the bus. The peaks were spectacular and beyond description. No one talked inside the bus; everyone's eyes were glued to the mountains to the east. Linda, for the first time, felt the mountain's magic in her heart. It felt so close, as if she could touch it by hands; she wanted to fly and be part of the mountains.

Everyone got down from the bus. The surroundings seemed to be of the eighteen century, with old brick houses standing in a cluster, and curious faces moving around with smiles around. In the distance, they could see rice seeds spread out to dry in the sun, strewn on huge straw mats.

The rays of the sun were very weak through the low-lying mist; the air was at its most pristine hue. The gentle walking of the group with a low murmur excited everyone in the true untouched area of life—as if everyone strolled on the ninth cloud. Linda felt magical and spiritual; a feeling of totality was exhilarating her. Her perception changed, and perhaps, she would not mind living in this country forever.

A tall, slender, thin square-faced guide voiced, "This city is known as the City of Devotees. It is filled with monuments, terra-cottas with carved wood columns, palaces, and temples with exotic and elaborate carvings, glided roofs, open courtyards dotted with pagodas and religious shrines."

Linda was not concentrating on the description, but enjoying the comprehensive sight and sound of the place with enchanting excitement.

After the exciting city stroll, the bus took the visitors to the scenic countryside road, passing through the rice terraces and a huge open area at the foot of small green mountains. Tall pine trees led to a ravine. With a sharp right turn, they approached the dense alpine trees, overlooking awesome mountain sights toward the east. The guide informed them they had come to Dhulikhel and would have an outdoor lunch with a stunning view of Mount Everest.

The place was enchanting. A clear blue dome sky and the mountains with smiling silver glitter made the whole atmosphere mystical and charming. The air was a little cooler, and one could smell strong fragrances of pines. Everything in nature was in perfect balance; the peaceful nature enhanced tranquility.

Karen looked towards Linda and smiled but said nothing. Perhaps nature's beauty was more essential than a talk at this moment of elation.

The group walked in different directions. Gazing at a huge meadow toward the east and holding the lunch packs in their hands, they seemed uninterested in food, and concentrated more on the spectacular blend of scenic, amazing beauty. Everyone was mesmerized and was looking towards the east on the mountain sight.

"That is Mount Everest, ladies and gentlemen. That is where you will be soon, as I understand." The guide was pointed towards the east even as he delivered the information, and everyone followed his finger's direction with curiosity.

Two nights stay in the most beautiful valley in Kathmandu City had a tremendous impact on Linda's mind. The whole city revealed itself as an eighteenth-century museum—an old structure with new dimensions. The artifacts, carvings, and shops with thousands of articles unknown to Linda created curiosity. In the distance, Linda occasionally heard the musical sound coming from a group of people carrying strange instruments. The fog covered and embraced the city, but when dim sunlight penetrated, it lifted up the city as if it gave the impression of a new bride slowly taking off her veil and exposing her stunning beauty. Linda noticed, when the faint rays of the sun exposed the city, everyone came out into the street and enjoyed the mild sunlight. She was told, as most of the houses were not heated, sunrays were the only source of heat during winter.

For Linda, the sights, sounds, architecture, and temples were something new, and she enjoyed the uniqueness and mystical atmosphere. The description she'd read about the city in *Tiger for Breakfast* was convincing, appropriate, and overwhelming. She could infer the true meaning of Shangri-La while walking and strolling across the city.

The two nights' stay in the medieval city energized and soothed her spirit and mind, and raised her perception to a new height. She developed a true purpose of coming on this trip and felt completely satisfied.

The next day, the group assembled at the domestic airport in order to take a flight to Lukla. The morning was crisp and cold, and it seemed the airport was not equipped with heating system. Outside, it appeared that the airport was covered with thick fog, and flights were delayed. Nobody had the clue as to when the fog would clear. They had no choice but to wait until the fog cleared away, and the flight to Lukla would commence. Around ten-thirty, after two hours' delay, the fog seemed to clear and the flight was announced.

The small plane left the airport, making a loud, piercing sound. It headed east with the beautiful city below and glittering snow-capped mountains on the left, and headed toward Linda's dreamland. Linda's mind was occupied with the fantasy of the trip, besides the joy of being close to these splendors of out-of-this-world sights. She wished, the plane would keep flying, but it eventually landed at Lukla Airport. Close to the airport, on its left side to be precise, she noticed houses that stood very close to the airport. People were watching the plane landing from their open terraces. Linda was surprised to see houses so close and within the airport vicinity.

Robert said, "Welcome to Lukla Airport."

When everyone in the group had assembled on a dirt road just a little away from the airport, Robert further announced, "We will have lunch in the Everest View Restaurant close by. After lunch and a little rest, we will move to Phakding, which will take around three hours."

Robert led the group to the restaurant, which looked shabby and old but clean and spacious.

The restaurant seemed to be busy as another group, maybe from Germany, was also having lunch. The tourists were seated at one large table on the left side of the dining hall. The group was noisy, laughing and having lunch at the same time. The hosts at the restaurant were gathering the scattered tables and trying to make one large table for Linda's group. They pulled in about six tables on the far right side of the dining hall and set up the chairs together. Linda's group started occupying the chairs one after another. Linda occupied a chair next to a graceful African tourist, who was also part of the group. In fact, she had never had a chance to talk with him.

After they had settled down, the African tourist said, "Hi, my name is Allure Okuba."

"I am Linda."

"Are you enjoying the trip?"

"By all means," Linda replied, looking directly on his eyes. "How about you?"

Allure shrugged his shoulders and replied, "It is magnificent and unique."

Allure was tall, with a smiling face. He wore glasses with silver shining rims, and bore a penetrating look. He had polish style of communication. Linda thought was a highly educated person.

"Mr. Okuba, may I ask you a personal question?"

"Call me Allure, and by all means yes, Linda."

"What is your profession?"

"I am in the medical field."

This was what Linda has speculated too.

"I work at Saint Jude Hospital in Los Angeles as a physician," the man added.

"Great! I had thought you were a doctor."

"What gave you that idea?"

"Your personality and my intuition." Both laughed.

When the lunch was served, everyone turned quiet and got busy with the food that seemed delicious, as the aroma was strong and inviting.

"Now we should head to Phakding, which is an easy walk, slightly downhill, without exertion," Robert announced.

The weather was perfect for the walk. The roads were narrow, and in some areas, they needed to form a single line to walk comfortably. Sometimes, on the right side of the road toward the ridge, yaks passed with a boy holding a stick in his hand. The yaks made noises with the strange bells that were tied around their necks, producing noise that echoed mildly in the close mountains and remained on your ear for a long time even after the animals had walked past.

The sound of air whipping was strong and noisy; it provided vigor that could only be experienced in beckoning silence. In the distance, Linda saw a gorge between the two similar-sized green mountains; the blue stream looked like a tiny river from this distance, flowing and making a narrow path down under the gorge. Robert explained about the village, the tourists walked smoothly, as everyone was submerged in the beautiful surroundings. Nothing but peace and tranquility with a totally spiritual decked the atmosphere.

"That is Phakding." Robert pointed toward a hilly area with some dotted thatch homes and a dark shadow of pine trees in the background. "We will have our camp here," he informed.

They reached the targeted spot for camping that night within the scheduled time. The spot was fascinating: a large meadow under the tall pine trees. On the left side of the ridge was a gorge, a river flowing downhill, making musical sounds with its water. It had a compelling, gorgeous sound that would help everyone to sleep soundly. Linda's impulses agreed perfectly with the choice of place. She'd had a vision of this kind of place in the past too. It was nothing but a piece of paradise on earth.

Tents were placed on four corners of the large meadow, and the remaining tents were placed together, within about six feet from each other, in one row inside the center. Linda observed the efficiency of the porters and the Sherpas. Together, they fixed the tents in no time. She was amazed to see their efficiency. A little further in the distance, a large tent they erected looked like a kitchen. A large dining table was placed in the middle of the tent.

Linda noticed a portable gas burner and a small propane cylinder close by. Some people were making ready-to-cook food for dinner.

"Madam, do you care for a cup of tea, coffee, or cocktail?" A husky boy with a stout build asked Linda. Linda had seen the boy in the group of porters who traveled in front of the group. He had a peculiar accent but spoke in a pleasing manner.

"Yes, please. May I have a gin and tonic?"

After a while, the same boy came with a tray on his hand and Linda took the cocktail of her choice.

The sun was setting slowly behind the tall mountains in the west and the golden rays reflected on the lofty eastern mountains. It created a lovely golden atmosphere. The humming and twittering of the multi-colored birds from the dense trees produced a melodious and intoxicating sound.

The river flowing down the gorge, the light smell of the pine, and the amazing scenery of golden mountains in the west touched everyone. Linda thought, this sight—if observed by great artists, like Rembrandt, Picasso, and Van Gogh—could have given Nepal international exposure through their immortal paintings.

Linda noticed Allure approaching her slowly. "Is it not hypnotizing?" he asked.

"Just perfect," Linda added.

"I do not know why the mountains always attract me," Allure remark

"Have you been to any other place with mountains?"

"A long time back, when I was sixteen, my father took me to Kilimanjaro," Allure replied.

"Were you born in Africa?" Linda questioned.

"No. I visited it. I was born in Los Angeles. My parents migrated to the States in the thirties."

"Which part of Africa are you from?"

"Middle of Kenya, from a city called Jos. My father is also a physician, and retired from the same hospital where I am working now."

"Great!" Linda gave a short remark and displayed a generous smile.

"I had been planning this trip for the past two years," Allure continued. "A group of nurses and physicians came down here from our hospital then; they talked about the visit constantly and motivated me."

"Did they come for this trip?" Linda was curious.

"No, they went to Pokhara. They had a medical conference and took the other trip of shorter duration, an easy one."

Linda saw a thin, tall man approaching them.

"Hello. If you don't mind, may I join you guys?"

Linda noticed, he had a very heavy European accent but had an attractive personality and an olive tan, long face, and thin moustache.

"My name is Alexander Kapatou."

"My pleasure to meet you." Linda showed her eagerness as she and Allure introduced themselves to him.

"We also have mountains but not as gorgeous as these."

"Where do you come from?" Allure inquired.

"Originally from Greece."

"Where do you live in the States?" Again, Allure put forth a question.

"Oregon," Alexander replied.

"Do you mind if I address you as Alex?"

"Of course not, Linda. In fact, all my family and friends address me with that nick name. In fact, I like it," Alex encouraged Linda. "These mountains revive my inner spirits." Alex seemed to be talking to himself.

"I have heard a lot of nice things about Greece. In fact, I have a strong desire to visit it some day," Linda expressed herself.

"Of course! I love Greek mythology, and the stories of Greek gods always fascinate me," Allure supported Linda.

"Alex, if you don't mind, may I ask you a personal question?" Allure ventured.

"Pleasure will be mine, Allure," Alex gave a confident reply.

"What profession are you in?"

"Timber. The same line of work I had in Greece before moving to the States about twenty years ago," Alex replied in one breath.

Allure looked at Alex's hand, which was rough and seasoned; he was convinced of his profession.

"Hi Linda, are you enjoying this setup?" Susan joined the small group. Looking toward Alex and Allure, she said, "Hi, I am Susan."

She shook hands with both of them with a subtle smile.

The twilight was disappearing slowly on the peak of the mountains; the camp was getting surrounded by darkness. The atmosphere was still awesome with fading birds' sound coming from dark pine groves nearby. The stream's murmur was growing louder. At a distance in the kitchen tent, a bright light had just sparkled. It exposed the porter's faces involved in the cooking. Linda could not help but gaze toward the handsome, youthful, smiling, bright face of Pemba.

"Does anyone know that the tall guy in the kitchen, wearing a long blue apron is the grandson of the cook who helped Hillary and Tenzing during their expedition?" Susan was indicating at Pemba.

"Indeed. I read that in their brochure," Allure added.

"People say he is a great cook," Alex said in agreement.

"Well, we are going to taste it tonight at dinner." At Linda's remark, everyone laughed.

Robert raised his hand and beckoned everyone to come closer, perhaps for some important announcement. When the group had gathered in a circle around him, Robert guided them to the middle part of the tent area.

"This tent belongs to the ladies. The ones a little further north and down south are for the gents, and the larger one in the southeast belongs to the porters and Mountain Travel personnel."

The beds were made neatly like the ones a maid prepares at a 5-star hotel. Although everyone's bed was a sleeping bag, they gave an impression of professional arrangement. The beds were cozy, attractive, and clean. Linda was fussy and picky about beds, especially the pillows. She couldn't stand the odor of another person. She often had hard times sleeping, if there existed some previous odor. Whenever she traveled in the past, she always carried her own pillow, but during this trip, it was not possible. She hoped, she would adjust with whatever was in store, and tried to manage a sound sleep anyhow, which was absolutely necessary for the next day's trek.

At dinner, everyone enjoyed the food. The main course was spaghetti with minced chicken, salads, wanton soup, and cheesecake for dessert. After dinner, coffee, liquor, and brandy were served. When they had dined to their satisfaction, everyone proceeded to their respective tents as tiredness of the walk followed by perfect food seemed to grip them with a deserving sleep for the first night in an open place with such an exotic setting.

Linda was the one who got up earlier than others in her tent after a sound and peaceful sleep. The birds' noise, smell from the pine grove, and the light murmur of the stream inspired her. Her feelings were exhilarating, and she felt perceptible changes in her body and mind.

After dressing casually, Linda came out from the tent and freshened herself up with refreshing water. The sunrise kissed the upper portion of the white mountaintops splashed with early golden rays.

Wherever she looked, the surroundings were utterly fresh and captivating. She strolled toward the southern part of the meadow. The grass seemed exceptionally fresh with morning dew sparkling on them as though they were nicely cut crystal drops. Linda's feelings compelled her to take off her slippers and walk on the meadow. The walk without the slippers energized and unusually freshened up her entire body and mind, which she'd never felt in the past. The closeness to pure nature and awfully fresh air mixed with pine scent, transformed her into a euphoric existence. She slowly walks towards the edge of the meadow's southern ridge on naked feet; a grass shrub or a piece of broken glass hurt her feet. She noticed a small wound on her right foot and tiny drops of blood flowing from her soft, white skin. She walks slowly towards the tent, occupied by Mountain Travel people and requested for a first-aid help for her wound.

Pemba came to respond and asked her, "What happened? How can I help you?"

Linda showed her right foot wherefrom blood was dripping slowly. Pemba hurried into the tent and came out with a small first-aid kit in his hand. He cleaned the tiny wound with a piece of cotton submerged in alcohol. After wiping it out, he put a bandage and covered the wound. Pemba was very compassionate, patient, and gentle during the whole process.

"Thank you so much, I should not have walked without slippers. Thanks again, I am Linda."

"Hello, I am Pemba. It is not your fault; these pines have sharp branches, and sometimes trekkers ignore our instructions to properly take care even of tiny pieces of broken glass left after the camp," Pemba consoled Linda. "I hope it will not hurt you during your walk."

"I will place a cushion of cotton around it, and I am sure it will not bother me," Linda assured Pemba.

Linda avoided direct look at Pemba's eyes. She was kind of nervous, and realized her face must be blushing. When he looked up, Pemba was directly looking into her eyes; their eyes met willingly or unwillingly, and both smiled at each other.

"Thanks, Pemba, again for your help," Linda said.

Linda walked toward her tent. The unusual and unexpected meeting with Pemba, she thought, was a divine incident as if God wanted them to meet in that delicate circumstance.

When Linda got back to the tent, everyone had woken up, and they were having coffee. Linda also requested for a cup of coffee from the boy passing through the tent.

"Linda, did you wake up early? You were missing from the tent," Karen asked.

"Yes, Karen, it was so refreshing, and the grass is so amazing. I went to walk in the meadow and had this small incident. I was walking without slippers, and I do not know how I stepped on a piece of broken glass. Pemba put on the dressing."

"Sorry, Linda! Will you be able to walk?" Susan sympathized, and expressed her concern.

"Oh, it's nothing. It will not bother me at all." Linda's expression was of self-confidence.

After about an hour, everybody assembled in the dining tent for breakfast. The breakfast that morning was simple porridge, fruit salad, orange juice, tea and coffee.

As everyone was having breakfast, Robert, who was sitting in the middle part of a table, slightly stood from the chair and said, "Well, I hope we all had a good rest last night. Today we will have about six hours' walk, and we will reach Namche Bazaar. We will have our lunch about halfway."

Linda's mind was not on Robert's information; she was thinking about this morning's memorable incident with Pemba. Whenever Linda tried to look toward Pemba, he was not facing her but was slightly diverting his eyes away from hers. Linda realized, Pemba was a very shy and modest person. She liked his behavior; young men, as her experience suggested, were normally aggressive and irritating. She thought Pemba was quite sincere. One thing she guessed was possible: he would never cheat her. Her feelings towards Pemba grew more and more profound and intimate, as time rolled by.

Pemba had almost forgotten the morning incident with Linda. He was busy with his daily chores and the usual stuff he did, such as dismantling the tent, bed and numerous other usual trekking gears and camping equipment that would be needed in Namche for the evening setup.

Namche reminded Pemba of a family trip they took up once during the Lohsar festival. His father bought lots of things for everyone in the family—beautiful dresses for his sisters, a colorful *bakkhu* for his mother, and nice dark blue pants for him. He used those pants for years until they wore out completely. He was always closer to his father than to his mother. However, he still remembers that when he was sick once, his mother took really good care of him. Since then, he had deep respect, love, and extreme compassion for his mother; the period of sickness created a lasting bond.

Pemba's family was at one of their aunts' houses in Namche. Pemba was nine years old then, but enjoyed family get-together. Everyone treated him like an adult. These memories impacted him throughout his life, and he still loved Namche. It still enticed him with its beautiful, gorgeous Himalayan ranges and typical Sherpa culture that entrenched the entire village.

***

CHAPTER SIX

November 1985

After a hearty breakfast, the group got ready to take a six-hour trip to the Namche Bazaar. Linda remembered Paul telling her that this trip would change one's perception of life. The nature, food, and hospitality of the people provided a fusion that would enhance and stimulate their inner spirit and confidence, and lead life into a new dimension. The mountain, detached from the worldly day-to-day busy routine, compelled one to think about life and beyond—to question the purpose of life and life after death, which one normally did not have time to think about and analyze. During this trip, while walking on your own—detached from phone, radio, television, traffic, offices, bosses and project deadlines—your mind is drawn extremely close to nature, mountains, river, trees, and beautiful landscape. This trek provided a meaning in life to Linda and touched the free spirit of her mind. Such eloquent atmosphere, remoteness, and unspoiled nature was possible only in this part of Nepal. Perhaps there is no place as this in the whole world for this kind of trekking activity.

Not only Linda, the entire team seemed to be in high spirits as no one had experienced this sort of setting before: tremendous landscapes with the dark-gray mountains on one side and towering white milky peaks all around on the other. The gorgeous, dark blue river flowing between the small dark red hills had an everlasting impact on the trekker's mind.

The trekkers were in their own small groups, walking together. Linda was with Susan, Allure, Alex, and an unknown Japanese trekker, who was also walking closely with them. Everyone had seen him in the group, but he had not met them, and everyone was staring at him curiously. The Japanese man in hefty boots—medium build, having an impressive personality with a round face that wore serious powerful expression—must have realized that he needed to introduce himself now.

"Oh, I am sorry. The fault is mine." With a pleasant expression, the Japanese man continued, "I am enjoying the mesmerizing nature and your conversation. So I did not want to disturb. My name is Mihara."

Everyone in the small circle introduced themselves. Mihara continued, "My father settled in Sao Paulo from Japan in the early thirties."

With that comment, Mihara tries to draw the interest of others on himself.

Linda, Alex and Susan were looking at Mihara closely, and their facial expressions were asking, "What else?"

Mihara, as if he understood them, continued, "After the death of my father, I sold the farm and moved to California to start a strawberry farming business." His polite manner, the cute accent and soft nature made Linda a close friend of him in no time.

After talking about the exclusively unparalleled beauty of Nepal, Linda asked a question to her group: "Does anyone know the population of Nepal?"

"I read some books on Nepal, but I am not sure of the exact population now."

Allure seems interested, and tried to join the conversation.

"If I may be of any help," Mihara tried to chip in politely.

"Of course, Mihara." Linda was exquisite.

"I think it is about sixteen million." Mihara was close to the real data.

"You know, Linda, Nepal had a strange beginning."

"What is that, Susan?" Linda expressed curiosity. "It's such a beautiful country, but I am not aware of its past and present."

"When the British were ruling India, they made a treaty with Nepal sometime in 1816. As per the treaty, some territory of Nepal was given to the British India. Nepal would have a British representative, and the British would have the right to recruit the Gurkhas in their army."

"How do you know all these facts, Susan?" Linda asked.

"I explored these things in my last trip to Nepal."

"Then you must know some interesting facts about Nepal."

"Not a whole lot, Linda."

"What is the per capita income, literacy rate, and tourism growth rate now?" Linda put three questions in a row.

"Before I give those answers, I believe you should know a little of the past history, which is interesting."

"Of course, Susan. Please go ahead."

Mihara and Alex also were interested to learn about the past as both got closer to Susan.

"Prior to 1951, the Ranas ruled under iron curtain. The people of Nepal felt the whole of the world was crammed within Nepal and nothing existed beyond its territory. No newspaper, no radio, no television was allowed; travel to foreign land was prohibited. Education, literature, libraries and anything that could enlighten the public, were completely banned. People were trained to follow their masters and work as slaves and respect them. Only after 1951, a Shah king took over power from that rigid oligarchy, and enlightenment and freedom were restored slowly. Sherpas, the mountain tribe, migrated from Tibet and brought Buddhism together with them.

"The iron curtain was lifted after a hundred and thirty-four years. This political change brought floods of interested hikers and mountaineers in large numbers into Nepal, which has eight out of the fourteen above eight-thousand-meter mountain peaks of the world. The tourists poured in, as most of them were interested in the Shangri-La fantasy. Culture and development had been restricted in the past along with technology, education, and scientific approaches.

The international community poured foreign aid for developments. American aid channeled through the education and agricultural sectors, trying to bring the country to a modern level."

Susan noticed that everyone in the small group was still interested to know more about Nepal. After a pause, she continued, "In 1953, Mount Everest was scaled by Edmund Hillary from New Zealand and Tenzing Sherpa from Nepal together. After that successful attempt, a parade of international mountaineers, hikers, and trekkers was attracted from Europe, Australia, and America."

Susan continued, "Hillary built a high school in Phaplu, and also a hospital. He also initiated the construction of Lukla airport. Now, the country is on the path of development and modernization. As you can see, the most effective aspect is the hospitality of the people, who are still simple, honest, service-oriented, and not very much attached to the materialistic world that we have in the West."

Susan's style of presenting the highlights of the country was effective, precise, and impressive. Linda said, "Thanks, Susan. You enlightened me about so many things in a short time."

No one noticed, but Allure also joined them quietly and seemed to appreciate Susan as well.

"Thanks, Susan, I am really impressed by your brief presentation," Allure commented.

"Linda, to answer your earlier questions…," Susan took her small compact notebook from her right side pocket and continued, "here it goes. The per capita is $167 and the literacy rate is 21 percent. In 1984, the total tourist arrival was 180,990. From the USA, there were only 19,370." Susan sounded like a teacher in the college, and her three 'students' were really happy.

Alex drew everyone's attention, pointing toward a peak. "Is that not Everest?"

Susan said, "No, Alex. It is rather confusing you see. That one, which looks smaller, and situated between the two taller peaks, is Everest."

The sight of the majestic peaks touched the hearts of everyone. In fact, the sceneries exceeded one's expectation. Everyone in the group preferred to divert attention to the mountains.

Linda was impressed so much with the pure, natural beauty around her that she was lost in a different world and imagined herself on the top of Mount Everest. She felt ecstasy and total bliss run through her body and inner mind. She wanted to get lost in these majestic surroundings and be part of the intoxicating nature forever.

"Well, if you all want to learn a little more about Nepal, may I suggest we sit together during lunch, and be able to consult my notes and tell you more."

Linda agreed enthusiastically to Susan's suggestion and was supported by Mihara, Allure, and Alex.

After another one hour of walk enjoying the view of the narrow road, the tourists saw the hair-raising sight of people and yaks walking in the narrow suspension bridge together, moving their bodies from one end to another end of the bridge. It was thrilling to see the dark green water with milky white foam down in the gorge. The exciting narrow roads, the strong whipping sound of the air passing through your surroundings, the yak's strange neck-bell sound tickling through the atmosphere added up to a unique euphoria for the trekkers coming from small and big cities of America.

Robert said, "Folks, that will be our wonderful picnic lunch spot." He pointed toward a hill about half a mile away, completely covered with small pine trees, looking like a meadow with small bushes all around. The place seemed attractive and soothing. The grass, though not so green, would provide a good, comforting cushion after three hours' trek.

The porters spread some kind of blanket mostly in the shady area under the pine trees. Nearby, a small stream crooned softly; the mountain ranges could be seen from where they were sitting. It was a gorgeous, attractive, and perfect setting for the outdoor lunch.

Susan, Linda, Alex and Allure gathered in one part of the red blanket area, sitting in a circle and facing each other. From where they sat, they overlooked dramatic canyons and a clear mountain view, and in the distance, downhill remote trails.

Susan took out her notebook, placed it in the middle and faced her group.

"Well, although Nepal is a small country, it has strange complex customs," she began. "Each ethnic group has its own outfit, language, tradition, and lifestyle. But each one of them has the capacity for high tolerance, the spirit of sharing, and unusual adjustment capacity. In Kathmandu City, almost all classes live and mix. They have never had a conflict on any issue: religion, language, or tradition. In fact, Nepal has one hundred and one ethnic groups and ninety-two different dialects and languages. To name a few, they are *Magar, Gurung, Tamang, Sunwar, Newar, Thakali, Chepang and Brahmin, Chhetri*. The caste system is deeply ingrained in the national psyche. But it is still parochial. Furthermore, there are few occupational castes that still prevail in the society. *Damais* are tailors, *Sarkis* are cobblers, *Kamis*, blacksmith, and *Sunars* goldsmith. Officially, the caste system was abolished by law in 1963, but in the villages and remote areas, it still prevails. They regard foreigners as casteless and do not allow them in some of the temples in Nepal. Also, they have the misconception that all foreigners, especially Americans, are of high status and immensely rich."

In the meantime, while Susan was explaining the interesting aspects of Nepal, Linda noticed Pemba approach with a tray of food for everyone in the group. He was now coming toward Linda's gathering area.

"Ladies and gentlemen, have a delicious fresh lunch with some fruits and refreshing lemon and orange drink."

Allure was the first to grab the lunch as he seemed more eager to have some food. He was followed by Alex and Mihara. After giving food to Susan, Linda, and everyone in the small group, Pemba approached the northeast area, where a small group sat.

"Mihara, is it not true you guys always prefer to have your own food while traveling?" Alex put a direct question to Mihara.

"Yes, Alex. The Japanese are conservative in that aspect, but while traveling, I prefer to have a variety of foods so that I can enjoy traditional tastes. Besides, travel should be a journey of adventure by all means."

Everyone appreciated Mihara's view on travel, and it showed his progressive attitude as well.

Linda expressed her gratitude to Susan, "My sincere thanks for your knowledgeable information."

"You're most welcome, Linda. I'll share more with you when we have some occasion in the future as well."

After folding the picnic camp, the porters and trekkers seemed to be ready for another three-hour marvelous journey in the wonderful setting of wilderness.

Linda was anxiously waiting for a suitable time to chat with Pemba again, but Pemba seemed to avoid her, as he was in a precarious situation not to be seen close with any client specially a lady in the group, as it was not considered a professional as per the policy of Mountain Travel management. They were very cautious to provide a high-quality service to international clients. Besides, Robert's presence as the head of the group put Pemba in a very risky situation. Linda realized this and did not want to jeopardize professional etiquette between them. So she needed to wait for a more suitable time for them to talk to each other. Linda was so eager to know lots of things about Pemba; she had learned a few things about his family setup, personal preferences and his attitude toward a foreign lady. But it was necessary for her to find his view about her, and sooner or later she was determined to getting it.

Linda knew, one did not always get what he or she desired in life; one had to face lots of difficulties and take life as a challenge one step at a time. So she needed to play a safe game and wait.

Pemba, on the other hand, was extremely busy with his day-to-day work. He didn't have much time left to think about anyone other than himself and his family. But Linda's behavior toward him was slowly catching his attention. He realized she had a soft spot for him and she seems to be attracted towards him. But he realized, it was hard to read the behavior of women from another culture from their peculiar acts. Overall, Pemba did not pay any serious attention toward Linda. He noticed she was extremely beautiful, with dark blue eyes and high cheekbones—a tall, gorgeous person with a smiling face and attractive, unusual charm. One thing Pemba liked about her was that she did not smoke and never misbehaved; in stead, she always consumed limited amount of alcohol which he found an unusual habit in a Western female. She also seemed to be of kind and religious type and had an unusually powerful attraction toward the Buddhist religion. Her impulse was genuine and intent; her conversation was articulate, and it reflected that she had decent understanding of human relation and a deep study of life through education or experience. Besides, she had an intellectual face. Occasionally, Pemba noticed that his feelings toward her were also exhilarating. He was also looking for an opportunity to get closer to her without the other members of the team or his peers noticing. He would wanted to professional courtesy all the time with the trekkers. He was extremely careful that his peers did not have any topic for gossip on his account.

The trekkers, as usual, were in great shape mentally and physically. Mentally, they seemed to have extraordinarily blissful moment in life as everyone was in best spirit and happy mood. Besides, the walk was not so hectic; the temperature was just perfect, the wind was calm, and the sky was blue, except for some clouds toward the bottom of the peaks.

Linda focused on the shape and beauty of the mountains. The trail they were traversing had dense forest on one side; white mountain peaks visible through the branches of the trees exhilarated the mind and provided mystical experiences. From the trail, Linda could hear water running. Down there, she saw a tiny stream cascading down the rocks. This part of the trail was cooler and had a strong fragrance of mint and pines. The pathway seemed quite narrow and had exotic plants with dazzling wildflowers and ferns.

In the distance, another hill approached with ruddy hills on both sides that were taller than the previous ones. The vegetation was scanty; perhaps the alpine climate was not suitable for the greenery of the surroundings. The sky in the middle was blue, but the thin clouds could cover the large part of the mountain soon, as it normally happened in the late afternoons. It impressed Linda, and she had a changed perception toward the natural beauty she was witnessing on this trip.

Slowly, Linda seemed to be lagging behind the group. She was the one floating back near the porters, who were carrying climbing gears, camping equipment, and necessary provisions. The porters talked in a local language, which Linda could not understand. The porters turned quiet when they noticed Linda getting close to them. She approached one of the porters for a bottle of drinking water. Pemba was also walking behind; he came up next to Linda, took out a small water bottle, and gave it to her. Linda thanked Pemba with the remark, "I am thirsty."

"Sure, walking makes you thirsty," Pemba said in agreement.

"Where do you come from, Pemba?" Linda posed a question.

"Oh, I am from Solukhmbu area, and I live in Phaplu village," replied Pemba.

"How far is that from here?"

"If you walk, it may take about two days."

"Is the place as beautiful as here?"

"Yes, I love the place of my birth."

"Have you seen the Dalai Lama yet?" Linda was curious.

"No, only in pictures," Pemba replied honestly.

"Would you like to see him in person?"

"Of course. That would be my greatest pleasure."

"I am planning to go to Dharamshala in India, where he lives. Once I met him in a Los Angeles monastery when he visited," Linda replied, looking directly into Pemba eyes.

"Oh, really. You are lucky." Pemba was brief.

"Would you like to go with me to India? It would be a moral support for me." Linda threw a curveball at Pemba, who was not expecting that question.

He just looked at Linda but did not reply.

"Pemba, I am going there alone, and perhaps you could be my guide," Linda expressed in a sincere tone.

"I am planning to go to my home after this trip and rest with my family in Phaplu for a few days." Pemba smiled but said nothing else.

"Please, just consider it. You will have some time to think, and we will talk again."

Linda realized, Pemba was not feeling comfortable in their conversation as porters were watching them. With that profound request, Linda moved, advancing and trying to catch up with her group.

The middle part of the sky was still blue with patches of scattered clouds here and there accompanied by a bright peach horizon. A small village in the west looked like a tiny dot in the background of these vast peaks and mountains.

Linda felt, she was drawing a spiritual power from her surroundings—an unspoiled, untrimmed, natural beauty. Linda joined the conversation that was going on between Susan and Karen as they walked.

"Linda, have you been thirsty?" Karen asked. "I saw you have some water."

"Yes, in that valley area; it was a little muggy and humid." Linda gave a soothing reply.

"We're talking about the lives of the Sherpas and the porters," Karen addressed Linda.

"What about them?"

"They are so simple, sincere, honest, and hardworking. We feel, they are utilized for excessive work with little compensation," Karen argued.

"Karen's right. I noticed in most cases, they lead you to the top of the summit. And in case both die, they mention the Westerner who dies in the press, but the Sherpa's name is not even mentioned."

"In my personal opinion, Nepal Government should determine their minimum wage, provide quality equipment and climbing gears, and manage a suitable compensation package for their surviving family members," Karen expressed her view.

"Yeah, for the Sherpas, the mountain is like their God. They never climb the summit. In fact, there is no word for *summit* in their dictionary. They worship and never disrespect the mountain by stepping on the top." Susan gave her expert view. She added further, "They also believe in the mountain forest; one can find all kinds of herbs that cure deadly human diseases. They even have faith that the mountain can provide herbs that could make man immortal."

"I understand, Linda, you have great faith in Buddhism." Karen faced Linda suddenly.

"Yes, I find the religion peaceful and fitting to my lifestyle." Linda was happy to answer Karen's question. "I am also planning to see the Dalai Lama after the trek."

Karen, with a surprised expression, said, "Really?"

"I am planning to finish my thesis on Buddhism."

"That is interesting, Linda." Susan seemed to like the idea.

While the three ladies chatted taking a steep climb on the gravel and stone road, they preferred to sit awhile next to a big rock under a medium-size pine tree. The sun was tilting westward slowly, making the shadows grow longer with the passage of each minute.

Linda had a sudden desire for a cup of coffee. She took out the small flask she was carrying with her and poured a little coffee in the cap. Both Karen and Susan declined the request. She began to sip the coffee; it had never tasted better. It was perhaps because of the pure water from the mountain. In fact, she had been enjoying every exotic and superb-tasting meal. She thought, she might gain a few pounds, but on the other hand, the daily hefty walk would shed the weight off her body. She was now one hundred and sixty-three pounds and wanted to stay in the same shape.

"Let's moves now; people are getting ahead of us," Karen said.

In no time, they rejoined the group.

"Thought you guys were lost." Alex approached them from the left side of the trail.

"Oh, no, we had a little rest under a pine tree." Karen was the first to answer.

In the meantime, they came across a steep, narrow gorge. After climbing the yellow stone slabs, they reached the top. Immediately after the high point, after stepping down a few steps, they came to a place where a narrow wire suspension bridge had been laid out. On the right side, a hill with lots of dark trees and bushes looked attractive. On the left, the flow of the narrow river continued uninterrupted, sending forth a wild but musical sound. A few locals were on both sides of the river, trying to catch fish. The movement of the bridge was making Linda's body squiggle, and the flow of the river was giving them a wrong impression, as if one was moving with the water. The swaying of the suspension bridge from left to right, the tranquility of the river making a strange murmur below, the whispering of the pine trees, and the closeness of the snowy peaks all combined into a shivering adventure.

After another forty-five minutes' walk, far in the distance, an oval-shaped mountain carved with dotted houses came into their sight. Here in the vast wilderness, nature occupied a large part in life's everything. Desires and ambitions suddenly appeared meaningless.

When they reached the border of Namche Bazaar, twilight set in. In the distance, pale lights glittered from the tops of the roofs, as if nature, especially the sun, was saying, "Have a great evening."

One could read the tired and faded faces when they came to the campsite. It would take at least an hour to set up the camp. In the group, everyone started sitting and lying down in the half-grass and half-gravel area. Some porters were in a hurry to set up the kitchen tent so that they could serve hot beverages as soon as possible. Robert and Pemba extended all possible help to the porters for unpacking and putting up the tents. The lights were coming alive slowly in the houses. Nearby, a Buddhist stupa and the tall buildings looked like a modern hotel for the tourists. Most people would rather have a camp with a tent in a situation like this, instead of a modern hotel. Mostly, the modern architecture was not a matter of interest as many of them were familiar with it.

Linda's group, again, had its own members sitting in a circle, and one could hardly see their faces.

"Let me get some tea or coffee for all of us." Allure proceeded to the kitchen tent area.

"There is a Sherpa cultural program after dinner," Alex broke the ice.

"Oh, it's exciting!" Susan was delighted.

"Yes, there is a community hall, and it is open for other trekkers as well," Mihara confirmed.

The porters fixed the tents, and as assigned, the group proceeded to the area to rest for about an hour before dinner. For the purpose of acclimatizing at this altitude, a light meal consisting mostly of soft food, fruits, and bread was to be served during dinner, and no alcohol was allowed. Dinner was going to be served early, and everyone was excited for that night's cultural program.

Namche was situated on the top of a hill. Kogde Mountain stood to its north. Beautiful houses had been built on the terraces, circling from one end to another in a row. The houses on the bottom of the mountain were thick, but they got thinner farther up the circle. Due to lack of sufficient light, it was hard to figure out the roof's color, but the houses were painted white. In the background, in the faint light of the moon, the peaks appeared beautiful, dazzling white on top, but the lower part was dark. In the distance, a white stupa was deckled all over with colorful banners that dazed in the dim light. A hotel building decorated with bright electric bulbs of many colors glittered in bright electric light, perhaps from a generator. The whole area looked majestic. A mesmerizing silence engulfed the area. It was hard for anyone to recognize the faces of every human; they had turned into a mystical shadow. Perhaps nature was trying to say that humans were nothing but a part of the shadow in this vast universe.

The night was damp and cold, and a piercing wind was blowing from the top of the mountain.

Dinner was simple. It was completed in a very short time. Robert led everyone to the community hall. The hall was large, with a wooden floor and high ceiling. A large bronze Buddha in sitting posture had been placed behind the stage. The stage and hall were decorated with expensive *thankas* painted with bright Sherpa colors depicting the human life cycle, and colorful banners spread out throughout the hall. There were two rows of seats—one on the left, one on the right. The middle part was left open for passage. The soft sound of a live drum sounded at the background. The hall was filling up gradually, mostly with the foreign audience. The murmuring low sound, melodious drum in the background, and low, mild yellow lights made the atmosphere very romantic.

One could read the unusual expectation in almost everyone's face. Perhaps they were witnessing a unique program, something they had not probably seen in the past anywhere. In fact, the Sherpa community had made remarkable contributions in all aspects of tourism in Nepal. Their reputation as porters, honest guides, effective climbers, and powerful, strong, and honest people was well-known. There were several short movies, books, and articles published all over the world depicting the Sherpa culture, their customs, and traditions. There was a unique attraction and interest toward this community from all over the world.

The program began shortly with a prayer chanted by a few Lamas. Everyone of them was in maroon robes, looking graceful and majestic. After the prayer, a fluid Sherpa song was presented. It echoed on the stage and produced a cheerful, lively duet. Following the song of joy, an attractive young boy, holding a *damphu* came dancing on the stage, while the melodious voice of a female came from behind. And that attractive couple performed a wonderful dance that impacted the whole audience.

After a couple of songs and dances, the program came to an intermission for fifteen minutes. Nonalcoholic beverages were served in the far corner of the big hall. Since the hall had not been heated, everyone felt a little bit cold, and occasionally, a dash of cold wave got inside the covered area whenever the main gate was opened and closed.

Most of the guests gathered at the corner table. Pemba also stood in one corner with a coffee cup in his hand.

When Linda, along with Karen and Susan, approached for beverages, Pemba put his cup down on the table and said, "What do you want to have?"

Linda and Karen requested for coffee, and Susan asked for a cup of tea. Pemba was prompt and efficient in bringing them the drinks of their choice. The three of them thanked Pemba.

"By the way, my fifteen-year-old niece is performing in the show on a Yeti in a mini drama." Pemba seemed happy to share the event with them.

Linda said, "Really?" She further added, "Pemba, can you take us backstage to see her after the show?"

"Of course, she will be happy to see you all in person."

In the meantime, the announcer informed them to take their seats so that the show could resume. Slowly, the audience occupied their seats and waited for the show. The curtain was up, and the show began with a short funny drama about the reaction of a boy on his first visit to the big city. The boy had seen cars on such a big road for the first time. The high overhead bridges, big billboards around, the parade of congested traffic and large number of pedestrians were all exciting to him. The reaction of eight-year-old boy was hilarious, convincing, and highly effective.

After a couple of songs and marvelous folk dances, the disk jockey announced the much-awaited mini-drama of a fifteen-year-old girl's surprise encounter with a Yeti, the snowman.

The opening scene showed huge mountains all around. The small girl went to the wooded area to collect dry wood for cooking. While collecting the wood, she heard a scuffling sound nearby.

She had heard about the Yeti. She hid behind a thick bush and watched. In the distance, she saw a tall creature about ten and a half feet tall, weighing about four hundred and fifty pounds, slowly coming toward her walking like a human being. It has a thick outgrowth of dark hair all over the body and face. The girl was scared; she hid herself deep in the bushes, and tried to cover her body. She noticed that the Yeti's face was not furious and ugly as it had been described to her. In fact, the face had a kind, loving, and gentle expression.

The Yeti came to her and said, "Tashi, do not be afraid. I am your friend, not an enemy."

Tashi could not believe the Yeti could talk like humans, and his sweet voice had tenderness and extreme softness. Still, Tashi was scared to come out of the bushes and face the large mysterious figure. The Yeti got a little closer to her.

"Come, my child; treat me like your friend. I am here to help you." The Yeti put his arm to her shoulder and held her hand softly.

Tashi noticed that the Yeti's hand was curly and dry, and his grip was firm but delicate.

"Let me collect some wood for you."

They walked toward a tall tree. The Yeti reached his hand to a high tree and started breaking the branches. Tashi saw the branches of the trees break off in an easy manner without efforts as though it was a child's play for the Yeti. In no time, enough branches were collected.

"Is this enough for you?"

Tashi could not reply as her voice was not coming out yet. She just nodded her head.

"Tashi, please do not be afraid of me. See, I am here to help you. Tell me, Tashi, do people talk about me?"

Again, Tashi could not speak. She just nodded her head, saying yes.

"Tell me, please, what do they say about me?"

This time, Tashi's low, slightly trembling voice came out. "They say you cannot be seen, that you only exist where normally humans are unable to reach."

"Interesting. Tell me something more."

"You are tall, furious, and harmful." Tashi's thin voice trembled.

"Really?" the Yeti seemed surprised.

"International effort is being made to research your existence, and numerous movies have been made about you."

"Is that so?" the Yeti was apparently happy.

"There is great interest in you, and sometimes people claim they have seen you. In fact, I have heard numerous stories from my friends, parents, and my grandma about you."

"What will be your opinion about me now?" Yeti question.

"I found you very friendly, polite, and helpful." First time Tashi spoke with confidence.

Tashi started walking toward her home, and the Yeti was followed her with a bundle of firewood.

"Let me tell you one thing, Tashi. I am here to help and take care of all the mountains and the Sherpa people. I am their guardian angel. Tell them, I will never harm them. Will you remember all this I told you?"

When Tashi turned to face the Yeti and thank him for his help, he was not there. The bundle of wood lay nearby.

The drama ended with a climax that sent forth high emotions and suspense. The audience gave a big round of applause to the girl who excelled in her performance and earned high appreciation for the wonderful act.

One could notice extreme happiness on the audiences' faces. Almost everyone had a cheerful expression for the ninety-minute show that had been highly successful, enjoyable, and professionally perfect.

The audience slowly moved towards the exit. Karen, Susan, and Linda waited for Pemba not far from the exit gate.

Pemba called, "Hi." All three ladies moved toward him.

"How did you like the show?" Pemba was curious.

"A great show! It was awesome," Karen replied.

"Are you ready to meet my niece backstage?"

Nobody replied, but quietly followed Pemba.

After a little walk to the back, they approached the dressing room of the actress. Tashi was at the door. "Namaste, everyone."

She still had the makeup on, and her face glowed with a smile. She looked more beautiful than on the stage. Her white face and both her cheeks had a tint of rose. Linda thought perhaps the rosiness was from her makeup, but actually, it was her natural hue. She had small, slight eyes, broad, attractive face, and was tall and graceful.

After a little chitchat, Tashi thanked them all for coming to see her. Pemba talked with her in their local language and left together with Linda. When they came out of the hall, the light was visible though a short distance down their path, but after coming further away from the community hall, the road appeared pitch dark.

Pemba led them with a torchlight to the campsite. Linda walked next to him, and the other two ladies, Karen and Susan, followed.

Linda spoke in a low voice, as if whispering to Pemba, "Did you think on my request?"

"Yes, Linda. I want to see Lord Dalai Lama but need to go to my home for a few days as my younger sister is sick."

Linda said, "How long do you want stay?"

"Maybe for two days."

"How will you go there?"

"By air."

"After the trek is over, we will staying for about two days in Kathmandu; why don't I go with you to see a new place?"

Pemba was completely surprised with Linda; he kept quiet and did not reply. They were both sure Karen and Susan were busy talking between themselves and had not overheard their conversation.

"Linda, let me have more time. I will let you know after three days."

Linda realized Pemba was feeling uncomfortable about their discussion. So, she changed the subject, "Pemba, thanks for taking us backstage and introducing us to your niece. She is really a beautiful lady."

Pemba simply thanked Linda, and they all walked slowly to the campsite, which was not very far now.

***

CHAPTER SEVEN

End of November 1985

The group was back from the phenomenal three-week trek to Mount Everest. The trip was a success in all respects. The trekkers felt that they received maximum excitement from the trip. Each of them was extremely happy.

It was the evening of the farewell dinner, and Mountain Travel had elaborately prepared for the same in one of the old Rana palaces that had been turned into a five-star hotel. Together with the dinner, arrangements were made for folk cultural program, as was the custom therein.

Linda was planning to attend the farewell dinner that evening. She was extremely content that Pemba had agreed to go to Dharamshala with her on one condition: she would also accompany Pemba to Phaplu for two days. Life sometimes takes strange twists and turns; most of the time, it goes as planned, but sometimes, things move without one's anticipation.

This situation—the sudden trip to Phaplu—was in a way a pleasure for Linda, though it was a totally unpredicted endeavor. Linda had no idea about Pemba's emotions and inner feelings, but for Linda, this was an opportunity to get closer to Pemba and his family. Perhaps during this trip, she might build a bridge between her and Pemba and his family and try to understand Eastern and Western cultures on a personal level. So far, she had found Pemba a tough, unemotional, and complicated person. Linda had had a hard time reading the expressions on Pemba's face. Normally, it was rigid, like a stone. Maybe, she thought, he could be softer, emotional, and kindhearted inside.

Linda was trying to choose the appropriate evening dress for the dinner but could not decide what her proper outfit would be. She decided to take Susan's suggestion, and went to room 347 to knock.

When Susan showed up at the door, she had an inquisitive expression. "Yes, Linda?"

"Pardon me for my intrusion. Susan, I am a little confused about my outfit this evening. May I seek your opinion? If you don't mind, could you drop by my place after you finish your makeup, please?"

"Sure, Linda, the pleasure will be mine."

"Thanks, Susan. I will wait for you."

Linda chose three outfits with different color patterns—one pink, the other light lemon, and the last one sky blue—and put them on the bed for Susan to pick one. All the dresses were made of cotton, and all of them were elegant evening long gowns. Linda wanted to look ravishing. Somehow, she had an intense desire to look the best she could afford. She had no idea whom she wanted to impress most. It might be Pemba or someone else. Anyway, a woman's prerogative and desire and motivation were a matter of mystery, and it was hard for a man to evaluate.

Linda heard a knock on the door. "Yes, Susan, please come in."

Susan moved to the dress display area, gave a critical look, and turned toward Linda. "If you really want to know my choice, Linda, I prefer the gorgeous pink dress."

Linda also had an inclination toward the one Susan chose. "Great, Susan. I really appreciate it."

"I hope to see you soon. I'll be waiting in the lobby."

"Thanks, Susan."

When Linda came into the lobby, all eyes were on her. Karen smiled with a remark, "Linda, the dress really suits you."

"Thanks, Karen. Susan helped me pick it."

The dinner hall was large with a white marble floor and a crafted, sparkling, colorful chandelier in the middle. The hall was not heated, but had a huge fireplace in the left corner that made the atmosphere quite cozy and warm for the guests. In the middle wall was a large Mountain Travel banner with a white background and dark blue lettering, carrying the slogan, "Always a step ahead" underneath. In small letters, it looked impressive and attractive. The large dining table of dark mahogany wood—covered with a milky white tablecloth and clustered with crystal cocktail glasses and an attractive flowery china dinner set—was decorated with a small dark rose vase next to each guest's place. The carved chairs created a pleasant and charming setup. In the far corner of the room, a huge portrait of royal figures stood on a tiger skin. It was like the one normally seen in the British art gallery.

Just under the Mountain Travel banner, a medium-sized stage occupied a higher elevation, about three feet from the ground. Linda guessed it had been prepared for the cultural program during dinner. In the background, a drum and some kind of sharp musical instrument were being playing. The soft, murmuring music and cocktails turned the evening into a fascinating event.

The guests were finally invited to the dining table, and they occupied the seats in an orderly and pleasing manner. The head of the table was occupied by Colonel Bradley. Robert, Dawa, and Pemba shared the chairs towards the middle area among guests so that there would be a good rapport between the guests and Mountain Travel management team. Robert was among the guests from Colorado. Dawa was in between three ladies and two gentlemen who included Linda, Susan, and Karen. Similarly, Pemba was among Allure, Mihara, and Alex along with two other ladies from California.

The dinner was served, and in the meantime, a typical attractive folk dance was presented on the stage. The sumptuous dinner, along with the compact cultural program, came to an end. Colonel Robert expressed his appreciation for choosing the Mountain Travel trek and wished all the guests a safe journey back home. On behalf of the guests, Karen expressed gratitude to Mountain Travel management for the wonderful trip and expressed deep appreciation of Pemba for being an exceptional guide, outstanding cook, and extremely helpful person during the entire trekking.

Most of the guests wished Linda a great time during her extended stay in Kathmandu along with a successful trip to Dalai Lama's place in India. Indeed, Linda was exuberant for the trip with Pemba.

But Pemba was in a difficult situation. He was in dilemma whether he should accompany Linda to Dharamshala or not because Linda was a client of Mountain Travel and there was certain decorum in dealing with the company's clients. He consulted Dawa on the matter, who suggested that he should get approval from Robert or Colonel Bradley. As advised by Dawa, he put a written request for official approval along with one-week leave from the office. Considering Pemba's character and reputation, the office granted his request.

Two days after the farewell dinner, early in the morning, Linda took a cab to the domestic airport for the Phaplu flight. She was somehow earlier than Pemba as she had not seen Pemba so far. After around twenty minutes, Pemba showed up.

"Morning, Linda."

"Hi, a very good morning, Pemba."

He then proceeded toward the check-in counter for the flight. Linda had a small backpack, and Pemba had a big, heavy duffle bag. After checking in on Linda's request, they approached a small coffee stall inside the eastern part of the terminal. Pemba had a cup of tea, and Linda, coffee with cream and sugar.

"Is Phaplu also like Namche?"

"More or less. My house is next to the airport and gets windy in the afternoon and night."

"How long is the flight?"

"About thirty-five minutes. The plane is small; hope you will like it."

"I have never been in a small plane. Is it smaller than the Lukla plane?"

"Yes, only seven seats. The plane was made in Canada." Pemba tried to convince Linda perhaps on the safety of the plane.

"Tell me what interesting things we can see in Phaplu," Linda said, showing her eagerness.

"Oh, there are not many things except a Wednesday market."

The airport inside the terminal was getting crowded with lots of trekkers, and Linda and Pemba noticed they had several mountain flights scheduled. The passengers were waiting for the fog to clear, and Pemba was busy talking with his people from the village. Linda was alone, walking outside the airport in a less crowded area. She loved to walk in foggy weather and feel like she was walking in the clouds. She realized the airport was at a slightly higher elevation than the valley, and somehow, the fog was thicker in this area. In the distance, she could see the top of the trees on the west, appearing as though they were growing out of the sky. Down below, the valley was covered with thick fog. Linda felt that she was blessed to see such an outstanding sight in such a mysterious and enchanting country.

Linda noticed that Pemba was approaching her in haste. She went to meet him.

"They are preparing to clear the flight soon."

"Great, I am ready."

Both of them rushed toward the terminal. The passengers and trekkers, mostly in heavy boots, appeared impatient for the flights to depart. Linda had felt the same while waiting for the Lukla plane three weeks back.

The fog seemed to be easing slowly as sunlight tried to penetrate. The crew members approached the aircrafts and occupied the cockpit.

But still, they all needed to wait for the departure announcement. The passengers were scattered here and there in small groups all around the coffee stall and cafeteria area. Linda overheard the conversation among the passengers waiting for the mountain flight. They seemed casual tourists who were doing normal sightseeing of the country, not pretending to trek or hike. The group was mixed, with Europeans, Asians, either from China or Japan, and a few Indians. They all seemed to be city dwellers and part of a business group. These tourists were typical and could be seen in all parts of the world traveling around for pleasure and regular sightseeing.

"Attention, please. The Phaplu flight is ready for departure. Passengers, please proceed towards the aircraft."

Following the public announcement, about six or seven people approached the small aircraft. Since Linda was the first one to board, she occupied the window front right seat after the pilot. Pemba took the next seat on the aisle. The aircraft had seven seats—three seats in each row and one at the end. Up front, the captain sat on the left, so the man at his right must be the copilot. Obviously, there was no need of a cabin crew, and there was none. Among the passengers and crew, Pemba was the tallest one, and of course, Linda came after that. The other passengers, even the crew, were shorter; in fact, Linda had never seen a pilot so short.

Linda had a peculiar feeling in this small aircraft. After takeoff, she enjoyed a close view of the mountains and spectacular sceneries. The aircraft swung rapidly, and she had a nauseous feeling. The short ride was not a pleasant one, but the adventure was worth taking. The plane landed on the airstrip, not completely tarmac. It felt like they had landed on the top of the mountain. The houses were on the slope, behind sharp ridges. They all had red and green roofs and looked beautiful, like the mountains in Switzerland Linda had seen in pictures and on the television. The air was windy and crispy. The sharp gorges down on the other side of the narrow road looked steep and were covered with tall pine trees.

Coming off the narrow, rough airstrip, they came to the compound of a white house with a green roof situated close to the airport. A narrow gate and a tall wall on both sides led the path to the main entrance of the house. The house looked stylish and had a touch of European professional architectural design.

"This is my house," Pemba was proud to announce.

"Oh, really? Nice house," Linda said in happiness.

"The house has one drawback," Pemba shared with Linda.

"What's that?" Linda asked.

"Due to some technical problem, we could not build a bathroom inside. Considering your comfort, I have managed your accommodation in my friend's hotel, which is equipped with all facilities, cold and hot water, and attached bath." Pemba continued, "In fact, it is a four-star hotel and was built recently by a French investor. Linda, you may like it because the interior decoration is entirely French."

"How about the food?" Linda was curious.

"They are building a restaurant, but in the meantime, food is delivered in the room. Why don't we go to the room and see it?" Pemba proposed.

The hotel, Eiffel, was situated next to Pemba's house.

The hotel had an interesting decoration, a mixed French-Buddhist style. The wooden beams were decorated with paintings that showed local religious life cycle in bright colors. The rooms were decorated with window glasses along with reflections of the Eiffel Tower and *Mona Lisa* replicas placed here and there. The lower wall of the hotel had been painted in black and the upper portion in white. The room selected by Linda was stunning. The crystal chandeliers decked almost all the prominent areas. The most impressive things were the replica paintings of Van Gogh, Monet, and Renoir seen everywhere. The interior of the hotel had French architecture, and the furniture was neat and attractive, revealing Danish style of finishing along with the neutral color pattern everywhere in the room.

Linda loved the hotel; she had never expected such a luxury in the midst of serenity. Pemba left for his home, and Linda started unpacking personal stuff.

She took a leisurely tub-bath to relax and enjoy. Pemba would be coming to the hotel for dinner along with his hotel partner Pasang, and his wife. But prior to dinner, she would again meet Pemba and go around the village briefly.

Pemba came back to the hotel after nearly two hours. In the meantime, Linda ordered a light lunch: a chicken sandwich and salad. Linda knew Pemba would have lunch with his family.

"How is everything with your family?" Linda asked Pemba.

"Good. My younger sister has overcome her cold and fever; she will be going back to school tomorrow. My mom has arranged a luncheon for you tomorrow and has invited my uncle and his wife too to join you."

"Great."

"You will have a taste of our typical meals, with chicken and deer meat. Now, if you're ready, let's have a round of our village. Do you prefer to ride a horse or walk?"

Linda had ridden horses during a school excursion at a camp during summertime, but she was not sure if she could ride one in a mountainous area.

"Walk," was her short reply.

The weather outside was sunny but cold and crispy. The wind was blowing rather strongly. Linda had hard times managing her hair, which bounced abruptly again and again, making her look more beautiful.

Phaplu was exposed to foreigners, mostly Westerners, and a few visitors that came from New Zealand and Australia. Pemba's walking with Linda did not surprise the villagers, in stead, most men were rather attracted to Linda. One of Pemba's friends, who was talking with them, gazed at Linda constantly.

After a downhill walk for about fifteen minutes, they reached the bottom of the village. A gorge and river could be seen from the narrow road. The houses were clean and fenced by wooden boundary wall around. There was no life seen in the village except for a few shop keepers, as if everyone had gone to work and would come back after sunset.

Pemba stopped by a tiny shop that had provisions such as cigarettes, matches, candles, candy, rice, and corn. A middle-aged man was inside the shop. Pemba went close to him and bowed his head.

They talked in their local language. Linda kept herself busy watching them from a distance. After a while, Pemba joined Linda.

"He is a distant relative of mine, an uncle from my mother's side."

"What did you talk about?"

"Nothing special. We talked ordinary things, like when I came, how long I would stay etc."

"Why are there no people in these houses?"

"Children are at school, men somewhere in the fields, and women in the river to take baths and clean clothes."

"It looks deserted," Linda commented.

"Yes, more or less."

Pemba pointed to a house with white paint and a green roof. "That is our Rodi-ghar."

"What does that mean?"

"A disco. A nurse from New Zealand brought musical instruments and we have good gatherings on weekends."

"Really? That is nice."

"Do you want to go further down to the river or return to the hotel?"

"It is easy to come down, but climbing back will be harder; so let's not go down further."

Pemba agreed, and they sat to rest under a tall tree for a few minutes. The resting place underneath the tree had been white; the chairs were made of stone. In the upper portion, a multi-color prayer flag fluttered in the wind, sending forth a strange but pleasant sound. The sound's echo was sonorous, as it was situated in the gorge between two tall mountains. Nature had lavishly made all efforts to make this place next to paradise. In the distance, Linda could see white waterfalls coming out of a dry mountain and falling nearly two hundred feet down. The vegetation was more downriver, and upriver, the land and mountain were barren.

The dotted white houses with the bright green and red roofs in the distance looked quite pretty in the sun, making Linda think of her life spent in this part of the world. Linda knew the people were simple, hardworking and not much exposed to material desires—the reason they were content with themselves. Linda knew to be happy was to control one's desire.

Linda had seen the roughness of the country, the people, and nature. She had never realized the happiness, peace, and the paradise one could find in this part of the world. People considered America a beautiful country. Linda had also thought the same way before coming here. But after seeing some of the highlights, she believed Nepal had all the criteria to be considered a true paradise. She admired the people; the natural beauty was beyond one's comprehension. The religious and the kind nature of the people made Linda think, God had perhaps inhabited this land in the past.

For some time, Linda and Pemba sat under the tall tree on the stone bench.

"Linda, may I ask you a personal question?" Pemba said.

"Of course, Pemba, by all means." Linda smile. A pleasing expression showed happiness at the question.

"Tell me your honest opinion about our country."

"Pemba, I am overwhelmed," Linda replied briefly.

Pemba, perhaps, did not understand the short answer from Linda; he opened his eyes wide and bore a confuse look on the face. Linda needed to reinforce the point.

"I wish I had been born here," Linda expressed her inner feeling.

For Pemba, it was hard to understand Linda's feelings. In fact, Pemba felt the other way.

"Pemba, I love the Buddhist religion and your way of life. In my country, there is a lot of crime, murder, and poverty, which is not exposed, but is a reality. Our society encourages people to be independent but selfish, breaking away from core values of religion and family." She was emotional. "In fact, American society is moving towards isolation; people think of nothing but me, myself, and mine."

"What do you mean?" Pemba tried to understand her point.

"I mean, everyone is becoming more and more selfish, thinking of the individual benefit only."

"Is that so? But our perception from here is complete opposite." Pemba did not seem convinced. "Yes, the grass on the other side is always greener."

Both laughed.

"How is the room at the hotel?" Pemba asked, as if he wanted to change the subject.

"Perfect. Luxury beyond expectation" Linda replied with satisfaction.

"Pasang and his wife will be at the hotel to host a dinner. Pasang had mentioned that your stay will be free as a part of a promotion, being an early guest." He continued

"How generous of him."

"Better thank him when you meet."

"Pemba, you asked me a personal question; let me ask one too, if you don't mind?"

"Yes, of course, Linda."

Pemba, how do Nepali men normally feel about foreign women in their life?"

"I can't generalize the answer, but in my opinion, it will not be an easy adjustment."

"In what sense?"

"The cultural difference is a major one—community, food habits, liking, disliking etc."

"Adjustment is required in every relationship," Linda interrupted.

"Adjustment is not a problem for Nepali men; they are adaptable in every way of life because they already come from a hard society and difficult living. In fact, Nepalese are settled all over the world, and adjustment is the key, which means they are extremely adaptable in all situations. Besides, we have another quality—patience."

Pemba's expression seemed to be normal; Linda did not interrupt.

"If we are not patient, it will be hard to climb the tallest mountain," Pemba argued to prove his point.

Pemba related a story about a friend who married a Japanese woman. They eventually divorced after having a baby girl, after five years of marriage. This was all because of cultural differences, and Pemba did not want to be in the same situation. Pemba knew divorce would destroy one's image, life, and even existence sometimes.

"But does it not depend on the nature of the two?" Linda was in the mood for argument.

"Yes, but time is so powerful that everything can change," Pemba said.

"The other powerful reason is religion that will help keep people together." Linda explain.

"In a way," Pemba agreed.

"Yes, but understanding plays a vital part to reinforce relationship" Linda said. "And what about love?"

"What do you mean?" Pemba ask.

"I mean, does the difference exist between lovers? As they say, love is blind," said Linda.

"I agree, but differences arise when love fades away," Pemba argued with practicality.

"True love dies hard." Linda echoed the thought in her heart as if she were trying to convince herself.

"Linda, it is hard to find true love in this world of compelling, diverse human beings."

As this interesting conversation continued, Pemba noticed the sun rushing westward. He held Linda's hand and requested she got up, as they needed to climb the hill toward the hotel and prepare for Pasang's dinner. It was twilight when they arrived at the hotel. The wind was picking up and blowing hard. Linda had hard times managing her composure while climbing, but Pemba helped her in many places, pulling her up and holding her hand. When they reached the top of the ridge, the golden sunrays' reflection on the white peaks looked dazzling and exceptionally attractive. The view in reality was so marvelous that Linda did not want to move from the spot.

Understanding Linda's interest, Pemba approached her.

"You know that peak, Mount Everest. The next one is Amadablam. A little further on the left is Lhotse, and the last one on this side is Makalu."

Linda was surprised at the mountain knowledge Pemba had.

After a brief description of the mountains, Pemba continued, "Further down on the right side there is the Sherpa village Junbesi. Actually, that is the beginning point of trekking from this area. Further up on a hill from Junbesi, there is a beautiful monastery and a Tibetan camp. I have been there a couple of times, and the camp has about two hundred monks. It's run by a high-order reincarnate Lama."

"What is the difference in starting a trek from here and Lukla?"

"Not much. These parts have more vegetation; scenic mountains are more visible. Khari Khola and Dudh Kosi River trail is spectacular. I personally prefer the basecamp trek through here. You must have noticed, the most fascinating view from basecamp is not the mountains but looking down below Khumbu's marvelous glacier, ice ponds, and several icebergs." Pemba explain further.

As it was getting darker and the velocity of the wind was rapidly increasing on the mountain ridge, Pemba virtually dragged Linda into the hotel. The hotel looked dark; perhaps there was no light.

The receptionist addressed Linda, "Good evening, ma'am. We are working on the generator for the lights; please use the candle in the room."

Pemba left for his home for a short visit and would be back for the dinner at eight. Linda quickly went to her room, undressed, and took a quick shower. She went to the bathroom but could not locate the shower cap, so she called the operator and requested for one. Shortly after the call, a boy stood outside her door with a few plastic shower caps in hand. She thanked him and gave a dollar tip.

It was now six forty-five. Linda needed a quick shower and had to select an evening outfit. Then she would be ready for the dinner. After showering, she picked up the lemon-colored long gown with light-colored suitable sandals and coordinated handbag. She put on neutral-colored light makeup, very mild fragrance, and combed her hair. In the end, she looked sexy but not overly dressed. It was just appropriate for the female company as well. She had no idea that she would be having conversation with Pasang's wife. She believed perhaps the lady would not be able to speak in English. God, she forgot to ask Pemba.

Linda had almost completed her dress and makeup when she heard a knock on the door. Pemba was standing outside with a graceful smile in a white shirt, blue Levi's tight jeans, and a light blue sport jacket. He looked amazingly handsome.

"Hi, ready?" Pemba asked.

"Almost."

Pemba looked at her closely. She looked simple, elegant, and extremely beautiful.

Linda gave a hefty smile and a ripple of passion flew through Pemba's entire body. Pemba had noticed, besides her abundant beauty, Linda also possessed a high level of ingenuity and intellect. Besides, she was well-behaved, highly disciplined, and a respected person by all means. Pemba thought, she must be from a religious, cultured and reputable family. In the entire trip, during three weeks of trekking, Pemba never found her behaving inappropriately with anyone. He was slowly but surely beginning to like her as a friendly, a down-to earth person.

The phone rang.

"Hello," Linda picked up the call.

"Your friend is waiting in the lobby."

"Well then, shall we?" Pemba made a polite gesture.

Both of them descended a staircase and found Pasang and his wife waiting in the far side of the lobby. Pasang came closer when he saw Pemba.

Pasang embraced Pemba in a very warm and affectionate way. They seemed close friends besides being cousins.

"Hi, my name is Linda." She extended her hand to the lady standing next to Pasang.

"You are most welcome to Phaplu and our small hotel. By the way, my name is Mingma." Linda shook hands with Mingma.

Since the hotel's restaurant was under construction, they had arranged a part of the lobby in the far left corner for the dinner that night. All four approached the area; Pasang led the way. When everyone had settled on their seats comfortably, Pasang broke the ice.

"Linda, first, we—I mean, me, my wife, Mingma, and also Pemba—welcome you to our small but beautiful village and to this moderate hotel."

"Thank you, Pasang. I find the place unusually beautiful and your hotel in no way a moderate. In fact, to be honest, I never expected such luxury here," Linda said, slowly but deliberately completing her sentence.

"We started building it about two years ago. As you can see, everything needs to be transported from the big city and it takes an unusually long time to reach here. The electric wiring and restaurant are still under construction, and we hope to make them ready by this January." Pasang continued, "I hope you would not have difficulty without electricity."

"Not at all. Rather, it looks romantic."

In the middle of the lobby, they had put a tall red kerosene heater that provided warmth in the room, and the arrangements of candles were concealed so that they would not have direct eye contact. The golden reflection in the front glass wall was that of the Eiffel Tower in the background, and it provided a Parisian feeling. On the right side, white walls had a Van Gogh painting of a beautiful tree in fall, and on the left wall, Linda recognized a Monet painting of a French lady walking with an umbrella near somewhere in the Sanjalise area. The reflection of rain and the shadows of walking people were vividly portrayed in the picture.

"How long are you staying, Linda?" Mingma put the question suddenly.

"Oh, not long. I'm leaving day after tomorrow. In fact, Pemba is taking me to Dharamshala to see the Dalai Lama."

"Oh my, you are lucky." A happy expression was on Mingma's face.

"Actually, I once met him in Los Angeles some time ago during his visit to the States."

Do you believe in our religion? Are you not a Christian?" Mingma was curious, and also surprised.

"Shall we order our beverage first?" interrupted Pasang.

A waiter approached soon. Pasang raised his hand. "Yes, Sir." The waiter responded.

Pasang, Pemba, Mingma, and Linda placed an order for two Scotch shots, one orange juice, and a gin and tonic for Linda. The drinks were brought promptly.

"I understand you have a French investor as your partner?" Linda told Pasang.

"Yes, Linda. He has a distillery just outside Paris that produces *Le Blanc* champagne and several brands of popular wines. He has the majority share in the hotel, and I am a care-taker with nominal partnership." Pasang continued further, "As per our law, no foreigner is allowed one hundred percent equity and needs to have a local partner."

"How did you meet him?" Linda was curious.

"I was also a guide, like Pemba, and I met him on his trip to Nepal. He was with his family and took a helicopter everywhere they went; they never walked. They even chartered separate helicopters: one for him, another for his wife, and another for his two sons to go and come back from the same place."

"Why did he do such a thing?" Linda was surprised.

Pasang said, "I asked him the same question. He replied that he did not want them all to die in case of an accident. He needed to continue his vast business, and having the next generation was important for him."

"How does he travel long distances?" Linda was curious.

"They all use different airlines separately. The children have a nanny to care for and travel with them all the time." Pasang seemed passionate about telling this interesting fact.

Linda faced Mingma. "Sorry, Mingma, what were you asking earlier?"

"Oh, I was just curious. Being a Christian, how are you inclined toward the Buddhist religion?"

"Near my home in Los Angeles is a Buddhist monastery, and I visit it very often. The visit of His Holiness the Dalai Lama and his preaching influenced me. Besides, I find it totally blissful, peaceful, and appealing to my lifestyle."

"Linda, may I ask you a question?" Mingma interrupted.

"By all means."

"What line of work are you in?"

"I am an executive secretary in a large law firm."

"That is nice," said Mingma.

"Pasang, where did you get all these French paintings?" Linda asked, glancing around.

"They were brought by Francisco, my investor. Do you see those empty spaces on the walls?" Pasang indicated to Linda.

"Yes, what are those?"

"Francisco is planning to bring some of the originals created by Picasso, given by his father as a gift, though some were purchased."

"Really? I love the work of Picasso. I have seen many of his paintings in Los Angeles museum."

"You will see lots of replicas of Picasso, Monet, and Van Gogh in the public area of our hotel and in guest rooms," Mingma added.

"Fascinating," said Linda.

"Among all paintings by Picasso, *Nude*, *Girl before a Mirror*, and *Les Demoiselle* are the most popular, and *Nude* was sold for eighty million dollars in 1976." Pasang clearly had deep knowledge of French artists and paintings.

"How do you know all this, Pasang?" Linda was curious.

"I lived in France, worked at a vineyard, and studied French Arts for two years."

"Pasang, I also want to know all the things about paintings, but my knowledge is limited as I took only a few optional classes during my college time." Pemba expressed his ignorance on the subject.

"Linda, if you are interested, Monet has the best paintings—*Impression, Sunrise*; *Woman with Parasol* and *Luncheon on the Grasses*. Each painting has a unique approach and style, but his *Impression* and *Sunrise* raised lots of criticism." This showed Pasang's passion toward French painting. He continued further, "And among Van Gogh's paintings, I like *The Harvest*, *Starry Night*, and *Wheat Fields* most. Van Gogh in reality introduced the 'tilt shift.' This produced real-world scenes on illusion in most of his paintings."

It was like a painting class. Pasang explained briefly what he had learned during his stay in France.

So far, Pemba had kept quiet and had not participated in the conversation. Finally, he spoke. "I am ignorant of most creations of great French and Spanish artists, although I have read briefly on all three, Picasso, Monet, and Van Gogh. The painting I like the most is Leonardo da Vinci's *Mona Lisa*."

"Agreed. That is the most popular painting in the world. Pemba, you have a great choice," Linda said, giving her view.

In the meantime, a person approached the table. Pasang introduced him as a popular French chef, who described the dinner menu to the guests.

"*Bonne soiree*, monsieurs and madames," he said in a heavy French accent, "this evening, we have a main course: it is *poulet basquaise*—a chicken comfort food with pepper and tomato. There is also *a l'oignon*, a superb French soup, garden green salad, and for dessert assorted cheeses with fresh fruits and homemade jam followed by red Bordeaux wine."

The way he presented the menu made it sound delicious and tantalizing.

"It sounds exotic," Linda remarked and thanked the chef.

The atmosphere in the lobby, especially the corner for this evening's dining, created a magnificent effect. Everyone seemed to be enjoying the cocktails and waiting eagerly for the superb French cuisine.

"I understand the airlines are trying to operate larger aircraft to Phaplu," Pemba commented, facing toward Pasang.

"Yes, we need more tourists as our hotel opens fully in January," Pasang said.

"We requested more flights with the tourism minister last month in Kathmandu; he is also planning to visit for the hotel's inauguration."

"Indeed, he is. Our uncle from this area should come," Pemba said to Pasang.

Mingma asked Linda directly, "Linda, do you really like our country?"

"What can I say? It is the paradise."

"We would like to visit America some day" Mingma said, expressing her feelings.

"Mingma, you are welcome to my place; you can stay with me."

"People say America is a paradise," countered Mingma.

"The grass on the other side is always greener."

"Yes, Linda, it is a dreamland for millions of people in Nepal," Pasang said.

"I do not know about that," said Linda.

The French delicacies started appearing with salad, followed by soup, the main course, and the delicious dessert with red Bordeaux wine. Because of the enticing aroma, delicious food, and rich wine, everyone was occupied with the food; they were not interested in conversation anymore.

Toward the end of the supper, Linda spoke again, "Mostly, American foods are flat in taste. Most people, including myself, favor ethnic food, such as Italian, French, Thai, and Mexican."

"That is spicy," Pemba remarked.

"Yes, but it has a pleasing and tasteful smell," Linda said.

Both Pasang and Mingma expressed their liking for Thai food. "Besides French, Nepali, and Indian, we may also add a Thai menu sometime in the future."

As all good things come to an end, everyone finished eating. Linda ordered brandy; Pasang and Pemba tea and Mingma, coffee with Splenda.

It looked like Pemba suddenly remembered something important and interrupted, "Pasang and Mingma, can you please come to my home for lunch tomorrow? Mother has arranged lunch for Linda."

"It will be our pleasure, Pemba."

On that note, Pasang and Mingma left the hotel for their home, and at Linda's request, Pemba had agreed to stay for short time stay.

The velocity of the wind was increasing rapidly, the sounds vibrant and even violent outside.

"Does the wind sound usually like this?" Linda asked, when they settled down in the room.

"Yes, in winter, from October to January, it sounds like this."

"Is your house windproof?"

"Yes, it has pretty strong doors and windows; some of them are without glass."

Linda noticed that the room had been remade; the bed was in the proper shape, and next to the pillow, two pieces of mint-flavored chocolates had been placed. Large candles were replaced—one in the bedroom and another in the bathroom. The candle's reflection on the chandelier glittered in the light and produced colorful rainbow images. The gold-colored Eiffel Tower image in the glass panel added perfection to the room. A Picasso painting hung above the pillow toward the headboard post and another painting of Monet hanged on the left side of the wall. On the right side was a large window covered with silky smoky color drapes.

"Relax, Pemba. Let me freshen up." With that request, Linda proceeded to the bathroom.

Pemba thought, *when ladies go to the rest room, they take an unusually longer time. Whatever they do in that place is their business.*

Linda came back after an unusually long time. Pemba noticed she had no makeup and had changed into her casual dress.

"We will be going to the market tomorrow," he reminded Linda.

"What is there in the market?"

"It is a village market that takes place once a week. We will meet almost all the village's people there."

"Is there anything particular in the market?" Linda inquired.

"It is a trading place. People come from far away to sell and buy groceries, clothing, animals, and things for daily use. We also have a play area for children; it's a colorful and lively event once a week," Pemba said.

Linda sat next to Pemba; their warm breath almost touched each other, and Pemba looked straight at Linda's eyes. Linda felt embarrassed when Pemba caught her watching him.

Pemba noticed that Linda was in a simple but sexy outfit and was looking immensely attractive and extremely beautiful. Linda sat on the edge of the bed, and Pemba, on the sofa.

"Pemba, tell me sincerely, what is your family's reaction to my visit here?"

"Nothing much; they are just curious and want to see you."

"What do you think of me, Pemba?"

"Well, you are a decent lady of high reputation with abundant beauty and good nature."

"That is all?" Linda tease Pemba.

"And very attractive, smart, and ingenious."

"Attractive in what way?" Linda asked again.

"Friendship, of course."

"That is all you want from me?"

"What else should I expect?" Pemba reaction.

"How about anything a man wants from a woman?"

Linda was getting closer to him. She extended her hand toward his shoulder. Pemba did not react but sat in the same place without moving. Linda got even closer, putting her right hand toward his thigh.

"Pemba, if you want, you may kiss me," Linda whispered in his ear softly and passionately.

Pemba was not expecting the offer. He gazed at her, agape, spellbound with her as she was. He shifted toward Linda; his growing uncertainty and anxiety on how to handle the unexpected situation was making him increasingly and obviously uncomfortable.

However, his erection was clearly visible through his jeans. Pemba could not resist the invitation for a kiss. He kissed her with his tongue buried inside her needy lips, passionately with vigor. She pulled him violently closer and brought his muscled chest closer to her breast. She felt the nudge of his manhood on the middle part of his body, which was filled with the need of being taken. He slowly kissed her moist lips, warmed her face, and moved his wet mouth to her neck and breasts, going down slowly and warmly to the white and majestic area of thigh, then to her clean pubic area, and to the center the body towards her genitals. Linda was hopeless; she could not do anything but moan, and the noise was getting louder. Her eyes closed, but her body was hungry, intent, and exceptionally warm.

She leaned forward to him. Pemba grasped her breast, and when Pemba wanted more, she pulled her breast away from his mouth, teasing him. In response, he pulled her hard into his lap.

Her back to his chest, he nibbled on her shoulder and squeezed her hard nipples through her thin clothes. She wished her clothing magically disappeared, leaving nothing between their warm body hot and naked skin. They both took their dress mercilessly and in rapid motion. He pushed hard from behind, thirsty inside, holding her hips with his strong hands, and she could feel his entire penis inside her large vagina. She felt her whole body melting; she had never felt this kind of raw and passionate lovemaking before in her life. It was wild but pleasant, so hot and so satisfying, and she was sweating. Each time he pushed himself into her, she would balance her body and put him closer between her thighs. His thrusts were getting harder, penetrating her, giving exotic, blissful feelings; she hoped it would never end.

Pemba was also sweating hard. Linda could feel his perspiration on her naked butt. The motion behind her was rapidly increasing, and she was feeling his hard, strong penis moving wildly inside her. Pemba's breathing was growing rapidly and becoming heavy along with Linda's each moment. She had not experienced such a divine pleasure in the past.

Now it was Pemba's turn. It was him that was moaning and slightly crying in a low voice. Time had come for both to express feelings of happiness together. Pemba could not control his body. He fell completely and heavily on Linda's back. He wanted to get up, but Linda pulled him back down and asked him to stay longer. Linda slowly flattened, facing Pemba, and whispered in his left ear, "I love you Pemba. Thanks for making love with me; it was heavenly, and I most enjoyed it."

Pemba, without moving his body from the top of Linda's body, gave a loving answer, "I love you too; you are amazing."

The two slept in the same position for a long time, holding and caressing each other, softly and slowly, all over their naked bodies. There was nothing but perfection.

When Linda got up in the morning, she found herself in the room, naked and alone. The sunlight was trying to reach the room, making her surroundings softer, brighter, and more cozy. She did not even notice when Pemba left her; she must have slept hard after the beautiful lovemaking last night. She needed and wanted to lie longer in bed, as her whole body was hurt, and she did not have the energy to get up. She looked at her watch; it was eight forty.

Pemba got up quietly from beside Linda's naked body, dressed in the bathroom, and left for his home without even saying good-bye to Linda, as she was in sound sleep.

Once home, he did not want anybody to know about his coming in the morning; he entered his bedroom and slept. No one in the house but his mother knew.

Linda got up from the bed slowly, lazily, and unwillingly, and made her way to the bathroom. She watched her full, naked body in the large bathroom mirror critically. She noticed her breast and genital area. Part of the body between her thighs was slightly bruised and red. She touched her breasts, which were still swollen from last night and looked tender. She turned on the warm water in the tub and went back to the room to get the flimsy nightgown which she had used last night.

The gown also looked used and wrinkled all over, like her body this morning. She took a leisurely warm bath, caressed her body all over, and massaged her breast and private area with French body soap. After a complete, satisfying bath, she asked room service for a coffee, which the waiter brought to her room promptly.

When she was dressing, she heard a knock at the door. The waiter who'd brought the coffee earlier was standing there.

"Madam, two young children are waiting in the lobby."

Linda thought they must be Pemba's sisters and had come to fetch her.

"Sure, please ask them to wait little longer."

The waiter ran back to the lobby to deliver the message to the little girls. Linda now knew she needed to finish her makeup quickly. Upon leaving her room Linda saw two beautiful baby girls, like dolls, sitting on the large sofa in the lobby. Both of them got up after seeing Linda and greeted her in thin and sweet voices, "Namaste!"

Linda returned the greeting, putting her hands together. "Namaste!"

Their faces were round, white, and very charming, very cute like two Chinese dolls. Linda hugged both of them, caressing their shoulders as if she was expressing her affection toward them. Linda held the sisters' little hands and asked, "How are you?"

The little girls were shy and blushed but replied in clear voices, "I am fine."

Linda walked along the long brick-tiled corridor, holding the little angels' hands. At the main gate, Pemba on the left and perhaps his mother on the right greeted Linda, holding both of their hands together.

Linda moved forward, bowed her head slightly, and returned their greeting, "Namaste!"

Pemba said, "Welcome to our house."

The entrance of the house led to a larger living area. The kitchen was on the far left side of the room. A large oak table had been placed close to the big French window. The wooden floors were clean and well-polished. A very impressive fireplace was situated in the middle part of the room, and fire was burning slowly, giving ample heat around. In the living room, an old man and a tall and graceful woman sat on the large black sofa. The two girls were seated in the cane chairs, far from the other people's sitting area. They were playing and enjoying themselves.

"Linda, let me introduce Mother and my uncle and aunty. This is Dorje, my uncle, and his beautiful wife, Dolkar. By the way, my uncle is the chief of our village and also an honorable member in the House of Representatives in Kathmandu. He has contributed a lot for the development of our district."

Linda bowed her head and greeted them in Nepali style, "Namaste." They all laughed at the gesture but did not say anything.

"How long have you been in the country?" Linda was really surprised when the uncle's wife, Dolkar, spoke flawless and unaccented English.

"I came here for three-week Everest trek through Mountain Travel, and Pemba was our cook and guide."

"How did you enjoy the trek?"

"It was superb."

"Where are you from?"

"California."

"No wonder you are so pretty."

"Thank you."

"Pemba told us you are planning to go to the Dalai Lama's place in Dharamshala in India?"

"Yes, I will feel secure in his company."

In the meantime, Pasang and Mingma entered the living room, and they also greeted everyone, saying, "Namaste."

"Linda, you are looking pretty and fresh this morning," Mingma remarked.

"Maybe because of your lavish French dinner last night," Linda said with humor.

Everybody laughed.

Pemba got closer to Linda and asked, "How are you?"

"I am fantastic."

"Do you know what my mother and sisters are saying about you?"

"What?" she asked with a naughty smile on her face.

"You look like a goddess in flesh."

"You must be kidding."

"Swear to God." Pemba quietly whispered, "Did you enjoy last night?"

"No, what about you?" A teasing question.

Pemba had a coy expression on his face and said nothing; he just smiled mischievously.

Pemba's mother came and said something to him in Nepali. Linda could not understand.

"My mother is saying we should have lunch; otherwise, we will be late for the market."

"What do we have for lunch?" Linda inquired.

"Our menu is *Phalughi* Sherpa stew, *momo* dumpling, green salad, chicken basmati rice, and carrot fudge. And to drink is *chhyang*, the rice beer." Pemba's description was brief and precise.

Everyone sat around the large dining table. The meal was kept in one corner and presented in buffet style. Linda seemed to be the center of attention. Everybody was asking her to take more food. Pemba offered her *chhyang* in a crystal glass.

Linda liked the food. It had a strange aroma but seemed quite nourishing and completely filling. After almost an hour, they were done with eating. They proceeded to the market, which looked so crowded, as if everyone from the villages had come there. Linda found the market a strange place of trading— like in barter time, primitive and crude. Chicken, goats, buffalo, even rabbits, were available to buy. There was a dusty corner for children to play all kinds of games. The scene was like what you would see in the *Indiana Jones* movies. Dirt, dust, a chanting crowd, some monks, children running everywhere, chickens flying in one direction and the owner running after them. One could witness very chaotic funny scenes everywhere.

Linda enjoyed the market as if she had never seen it before in her life. Exhausted and completely worn out, Pemba and Linda left the marketplace without buying anything. When they arrived at the hotel, it was past twilight.

Linda asked Pemba to have coffee or something to drink, but he declined and wanted to rest at home after a shower. Linda, left alone, went to her room and took a warm bath and a nap. She got up around eight and ordered a simple meal of spaghetti, soup, and salad. She needed to sleep early as the flight would leave around ten in the morning.

After dinner, she put a request for a wake-up call at eight to the receptionist. She got the new Forsyth book *The Fourth Protocol* from her backpack, which she'd purchased at the Frankfurt Airport, and lay down with the book in a relaxed manner. She slept well because of the hectic market trip.

She got up when she heard the sound of a knock at the door—her wake-up call. Without opening the door, she said in a high-pitched voice, "Thanks."

The noise subsided. Linda put warm water in the tub, got naked, and immersed herself and felt heavenly refreshed after the sound sleep last night. The memory of her divine sex with Pemba the other night was still fresh inside her private parts, and that made her shiver still.

Pemba's sisters were waiting in the lobby again this morning. When they saw her, they greeted, "Namaste," both together.

"We are here to take you to the airport." Linda laughed inside; actually, the airport was at their doorstep. How funny!

Pemba's mother was there with a white silk scarf. Pemba looked like a dashing prince next to his mother, with blue Levi's jeans, a yellow shirt, and an iron-colored sport jacket. He looked just gorgeous. His mother smiled at Linda and put the white silk scarf around her neck. She then spoke something in her language to Pemba.

"Mother is really happy that you came to our village and house," Pemba translated. "She wishes you a pleasant and safe trip back to your home."

Linda, at that moment, became really sentimental. It brought tears to her eyes, and she could not say much, except a "Thank you," and embraced his mother and sisters warmly. She gave one hundred dollars to each of the sisters, which they accepted, bowing their heads with "Namaste" again.

***

CHAPTER EIGHT

December 1985

Linda seemed more comfortable and happy in Pemba's company after coming back from Phaplu. They did their own chores. Linda went shopping, and Pemba went to his office. The next day they had their flight to Delhi and then to Dharamshala day after.

Pemba was coming to Linda's hotel at Yak & Yeti. They planned to have supper together somewhere in Thamel that night. Linda bought a few gifts for her coworkers and friends—mostly Nepali handicrafts, some Tibetan *thankas,* a few artifacts, and a beautiful emerald Buddha sculpture for her living room.

She was about to finish her packing when she heard a knock on the door.

"Hello, dear, how was your day?" Linda was pleased to see Pemba.

"As usual. Nothing remarkable at the office. Finished packing?"

"Almost. Give me a few minutes. Let me freshen up; are we going now or a little later?"

"In about half an hour."

"Okay, great."

Linda proceeded to the bathroom, and Pemba turned on the radio to listen to some music. Linda joined him nearly twenty minutes later with fresh makeup, in jeans and a white top along with a blue cardigan.

"Oh my, you look awesome. Let me have a kiss." Pemba got up and kissed her passionately.

"Pemba, where did you learn to kiss? Your technique is sensuous, and I never want to let you go."

"You must be joking." Pemba reacted.

"Oh God, I am not lying."

"You mean, you just like my kiss, nothing else?" Pemba answered in a teasing manner.

Linda gave a mischievous smile but kept quiet. Pemba moved closer to Linda. This time, he held her hand and kissed it.

"What's that for, Pemba?"

"You are a superb person, and I feel I am growing a soft spot for you."

"What do you mean by soft spot? Do you mean you love me?" Linda wanted clarifications.

"That confession may be premature," Pemba said.

"Tell me when you are ready." Linda took it lightly.

Pemba gave a mysterious smile but kept quiet.

In front of Hotel Yak & Yeti, they picked up a cab and went to Thamel tourist area for dinner. Pemba knew a Tibetan restaurant there. After the taxi dropped them in front of the restaurant, Linda asked, "This is it?" Pemba just nodded.

The inside decoration of the restaurant was amazing; it felt as if you were entering a palace. The carpet on the wooden floor looked soft, colorful, and gorgeous. The setting was like that of a monastery, with light drums playing in the background. There were about ten large Buddha sculptures scattered all over the rooms. The lighting was conceived in such a way that it did not hurt to look at it directly; the reflections and the paintings on the ceilings depicted a museum-like setting. Everywhere in the restaurant, rich Tibetan heritage and artifacts were on display in a very attractive manner. The waiters were tall and beautiful. All had colorful *bakkhus,* and were welcoming the guests with mild smiles and pleasant gestures, gracefully bowing their heads in an eloquent manner. The restaurant was half empty—perhaps they were a little early—and occupied mostly by Europeans, except for a few Japanese in the farthest corner.

The moment the waiter noticed Pemba, he ran inside and informed Lopsang about Pemba and Linda's arrival. He came out, shook hands and led them to an inside private room, which seemed to be prepared for special guests. The room has also been tastefully decorated. It had no table or chairs but a sunken place in the middle and a Japanese-style low table for food. Linda liked this kind of sitting; she could put her leg down and feel comfortable while eating. The room was cozy with carved chairs and table, soft, concealing light, and some kind of Nepali instrumental music in the background.

"Good evening," a waiter addressed Pemba.

"Good evening. Please, a Heineken for me, and you?" Pemba asked Linda.

"Gin and tonic with a twist of lemon."

Pemba checked the menu. From the list, he selected wanton soup, fried dumplings, chicken chop suey, and rice pudding. Linda supported Pemba's choice for the meal.

In the meantime, Lopsang entered the room, smiling with the question, "Have you ordered?"

"Yes."

"I heard, you are going to Dharamshala?"

"Yes, Linda has planned it for a long time."

Facing Linda, Lopsang asked, "Do you have faith in the Buddhist religion?"

"I do." She gave a short reply.

"Okay, I wish you all the best for the trip; enjoy the food." Lopsang left them.

"Pemba, I would like to go to the Taj Mahal too. Should we plan that after Dharamshala?"

"Of course. We can make a day trip or stay overnight in Agra."

"I prefer to stay."

"Then we need to take the Taj Express train from Delhi."

In the meantime, several of Chinese, Nepali and Tibetan dishes were brought by the waiter and placed neatly on the table. The strong spicy aroma from the food tickled the air.

Linda was getting used to the half-spicy food from Nepal. She liked the taste ordered by Pemba.

After the tasty and delicious food, Linda made a remark.

"Thanks, Pemba; your food selection is great."

"Really? You like them?"

Linda nodded in approval.

After thanking everyone in the restaurant, especially Lopsang, Pemba and Linda took a cab back to Yak & Yeti Hotel. They both entered the coffee shop, which was open twenty-four hours for snacks, and took a small table next to the large French window in the far corner. "Yes, Sir?" the waitress asked.

"Two cups of coffee," Linda ordered.

"The flight is at ten thirty. I will come to pick you up at nine for the airport," Pemba told Linda. "We will make all arrangements after arrival in Delhi."

Linda nodded and looked at Pemba; she found him very attractive this evening.

"Why are you looking at me like that?" Pemba questioned.

"Just you look very attractive."

"You are looking charming too," Pemba said.

Both complimented each other and sipped the coffee slowly, enjoying the other's presence. Pemba left after they had finished. Linda went up to her room to finish packing, and prepared to sleep.

Pemba was at the lobby at nine sharp. Linda was almost ready when she received a call from the reception desk downstairs. She called Pemba to the room to get some last-minute help.

"Hi, dear, good morning."

"I am ready, almost." Linda came close to Pemba and kissed him passionately.

After a quick visit to the restroom, she joined Pemba. The cab dropped them outside the international airport terminal and they proceeded to the check-in counter for the airlines. Everything proceeded normal. After some time, they boarded the aircraft.

Delhi Airport was larger than the airport in Nepal and seemed more crowded. Linda noticed the piercing look of the Indian men towards her. The immigration and custom procedure was normal and without event. A cab hailed outside took them to Claridge Hotel, somewhere in the southern part of Janpath Road. The hotel was medium-sized, with a quiet and attractive lobby. They had two separate adjacent rooms on the seventh floor. The elevator made an uncomfortable noise while going up. The back area of the hotel had lots of trees with a swimming pool and beautiful green grass. As a whole, the hotel was awesome: centrally located, and the staff's hospitality was superb, with polite and efficient service.

While checking about the train for Dharamshala, the hotel receptionist had all the information about the train. She informed them that the train would leave overnight and reach Pathankot in the morning, and then there was the option to take a bus or a taxi to go to Dharamshala—which was about eighty-five kilometers. There were several type of accommodations of various tastes fitting for own budget in Dharamshala. As per the receptionist, it would be a hassle for them to go to the railway station and buy tickets, but they could get first-class tickets for the train the following night for a nominal service charge. Following the receptionist's suggestion, they agreed to get the ticket through them for the following night. For that afternoon, they booked a half-day sightseeing tour that would take them to Connaught Place, Lodi Garden, Jantar Mantar, Qutab Minar; and on the way back, they would shop around Janpath Market.

The tourist bus came on time. They completed the tour as planned and, towards the evening, enjoyed a fabulous shopping for Indian arts and crafts. Pemba bought a beautiful silken *kurta-salwar* for Linda—in return for which, she bought a long silk *kurta* with lots of embroidery work in the neck area for Pemba.

For dinner, they chose the Indian cuisine restaurant inside the hotel, where they saw a performance of wonderful Indian song and folk dances. The show was glamorous and performed in a highly professional manner. Both Linda and Pemba enjoyed the performance immensely. Even after all the activities, neither of them was tired; so they decided to go to the hotel disco a little later. In the meantime, they preferred to walk into the hotel garden by the swimming pool to relax and have a couple of cocktails. The atmosphere was just intoxicating. The flowers and ambiance were wonderful. The weather was on the chilly side, but a great bonfire had been started in the middle of the garden. The tourists were sitting in the circle, sipping their cocktails. Linda and Pemba preferred a quieter place far from the tourists, closer to a large tree.

After they had settled down at the comfortable iron table, a waiter approached and took their order for a drink. Linda looked just perfect in a smoky gown with a dark-colored, charcoal cardigan. Pemba had a blue dapper cap, black boots, brown belt, blue-striped collared shirt, cream-colored jacket, and dark slacks. He was looking gorgeous too.

After they got comfortable, Linda asked Pemba a question. “Pemba, if you have an opportunity, would you like to visit or stay in America?”

“I haven’t thought about it.”

“Suppose if I invite you. Will you come?”

“For a visit?” Pemba questioned.

“Maybe to live for some time.” Linda clarified.

“I am not sure, Linda. My family is here.”

“Wouldn’t you like a better life for yourself and your family?”

“Depends.” Pemba seemed reluctant.

“Depends on what?”

“On the kind of job I will have, and the place I will get to live in,” Pemba said.

“You may stay with me.”

“What will our relationship be?” Pemba was curious.

“Suppose I invite you on a fiancée visa.”

“It is tempting, but it will be hard for me to understand a person from another culture and upbringing.”

“Pemba, so far, how much have you understood me?” Linda put a direct question.

“You are an extremely nice person as a friend for a short time. I will need time to think it over for a lifetime. Besides, I have to protect and see to the welfare of my family.”

"I can't do much for your family, but I can guarantee their financial protection on a monthly basis as far as their expenses are concerned." Linda tried to assure.

"I really appreciate it, Linda, but I can't burden you on financial obligation for my family."

"Why not, Pemba? Treat that as a loan, and you may pay me back when you are able to."

"Let me think over your proposal, and I will let you know before you leave for the States." Pemba gave final answer.

"Indeed, Pemba, that is what I expect. May I kiss you?

While kissing, Linda whispered in his ear, "It is not my fault. You look alluring this evening, and I may even seduce you tonight." Linda laughed.

Pemba could not reply but just wore a shy expression. He looked sexier in his silent mood.

"Pemba, my man, let us go to the disco. It is about time."

The disco was of medium size with a sophisticated sound system, wooden waxed floor, and dark light for perfect dancing. Western music was on air, and there were about eight couples on the dance floor. Linda bought two drinks, one for herself and the other for Pemba. They sat in a corner curling and holding each other, and tried to warm themselves up. After some time, they were both on the dance floor. Surprisingly, Pemba happened to be a good dancer, which impressed Linda. They danced till they dropped around 1:00 a.m. Both felt they had enough and moved to their rooms.

Linda whispered to Pemba in a very sexy voice, "I am going to seduce you; let's go to my room." Linda virtually dragged Pemba to her room.

They slept till ten the next morning, both exhausted from last night's disco and wild, delightful sex. Both had orgasm and felt completely satisfied with each other. All night, they held each other and enjoyed each other's naked body.

Pemba hardly allowed Linda to get up, but she whispered, "Darling, I need to go to the restroom, and it is urgent."

Pemba reluctantly let Linda out of his warm embrace. For her charm, her intoxicating body essence, and the light perfume she used along with her magnificently curvy body shape—Pemba could hold her twenty-four hours without any kind of interruption. He was getting crazy for her body, her mild nature, and her soft style of dealing with everything. Only God knew what would happen in his life, and where it might take him.

Immediately after using the restroom, Linda came to submit herself in Pemba's warm and inviting embrace. They stayed another hour in bed, enjoying each other and caressing their soft and naked bodies. Both seemed like they would never be satisfied with each other and would always crave for each other.

Pemba felt a slight squeeze in his stomach, which was an indication of hunger. Perhaps it was high time for brunch.

"Linda, darling, should we go to nibble something? I am hungry." Pemba proposed.

"Of course, I feel the same way."

In a short time, they had showered and changed. Linda had put a casual makeup with white slacks, a white top, and a straw hat. Any kind of dress was a gift for Linda's body; it suited her, and she looked amazingly beautiful.

"Where would you like to eat?"

"Let's go to Mayuri Intercontinental."

"Where is that?"

"It is a fabulous restaurant for authentic Indian meals."

"Oh my God; it sounds tempting. Let's go."

Pemba, in the meantime, remembered that they were supposed to check out of the hotel at noon. If late, the hotel may charge for another night. They approached the reception area and requested for late checkout.

"What time do you think you may be able to check out?"

Linda replied, "We have a train tonight; is it possible to check out at five?"

"No, madam! The latest we will allow is three."

"That is fine. We will be back before three, and thanks."

They hailed a cab outside the hotel porch and drove to Intercontinental Hotel. On arrival, a very tall man with a bright red turban, full beard that cover the face and a long red coat opened the cab door. Linda was very impressed; she had never seen a tall, well-dressed doorman opening her cab door. She reached for her purse and gave one hundred rupees. The doorman was so happy with that kind of exuberant tip that he saluted her vigorously and showed clear happy expressions on his face.

Pemba knew the location of the restaurant; so they proceeded to the tenth floor. Linda noticed that the internal decoration of the restaurant was like a Mughal-fashioned dining room. It was decorated with classic pictures and ancient pot artifacts. A portion of the floor was covered with a big head of a tiger's skin covering the area as a rug. Everything was pleasing, aristocratic, and had a royal, elite taste.

A waiter approached in a beautiful, pink embroidered dress. Pemba ordered gin and tonic for Linda, and for himself, a dry martini. For lunch, he ordered a chicken sizzler, two *nan bread*, typical Indian flat bread, lentil soup, and *rasmalai*, an Indian sweet. Linda enjoyed the tasty but spicy food. She was getting used to this type of spicy food and happened to like it more, as she tried it every day. It might be hard to get this kind of food in Los Angeles.

After the out-of-this-world food, they returned to the hotel and started packing. Linda thought, instead of carrying all the suitcases, she preferred to leave the two big suitcases in the hotel and carry an overnight bag to Dharamshala with the proper kinds of dresses—normally long gowns that covered the full body. The colors she chose were yellow, white, and gray. After packing, they dropped the two suitcases in the hotel's custody until she came back after three days to collect it upon coming back from the trip.

It was good that the train had a sleeping area in the first-class compartment. Linda chose the upper berth. They covered it with bed sheets, which Pemba had brought with him, and prepared to sleep overnight.

The station was crowded as usual. In India, a lot of people travel by train. They were on the move for all events—marriage, pilgrimage, tour, and other important social events. In fact, India was alive with the train as it covered almost all the big and small villages all over the country. The train was the main source of keeping the country powerful and progressive, and the way poor and middle class people traveled. One could travel day or night at any time, and all the time, 24-7, almost to every part of the country.

Pemba and Linda hired a taxi from the train station to go to Dharamshala, which was just over fifty miles.

The cab took nearly two hours to reach Dharamshala along a scenic uphill-and-downhill road. The hills and mountains were visible clearly in the morning sunrays and looked beautiful. The weather was slightly cooler in this mountain range. One of her friends had suggested Linda that she should stay in the Grace Hotel during the congregation in the Los Angeles monastery, and Sonam had also mentioned the hotel. Linda requested the cab driver to take them to Grace Hotel. The hotel seemed to be pretty small, but looked elegant and seemed to be built keeping in mind the traditional hill architecture. The backdrop of dense forest on the hill was set amidst majestic Himalayan ranges, which were clearly visible from most parts of the hotel. The reception area was quiet cozy. A fireplace with burning wood occupied a corner and was inviting to all incoming guests. The receptionist was a charming middle-aged lady who spoke in a clear and pleasing British accent.

"Welcome to Grace Hotel," she said, and she offered a chilled mango drink to Linda and Pemba.

The drinks refreshed the new guests. In the meantime, a distinguished-looking, tall gentleman with salt-and-pepper beard all over his face and wearing a dark suit, a bowtie, and a blue turban emerged. "Hi, my name is Khurana, and I am the manager of this elegant hotel. It will be my pleasure to give you a brief tour of the hotel prior to showing to your room."

Linda said, "It will be our pleasure, Khurana."

"Which country are you from?"

"America."

"We really love to have the Americans as our guests."

"And this gentleman is from Nepal."

"How nice! We get lots of Nepali, and this part of Dharamshala has become home for a large Tibetan settlement. Believe me, Linda, they are the most peace-loving and nonviolent people on earth."

"Yes, I know." A short remark came from Linda.

"Well, about Grace Hotel, it was the residence of the late prime minister of Kashmir, built about two hundred years ago. The prime minister's son later restored his ancestral home and adopted it to the Welcome Heritage Hotel Group. This establishment is rooted on rich, traditional, and royal culture rooted in imperially outstanding Kashmiri hospitality. All guests appreciate the enchanting setting, excellent food quality, and hospitality of the hotel. We have many repeat clients. This is one of our guest rooms, which offers beautiful and exotic furniture and breathtaking views of Kangara Valley and Pongdam Lake."

In conclusion, Khurana summarized, "The old charm of Grace Hotel, its ancient charm—the surrounding beauty of the magnificent mountains combined together—makes it a perfect and magical place. I am sure you will enjoy your stay here."

The manager left them outside their rooms. As in Delhi, they occupied two separate rooms.

"Oh, Pemba, we need to contact Sonam and inform him about our arrival here. Can you call him; I have his phone number."

"Sure. Let us get refreshed and will call from the lobby downstairs."

"Of course, Pemba."

After an hour, both met in the lobby.

The call did not get an immediate response. Pemba left a voice mail about Linda's arrival from Los Angeles. Then they wanted to explore the charming city. They could not see a cab; so they hired an auto rickshaw and went to the center of the town. The town seemed not so organized; the traffic was heavy and running in a haphazard manner. People were not following traffic rules; overtaking and honking seemed to be the norm here. Local people and lots of Lamas seemed to be shopping in the crowded market. The whole city looked like a colorful, religious, spiritual, pious, and peaceful place.

Pemba and Linda planned to have lunch in the city somewhere. Linda preferred not to eat meat during her three days' stay here. She wanted to be a complete vegetarian and avoid sex.

After searching for some time, the duo found a Marwari restaurant, pure vegetarian. Pemba suggested trying that place; it did not seem so clean and air-conditioned, but as per Pemba, they provided excellent vegetarian food. Linda really liked the food; it was fresh and delicious.

After lunch, they returned to the hotel in an auto rickshaw, as taxis were scarce. They were curious, and checked with the receptionist at the hotel, who confirmed that taxis were limited and expensive and suggested using auto rickshaws. There was a message from Sonam to call back. Pemba called Sonam; they spoke in their dialect. Linda could not understand. After a while, Pemba handed over the phone to Linda.

"Hi, Sonam, how are you?"

"Hi, Linda, welcome to Dharamshala. I will check His Holiness's schedule for the next three days, and will inform you when I can get you an audience with him. A one-on-one will not be possible but it will be usually with the group of devotees from Europe, Thailand, Sri Lanka, and Burma. By the way, how many days are you staying?"

"Three."

"Well, I will let you know tomorrow. In the meantime, I will be sending you the brochure in the hotel that will explain about His Holiness's teaching procedures. Your seat will be a special one, and someone will come to take you to the gathering and provide a radio for translation as His Holiness teaches in the Tibetan language."

"That's fine. I will wait for your Lama to escort me."

"Great, and bye for now." Sonam hung up the phone.

Linda briefed Pemba about her conversation with Sonam in detail. After almost two hours, Linda got the booklet, which explained about His Holiness' teaching hours, place, duration, shoe placement style, and how to listen to an interpreter through the radio simultaneously. She also learned the method of offering donation to the monastery and learned how mass tea was distributed during the teaching. It seemed everything was well-organized so that everyone would be able to get the most out of His Holiness's teaching and enjoy it hassle-free.

There were radios for all the foreigners, who obviously would not understand Tibetan. Normally, the radio would simultaneously be broadcast in English, French, Japanese, or any other language depending on the availability of the interpreters. The shoes were not allowed; one was required to place them under their seats. In the gathering, due to security concerns, no outside electronic gadgets were allowed. Seating was on the ground and provided on a first-come-first-serve basis. For the special guests, separate chairs were allowed close to His Holiness—normally on the sides, without hampering the front view. It was necessary to register if you were planning to attend.

All attendees were required to register in person, due to security reasons, at the Tibetan branch security office near Hotel Tibet. Normally, registration began only three days in advance to the start the teaching. The Tibetan security required the public to present a passport and two photographs in order to be admitted in the teaching ground. Several thousand devotees might attend a session, and it was always advisable to arrive at least three days in advance to secure their accommodation.

There was a note from Sonam together with the information brochure. It explained that some Lamas would be coming to fetch Linda and Pemba the following day at eight and take them to the teaching ground in a special area of sitting for the foreigners. Linda felt happy and at ease and explained the note to Pemba as well. She also explained the procedure for the following morning. Pemba also felt happy that he was getting a special privilege due to Linda.

The Lama Sonam sent was in the lobby at eight to pick them up for the teaching. Promptly, both Linda and Pemba came to the reception desk to meet him. The Lama was in the maroon robe and was very polit. He greeted them with modesty. Sonam had sent a Toyota jeep to pick them up. After they all had settled, the Jeep moved slowly up and down hills. The road was rough and a little muddy due to last night's rain. It seemed the Jeep was a four-wheel drive and had a hard grip on the road.

After driving for nearly twenty minutes, a big ground came to their sight. The whole of the ground was occupied by devotees sitting on some kind of cloth-mats. The congregation seemed colorful and orderly, without any shade atop their head. Yet, they looked extremely disciplined. In the center, there was a huge platform about three feet above the ground decorated with colorful banners. A huge sitting Buddha statue with lots of flowers, oil lamps, and candles around was in the right side of the platform.

The attractive platform had been prepared for His Holiness with a small but powerful microphone installed. Everything looked very pretty and the decoration was pleasing and religious. The whole atmosphere had an aroma of incense sticks; some kind of uniqueness had been created in the congregation.

On the right side, there were a few chairs that were occupied by foreigners and distinguished followers from Japan, Sri Lanka, and Thailand. Linda and Pemba were asked to take the empty chairs among the distinguished guests. Linda and Pemba were also supplied the interpreter radios as Pemba also did not understand Tibetan.

His Holiness the Dalai Lama is the 14th Dalai Lama incarnate. He was born in 1935 in the northeastern part of Tibet and wants to recognize himself as a simple Buddhist monk who has come to stand for peace and compassion in the world. The Dalai Lamas are believed to be manifestations of *Bodhisattva* who are again believed to be enlightened beings who have postponed their own nirvana and chosen to take rebirth in order to serve humanity.

In 1959 due to the uprising of the Chinese troop, the Dalai Lama was forced to leave Tibet escape into exile. Since then, he has been living in Dharmasala, northern India. Because of his leadership in the non-violent movement to free Tibet, he is recognized as a peace loving person, who was awarded the Nobel Peace Prize in 1989. His Holiness has traveled sixty-seven countries of six continents. He has received numerous awards in recognition of his powerful message of non-violence, peace, inter-religions understanding and compassion. His recent initiation of dialogue with the scientists mainly in the fields of cosmology, quantum physics, neurobiology and psychology, in moves for the collaboration between monks and world-renowned scientists are attempts to help individuals achieve peace of mind. His Holiness is not only a spiritual leader of the Buddhist but also an apostle of peace for numerous people of the world. So, even people from other faiths respect him as a man of peace and compassion.

Normally, His Holiness prefers to deliver simple teachings which could be useful for everyday ordinary life. But during his deliberation among the Lamas inside his circle, he prefers to enlighten with complex analytical talks and wrestle with complicated doctrines and highly thoughtful, resourceful issues.

That day, his deliberation was on nirvana.

His Holiness began his lecture, "The important thing in life is to scatter and not accumulate."

Then he compared Western and Eastern philosophies. "The people in the West are normally accumulating wealth and materialistic things, forgetting that this is not our home. Eventually, our home is only after our death, when we reach nirvana. So in life, we should collect the things that will enlighten us and relieve us from reincarnation."

When His Holiness delivered the speech, the entire congregation was still, silent, and hypnotized. Linda had not seen such an attentive, extremely devoted and humble crowd before. She was highly impressed with the deliberations, management of the congregation, and undivided attention; the respect toward His Holiness was unprecedented. The teaching lasted almost two hours, and almost everyone had a smile on his or her face. There was some kind of enlightenment clearly visible on the devotees' faces. Linda enjoyed and learned so many things from the teaching.

"Hi, Linda," Sonam said, as he approached her.

"Oh, hi, Sonam. By the way, this is my friend, Pemba, from Nepal."

Pemba and Sonam spoke in Nepali language, which Linda could not understand.

"Linda, I have arranged a group audition with His Holiness tomorrow morning at eleven. I will send a Lama together with a vehicle. Please come and bring Pemba with you."

"Sure, Sonam. We'll do as you said."

After that brief discussion, Sonam left their company. Pemba and Linda returned to the hotel in an auto rickshaw. Upon arrival, they both went to their respective rooms with the plan that Linda wanted to go for brief shopping for Tibetan artifacts and handicrafts toward the evening.

The downtown looked glamorous; the shops were crowded with people everywhere, hustling and bustling. On the street, Linda saw lots of vendors selling Indian food, sweets and fruits. Pemba was looking for a Tibetan shop that sold handicrafts and gifts. Pemba found one on the upper floor of a cemented three-story house that was connected with a ladder from outside the building. The shop was well-decorated with all sorts of Tibetan *thanka*, and Buddha sculptures made of marble, jade, silver, and metal. There were so many things Linda did not recognize—in fact, all of them. The good thing was that, the shop had fixed prices, and haggling was not allowed like in other Indian and Nepali shops. And the best part was, the shop owner accepted American Express credit cards.

Linda selected a few things for her own decorations in the living room and some gifts for the office friends and family members. She was pleased with the selection, and everything was done under one roof. She liked the owner, who seemed very honest. The owner, Lakpa, was also from Tibet whose family came with His Holiness Dalai Lama together, and His Holiness helped his father to establish this shop. Although the father had passed away now, his son was taking care of the family business. The young man was very polite and sincere, and really knew how to treat a client.

After the brief shopping, they came back to the hotel, took dinner together, and went to sleep early. They both retired in their respective rooms and visualized the next day's meeting with His Holiness.

The next morning, at ten thirty sharp, a Lama came to the hotel with a Jeep came to pick Linda and Pemba. They both were happy to take the ride of their lifetime to see His Holiness.

The Jeep came to stop in front of large three-story house brightly painted yellow color inside the camp surrounded by dense trees, green meadows and beautiful landscape decked by a variety of flowers. On arrival on the foyer, Pemba and Linda were taken to a large waiting room. The distinguished devotees from Japan, Sri

Lanka, and Thailand, along with some foreigners, had assembled in the room. Everyone seemed anxious, quiet, and eager.

Almost fifteen minutes after eleven, a tall Lama emerged into the room. In a very soft, polite manner, he said, "His Holiness is ready to see you."

He led everyone, about twelve people, who followed him quietly and in an orderly manner. After walking along a corridor decorated with rich Tibetan colorful, soft, and very attractive carpet, all entered a narrow but well-lit room and were requested to wait for a moment. The tall Lama quietly knocked at the door and entered through a large, well-polished wooden door. A few minutes later, he signaled everybody to enter the room. It was a large and bright room. On the left side of the room was a coffee table, and it was filled with bouquets of fresh, colorful flowers.

Behind the flowers was a large wooden showcase with a big yellow metal sitting Buddha placed inside. In front, lots of oil lamps, candles, flowers, and numerous small Buddha images were decorated along with flowers and a silk white scarf. On the right side of the room, a yellow upholstery, cozy and comfortable sofa had been placed, and a golden lamp-stand had been kept towards the wall of the room that had bright light covering the entire room.

Alongside a large, comfortable chair with matching colors, in a wooden credenza, lots of books and valuable manuscripts of religious doctrines were lying and were visible to all guests.

On the right side of the large and comfortable-looking chair, a beautiful looking coffee table had lots of books arrange nicely. Some of them were opened as if they were in use. Under the sofa, a large, colorful flower-patterned thick carpet which could easily hold up to fifteen people for sitting position comfortably. The wooden floor was polished and waxed and really looked clean and new.

His Holiness entered the room with folded hands, a smile on his face, and gave a deep and warm welcome gesture toward the guests. He seemed a very simple, spiritual, and down-to-Earth person. The guests greeted him with respect, bowing their heads slightly and bending forward, facing His Holiness. When His Holiness occupied the single seat placed in the room, the guests all sat down on the carpet, facing him. As requested, a self-introduction started from the right side of His Holiness. Each guest slowly and clearly gave their name, where they were from, and how long they have been inclined toward the Buddhist faith. In total, there were two from Japan, two from Australia, three from Thailand, two from Burma, one from France, and Linda and Pemba.

A good combination of countries devotees were assembled. His Holiness had a small conversation with everyone on personal basis.

"It would be my pleasure to discuss three aspects of religion in this gathering today. One is the message of love, compassion, tolerance, and contentment, which all religions have in common. There is also the philosophical aspect, which each religion differs from one another in tradition and beliefs. Basically, it is the common belief that if you do good deeds, you are entitled for happiness. On the other hand, if one does bad deed, he will have bad consequences and suffering in life. Both Buddhists and Hindus call it karma."

His Holiness used his sense of humor and gave examples of ordinary people—without knowing their past deed, always tried to blame something else, and they trust their destiny was out of their control. But in reality everyone could control their destiny in life if they tried hard.

"The Buddha was always against the caste system in India. He suggested the spiritual leaders should try to reform. Similarly, on the cultural aspect of religion, he has raised the issue that needed to change. One aspect is the equal opportunity between men and women, but until now, male dominance prevailed. The spiritual leaders and our political leaders need a revolution in our society, and we need dramatic legislative changes to allow equal opportunity in all aspects after God created us equally.

"My job, as you know, is to promote Tibet's warm, deep concern to preserve the value of a culture of peace, nonviolence, and compassion that can be beneficial to everyone. Besides, Tibet has a treasure of natural ecology and needs to preserve the glaciers, which turned into river in Asia, and that is a crucial water supply of billion people."

In conclusion, he outlined that the inner value as the source of happiness was crucial; and interreligious harmony was necessary for the peace and preservation of Tibetan language, culture, and environment. These were essential.

After the hypnotizing lecture, the floor opened for questions for fifteen minutes. Extremely thoughtful and serious questions were put to His Holiness, who answered the questions in a very calm, convincing, and logical manner. The question-and-answer and brief discussion all took over ninety minutes, and every guest greeted His Holiness and thanked him for the enlightenment.

Prior to departure from the small congregation, there was an announcement that the lama, who had brought them in there, would lead a tour of His Holiness's residence. Just outside the narrow corridor led to an open large terrace; dense tall trees built a natural canopy. The railing in the terrace was painted with sky blue color that provided a glamorous atmosphere, and one could see the plateau to further distance and enjoy the marvelous view.

"This is where His Holiness spends mornings and sometimes evenings when weather is at its best. Here, His Holiness can see the Himalayan Valley that separates the Indian subcontinent from Tibet."

It was such a delightful sight from the terrace, and no wonder His Holiness had built the residence in such a place where he could have a constant view toward his beloved motherland, Tibet. After spending enough time in the beautiful terrace, the group entered a large room on the left side. The room was decorated with ancient books on Tibetan religious doctrine. In the middle, a tall place was built, like a small podium with lots of colorful carpet and an attractive sitting place. On both sides, the floor was covered with carpets, and on the top of the carpet, several floor seats were arranged, all facing the tall podium.

The room decoration pattern was pleasing with bright cream color, and several *thankas* were hanging in the wall— some small, some large. The room did not have windows, but it was brightly lit with light that came from the ceiling and covered all corners of the room.

"This is where His Holiness preaches and discusses complicated issues related to Buddhism with senior and highly respected lamas."

On the way out of the large residence, the kitchen was clean and airy. The dining area had a large table in the middle and lots of fresh flowers around. The group was escorted out of the residence with very polite expressions, and the Lama thanked everyone for the visit.

Linda and Pemba were dropped off by Sonam's Jeep at the hotel. After lunch, they had to catch the evening train to Delhi.

CHAPTER NINE

January 1986

After coming back from Delhi, Pemba had to catch up with lots of pending paperwork at the office. Also, January was going to be pretty busy as they were expecting three American and two Australian trekking groups. The hotels were a problem too, as the American group wanted to add a few people to their group, but they had declined the dearth of hotels. Regular meetings, a checklist for the trek, porter recruitment, and dry grocery collection from the market had become daily routine in the office.

Pemba went to the office early and stayed late for all management preparation work. He and Dawa were constantly busy; sometimes they took lunch at four in the afternoon.

They had received the new company brochure that had been printed in Thailand. All pictures and materials were attractive and printed on high-quality paper.

As usual, that evening at nine, Pemba managed to leave the office. Both Dawa and Pemba left the office together. Dawa suggested that they both go to his place to cook dinner together and then get to sleep early. Pemba accepted Dawa's invitation for dinner at his place.

On the way, Dawa asked Pemba, "Have you heard anything from Linda?"

"No, not yet. She also might be busy in the office like we are here," Pemba said.

"Maybe. Do you miss her?"

"Not really. I hardly have any time to think about her; as you see, we are so busy." Pemba explained his friend.

"Is she sending a fiancée visa for you?"

He had kept that secret from his family, office and everyone except Dawa. Pemba shared his personal matters with him and considered him his mentor.

"I have no idea, Dawa. You know how women are, and she might change her mind."

"But if the visa comes, are you really going to go?" Dawa wanted to know Pemba's feelings.

"I have not thought about it seriously; it may take a while," Pemba replied.

"Pemba, who is going to support your family?"

"We have discussed that problem; she has promised to send four hundred dollars a month as long as I will not be earning," Pemba revealed.

"Really, that is very nice of her." Dawa liked the arrangement.

"She will provide it as a loan, and I will return it after I find work," Pemba clarified.

"I like that agreement. Let me ask you one more time, do you really love her enough to get married?"

"Dawa, you are like my brother and mentor. She is extremely nice to me, and she is a very warm, lovely person. Seriously, I have not found a fault in her." Pemba was sincere.

"Pemba, you know about our friend who married a Japanese woman."

"Of course. I have told her about them, but she has faith in herself and in my love."

The dinner was ready with noodles, veggies, and chicken. They ate a lot, as both were very hungry. Since both needed to get to the office early, Pemba departed soon after dinner. In fact, the past month had kept Pemba so busy that he hardly had any time to think about Linda. He also had not received a letter or any kind of news from her; perhaps he might get it in the next few weeks. In his sleep, he dreamed he and Linda were together in a new place. Perhaps, he thought, it might be somewhere in Los Angeles.

Linda was in a blue dress, looking very pretty, and he was in blue faded jeans and a pure white shirt. They both were happy and sitting close to a lake in a park with lots of colorful flowers. The landscape was attractive with trimmed and soft green grass. In the middle, there was a white gazebo covered with small and soft green branches all around; a white marble fountain looked awesome in the middle of the grounds. Some very lovely white doves were playing in the fountain. Adorable children were trying to catch the beautiful butterflies hovering in the fresh bursting flowers. The whole atmosphere was aromatic, tantalizing, and soothing. Pemba and Linda were engulfed in each other and lost in that wonderful euphoria.

When Linda was about to kiss Pemba, the alarm went off and indicated that it was six in the morning. Pemba lay for a while, remembering the fresh and heavenly dream. He thought Linda still loved him, and that the dream was some kind of indication he might get some news from her soon.

The office was busy as usual. Robert prepared a to-do list for the day and placed it on everyone's desk. Pemba glimpsed at the list; it was overwhelming, and he felt he might not finish on time. He started from the beginning, compiled the files of the group which was arriving next week, filled out the trekking permit forms, checked the porters' situation, and compiled their list.

It looked like they needed two more porters for that group. He informed Dawa, who reassigned two more porters. He checked the accommodation list along with the room list at Hotel Soaltee, so on and so forth. Pemba's whole day was just coming to an end and he had hardly finished a little more than half the items in the list. In the meantime, he heard constant coughing and sneezing from Dawa, who was suffering from flu. Robert came to his table and requested Dawa go home and rest. Dawa was actually not feeling well; he was forcing himself to finish some of the work, but his uncomfortable situation was clearly visible.

After Dawa left, Robert asked Pemba to come to his room, and they discussed about distributing Dawa's work among the four of them until he returned to work. Pemba realized they all were going to be more hectic and busy in the office. He needed to stay longer in the office by coming earlier and leaving late; there was no other option. Robert issued an office internal memo that for two weeks, he would manage lunch delivery from a local restaurant, and all the administrative staff were not allowed any leave so that they could finish their daily work on time. He also canceled all leave except for the sick in the entire month of January.

The next day, Dawa got very sick in his apartment. He called Pemba at about eleven at night. Pemba took him to the emergency room. The doctors, after diagnosing Dawa, came to the conclusion that he had severe flu and was running a high fever. They suggested he be admitted to the hospital for at least the next three days. Since Dawa's family lived in Solokhumbu, he had no family in Kathmandu. Pemba assumed the responsibility to take care of Dawa until he was cured. He left his phone number at the reception desk and with the concerned nurse to call him for any kind of emergency.

As Dawa slept in the hospital bed with the medication, Pemba left for home almost at one in the morning. Overwork in the office and now another tension of Dawa had almost exhausted Pemba. He phoned the hospital early. Since there was no phone in Dawa's room, the nurse informed Pemba that he slept well last night, and the medication was working on him.

Pemba was satisfied with the result and prepared himself to go to the office.

He was late, and Robert asked him what had happened.

"Last night, Dawa turned seriously with flu, and I took him to emergency."

"How is he now?" Robert asked.

"Much better, still sleeping."

"How long might they keep him?"

"Maybe for three days," Pemba replied.

"Please take care of him," Robert suggested.

"I will, Sir."

Pemba became busy with his regular work. He had realized it was already getting dark outside; he put a call to the hospital. The receptionist kept him on hold. After a long hold, a nurse came on the line. "Hello."

"Hi, I am Pemba. How is my friend, Dawa?"

"He is much better. His fever is down and he ate his food this evening."

"Can you tell him I will be there in a short while?"

"Okay."

On the way to the hospital, in front of a restaurant, Pemba saw a friend of Dawa and him, stopped his motorbike.

"Hi, Pemba, how are you, man?"

"I am just fine. Hey, Dawa is sick in the hospital. Won't you like to see him?"

"Of course. I have nothing to do this evening. What happened?"

"Just flu and high fever; he is much better today."

The mutual friend, Lakpa, hopped on the back of Pemba's motorbike, and they moved toward the hospital. At this time of evening, the traffic was heavy; they reached the hospital after some time.

"Hi, Dawa, what happened?" Lakpa inquired.

"Nothing much, my friend, just a bad flu," Dawa answered slowly. Facing Pemba, he asked, "How is everything in the office?"

"Very hectic and too busy."

"I can understand; it is a peak season."

"Robert asked you to submit hospital expenses to him when you come back to the office."

"That is nice of him." Dawa seemed happy.

"Lakpa, when are you planning to go to Phaplu?" Pemba asked.

"Not soon, maybe after the end of the month."

"Will you do me a favor?"

"Yes, Pemba."

"Will you carry a letter to my mother?"

"With pleasure, Pemba."

"What else is new?" Dawa obviously was curious.

"Nothing much. I received a letter from Linda and Jack from Denver today."

"How are they?"

"Great."

"Pemba, I understand you took a nice American lady to Phaplu," said Lakpa.

"Yes, she was there for two days and enjoyed the visit."

Pemba asked Lakpa, "How did you know?"

"Are you kidding me, the whole village is talking about it." Pemba became quiet.

"Was Colonel Bradley in the office today?" Dawa asked Pemba.

"He had some guests who came late in the afternoon."

"Lakpa, how is your computer school coming?" Pemba asked.

"It is pretty good, Pemba. By the way, how long are you going to stay here?"

"You both may go now. I am fine," said Dawa. "Pemba, do you need to go to office early?"

Pemba nodded his head in acknowledgement; with a formal good-bye, they left the hospital. Pemba dropped Lakpa off in the same place he'd picked him from earlier.

Upon arriving at his room, Pemba first opened Linda's letter, which was pretty long. It had almost four pages and began with, "My darling."

It was a love letter that covered their love situation in Phaplu and Delhi Claridge Hotel in detail. She used powerful, passionate words and explained everything in a very attractive and exciting manner. When he had finished reading the letter, Pemba had a hard time controlling his romantic emotions.

She had become busy at work after arrival in Los Angeles but took three days' rest to overcome the time change which had resulted in extremely bad jet lag. In every sentence, she mentioned how much she missed him and would like to be together soon. She also mentioned that she was working on a visa petition and asked him to send his birth certificate with a few copies of current passport-size photos, along with his parents' date of marriage, date of his father's death, etc. She had already talked to a lawyer, and he had asked for those documents as soon as possible. As per the lawyer's advice, the process of getting a visa might take between six to nine months.

Linda also mentioned that she had transferred some money into his account, which might take a week to ten days, and had asked him to check his bank account regularly. After reading the letter more than three times, Pemba set it aside and opened Jack's letter from Denver.

Jack had constantly asked him to visit the States as his guest, and if he liked, he had a job waiting in his white water rafting company. Jack sent a few hundred dollar bills inside the letter, folded in a concealed manner. Pemba carefully folded the letters and put them inside the locked drawer of his table and started cooking his food.

The next morning, he could not remember everything that had happened the previous night. Oh God, he was so tired and slept soundly, felt fresh, and rejuvenated. That day, he needed to go to Rastra Bank, to get some important things, to the immigration office to get arrival cards for the guests, and to his own bank, to check his accounts. He would be running errands and it could be only in the evening he might reach office. This evening, he did not need to go see Dawa at the hospital as he was going to be discharged the following day. But he needed to buy some personal things, such as underclothes, toothpaste, and groceries. He had not had leisure to do his personal shopping for a long time. He had been busy making trekking arrangements. Trips to Phaplu, Dharamshala, and Delhi had kept him quite busy, though he still had fresh memory of the lovely time he spent with Linda.

Pemba tried to think about and analyze his relationship with Linda. Was it true love or infatuation? He found that Linda was perfect in every way. His mother, sisters, all his relatives—aunts, cousins—liked her. Although, Linda drank socially, she never smoked, and everything she did was within limit and moderation. Pemba found her always soft and polite and extremely gentle. Besides, she loved the Buddhist religion and its way of life. There was more similarity than disparity.

Moreover, she had genuine love toward him and was willing to spend money to support his family. The more he thought and tried to find negative aspects, the more helpless he grew, as he could spot no flaw in Linda. It would be a disgrace, disrespectful, and unfair act to reject her proposal and love. He would be regretting it if he let this opportunity pass by. He had talked with Dawa in detail about this, and he also had advised him to marry Linda. He had not broken the news to his family so far and was waiting for the appropriate time. He would wait until the visa arrived and the embassy approved of it.

Until then, nothing was certain. Linda could change her mind any day, not send the visa, or who knew, the visa people might not approve of the petition after the interview. He had many reasons to hold the information from his family, office, and other friends.

In spite of all these apprehensions, Pemba felt deep down that he loved Linda. He had full faith in her love, and his liking was not based on superficial notions. Dawa had warned that their relationship might turn sour after a few years as they came from completely contrasting cultures. They should be careful that such a situation did not develop between them. They must make sure that the American community accepted Pemba without prejudice, as Pemba had no basic idea how the American culture was under the surface and how liberal they were in reality. In general, most people liked the Americans and embraced their culture as it was, as it was based on liberal freedom, equality, and mutual respect. But Pemba knew there were lots of conservatives in the society who did not permit marriage other than between Christians. Besides, Pemba had studied about the Republican Party, whose members were normally hard-liners and wanted to continue with their old tradition without much change in the society. They normally followed traditions and conservative values. Perhaps, Pemba thought, he might not be able to fit in among that group.

Pemba knew, his marriage with Linda posed lots of challenge in his life. He would be required to make adjustments with the new society, new world, new culture, and totally new lifestyle. But he was determined and willing to face the challenge only because he loved the woman. It was pure love, unselfish, with total devotion to each other. Pemba also visualized the concept Buddha preached, that in the world, nothing was static; everything was dynamic and changed with time.

Pemba did not know how long the relationship between them would last. It might last a lifetime or dissolve. But he was willing to take the chance; he knew he had to go for an adventure and improve the quality of his life for himself and his family. He was going to a developed country that offered abundant opportunity. If he was capable, he should be able to open that Pandora's box with or without Linda's love and support. He had faith in his confidence, attitude, and skills. Besides, he had financial support from Linda until he would be capable of generating some revenue. If anything went wrong, he would get the support of his close friend Jack, who was willing to have him with open arms.

After his errands, Pemba was back at the office. His table was covered with a number of papers. He compiled the papers and gave a quick look, sorting important ones separately in one folder.

"Pemba, could you please double-check the accommodation for our American group arriving on January 21st? I understand they have overbooked the room in Shankar Hotel," Robert said.

"Sure, I will go to Shankar Hotel tomorrow with the list and check with them."

"Thanks."

Pemba checked the list. The group needed three double and fourteen single rooms, including for a tall man of almost over six feet. Perhaps he would have to make a request for special bed. Normally, Dawa took care of all the administrative works, and Pemba got the overflow work, but in Dawa's absence, he needed to cover everything. He did not mind working hard when it was needed, but last week had been extremely out of the ordinary, and it would be much better when Dawa resumed his work.

The next day, at Shankar Hotel, he was sitting with the manager across the table.

"Rameshji, I will need three doubles and fourteen singles along with a larger bed for a man over six feet. Their check-in is January 21st, and checkout is January 24th."

"Pembaji, we are overbooked on January 23rd. Are you sure you need all the rooms?"

"Certainly, we have rechecked, and nobody has canceled so far."

"Okay, I will see all your guests are accommodated here."

"Great, we appreciate your efforts."

Pemba needed to go to the bank and send some money to his family in Phaplu. He dropped by the bank on the way; then he would have a quick lunch and go to the office immediately after.

As soon as he reached the office Pemba went to see Robert.

"May I come in?"

"Yes, Pemba."

"I have just come from Shankar; the rooms are reconfirmed."

"Great. I was told they are overbooked."

"Yes, they are, but they will adjust some other way without splitting our group."

"Thanks, Pemba."

The moment he sat at the desk, he received a call from the immigration office.

"Pembaji, your permit for the group leaving on January 25th is ready; you may pick it up."

"Thanks, I will be there probably tomorrow."

After the office, Pemba needed to go to Kalden's house to collect the letter from home. Kalden was on the portico. They both hugged when Pemba approached him.

"When did you get back?"

"Day before."

"How is everything at home?"

"Great! They send all their regards."

"When do you plan to go to Hong Kong for business?"

Kalden frequently took few people along with him to Bangkok and Hong Kong and brought lots of commercial goods for trade in the city. He dealt in everything in wholesale and sold to retailers for profit.

"Kalden, I came from the office directly. I'm tired and need some rest at home."

Pemba thanked Kalden again and left for home.

Those three days' rest after the trip totally relaxed Linda. A couple of times, Kathy called her and updated her on the office situation. As told by Kathy, most of the partners and office colleagues, including Smith, were missing Linda. Everyone in the office was eager to see her back as soon as possible. After coming back to work, Linda had a hard time adjusting everything. The time seemed to be moving pretty slowly. But after a few days, and now after weeks, everything was under control, and Linda was handling the entire situation in the office normally.

The office became busier; things were moving at a fast pace. The franchisee law project was gaining rapid momentum, and Linda had lots of things to check and keep herself up-to-date on.

Now, it was only the middle of the week. Linda was looking forward to the weekend, especially Friday evening; she had a date with Amanda at the Marriott for happy-hour time.

The phone rang on the outside line.

"Hi, Linda, how was your trip to Nepal?" It was a call from Mountain Travel in San Francisco.

"Awesome. Your organization has my best compliments and regards; everything went smoothly."

"We will be sending you a post-trip survey form; will you complete it?"

"The pleasure will be mine, Lisa."

"Okay, you will find it in the mail within a couple of days."

"Thanks, Lisa."

While going through the files, Linda remembered that Kathy needed a file on John from the confidential rack this morning. She sorted out the file and carried it to Kathy's cabin.

"Thanks, Linda. He is coming this afternoon."

Linda noticed Kathy was busy and, without talking further, settled back at her desk.

"Linda, could you please prepare a progress summary on the law franchise project? I have an interaction program with Los Angeles Jaycee's organization next week."

"Of course, Mr. Smith."

It was almost lunchtime. Kathy and Paul had requested Linda join them in the office lunchroom. Linda had a close relationship with those two partners, and they both were fond of Linda.

"Almost ready? We'll be waiting." Paul knocked on her door before going to the lunchroom.

Linda gathered her papers from the table, tossed them properly in the safe area inside the desk, and left for lunch.

"Hi, Linda, the trip has made your complexion a little tan. It's charming."

"Thanks, Kathy."

"Tell me your trip highlights," Kathy insisted, and Paul concurred.

"Well, where should I begin… The trip was just what Paul explained to me earlier. It has rejuvenated my spirit, body, and emotions."

"Now it will be my turn then," Kathy seems to like the trip and she may also plan in the future.

"Really, Kathy, you need to have your own experience; there are many things that are hard to explain."

"Will it not be a lifetime experience?" Paul's statement was not a question but his conviction.

"Yes, Paul, it has deep meaning and tangible value," Linda gave her opinion. "Kathy, excuse me for changing the subject, but how is the support for the franchisee in the public and press?"

"You mean, nationwide?" Kathy asked Linda.

"Yes."

"So far, it has had positive reception nationwide. Small lawyer's associations expressed their resistance."

"I am sure it will produce a historical impact." Paul had confidence in the project.

"So, Linda, did you also go to the Dalai Lama's place?"

"Of course, Kathy."

"Thanks, did you purchase the gift you gave me in ….um."

"Dharamshala."

"I adore my gift also, Linda."

"Thanks, Paul; glad you like it."

Linda remembered the visa for Pemba and asked a question to Kathy.

"Kathy, perhaps have information on the process of getting a fiancée visa."

"For whom do you need?"

"For me."

"Are you serious, Linda?"

"Yes, Kathy, I want to bring a man from Nepal."

"You mean, eventually, you will marry this person?"

"Yes, Kathy."

"Who is this person?"

"A Sherpa from Nepal."

"Really, Linda? I love the Sherpa people. In fact, they are an overworked, underpaid breed in the whole world." Paul gave his opinion.

"Are you in love with this man, Linda?"

"Very much, Kathy."

"Okay, I have the information in my computer; I will give you the documents that you need to process for the visa."

"How long will it take, I mean, to process?"

"It will take between six to nine months. In fact, talk to our immigration specialist, he will be happy to take your case and expedite it."

"Thank you, Kathy. I will talk with Chuck."

"Best of luck, Linda."

"I need that, Kathy."

"I am glad you enjoyed the trip as well as found a future husband."

"Yes, Paul. It is because of your strong motivation I took the trip."

"Okay, good luck."

Kathy and Paul left for their room

Linda, after some time, slowly came back to her workplace. The phone was ringing, and she responded, "Hello."

"Oh, hi, this is John from Chicago. Can you please make me an appointment with Mr. Smith on next Monday please?"

"Sure, please hold for a moment, John…Yes, next Monday at eleven."

"Thanks."

The internal line rang in the meantime; the switchboard receptionist was on the line. "Phone for you, Linda."

"Thanks, please put me through."

"Hello, Linda. I am just reminding you about tomorrow evening's gathering."

"Sure, Dorje, I will be there. What time is it?"

"Six."

"Thanks, see you tomorrow."

Linda was happy she was going to the monastery the following day. She would share about her visit of His Holiness, and people would be eager to hear. Linda thought to herself, so many things were moving in her life, and she needed to prioritize one at a time.

The phone rang again.

"Yes. Oh, hi, Dr. Allure, how are you?"

"I am fine, Linda. Hey, Mihara called me the other day and wants to meet the three of us for cocktails."

Linda thought for a moment. She did not have much time to spare as she was very busy in the office and her personal life.

"How about we meet at the Marriott on Boulshire Boulevard at seven on Friday? I will have another girl friend with me, and we will have a mini-reunion."

"That sounds great, Linda. You have been working hard and need a break. I will inform Mihara."

"Okay then, that's set."

"Thanks, Linda. Bye."

That afternoon in the office, a serious and confidential meeting was taking place in the small meeting room. As far as Linda understood, a client recently lost a big case, and he was blaming some partners and the firm for gross negligence. The client had a lot of powerful political contacts at the state and federal level. He was creating a bad image for the firm in general. The meeting's objective was to find a pragmatic way to solve the problem and control the damage. The main switchboard operator and Linda were advised not to transfer calls to partners this afternoon until the meeting was over. There was an invisible tension prevailing in the office.

Linda suddenly had a memory of Pemba. She realized her pain and agony in his absence. She had not disclosed Pemba's presence in her life to her family. She knew her father would not mind a cross-cultural marriage, but her mother would never leave her in peace. She would be nagging every time they had a phone conversation—the reason she was waiting for the appropriate occasion to expose the matter. A face-to-face talk with her mother might be the best way to convince her, but it was not likely to happen soon. She had already told her office colleagues; sooner or later, her family would come to know. The best way would be direct communication with them sooner rather than later.

It was almost five thirty. The partners' meeting had not adjourned; an internal memo was issued earlier that no one was to leave the office until the meeting was over. Linda had no idea how long the meeting would continue. She had no option but to wait in the office. Close to six, the partners' meeting was over, and Linda observed relief on everyone's face; they all seemed happy.

Mr. Smith came back to his room and asked Linda to come to his chamber where he dictated a confidential memo to all the offices.

"Please see that the content remains confidential, and no one in the office should know about it."

"I will keep it confidential."

Linda returned to her room, finished up some opened files, made a to-do list for the next day, and put it all inside the drawer and left the office.

That day, there was no special event in the office. Everything went normally and quietly. Linda left the office at 5:15 on Thursday evening. She always had a yellow bouquet of fresh flowers, which she picked from the flower shop, and proceeded to the monastery for that evening's congregation.

As usual, Dorje was at the main gate, receiving guests.

"Hi, Linda, welcome back."

"Thanks, Dorje."

"Linda, we are going to start our program soon. Do you want to say something about your recent trip to His Holiness?"

"Yes, Dorje. I will speak briefly on my visit."

"Sure, Linda."

"Oh, before I forget, I have two small jade Buddhas, which are a gift from me."

"Thanks, Linda. I will find a suitable place for the gift somewhere here."

The program began with meditation. The room was filled with a soft, wonderful aroma of the incense coming out of the small lamps placed in front of the large Buddha statue. The atmosphere was subtle, holy, and spiritual. Linda sat in the third row from the left.

Dorje opened the floor, welcoming the guests, and gave a brief narration of the day's program.

The highlight was the visit of respected, high-level Lama Mingma, who was from a popular monastery about thirty miles east of Toronto and would provide the day's teaching.

A tall person in a maroon robe, the Lama came out. He was clean shaven, had a large-size head, big, dark, sparkling eyes, and long arms—and delivered the teaching for about half an hour. His attractive personality, with a flawless British accent, was hypnotizing and interesting. His style of talking, presenting his views, and analyzing logics was of international quality. The way he explained nirvana was especially noteworthy in its simplicity and the selection of his words. The Lama had enormous knowledge of Buddha's teachings and doctrines, and according to him, some of the principles were highly pertinent and even practical to our daily life.

Linda was very much impressed by the Lama's teaching and by his wonderful knowledge on most of the religious doctrines. After the program, Linda had the opportunity to meet Lama Mingma privately, and he asked Linda, "Did you have a one-on-one meeting, Linda?"

"No, it was in a group of about ten people."

"How was your experience?"

"Highly spiritual and divine."

"I also had the same experience when I met him about three years back." Mingma shared his feelings with Linda. "Linda, if you ever visit the East Coast, please come to our monastery. It is one of the unique ones in North America—vast, serene, and celestial."

"Of course, I will keep that in mind. Thanks for your invitation."

After the program, Linda felt tired and needed to go home for early retirement as this week had been crazy and tiring. On the way, she stopped at a diner and ordered a sandwich, Coke, and fries for her dinner. Afterwards, she immediately went home as she needed sleep badly, and oh God, one more day at the office tomorrow.

It was almost lunchtime at the office; the mood was festive and much better than it was the day before. Even the partners were in a good mood, and Mr. Smith must have done something dramatic to bring back and boost the office morale.

Being a casual Friday, Mr. Smith had ordered lunch for everyone in the office from one of the eateries not far from the office. The free lunch and casual clothes brightened the office mood and boosted the employees' morale. Linda was especially happy because she was meeting Amanda and her two co-travelers, Allure and Mihara, for cocktails that evening.

"Linda," Mr. Smith was on the internal line, "will you please announce on the public speaker that everyone joins the lunch in the large conference room? We will also be celebrating the birthday of Kathy at twelve thirty."

"Sure, Mr. Smith."

The food was there in the conference room, and all the office employees gathered and waited for Mr. Smith. After a while, Mr. Smith and John entered the room.

"Have a seat, please," Mr. Smith requested. "We are taking this opportunity to share with you the progress we are making in our law franchisee project." He continued, "In fact, we are getting an encouraging national momentum for the project. TV, newspapers, and radio talk show hosts in national media are keeping close watch of the progress of this project. We are promoting Linda to senior level, and she will oversee the recruitment part of the project; she will be directly responsible under the HR manager."

Everyone clapped to welcome the news.

"Furthermore, a Japanese firm from Tokyo wants to hire us to handle the legal aspects of their multiple companies doing business in America; we signed a contract last week. We have the good news that Paul is getting promoted as our vice president, and he will have added responsibility to promote the franchisee project and media relations."

When everyone had clapped, Paul got up from his seat and said, "Thank you, everyone."

"Before I close up the meeting, from the bottom of my heart, I would like to thank Kathy for adding a few new businesses last month and wish her the best on her birthday."

The meeting was adjourned, and everyone turned towards the food. The office atmosphere turned festive as dress-down on Fridays provided some charm on everybody's mind. Besides, it added colorful dimension with free lunch and some good news.

The promotion came as a surprise to Linda, as she was not expecting it so soon. During the lunch, she expressed her happiness to Mr. Smith. The party came to an end and Linda returned to her office to finish the day's work. Before she forgot, she put a call to Amanda.

"Hi, Amanda, I just want to remind you, I am on my way to the Marriott. Please make sure you come on time. I have invited two of my co-travelers at seven."

"Well, you know my office. I will try to be there on time. I am dying to see you."

Linda as well as Amanda seemed excited to see each other and to share so many things that had happened in between. When Linda reached the Marriott, the hall—usually crowded during the happy-hour—including the large counter, was almost empty; she noticed she was a little earlier than the usual time. She looked for the barman; even they were absent. Linda decided to wait for Amanda. She walked out from the bar toward the lobby area and strolled on the hotel's garden, enjoying the lovely roses and various flowers around. She took a seat further down in the garden, next to a big white gazebo. The fountain was situated in the middle of the garden, with a flying angel, and one part of the fountain was flowing through her hands, making the sight very attractive. Linda watched the angel closely and felt a strong similarity that she saw the same figure in her dream up in heaven. She could not believe this was some kind of coincidence. She must share this experience with Amanda and show her this blue angel fountain.

After that amazing, sudden, unexpected sight, Linda realized that Amanda should have come by now. She had spent almost twenty minutes in the garden.

She walked back to the bar, through the main hotel lobby. She noticed that Amanda was coming in from the main entrance of the bar. They hugged for more than a minute, and both expressed, "Missed you so much," as if good lovers were meeting after a long time.

"Hey, Amanda! Look; why don't we talk about our personal stuff before my two co-travelers join us?"

"Sure. First, let us get our drinks, as usual?" Amanda asked.

In no time, as the bar was not crowded, Amanda brought gin and tonic and a regular drink Amanda loved to have.

"So tell me, what happened? No letter, no news, nothing for almost over a month," Amanda expressed her anger.

"Listen to me; there is no viable communication between Nepal and here," Linda tried to explain.

"Tell me first what happened with that guy. Did you meet him?" Amanda seemed impatient.

"Of course."

"Did you sleep with him?"

Linda kept quiet. She blushed, and her face became red.

"I know you did." Amanda seemed more excited than Linda.

"I am bringing him here on a fiancée visa."

"No kidding." Amanda reacted.

"I am serious."

"Have you told your parents?" Amanda asked.

"Not yet."

"Was he as you imagined?" Amanda asked again.

"More than that."

"How long will the visa processes take for him to come?"

"Six to nine months," Linda replied.

"Have you thought of what he is going to do?"

"Not a clue; he may go to school or work. How is your boyfriend?"

"David?" Amanda asked.

"Who else?" Linda threw a suspicious glance at Amanda.

"Linda, it is not easy to find another one."

"So you are doing okay?" Linda asked.

"Yes, in a way, but when mixing with my culture, he is having a tough time."

"So?" questioned Linda.

"I think adjustment may be tough. How about you?"

"I have never attended his social program with his family."

"If he loves you enough, I am sure he will try to adjust," Linda supported.

"Depends; time will tell." A hesitant answer came from Amanda.

"Tell me about the trip." Amanda changed the subject.

"I felt leaving the country was coming out from paradise. It was wonderful by all means." There was a bright expression on her face.

"Of course, one of my coworkers had been there, and she adored it."

"What else is new?" Linda asked.

"Oh, one of my articles and photographs have been selected for a Pulitzer Prize nomination."

"That is just fantastic, Amanda."

"Not yet; it is just for consideration."

"I am sure you are a genius," Linda commented.

"Wait till they announce it next month."

"Amanda, did I tell you about the heaven dream I had?"

"Sure, you did."

"Just in the hotel garden, I saw the same angel in the fountain statue," Linda reported.

"You mean the one that took you up?"

"Yes, I must show you on the way out." Linda was excited.

"I would love to see that statue."

Far away, in the corner at the hall entrance, Linda saw Allure coming toward the crowd. Linda raised her hand, and he approached her. Mihara was following him.

Allure was wearing a dark business suit, light blue–colored shirt, and matching tie with small white stars. Mihara was in Wrangler jeans, an ash-colored shirt, and thin black leather jacket. Both looked smart and handsome in the outfits.

"Hi, Linda." Allure gave Linda a hug.

"Hi, Allure, this is Amanda."

"Amanda, this is Allure, and this is Mihara."

Amanda shook hands with both of them.

"We had a wonderful time on the trip. Amanda, Allure is a physician at the local hospital, and Mihara moved from Brazil and has a strawberry farm."

"How far are you from here, Mihara?" Linda asked Mihara.

"Nearly three hours, in Santa Maria."

"I would love to come to pick strawberries sometime," Amanda said.

"Mihara, are you going back tonight?" Linda expressed surprise.

"No, my sister and her family live in the city."

Linda and Amanda's first drink was almost finished. Amanda asked both the guests for their order and moved toward the crowded bar area.

"I understand Allure is busy at the hospital. How about you, Mihara?"

"Not so much; I have enough people to work on the farm."

"Are the field workers from Mexico?" Linda asked.

"Yes, mostly, though a few are from Guatemala, Cuba, and some are locals."

"Are they good workers?"

"Pretty much."

"I know; the Japanese are very good farm workers as well."

"Yes, I am running our second generation in this business."

The crowd, their noise, cigarettes, and smoke inside was suffocating for the people who did not smoke. Linda was not feeling comfortable inside. She saw an iron table and chairs just outside the large hall, so she dragged everyone outside and occupied the chairs. Allure accompanied Amanda to get the next round of drinks.

"Mihara, what is it you like here better than Brazil?"

"Organized work pattern, better climate, and well-established marketing system," Mihara replied.

"How are the products themselves?"

"Juicy and sweet," replied Mihara.

"Do you export to Japan?" Linda asked.

"Not directly. I sell in the wholesale market, and they export all over the world."

"Are you single or married?" Amanda asked.

"Married but separated, now divorced. My mother-in-law was sick, my wife went back to Japan, and she never came back."

"Have any children?" Linda questioned again.

"No."

"Have a girlfriend?" Linda seemed curious.

"No, steady one." Mihara replied.

"Do you plan to get married again?" Linda questioned.

"Yes, though not to a Japanese."

"Why?" Linda asked.

"Had a bad experience."

In the meantime, Allure and Amanda both came with cocktails in their hands.

"This place gets crowded all the time on Fridays," Amanda remarked about the growing crowd.

"Yes, it must be happy hour," Mihara said.

"Until eight. Then it goes back to normal price drinks," Allure confirmed.

"Amanda, what line of work are you in?" Mihara asked.

"I am an investigative journalist."

"That is interesting."

"Do you cover a certain area?" Allure put a question.

"Yes, international politics, mainly Israel and conflicting areas in the Middle East."

"Are you a Jew?"

"How do you know?"

"That drink."

"Is it that Jewish?" Amanda asked.

"Yes, I have a friend at the hospital; he drinks this kind of drink all the time."

"It is refreshing," Amada claimed.

"I want to try one." Mihara was tempted to drink.

"I love my gin and tonic," Linda said, showing her profound liking for the drink.

It was getting darker, and the sky was overcast. It was likely to rain that night.

"Guys, I have news."

Everyone looked on Linda's face intensely and curiously.

"I am bringing Pemba on a fiancée visa."

"That *is* good news." Both Mihara and Allure were happy.

"He is a fine and handsome gentleman," Allure remarked.

"Indeed," Mihara agreed.

"Let us have a toast," Amanda proposed.

"Great, thank you, guys," Linda acknowledged.

"Thanks, everyone, but I have to go now as I promised that I would be there during dinner." Mihara tried to get up.

"We will all leave after fifteen minutes, Mihara," Linda assured him.

"Let us have a last round," Amanda proposed.

Allure and Mihara brought the drinks after making the usual tussle to the counter due to the tremendous crowd toward the peak of happy hour. Mihara also had the same Jewish drink like Amanda, one gin and tonic, and one Bloody Mary for Allure. The four of them seemed to have a wonderful time; they liked each other and had mutual respect and helpful attitudes. In a short time, the four of them had become close friends and valued each other's friendship. Being from different ethnicities— one of them a Jew, one African American and another an Asian—it was amazing, three people from different background, three different cultures, three different languages, coming together! And this was truly a melting pot. This was what made America a great country.

"Listen, Linda, I do not want to leave, but tomorrow I have an important presentation at the hospital," Allure said.

"Sorry, my sister and her family will get upset if I do not leave now." Mihara also got up reluctantly.

"Great, thanks for coming. We will stay here a little longer." Linda understood their urgency.

After some time, when both Allure and Mihara had left, Linda asked Amanda, "How do you like them?"

"Honestly, I like them both."

"They are good human beings," Linda agreed.

"Tell me, if you want to choose your boyfriend, out of two, whom do you prefer?"

"Obviously, Mihara. Allure is married." Both had a good laugh.

"Tell me more about your trip."

"Well, another highlight was the visit to His Holiness the Dalai Lama in India."

"What did you experience?"

"A profound inner peace."

"Wonderful."

"It is something I cannot explain; one has to experience it themselves."

"Well, tell me one thing. When are you going to tell your family?" Amanda asked.

"You know my dad; he is liberal and won't mind me marrying a foreigner. It is my mother who is hard to convince."

"Are you going to see them?"

"I have no time. Oh, by the way, they promoted me at the office."

"Congratulations."

"Thanks, I was not expecting it so soon."

"There is a commotion in the media regarding some kind of franchisee law project." Amanda was curious.

"Yes, it is a Smith law franchisee project schedule to be implement from the year 2000. The way things are moving, it could be finished in the next five years."

"That is interesting," Amanda supported.

I also might be going to Israel next month." Amanda also disclosed her news.

"Is it an office assignment? For how long?" Linda was curious.

"A couple of weeks."

"What will you be doing in Israel?"

"I have a couple of interview in Gaza area, also plan for an interview with Israel's Prime Minister."

"I am going to miss you." Linda was sincere.

"Me too," Amanda added.

"What do you think, should we go now?" Linda suggested.

Linda did not forget to take Amanda to the particular place in the garden where the blue angel was holding the beautiful water fountain. She showed the angel and described the face she'd seen in the dream, closely and clearly similar with shapes of the eyes, mouth, and facial expression what they were watching now.

"Are you sure this one is the same? You might be having a vision?" Amanda questioned.

"Swear to God, Amanda, it is just similar, has the same style and facial made like Sophia."

***

CHAPTER TEN

November 1987

Wednesday was that day of the week that normally was a lucky day in Pemba's life. Most good and fortunate events mostly occurred on Wednesdays.

Pemba received a letter from the American Embassy, which happened to be on a Wednesday. He had not disclosed his plan to go to America. Neither his family nor the office, except for Dawa, knew about it. The Embassy asked him to come for a visa interview along with all the documents and photographs the following week, Wednesday again. He was determined that, unless he got a visa, he was not going to tell anyone. Who knows, he thought, he might be turned down!

"Pemba, are you going to the post office today?" Dawa asked, snapping Pemba out of his thought process.

"Yes, Dawa. Do I need to get anything besides the register letters from the post office?"

"Yes, please get some stamps."

"Sure." Pemba replied.

After finishing a couple of files about the group arriving on November 28th from Australia, Pemba left the office at around one.

He remembered he also needed to get the trekking permit for the group leaving for Annapurna two days later from the immigration office.

It took him about two hours to complete all errands for the office, and after coming to the office, he had some more time to finish his pending desk work.

It was again a Wednesday. Pemba took morning half-a-day leave from the office. The interview time was set for nine at the US Embassy. He had eggs, bread, and orange juice for breakfast, and prayed for a few second. He arrived at the Embassy in Panipokhari fifteen minutes earlier.

The waiting room was narrow and congested, with more than ten people waiting for the process. At nine sharp, a guard escorted Pemba to the inside of the Embassy garden through a narrow path into large waiting room. The room had about four other people may be waiting for interview like him. A white lady approached Pemba and escorted him to a small office room stuffed with a kerosene heater burning on the right side of the desk. The polished, good-looking oak desk was overstuffed with files and numerous loose papers scattered around.

"Hi, my name is Gloria," the white lady introduced herself and shook hands with Pemba.

"Hi," Pemba responded.

"How did you meet Linda?" Gloria asked.

"During the trek." Pemba gave a short answer.

"You are with Mountain Travel?" Gloria asked again.

"Yes."

"How long?"

"Over three years." Pemba replied.

"Where did you become intimate with Linda?"

"In Phaplu." Pemba replied.

"Is that place part of the trekking?"

"No." Pemba

"Why did she go there?"

"To visit my family." Pemba said.

"Did you have intimacy with her?"

"Yes."

"May I see some of the pictures of you with Linda, if you have them?"

Pemba gave about ten pictures that revealed closeness between them. Out of ten, Gloria chose three.

"Do you mind if we keep these in the files?"

"Of course not." Pemba replied.

"Great, congratulations, your fiancée visa is approved. Please leave your passport, and pick it up after three days."

At that moment, Pemba had a mixed reaction about the visa approval news. In one way, he was happy; and in another, he was still reluctant to leave his family entirely on their own without proper family support when they needed help.

Not far from the Embassy, he chose a restaurant and ordered a typical Nepali lunch. He wanted eat a satisfying lunch for achieving an important thing that day. He was not sure his visit to America would be an achievement or a disappointment. He had to learn lots of facts about history, culture, basic human nature, and ways of life in America. He needed to read books on facts and myths of America, along with history and politics.

Until he had his passport and visa with the approval stamp on it in his possession, he would not tell anyone but Dawa. He would take Dawa for a drink after work this evening and share everything with him.

Pemba knew a nice bar on the second floor somewhere near ring road close to their office, operated by the Gurung family. It was an ideal place to have some drinks and a conversation without loud music. Dawa liked the place; it had soft light coming from wall lamps, a stereo playing soft music, and an attractive ceiling painted with snow-peaked mountains. It produced a glamorous, distinguished, and dramatic image of true Nepali culture. Dawa noticed, at some other tables, people were drinking not from glasses but from yellow fancy metal tumbles that carried significance of their rich culture and heritage and it was a traditional drink-ware.

"This is a very nice place," Dawa remarked.

"Yes, I like it."

As usual, they ordered *chhyang*—the typical beer of their community. Both liked to drink it in place of imported or other local liquors. A smart-looking, pretty girl brought the drinks and placed them on the table. They both felt the fresh aroma of the flavor of *chhyang*.

"Cheers." Dawa raised the yellow shining glass.

"I want to toast with you for the good news today."

"Really, what is that?"

"My visa is approved."

"Indeed, very good news. Congratulations. Let us drink for the happy news."

Dawa raised the shining yellow glass and toasted again. "So you have decided to marry Linda?"

"Of course. There's no other option; we have to marry. That is the condition of the visa."

"Do you have any idea how long you have to decide?"

"I must get married within ninety days after my arrival in America."

"When are you planning to leave?"

"Not until March next year."

"Why so long?"

"I need at least four months to arrange everything for my family."

"Who is going to take care of your family in your absence?"

"My uncle, Dorje. I told you Linda is sending four hundred dollars a month for my family expenses as a loan until I will have my own job"

"That is very thoughtful on her part."

"Yes, she is a nice person."

"Good luck to you."

"Thanks, Dawa."

"When are you planning to resign from work?"

"A month before I leave."

"I am going to miss you."

"Me too, very much. Why don't you plan to come sometime to stay?"

"No, I cannot. My parents are old. In fact, I need to be with them in Solokhumbu."

"Dawa, when are you planning to marry?"

"My mother is insisting this coming March."

"Who is the lucky girl?"

"You know Choden; she is from my village."

"Best of luck."

"I hope you will stay until my marriage."

"I hope so. It depends on Linda, but I will try my best."

"Should we go now? It is getting late, and I have to be in the office early."

Pemba asked for the bill. Upon arrival, the bill was paid promptly with a hefty tip as they'd had a couple of fried chicken dishes and the service was excellent.

Everyone in the office was extremely busy because of high season for trekking. Pemba had lots of work to complete, and he had some outside errands for the office as well. In fact, most trekking organizations earned all their yearly revenue within six months, between October and March; during summer and the monsoon season, they operated with a skeleton staff only. Pemba had a passion for trekking, and for the beautiful and awesome mountains. He got inspiration in life through mountains. His life in America, without being close to tall mountains, might not be that good, and he would always miss these mountains.

But now he missed Linda, her soft nature, soft body, soft and loving words, abundant beauty, kindness, selfless love, and total submission. He had enjoyed being with her in Phaplu and in Dharamshala. He cherished every moment with her and would treasure it throughout his life.

He needed to write a long letter, expressing his true emotions and suffering he was experiencing without her company. Perhaps he might have time to write tonight. He had no idea about Linda; she also might be missing him too.

After collecting his passport and visa to America, Pemba had an obvious expression of happiness on his face. Dawa must have noticed.

"You have the passport?" Dawa asked.

Pemba gave a meaningful smile and just nodded his head without reply.

"Congratulations."

"Thanks."

They both became very busy with the paperwork and began to work quietly in the office. Pemba, as much as possible, wanted to keep quiet about his coming trip until he was ready to announce the news. He had a tentative date of departure sometime during the last week of March. Within four months, he needed to complete his affairs, meet his Uncle Dorje in Phaplu with the family, and open a bank account in his uncle's name.

It is hard to predict where life takes you, but one thing is certain: you need to struggle and survive for existence in every situation. Pemba had faith and self-confidence that he should be able to survive whatever situation, good or bad or even worse. His tough upbringing, his culture, and his race would provide faith for strong determination, and he may survive in almost all the condition though he may not be able to progress much his life.

Pemba was facing a tough situation about breaking the news to his mother and sisters. Pemba knew his mother would cry and try to stop him and request he change his mind. He needed to explain the situation to his uncle and convince him to be a guardian of the family. Perhaps his Uncle Dorje would understand his predicament and try to convince his mother. First, he needed to see Dorje, and after bringing him into confidence, face his family. His uncle's support would boost his morale and confidence.

But first, he needed to prepare a resignation letter to his office and announce to them his intention to go abroad, and effective date of his resignation should be first week of March. He would need to consult Dawa first and proceed as per his advice. Pemba would be busy in the office until next week; then he thought he would go to Phaplu to convey his decision to his family. Otherwise, it was possible they might get the news through some other sources. In such a situation like the present one, it would not be wise to wait further.

Pemba decided to go to Phaplu that weekend and stay for three days to sort out his entire family problem. He booked a flight that would leave on Friday at eight thirty in the morning.

As usual, the airport was crowded but the flight was on time as there was no fog and the weather was good. The flight left on time. He had a big duffle bag and lots of clothing, shoes, and other necessary daily materials for his sisters and mother. Upon arrival, no one knew about his coming home. His mother was cooking something in the kitchen, and his sisters were at the school. The mother expressed surprise when he walked into the house.

"Oh, Pemba, I am really happy to see you all of a sudden."

"Yes, I have to discuss many things with you."

Pemba did not like to share his intention of going to America yet by himself. He needed to bring his uncle with him to explain the complicated matter so that the reaction of his family would be less alarming as Dorje, his uncle, would explain in a proper and mature way.

"If the meal is ready, I will have one after a bath, and I need to go to see Uncle Dorje."

"Yes, take a bath, and I will prepare a meal for you." His mother assured him.

Without waiting further, Pemba proceeded to his room for a change of clothes and a bath. After almost an hour, the meal was ready. He sat in the kitchen with his mother. The food was tasty, and he appreciated his mother's meal.

Without further conversation, he was on his way to his uncle's house that was nearly an hour's walk. The house was on the hill, and around the house were tall, thick pine trees. Whenever Pemba came to this house, he enjoyed the chirping of the birds coming from the dense pine trees.

Thank God, Pemba thought, *Uncle Dorje is home*. He was extremely happy to see uncle home this time of the day so that he would be able to explain him everything properly.

The servant opened the door and welcomed him. After the usual greeting, he sat next to Dorje on his right side of the sofa.

"This is a surprise. Welcome, Pemba."

"Thanks, Uncle. I have come to seek your advice on a very important matter."

"Go ahead; I am listening."

"Linda sent me a fiancée visa to go to America."

"You mean; you are going to America to get married with her?"

"Absolutely." Pemba replied with confidence.

"Who will take care of your family here?"

"That is why I've come to seek your advice."

"What do you want, and how may I be of help to you?"

"Linda will send four hundred dollars a month for my family expenses."

"Great!" Dorje liked the idea.

"Until I am able to earn my income."

"That is very nice on her part." Dorje seemed glad.

"I will be grateful if you would be their guardian in my absence."

"When are you leaving?" Dorje asked.

"At the end of March. I would like to open a separate bank account in your name."

"I have an account with Nepal Bank." Dorje explained.

"That is great; we can use your existing checking account, and I will be sending money every month for my family expenses."

"I do not see why that will be a problem."

"Can we go on Sunday to open it?" Pemba asked.

"Sure. It will not be possible for me to visit your place regularly as you can see I have pain in my left leg. I will manage my boy to visit your family once or twice a week."

"That sounds great. I have no courage to tell my mother about moving to America without your support." Pemba put forth a request.

"What do you want me to do?" Dorje asked.

"I would be much obliged if you could come to my home tomorrow morning and convince them that my move to America is good for all of us and this step is necessary."

"Of course. Besides, Linda is a very good person." Dorje supported Pemba's decision.

"I would like both my sisters to have good education."

"That is a good thinking," Dorje said.

"Okay then. I will wait for you tomorrow."

"Pemba, it will be my responsibility to look after your family in the absence of your father."

"Thanks, Uncle."

Pemba had two days to see all his friends, say good-bye, and tell them about his move to America. He was sure most of his friends would like the idea, and some of them would be jealous of him.

He visited his friends on the way to his home and met about four of them. When he reached his home, it was almost dinnertime. His sisters were really happy to see him; they had dinner together and talked about school and their activities there.

After dinner, Pemba played a couple of Ludo games with his sisters and enjoyed their company.

The next morning, at around nine, Uncle Dorje, accompanied by his boy Dote, came to Pemba's house around nine. His mother had prepared a typical breakfast with homemade bread and omelets with lots of tomatoes and green chilies. It smelled good and they all ate together. The boy Dote was twelve years old, tall for his age, with a pleasing face and stout build. Pemba's sisters liked him, and they were friends at the school as well.

"You have good news," his uncle began, facing Pemba's mother.

His mother had no idea what the news was; she was just curious and happy.

"What news, Uncle?" Pemba's younger sister asked.

"For a better life for him and you, Pemba is going to America for few years."

No one in the family said a word; they all were quiet and astounded.

After the unusual silence, his uncle continued, "He is going to marry Linda, and she has sent a visa."

His mother had a hard time facing his uncle. She bent her head down, and after a long time, she asked, "When is he going?"

"In three months, but he will not have time to come and see you all again," Uncle Dorje said. "He needs to take care of his trip, his office, and so many other things before leaving. Pemba will be sending money every month, and I will give it to you. You do not have to worry, he is taking this venture for everyone's better life and happiness."

Until then, Pemba had been quiet. Now he opened his mouth, "I want both of my sisters to have higher education and not to marry until they complete their education. Uncle Dorje will be your guardian, and Dote will visit here once or twice a week and whenever it is necessary. Uncle will also visit on a regular basis."

"What will happen if someone is sick in the family?" his mother questioned.

"Uncle will take care of it."

"You do not have to worry in such matters, Dolma. You, even at present, I am taking care of such situations as I did in the past." Uncle Dorje reinforced his commitment.

"Linda is a very nice lady. I am sure Pemba will have a good life. He has had a difficult life here," the uncle said, trying to convince his mother.

"If you need or want anything, please tell Uncle," Pemba consoled his mother.

Pemba noticed his sisters were unhappy, but his mother perhaps had no idea and was unable to tolerate his absence from the family. But his uncle handled the complex issue in a very mature and delicate manner and even his mother seemed to be convinced of her son's decision to move to the other side of the earth.

After lunch, Pemba accompanied Uncle Dorje to his home, and thanked him for his handling the tough problem in a simple and easy way. While coming back, Pemba saw Pasang outside in the garden of a hotel and dropped by his place to say good-bye. He was sure his decision to move would surprise him.

"Hi, Pasang."

"What a surprise! When did you come to Phaplu?"

"Yesterday. I am leaving Monday; I just came to say hello and a long good-bye."

"What do you mean?"

"Within three months, I'll be leaving for the States."

"You mean; Linda has invited you?" Pasang asked.

"Yes, I have the fiancée visa already."

"Congratulations. I really envy you. Hey, Pemba, I am a little busy now; is it possible to have a quick drink this evening?"

"Sure. I will come around six. Is that OK?"

"Perfect."

Reluctantly, Pemba took his first step toward home. He needed to face his mother, and surely, she would be nagging and have millions of reasons to bar him from sneaking into America. Pemba went to his room quietly and lay down in his bed. Perhaps he needed a rest and quiet time to evaluate himself. He slept for nearly two hours. His younger sister was knocking on the door.

"Brother, Uncle Pasang is inviting you to the hotel."

Quickly, Pemba freshened himself, put on a decent outfit with blue jeans and a light blue shirt and a sweatshirt on top, and walked out.

"Sorry, Pasang; must have been tired, I overslept."

"No problem. So how did it happen? I knew that lady was in love with you but was not expecting this to happen so soon, man."

"Yes, I was also surprised when she sent the visa."

"When are you planning the wedding?"

"As per immigration regulations, it should take place within ninety days of arrival. Linda is planning in June." Pemba replied.

"Good luck; she is a fabulous lady."

"Pasang, I have a request."

"Shoot."

"Since you are close to my house, will you please keep a close watch? Uncle Dorje lives far from here."

"Of course, Pemba, you do not have to ask me; it will be a part of my responsibility."

"Thanks."

"When do you think you will be visiting from America?"

"I do not know. I have no idea what is going to happen there. It depends."

"Anyway, do not forget us." Pasang remind him.

"No way."

"Another thing, Pemba, please try to promote this hotel in whatever way you can."

"Yes, give me a few hotel brochures. I would love to carry them with me." Pemba seemed happy.

"I will send some to your house tomorrow."

"Great. Please give my regards to my sister."

"Of course. She will also be happy and surprised by your travel to America."

"Okay then, my mother must be waiting for dinner. Thanks for the drinks."

They hugged each other for a long time and parted with a promise to see each other sometime in the near future, though they both knew, that time might never come.

Pemba was surprised to see the house brightly decorated with ample candles just about everywhere—in the windows, staircase, around the dining table, and all over the kitchen doors and the entrances to all bedrooms. Knowing that Pemba was not coming back again before his trip from America, his mother had obviously put up this illumination, wishing for his success overseas.

His sisters had new dresses, and his mother a *bakkhu* he had brought her from Katmandu. The house looked bright and pleasant with the aroma of the incense sticks, which he'd found in the city. His mother also prepared a variety of typical dishes that were Pemba's favorites, and since this was going to be a kind of farewell dinner, everyone sat at the table as if it was Losar festival— which marked a new year and generally felt near or the same day as the Chinese New Year. His mother also prepared a fresh *changkol*—known in Tibet as *chhyang*, a local beer made of rice.

Everyone in the family ate the dinner quietly, and his mother occasionally broke the silence—mostly regarding his sisters' naughty behaviors in the house.

"Your sisters are now growing; they want more beautiful and expensive dresses."

Both the sisters lowered their heads, as if afraid to face their only brother, who behaved as their father and took care of their demands. They were really obliged to their brother, who was kind and never got angry with them.

After the dinner, the siblings played their favorite game of Ludo while their mother finished up the dishes in the kitchen. Pemba enjoyed the game with the sisters, and they spent a good time with their brother, who was going to a faraway country for a long time; they would not have the same opportunity again.

After several rounds of the game, the youngest sister felt sleepy and wanted to go to bed. When both his sisters had left, his mother came to his room and started talking her son politely, "Pemba, I don't understand why you want to leave us to go to America. You have everything here—a house, a family, and land down there near the river where we can grow enough food for the whole year."

Pemba was expecting this kind of argument from his mother. He slowly but deliberately explained his mother in a simple language so that she could understand his intention.

"Look, Ma! In the first place, I do not want to go away, leaving this family, which I love so dearly. My heart is not happy, but if I go there, it will be for everyone's benefit. If I could earn enough money within a short time, I will come back. Besides, until I earn by myself, Linda is sending four hundred dollars per month for the expenses of the family in my absence."

His mother interrupted, "I know Linda is a nice lady, and you should be happy with her, but money is not everything. Family support is necessary during sickness and hard times."

"Mother, Uncle Dorje has promised all the help as a close family member. I am positive he will do everything."

"I know, Pemba. I am sure I will not be able to get everything from Dorje which I can get from my son." Pemba noticed tears in the mother's eyes.

"Well, you trust him. You might be surprised that he is a good man with lots of influences in our community. Sunday, I am going to the bank to open an account in his name and depositing enough money before I leave, and every month, you will get that money from Linda for your expenses."

"Thanks, son, but how am I going to get your information on a regular basis?"

"Through letters, and I will find some other sources soon. Dawa will be one good source of contact for me, and I will keep him informed."

"Pemba, my dear, I am scared that I may not see you again."

"Ma, I will miss you more than you will miss me."

His mother gave a hug to her son for a long time and whispered, "Son, remember, I love you very much."

After that emotional hug, she could not stay in the room any longer. She ran toward her own room. Pemba knew she was crying. Pemba's eyes were moist too with tears; he had not felt so close emotionally with his mother as he was feeling now and felt bad himself. He could not go to sleep for a long time, thinking about his future, uncertain life, and the hard feelings of separation from his family.

Pemba got up with the sound of birds' chirping in the early morning. The house was quiet. Everyone in the family was sleeping, as his sisters did not have school on Saturdays. He was surprised even his mother was not awake. Normally, she was the one who got up early. Perhaps she also did not have proper sleep last night, must be crying in the bed until past midnight.

Pemba got a glass of water from the kitchen and came back to his room. He was reading a Thomas Hardy novel, *Far from Madding Crowd*. He loved the romantic story, and he was now through more than half of the book. The setting of the story, plot, and characters were vivid, lively, and heartwarming.

Pemba planned whole-day's activities and concentrated more on meeting all his friends from Phaplu, Salleri, and close-by villages. Besides, he had to meet some of his close relatives also in the remaining time. He wanted to spend quality time with his family as well.

Morning and afternoon passed by; he was traveling from one place to another. He met lots of old friends, close relatives, and eminent village people. He was back home toward the evening—tired, exhausted, and thirsty.

His mother came with a cup of cold *chhyang*, which Pemba appreciated very much. He spent all his remaining hours at home, playing Ludo with his sisters, talking with his mother, and giving a brief report to her about meeting with his close relatives and their status. His mother was happy to learn about her relatives scattered all over the villages as she hardly traveled these days because of her foot pain.

Sunday morning, Pemba knew his Uncle Dorje would be at the bank around ten; so he needed to be on time. After a light breakfast, he left for Salleri market, where the bank was located. It was not a surprise that his uncle was waiting for him.

Pemba knew the bank manager and completed his procedures on time. They asked his uncle to get the checkbook next week. During that time, he hoped for it to be ready. Also, every month, after getting the bank draft from Linda, his uncle needed to see the manager, who would deposit the funds to his uncle's account. Everything was completed with the help of the manager, and within a short time, his uncle left Pemba to run another errand.

Pemba took care of all family finances, met his friends and relatives, and said good-bye to them. The whole village wished him good luck and prayed for his happy life.

Monday morning, Pemba was not worried. He had a flight to take, because the airport was like his private one. It was at his door; there was no need for a taxi or any other transportation; he just needed to walk two minutes from his bedroom. Pemba was sure no one would have an airport inside his yard in the whole world. He felt lucky he had this privilege in life, which he was going to miss now.

At home, almost all of his friends and close relatives from the village assembled for his departure, holding a white silk scarf each. The house looked like a gathering place for an event. There were a number of small children and women in typical colorful dresses, and men were in their best outfits. His departure was like an important occasion and turned into a grand festival. The Lamas were chanting and praying for Pemba's safe and happy journey all the way to America.

A person from the airport informed them it was boarding time. The tiny aircraft was parked on one side of the airport; when the big, colorful procession approached, led by Pemba, everyone—including the tourists—gazed at Pemba and thought he was a very important person.

After everyone had wished him good luck and given numerous hugs, Pemba boarded the aircraft. The people who came to see him off waited on the left side of the airport close to his house. They all waved at him when the aircraft moved to the other end of the airport for takeoff. Pemba could see the numerous friends and family still waving at him when the plane took off.

In his office in Kathmandu, Pemba became extremely busy. Two and a half months had already passed. In two weeks he would be leaving from Kathmandu. He had got flight ticket from Thai International with the flight routing to Bangkok, two-night stay, then to Los Angeles nonstop, and he had got a very good discount being an employee of Mountain Travel.

Two days before his departure, the office arranged a nice farewell get-together for Pemba at Colonel Bradley's residence. In the meantime, Linda sent a list of things she wanted to have, and he was going to be busy in the market, shopping for Linda and himself. Furthermore, he planned to get special gifts for his in-laws' family as well. He would also buy something nice for Jack and send it to Denver after his arrival. Jack would be happy that Pemba was in the States. He had his number; maybe Pemba could call him. Anyway, Jack regarded him as a close friend.

That evening was the get-together at Bradley's residence. Besides Pemba's coworkers, Bradley had invited a few of his personal friends from the immigration and tourism office along with hotel owners and some British Embassy staff for cocktails. Dawa planned a dinner for Pemba in one of the Sherpa joints along with some of their close friends following the cocktail at Col. Bradley place. The cocktail went well, and towards the end, Bradley made an important announcement.

"I am happy, and I welcome you all to this cocktail hosted for Pemba, who is leaving tomorrow for America as an immigrant. He is planning to marry Linda in Los Angeles, who came for one of our treks a few months back. We wish for his wonderful life in the dreamland."

Dawa's dinner followed by cocktail became even livelier with their close friends as there was no formality like at Bradley place. It was among friends, and everyone had a good time. It was all typical Sherpa meals in flavor and taste. Toward the end of the dinner, everyone seemed to be drunk with stammer talks and slouched bodies.

On the day of his departure, only Dawa and one other friend from the office came to see off Pemba at the airport. He remembered the big, colorful procession at departure from his house in Phaplu. There was no comparison, but he could not expect that crowd here.

When the plane left in the middle of the day, he could see the mountains' gorgeous ranges toward the east and the awesome landscape underneath, with numerous gray and green splendid mountains all around. He felt he was leaving a piece of paradise on earth.

***

CHAPTER ELEVEN

March 1988

Pemba arrived in Bangkok on the Thai flight, which he liked very much. The cabin services were marvelous; the food and the flight were just perfect. Although Pemba had heard about Bangkok City many a time, he had never been there before. Dawa had cautioned him about the girls, as one could easily catch HIV through them in one night. Pemba knew several Nepali men who had caught AIDS from Bangkok.

Pemba asked the taxi to take him to Asia Hotel. As per Dawa's suggestion, it was a very nice middle-class hotel. The taxi driver did not know much English, but he tried to be friendly with Pemba and suggested he could get a nice girl for him in the hotel. Pemba politely declined his offer, saying he was a married man.

The hotel was in a quiet part of the city and the way the lobby was decorated had an impressive look. It was a magnificent hall with a high ceiling. A large, colorful chandelier hung in the middle of the hall. The check-in counter was on the right side. There was a gorgeous fountain in the middle and a pond that had several gold fishes.

Pemba was highly impressed with the efficiency of the check-in system, which was done promptly. He saw tour counters on the left side of the lobby; two girls were chatting there. Pemba approached the tour counter and inquired, "Hi, do you have any tours after lunch today?"

"Yes, Sir. Would you like a half-day city tour or the rose garden tour for about three hours?"

"How about rose garden; what will I be seeing there?"

"Thai cultural program, a glimpse of different Thai ethnicity tribes, how they live. You will also see the elephants, the way they lift heavy logs and work in the forest. This brochure will explain to you in detail, and I strongly suggest taking this tour, Sir."

It sounded interesting, and Pemba would spend three hours properly. He purchased the ticket, and as per the tour girls' suggested, prepared to take the bus that would be in the lobby to pick him up at two in the afternoon. He hardly had time for a shower and quick lunch at the restaurant.

After his chore and nice, delicious lunch, Pemba waited for the bus in the lobby. The bus was on time.

After about a half-hour's drive, they reached the rose garden. It was a surprising and refreshing garden covered with lots of green field and fabulous flowers, mostly roses of different colors. Pemba had never seen so many varieties roses before. It was not only attractive but had such a fascinating aroma that spread all over the garden. The landscape was kept meticulously clean, and it was extraordinarily beautiful. Pemba's mind and body were refreshed with the garden sceneries.

The guide took them to a large, open, circular area where all the ethnic groups of Thailand had been housed. They demonstrated their everyday lifestyle and habits of their living and their housing structures vividly. The guide clearly explained how they lived, what they ate, and how they performed social events.

It was very interesting, educational, and academic to learn and study in a short time in the most effective manner.

Pemba thought, *Nepal also has 102 ethnicity groups with different cultures and languages, and there are five religions. If we were related in a similar manner, it could be an attractive and interesting tourist attraction.*

The huts for the variety of tribes were built in an economic manner, but they looked so attractive that the surrounded with beautiful pond in the middle, and large white ducks swimming in the pond bequeathed an added impression on the mind of the visitors. The flowers were magnificent and enhanced the beauty of the garden. Pemba was surprised. Thailand also had such a variety of tribes. He was glad he had learned a new thing today that had an educational value.

After the beautiful and enchanting circle of the pond, the tour was back at the place of the entrance. Pemba noticed lots of elephants in chain, tied to big logs in a small stream. They were showing how the elephants carried the large logs through rivers and land from one place to another in Thailand. It was so fascinating to see the elephants do all the hard work.

In another area far from the pond, in a large meadow, there were goalposts in two different areas, like the ones in football-soccer fields, and four elephants were divided—two each in one team—and they were playing soccer. The team members passed the soccer to their own team and took it to the other post and made goals inside the goalpost. The game was not only fascinating, it also gave much pleasure to everyone, though it were the children that enjoyed the game most.

After the soccer game, they went to see elephants in other group where they were painting beautiful flowers with their trunks. According to the guide, the elephants exhibited these paintings all around the world. Pemba observed this awesome creation of artwork by the elephants, and he was surprised with the trainers for providing such magnificent training. The paintings were mostly of tulips flowers completely with lifelike color. Pemba had never seen such magnificent creation of artwork by an elephant.

After the awesome display of elephants, they all moved on to a large hall, where seating was arranged like in a stadium style. After a while, the announcer from the middle of the stage briefly covered about the culture program description that was going to be presented in the next hour.

The hour-long program was interesting with songs, dances, and various Thai tribes' glimpses. They were presented in a very professional and efficient manner. The audience—mostly tourists from Europe, America, and Japan—seemed to like the show and, in whole, the rose garden's three-hour tour. Pemba returned along with the group of tourists in the bus.

Upon arriving at the hotel, the tour counter was still open. Pemba inquired about the tour for the following morning. The girl in the counter was so pleasant and eager to explain about a tour of floating market in the morning.

"This tour of floating market is a unique tour of the world."

"In what way is it unique?" Pemba was curious.

"Sir, you can see all the market for food, fruits, and other things' trade from boats."

"You mean; it is on the river?"

"Of course."

"What time does the tour leave?"

"It is at five."

"That early?"

"Yes."

Pemba had never seen such a sight in his life before; he visualized it and thought, it should be interesting.

"Thanks, will be here before five."

Pemba took a tour brochure with him; he would read it at the room before he went to bed and find out more details about the tour. After a quick shower, he changed to light cotton gray slacks, half-strip shirt, with a loafer shoe, and came out of the room.

He noticed a hotel boy following him and asked, "Very beautiful girl; do you want in your room tonight?"

"Sorry, I am married."

"Your wife not here," the waiter was talking in broken English, and Pemba had hard time understanding him.

"No, thanks."

He walked faster than the waiter and ignored him. He liked the food he had at lunch and would love to try similar Thai food for dinner. He visited the same restaurant he had lunched at that afternoon; it looked very different—vibrant, stunning, and colorful—maybe because of light decoration, or maybe he just did not notice during at the daytime. On the left side, there was a large bar counter decorated with multicolor bottles placed in the tall glass rack that attracted the people who loved to have various cocktails. After the entrance gate, Pemba came into a large hall with a high ceiling had numerous chandeliers around the ceiling. In the middle, a huge hardwood dance floor was polished and was shining with wax, looking very inviting. A few couples were dancing. In front of the dance area, a very tall, gorgeous-looking Thai girl was singing a melodious love song with live music. The tables were arranged, surrounding the dance floor. The table Pemba occupied was on the right side, where the lovely lady was singing. The table was covered with a white cloth, and in the middle, a maroon-colored piece of cloth had impacted the table's decoration. Moreover, the small, aromatic cute-looking candle and a dark red rose along with cutlery and mostly empty cut glittering glass images in the dim lights totally enhanced the table decoration. The atmosphere was smooth, mild, and relaxed. Pemba really loved this place.

He ordered a typical world-famous tom yum soup, egg fried rice, green vegetable curry, and some kind of Thai ice-cream known as rim sweet for dessert. The food was heavenly—the wonderful taste, enticing aroma, and different kinds of spices brought out a wonderful perfection. Pemba had never had this kind of food in the past, but he was becoming crazy about it. Moreover, the beautiful waitress's soft-spoken style and polite service and presentation were outstanding.

Pemba had never seen such a sophisticated delivery of services in the tourism industry. Thai tourism products were of high quality, and their delivery of services was the best in the world—the reason Thailand was turning into a great tourism destination in a very short time. Pemba knew Thai Airways was nourished by the SAS, and in the beginning, the SAS had the majority and Thai Airways had only limited shares. Gradually and dramatically, Thai Airways grew to Thai International and earned a reputation as one of the best airlines in the Far East. Pemba appreciated their tourism promotion efforts, quality service products, and delivery of the service in a professional manner.

Pemba was witnessing and experiencing the tourism products such as sight-seeing places, transport quality, and service delivery. He noticed that 1987 was a Visit Thailand Year, and in the year, there was an intense focus on tourism, and they were hoping to draw one million more tourists another year because of these efforts. As per statistics, they had around 2.8 million tourists, and hoped to bring 3.8 million in the next years. It was an aggressive and attractive tourism promotional effort.

The food smell and clattering sound of cups, plates, and glasses were growing louder along with music. The restaurant was in full swing. A couple of times, Pemba was approached by the beautiful Thai girls for a dance. Dawa's warning was still fresh in his mind, and he politely declined such requests.

Further away from the corner of the restaurant, a tall, slim, and very sophisticated girl watched Pemba for a long time. She slowly approached him when he refused several girls to dance. She found him unusually handsome and attractive but he was resisting dance request from girl, and this, she thought, was an unusual behavior.

"Do you mind if I sit with you?"

"Yes, please."

Pemba could not believe his eyes. The girl in front of him was stunning, very sweet, great looking unusually tall and was perfect in all respects expected in a perfect woman. He had not seen a lady this beautiful in his entire life.

"Is this your first time in Thailand?" the girl asked.

"Yes," Pemba replied briefly.

"How long are you staying?" Another question.

"I'm leaving the day after tomorrow."

"What do you want to do tomorrow?"

"Mostly shopping after the morning floating market tour."

"Great. I am free tomorrow; can I be your shopping guide?"

"Sure. I need to purchase some gifts for my wife, maybe a female could pick up nice gift choice."

"What is your name?"

"Pemba."

"Where are you from?"

"Nepal."

"Are you going back to Nepal or somewhere else?"

"I'm going to America."

"Are you looking for company tonight?"

Pemba had never expected such a direct question from her. He avoided the answer and changed the subject. "What is your name?"

"Elisa."

"Pretty name."

"Thanks."

"Okay, Elisa, I am going early tomorrow for the tour, so what time are you free for shopping?"

"How about three in the afternoon? I will be waiting here for you."

"That sounds great."

"Have a great night, Elisa."

"Thanks."

It was almost midnight. Pemba, after paying the bills with good tips, left the beautiful place reluctantly. In no time, he was in his comfortable seventh-floor room for sleep. He had a hard time going to sleep and remembered that beautiful girl and her offer.

The first sight of the floating market was like a dream—numerous boats laden with fruits, commodities for trade, and a small cooking area inside the boats was bursting with the aroma of lemon grass and other spices. The sight and sound was out-of-this-world and provided a unique vision for artists and poets. Numerous tourists were taking photos and videos of this marvelous view, and it might be an excellent investment for memory in the later part of life that could be shared with children and grandchildren. Pemba was not certain about his future, because the children were the dream of later part of his life.

The tour took nearly two hours in the floating market and now they were on the way to a place of elephant riding for the tourists. Pemba had had several elephant rides in the past during his safari jungle tour in Chitwan, Nepal. The children looked like they are from Australia; they seemingly loved this part more than the floating market. They seemed to have a unique kind of ride, perhaps they had never had it in their life before. One cute child of about eleven years had taken the ride three times, and he still was not satisfied. One could easily read it in his facial expression.

The bus arrived at the hotel lobby close to one. Pemba rushed to his room to have a quick shower and changed to cotton khaki slacks, a gray half-shirt, and white walking tennis shoes. He chose the same table for lunch he had had last night for dinner at the restaurant.

This time of the day the place was not pretty and had only a few tables occupied. There were about three groups of girls scattered around the tables without men, eating lunch.

A pretty waitress approached with a large menu in hand. Pemba looked at her.

"Well, I had a wonderful dinner here last night. For lunch, I would like to go as per your suggestion."

"Sure, do you like Thai or Western dishes?"

"Thai, of course."

The waitress gave a half smile. "Okay, I will bring it shortly. Anything to drink?"

"Yes, one Thai beer, Singha, please."

The beer was cold, and Pemba liked its taste. It was mild, soft, and smooth like the Thai people. The food was also placed on the table earlier than expected.

Pemba had no idea about the food. Whatever it was, it had a good flavor. So without asking further, he started eating with blind faith.

After a few meals at the restaurant, Pemba had started having great faith in the quality and standard of the food preparation in Thailand. Since he also was a cook, he longed to meet the cook in the kitchen and see their recipes for such tasteful meals. Maybe tonight he could meet them if he got back to the hotel for the meals, after the hectic shopping. He had already compiled the shopping list for everyone, including his in-laws, and for Mihara and Allure, as they also lived in Los Angeles. He really needed an exotic gift for Linda, a sexy and quality material, perhaps a nighty.

Elisa showed up, as she knew the place and spoke Thai language. God, she was awfully beautiful and attractive by all means.

He was about to finish his meal and the time was close to three. He was very excited to see Elisa at the entrance door coming toward him.

"It's my pleasure to see you."

Pemba took her hand and gave a warm kiss with courtesy and bent his shoulder toward her.

Elisa expressed a very pleasant and tantalizing smile. She came closer and gave him a warm and soft kiss. It was a heavenly experience for Pemba. Her light makeup, with khaki shirt, and full cream trousers with a fascinating straw hat, red belt, and canvas walking shoes were a perfect match for a perfect lady. Pemba looked at her, maybe more than a minute, without a word escaping his lips. They both seemed to talk through their eyes in a language that was universal. Maybe in the West, they could have hugged and exchanged passionate, warm kisses, but they were Easterners and both Buddhists. They had to maintain public decency.

"How have you been? How was the floating market tour?"

"It was fascinating; I had never seen such a sight in my life."

"Yes, it is something of typical Thai culture."

Pemba took out a shopping list and gave it to Elisa. "This is all I need to buy."

"No problem, first we will go to Central Department Store and then to Daimaru."

"Well, you lead. I will follow you with pleasure."

Elisa had been closely watching Pemba for the last days. She was somehow attracted to Pemba's polite behavior and his rejection of dancing with the ladies at the restaurant. She had a special quality to pick up the right kind of men for her company, and she had never failed in the past; the reason she never had a problem with the law. She was grateful to the Buddha for that kind bestowal on her, and spent at least a half hour praying every day in the morning. Because of her unusual power, she had never had to go through any kind of trouble or unnecessary hassle in her profession. She had seen many of her friends become victims of drugs and other unnecessary elements.

She had observed special qualities and unusual behavior in Pemba—the reason she was inclined toward him. She earned her living sleeping with men, but she had standards in picking the right kind of gentlemen like Pemba.

They were in the Central Departmental Store. Normally, this store carried all sorts of nice merchandise at a reasonable price and without the hassle of haggling. Pemba picked up lots of gifts in the store, but he could not find a gift for Linda and her friend, Amanda, there.

After the Central Departmental Store, Elisa suggested going to Daimaru Japanese Department Store for sophisticated gifts for ladies. They reached Daimaru after twenty minutes by a taxi. Apparently this store was of high quality, and prices were much higher than at the Central, but things were of quality and good-looking as well.

Pemba liked this store better than the other one. As per Elisa's suggestion, he chose a black silk embroidered night dress for Linda. The dress was elegant, soft, and extremely sexy and attractive. For Amanda, Elisa picked up a fancy handbag that was made in Italy, which was simple but gorgeous in style.

Pemba also picked up a few slacks and some shirts that were made in Japan along with a sky blue jacket for himself. He insisted on choosing a gift for Elisa, but she refused. But when Elisa was in the restroom, he bought a blue blouse with lots of embroidery work in the neck area. He purchased it for Elisa and put it inside his bag quietly.

When they left the Japanese store, it was already dark outside. They hailed a taxi and collected all the shopping bags together, putting them in the taxi and leaving for the hotel. Elisa hesitated to go to Pemba's room, but after his hard persuasion, she agreed and helped him carry the bags into his room.

"Elisa, I will pack these tomorrows. It would be an honor if you could dine with me tonight."

"Okay, but not at the restaurant downstairs. I will take you to an authentic place in Siam Square."

"Of course, the restaurant choice is yours. I love Thai food and ladies."

"But you are a married man."

"I will tell you the whole story during dinner."

"Is that a deal?"

"A sincere deal." Both laughed.

They hailed a taxi to go to Siam Square. Pemba did not know this was one of the posh areas with authentic Thai restaurants. It was a nice place to spend some time, and they also had several movie halls in this area.

Elisa held Pemba's hand. "I hope you do not mind."

"The pleasure is mine, Elisa. You have such an elegant and soft hand—I wish to hold it forever."

"You must be kidding."

"Try me." They both laughed again.

The Thai restaurant Elisa chose was small and not so spacious but had been decorated with Thai arts and artifacts. Pemba felt it looked like a Thai house rather than a tourist restaurant—small, cozy, simple, and comfortable.

Pemba had nothing to do here but follow Elisa. She gave the order for the food. When the food arrived, it was all in clay pots that were polished and clean. Oh, the food's smell was stronger with lemon grass and several Thai spices. The taste of the food was awesome. Pemba felt perhaps there was no other place on earth besides Thailand for the best food. The soft chicken, rice, and red curry was fantastic. Pemba liked the food very much and ate to his complete satisfaction. He was full, most satisfied with the aroma and taste of the food he ate just now. He had no suitable words to express his gratitude to Elisa for coming to this hidden place.

"Hey, Pemba, how do you like the food?"

"It is the best food I've ever had in my entire life."

"What do you prefer for dessert?"

Pemba whispered to Elisa softly, "You!"

"I am going to tell your wife."

"She is not here."

Both laughed loudly.

"Okay, Elisa, I will be frank with you. Do you trust me?"

"I do, because you are a nice person."

"Linda is my fiancée, not my wife. We are going to marry in June."

When Pemba showed the picture from his wallet, Elisa could not believe she was white and exceptionally beautiful. She noticed Linda was more beautiful than her and had more loving face. Elisa got jealous of Linda only because she was more beautiful than herself. It is a common human weakness. Ladies are jealous of each other, nothing more.

After the food, Elisa suggested they go to a movie in Siam Square, which was within walking distance. The new movie that was running was *Karate Kid Part II*. They both wanted to see the movie. The movie hall was of average size, but the sound system was awesome as the trailer for the movie *Empire of the Sun* began, which would be released in the later part of the year.

Just before the screening of the movie, a large portrait of King Bhumibol came onto the screen, and everyone in the movie hall got up and bowed their heads in respect as the Thai national anthem began. Pemba followed the same gesture along with Elisa and everyone else in the movie hall.

Pemba asked Elisa in a low, whispering voice, "Do you really respect the king, or is this just pretend?"

Elisa put her finger to his mouth and warned him, "Be careful on what you say about the king. King Bhumibol for us is next to the Buddha. We all love him, and respect comes from our heart."

"We also have a king, but nobody shows this much respect in a movie hall."

"We will talk about this later," Elisa cautioned Pemba.

The movie was not that bad, and both enjoyed it. They hailed a cab.

"I will drop you at the hotel."

Elisa accompanied Pemba. It was almost eleven thirty at night. The hotel restaurant was about to close; so they found a place at a coffee shop that was open until 1:00 a.m.

"Pemba, I will stay at the hotel with you, just to have your company, if you don't mind."

"Of course, Elisa."

"But there is one condition."

"What?"

"You will sleep on your side of the bed; I will sleep on my side of the bed. You cannot touch me."

"Okay, I will follow that rule."

They both were on the seventh floor. The floor boy who had offered a girl to Pemba earlier looked at him sarcastically when they entered the room. Elisa made a restroom trip the moment they entered. Pemba was now waiting for Elisa on the sofa. The bed had been remade; it now had a clean look. A fresh bottle of water had been placed on the desk in front of the bed. Pemba was surprised at the room's luxury, and the charge was only thirty dollars per day.

In the meantime, Elisa had come out from the restroom.

"Hey, Elisa, may I ask you a personal question?"

"Go ahead, Pemba."

"What is your religion?"

"Buddhism, of course."

"How come your name is Christian?"

"There is a story behind it."

"What is your Thai name?"

"Ubon."

"What does that mean?"

"Lotus flower. My sister picked it for me while we were in school."

"To be honest, I'd rather call you Ubon than Elisa."

"Yes, everyone in my family calls me by that name."

"Then change to that name."

"My clients prefer Elisa over my Thai name."

"I am not your client."

"I know that."

Elisa got closer to Pemba and briefly kissed him on his cheek.

"Why there, could be much better here." Pemba pointed to his mouth.

"No, you are honest, pure, and a gentleman about to get married."

"I respect your true feelings toward me."

"Pemba, may I ask you something very precious, and this is my sincere request."

It surprised Pemba. "Anything, Ubon."

Both laughed at Pemba's mention of her Thai name first time in peculiar manner.

Ubon kept quiet for a long time. Pemba looked at her face—still no expression. He thought this must be important to Ubon—the reason she was taking a long time to utter her words. Ubon's eyes had become watery; her voice was trembling when she spoke.

"I hate my current profession but need to take care of my family. I have responsibility toward them."

Pemba did not interrupt. He gave space not interrupting her so that she would bring out her emotions.

"I like you very much; you are a person of my dream."

"Really?"

"Can you promise me one thing?"

"What thing, Ubon?"

"I insist, if something happens later in your life with Linda and you become alone, will you come to me?" Ubon continued, "We have farmland in the province. My father is sick; he is not able to spend his time at the farm, so he has given it to another person to work on fifty percent income basis. In addition, I have about ten million Bhatt savings in the bank. We could live in the province, and you be my man."

Pemba just smiled, but said nothing. For quite some time, Ubon gazed at Pemba's face, but it was hard to read what was on Pemba's mind.

After some time, Ubon put a direct question, "Pemba, do you not like my proposal? This is my first time proposing to a man."

Pemba slowly but deliberately tried to give an answer to Ubon's proposal. "Ubon, my dear, you are more than a friend to me. I do not know how we became so close that we could share our emotions within such a short span of time. To answer you, first of all, your proposal is hypothetical—it has a big *if.* Your request is very reasonable and practical, and for me, it is a huge opportunity you are providing. I truly like Thai people. They are honest, soft, polite, and generous.

Second, I love Thai food—so delicious and fulfilling. Third, if I get any such opportunity in life, I will be happy to accept your proposal."

"What time is your flight tomorrow?"

"I have to be at the airport at 9:00 p.m."

"Could you go to my home and meet my family tomorrow?"

"Ubon, the pleasure will be mine."

Ubon got closer to Pemba and gave a warm kiss on his mouth, short but sweet.

"Ubon, try to understand my situation in America. It is a new country, with new people, and completely foreign, and I am going as an immigrant. I am totally depending on Linda, at least in the beginning, and I need to fight for my existence, identity, and livelihood." Ubon was feeling and understanding Pemba's deep practical emotions. "Besides, I also have a family like yours, who are totally depending on me."

"I understand, Pemba. Let us have a good night's sleep. We will talk more tomorrow."

With that remark, Ubon kissed Pemba and slept on her side of the bed.

From the eastern window, bright rays of sunshine penetrated the room. Ubon got up and went to the restroom. Pemba also got up and asked for coffee from room service. The coffee was brought by the same floor boy and left on the wall table next to the mirror desk. In a small white flower vase was a fresh dark red rose, which brought a fresh atmosphere into the room. Pemba gently knocked on the restroom door.

"Ubon, coffee is here."

"Thanks," a frail, sweet, thin voice came from inside.

When Ubon came out, she was wearing a beautiful, soft cotton nightgown with tulip flowers printed all over, and she looked like a tulip itself—very pretty, delicate, and beautiful. Pemba and Ubon sat together and observed each other, exchanging a meaningful glance. Although Ubon was not wearing any makeup, she had a strong personality and naturally commanding beauty.

"Well, let's take a bath me first and after breakfast, I will take you to my home on the river."

"Do you live on a boat?"

"No, but have to go through boat in the river."

"Great, let us be ready then."

After having breakfast at the coffee shop, they took a taxi that took them to Canal Street. A boat was hired. After Ubon said something in the local language, the boat moved to the northeastern part of the city. After nearly half an hour, the boat stopped in front of a two-story wooden-framed house. Two small girls, aged about ten and twelve, were at the gate. They both gave a heavy, tight embrace to Ubon. An elderly lady, aged maybe around fifty, in a nice dress, embraced Ubon, and they exchanged words in the local language. An elderly man in the next room was lying in a small wooden bed. He looked sick, feeble, thin and yellow skinned. He greeted Pemba. Obviously, this sick old person was her father.

Pemba sat in the chair close to the sick old person and extended his greeting with respect and in an extremely polite manner. Ubon introduced her father, mother and two sisters in the family, and stepped into the kitchen to prepare a light lunch for everyone. It seemed Ubon brought smiles to everyone's faces in the family when she came to them. Mostly, she was out in the evening and nighttime and came back home in the morning when they had good family reunion every day for lunch.

Ubon was like a boy in the family, who brought income after selling her body every day. Pemba felt the family should know what Ubon was doing, but everyone took it as a profession. Pemba liked Ubon very much, but he was unable to do anything in the current situation.

It seemed the old man was asleep. Pemba slowly went to the kitchen and knocked on the door.

"Hi, it is me."

"Oh, come in; we're just trying to cook meal."

Ubon was working together with her mother, and they were cooking something nice with great flavor and taste.

"How far away is your farm?" Pemba was curious.

"About fifty miles from here. We get all the grain, vegetables, and fruits from there. We just buy some fish, chicken, and spices from the local market."

Food preparation took about an hour. They all sat at the large wooden table outside. Everyone sat, except Ubon's mother. She gave food to her husband who'd gotten up now. Ubon was on the left side of the table, Pemba, next to her, and the sisters sat across. The food was placed in the middle of the table. As usual, it had the same great smell and taste like the food in the restaurants.

The sisters watched Pemba eat the food slowly, smiling, and with shy expressions on the face. They were very pretty and delicate, and had innocent looks on their faces. Along with the food, Ubon opened Singha beer from the refrigerator. She also brought a glass of water for herself. Obviously, she did not like beer in the daytime and in front of her parents and sisters.

Pemba liked the house on the river; he had never seen such houses in the past anywhere.

Ubon's mother was a simple lady with a very good smile, and she had great quality to welcome guests in the house. It was obvious that Ubon had not brought many men to the house. She might not trust everyone but a few like Pemba, to whom gave her heart and mind, not her body.

Ubon had more trust and respect toward Pemba since this morning. He did not touch her body, not did he make any efforts to get her. They just slept as brother and sister in their beds.

After staying almost five hours in the house, around four, they left the house via a boat again and were in the hotel at four forty-five. They again stopped at the coffee shop for snacks and, of course, for coffee.

"I really appreciate your visit to my house; my mother and sisters like you very much."

"Great, give me your address and phone number, if you have, postal house address, I will send you postcards and maybe call you sometimes."

"I'd love that."

"Regarding the future, as I told you I am not sure what is going to happen with me. I am going to an uncertain future."

"I understand your situation, but only remember, I am here for you in case."

Ubon wrote her home address and phone number on a piece of paper. Normally, lovers wrote love letters in Thailand.

They stayed for about an hour, and Ubon asked, "Do you want to have dinner here or in the hotel or airport restaurant?"

"Will be better here around seven and take a cab after that."

"Let's go to your room to pack your things."

They spent around thirty-five minutes packing two large suitcases and one handbag. Ubon's packing was so efficient, like a professional, and utilized every inch of the suitcases to look really neat and tidy.

Close to seven, they came down to the restaurant and ordered the food as per Ubon' suggestion, as she had great experience in selecting quality of food. Pemba ate like there was no tomorrow and maybe the best food for the last time in Thailand.

Pemba felt it would be unnecessary for Ubon to come to the airport to see him off in such nasty traffic at the peak of the rush hour, but Ubon insisted. From one small bag, he took out the gift for Ubon—who just jumped and thanked him very much.

The taxi was ready, and Ubon was waiting outside in the portico of the hotel. After checking out from the hotel, Pemba entered the awaiting taxi, where Ubon was already sitting in the backseat. The taxi was filled with a very mild lady fragrance, and Ubon was looking unusually beautiful.

When the taxi moved to the main street, Pemba could see nothing but cars all over the place. It must be a great jam. He drew close to Ubon and whispered, "You are looking awesome."

With a shy expression, Ubon said, "Thanks," and gave him a warm kiss.

On arrival at the airport, there were big lines at the check-in for Thai International flights going to Los Angeles.

Pemba asked Ubon to move to a less crowded corner and gave her a manly hug and warm kiss, and he took the envelope from his jacket pocket.

"My Los Angeles address and a few dollars are here for your expenses. I hope you have a great life. Until next time, thanks for everything."

It was such a simple but memorable departure at the crowded airport. Pemba as well as Ubon raised their hands until they could see each other. After that, Ubon got lost in the crowds, and the face got lost among many faces therein.

***

CHAPTER TWELVE

April 1988

The Thai flight left on time for the Los Angeles airport.

Pemba relaxed on the flight. As Linda had told him, if he got sleep during the flight, he would have less jet lag; otherwise, it might take longer to overcome.

After the fabulous dinner, Pemba had become addicted to the Thai food that was served onboard, which was also like the one he ate in Thailand. With a couple glasses of red wine, he completed the meal and was satisfied. Although he had not been on international flights except to India a couple of times—this flight, cabin services and their dealings with the passengers were delicate and charming. Their soft way of talking impressed him a lot.

Pemba tried hard to get some sleep but somehow he felt jittery and could not sleep at all. He concentrated on his book and the movie that was playing. The music was good but sleep was distant away.

Many times, the stewardess stopped at him and asked politely, "Do you need anything?"

Pemba knew what he needed was sleep, and they could not deliver it to him. He joked, "Yes, sleep," and they both laughed.

The whole cabin was dark except for a few spotlights here and there, where people were reading books, while most of the passengers were watching some movie on the big screen. The low, humming sound of the jet engine could be heard from inside the cabin. Pemba visualized himself on top of the Pacific Ocean somewhere. It was pitch dark outside, both below and in the sky, except for the anti-collision lights that flashed occasionally. At the back, he heard a baby crying, maybe just after walking for sleep or perhaps the pacifier was missing from his mouth.

The cabin had a very sweet perfume. The stewardesses were relaxed in their seats, as it was not time to be busy. Most of the passengers were asleep, reading books, watching the movie, or listening to music. Only a few of them, like Pemba, were doing nothing—just impatient and excited. Of course, Pemba was excited because of the new life he was going to face in a new land with a new set of people. But Pemba had deep confidence that he would be able to handle whatever came in his life—good, bad, or even worst.

A light ray of sunshine was visible from the window near the front of the cabin. Smells of fresh omelets lingered in the cabin. Perhaps they were preparing breakfast. With the cabin's bright light, people were waking up. The stewardesses passed around fresh, nice-smelling wet towels to wipe their faces and get ready for the breakfast. The atmosphere inside the cabin brightened and half-sleep faces of the passengers started brightening up. The crew announced that they would be landing in Los Angeles in ninety minutes. The cabin crew gave the ground weather information, which was calm air with good visibility, the arrival temperature being seventy-six—which was perfect, neither hot nor cold.

When Pemba arrived in the large lounge of the airport after customs and immigration formalities and a mindboggling, exhausting flight, he was more than happy to see Linda. The two hugged each other for a long time, as if they did not wish to part.

"Welcome to America."

"Oh, man, it was such a long flight. Love you very much."

Pemba lifted the luggage, both the suitcases, and Linda took his handbag. They proceeded to the parking lot. Pemba could not even imagine that the parking lot was so large that they had to take an elevator to the tenth floor and walk about five minutes to find Linda's car.

After placing the luggage in the trunk, Linda sat in the driver's seat, Pemba next to her, and they left the huge parking lot. The open road was something Pemba had never imagined. Traveling along an eight-lane highway in the most luxurious Impala felt like he was traveling in a luxurious boat rather than a car. It was so fascinating to look the way Linda was driving on such a busy freeway. Pemba thought he would never be able to drive on this busy highway filled with numerous cars, keeping the right lanes, and being in that amount of control. It was amazing just to look at. Besides, Pemba had never seen a woman driver in his life. Now, his would-be wife was driving on such an amazing highway in America. This was like a dream for Pemba. He moved closer to Linda and kissed her on the juicy mouth just to come out of the dream. Linda loved that kiss.

"Pemba, I will go to work at two. I am sure you will need some sleep, and I'll make a quick lunch for you before I go."

She made a chicken sandwich, fresh salad, soup out of a can, and a piece of cheesecake. Linda had lunch with Pemba, and immediately after lunch and a quick shower, she guided him to sleep in her guest room.

Within a very short time, Pemba was in a dreamful and sound sleep. Linda left a note on the fridge about his dinner—rice, chicken curry, and some vegetables—and asked him to heat it in the microwave and eat if he was hungry; otherwise, she would join him at dinner.

When Linda came back from work, she checked Pemba he was still sound asleep. She prepared some dinner for herself, ate, and went to sleep in her bedroom. After a while, she again looked at Pemba; he still was asleep.

The phone rang in the living room.

"Mother, he is still asleep. Don't you remember I slept for three days after my trip?"

"Your Dad wants to talk with him."

"I will ask Pemba to call him once he is fully awake."

"Okay, I will tell him."

"Thanks, Mother."

The phone cut off as Linda was getting a little irritated at her mother's behavior.

Linda needed a shower before bed. As she was about to take a shower, the phone rang again.

"Hello."

"Oh, hi, Amanda how are you?"

"Great."

"Listen, Mother is planning a wedding in Ohio during Father's Day sometime in the third week of June."

"What do you expect from me?"

"As a best friend, I want you at my wedding."

"By all means, Linda, I will be there."

"That is great. Should we drive?"

"Well, I have some time to make decision on fly or drive situation." Amanda was brief. "I want to see Pemba before that."

"He is having jet lag. I will make a plan for a get-together, along with Mihara and Allure."

"That really sounds great; please let me know."

"Of course. I will call you, Amanda."

"Okay, bye. Talk to you soon."

Finally, Linda had time for a shower to refresh herself. After the shower, she did not remember when she went to sleep and got up in the morning. Again, she checked Pemba's room. He was still asleep. The food from last night was untouched and he was snoring softly. Linda tried not to wake him up, made some breakfast with fresh scrambled eggs for herself, left a note about breakfast in the fridge, and left for the office around seven.

This morning, Linda was earlier than most of the staff in the office. She needed to prepare lots of files for review by Smith and also make a trip plan for him early next week to Chicago. She had lots of work; moreover, the personnel issues for the franchisee law project were moving fast, and she had a hard time coping with all the tasks and deadlines.

"Hi, Linda, what's up?" Kathy poked her head inside the room and asked.

"Nothing much, Kathy"

"Has your guy arrived?" Kathy asked.

"Yes, yesterday. He's sleeping—jet lag."

"Great, when are we going to see him?"

"Perhaps soon, Kathy."

"Ok. I am excited to see him." Kathy remarked and left.

Linda got busy with her paperwork. She noticed that lunchtime had passed but she had no feeling for food. She remembered to call Pemba, but there was no response even after a long, continuous ring. The guy must be sleeping, otherwise, he might have picked up the phone.

Linda took a break from paperwork and ate some salad and two pieces of sandwich bread she'd had since yesterday. She finished her lunch promptly and returned to her cabin to complete the pending paperwork.

Half of her mind was with Pemba and the other half in the office. She had to balance her life in the next three months until she got married. She did not want to provide a neglectful attitude toward Pemba. Pemba might not understand the lifestyle in this country; he should be educated on American lifestyle, culture, and the basics of core relationships and mutual understanding.

Foremost, he had to learn to drive. Linda was pretty sure he would pick it up fast as he drove a motorbike and Jeep in Nepal. He should become familiar with basic highway driving and should have control on traffic-congested road, typically in Los Angeles. After learning to drive, he needed to find a suitable job to his liking. Close to her home was a Home Depot store; perhaps Pemba might look for a job there after getting a driver's license.

Linda' mind was occupied with Pemba.

"Linda did you have time to check my flights to Chicago next week?"

"Yes, Mr. Smith."

That was the brief question Smith had for Linda.

Linda checked that afternoon's schedule. A client was due for Mr. Smith at three; so she picked up the file, walked into his office, and dropped the file off. Smith noticed the files and the name on the front.

"Thanks, Linda, what time is he due?"

"Three."

Linda went to her room immediately. She was a little impatient. She called Pemba again but no response on the phone. She needed to keep busy for another two hours in the office, and it was also necessary to do some quick grocery shopping in order to pick up rice, vegetables, and meat for Pemba. Maybe he would also like some beer and bourbon.

When it was around five, everyone left the office. Linda also packed her files and locked important papers and files in the credenza and left. She was familiar with the grocery store; she picked up everything along with some fresh vegetables.

Linda entered the house without making noise. Pemba's bedroom door was closed.

She entered her bedroom, casually undressed, and got in the restroom for a quick shower. She needed to cook a little rice, and Pemba loved green vegetable and potatoes. She kept herself busy cooking. Linda had a feeling that Pemba should be awake by dinnertime, if not earlier.

While Linda was occupied with cooking, Pemba startled her, holding her from behind, kissing her neck madly and holding her breast tightly.

"Oh my, I thought you were going to sleep the whole week. Did you have a good sleep?"

"Great, I have never slept like this before."

"I did not go to the office for three days; I just slept the whole time. Are you hungry?"

"Not for food," Pemba answered.

Linda had a silent question, and looked at his face. Pemba pointed at Linda's nose. Linda understood what he wanted. Both had a good laugh.

"Pemba, go take a quick shower, you smell like a rat."

Pemba gave a mischievous half smile and left. When Pemba returned after the shower, Linda had prepared food and placed it on the table. They both sat at the dining table and started their first dinner together. Pemba liked the food—rice, some kind of yellow lentil, and okra. It was really tasty. To drink, Pemba had bourbon, and Linda some beer.

"I should be okay after tonight's sleep. You go to office; I have nothing to do in the house?"

"Mom had called yesterday. Dad wants to talk with you. Amanda also called; she too wants to meet you."

"Give me a few more days, and I will be ready to talk with everybody," Pemba said.

"Pemba, next week, I suggest you go to driving training. I know a driving school, which is close to our place. They will come to pick you up and the instructors will drive you back."

"I know how to drive."

"Of course, Pemba, but they will be teaching you everything. The traffic is congested here. They will teach you how to merge in the highway and get out. Besides, you drove in the right side of the road in Nepal; here, driving is on the left side. I feel, Pemba, you should be able to learn everything after about eight hours of training."

"That sounds good."

After dinner, they moved to the living room, and Pemba seemed to be attracted toward the television as there was no TV in Nepal.

"What would you like to watch, Pemba?"

"I love movies."

"Let me show you one. Go to channel 125 onward, and you will have old and some new movies. There is a Clint Eastwood Western cowboy movie —*The Good, the Bad, and the Ugly*, do you want to watch that one?"

"Oh, yes, I love Clint Eastwood."

Linda chose that movie for Pemba and went to take a quick shower. Pemba relaxed on the sofa and watched the movie. He had not even noticed when Linda returned.

After a quick shower, she kissed him good night and invited him to come to bed whenever he got through the movie. Pemba had thoroughly enjoyed the movie, continuously scanned the channels one after another and slept in the living room.

Linda got up around six in the morning; she had noticed that Pemba slept in the living room. His cover had fallen down from his body onto the floor. Linda managed the cover on his body and let him sleep without waking him up. She realized his sleep pattern had still not adjusted properly. He slept at daytime and woke up at nighttime. This was totally opposite of day and night in two countries. This was what they called jet lag perhaps.

After the shower, Linda made herself ready for work after making a breakfast of omelet, sausage, and toasted bread with orange juice. She also made a plate for him and kept in the refrigerator, left a note on the dining table that she was going to the office and his breakfast is inside. She wrote, "Warm up and eat; will call back later."

Pemba woke up at around eleven and noticed that he'd slept in the living room. Perhaps, he thought, Linda had minded his sleeping in the living room last night.

He read Linda's note and ate the breakfast after heating it in the microwave. He had a shower and looked for something to do in the house to kill some time. He noticed that the patio flowers needed water and could look better if he could trim them. He checked the garage. There were two bags of potting soil. He could use it for the plants. He noticed there were exotic plants in the garden and walkways; he could trim those dazzling plants and beautiful ferns. He manicured the garden, patio area, and surrounding walkways. He changed the garden set up in an attractive and pleasing manner. In fact, Pemba's work was like that of a professional landscaper.

Pemba heard a phone ring, and he picked it up in the living room.

"Hello."

"Hi, Pemba, you woke up?"

"No, I am still sleeping," he said, jokingly.

"Listen, darling. Did you eat breakfast?" Linda asked.

"Of course. I am sorry, Linda, last night I slept in the living room."

"Pemba, darling, you don't have to explain that to me. It must be the movies and your sleep pattern. What are you doing now?"

"Taking care of your garden and patio."

"Darling, don't say yours; it is ours," Linda reminded.

"Okay, I am taking care of *our* garden."

"Do you love me?" Linda asked.

"Why are you asking that stupid question? Of course; otherwise, I would not be here."

"Just have to make sure." Linda reinforced.

"Darling, please do not leave me in the living room tonight," she joked again.

"Of course not, silly." Pemba assured.

Linda hung up the phone after saying, "Love you again," as she needed to go to Mr. Smith with some important files.

Pemba finished the remaining work in the garden and walkway and the patio. He brought the plants from inside and added soil and water, and trimmed them.

It was almost lunchtime. Pemba checked the fridge, took out two pieces of sandwich, with some salad, and ate with a glass of orange juice.

In the middle of the garden, there was a large avocado tree that required lots of trimming. Some parts of the garden needed to be mowed.

He liked the weather; it was just perfect, neither hot and nor cold. Perhaps he would like to get a job working outside.

After finishing the garden and patio work, Pemba entered the house and proceeded to the restroom for a quick shower as he felt dirty.

Linda parked her car in the yard and was extremely happy with what she saw up front. She had the curiosity to check the garden area also. She was impressed, Pemba had worked hard to keep the patio and garden in attractive manner.

"Hi, dear. It looks beautiful." Linda was pleased.

"Do you like it?" Pemba came forward and kissed the back of her neck.

"Of course, it has a professional look."

"Thanks."

"Do you need to pick up personal things from the market?" Linda asked.

"Yes, I need some things, such as toothpaste, a brush, and undergarments."

"Great. Let me change and I will be ready." With the remark Linda changed her dress.

The minimarket was close to Linda's house. It took just seven minutes to reach. Pemba picked up his required things, such as after-shave, a nice Gillette razor, shaving cream, socks, and undergarments. Linda picked up some lipstick and cosmetics for her use.

On the way back to the house, after the casual shopping trip, Linda asked Pemba, "What do you want for dinner, Pemba?"

"What do you mean?"

"I mean; would you like to eat out or at home? How about Japanese food?" Linda suggested.

"Good, I love sushi."

Linda changed direction and entered the highway. After driving for about twenty minutes, they came to Benihana Restaurant. They chose the sushi bar for drinks and snacks. Linda ordered Sapporo beer, and Pemba asked for Shochu along with sushi, shrimp tempura, and teriyaki wings.

"Did you know, Linda?"

Linda did not reply; she only turned her face to Pemba as if asking, "What?"

"In Japan, when they drink together, they care for each other by pouring drinks and watching that the other person's glass is not empty."

"You mean, the other people sitting with you takes care of the other person's drinks?"

"Yes. At the same time, you make sure your company is not drunk."

"That is an interesting tradition."

"So I will take care of you here, and you take care of me."

Both laughed simultaneously. Pemba got closer to Linda and kissed her warm face and hands. After a couple of drinks, the waiter asked them to move to the chef table, where the knife food-cutting demonstration, Hibachi, was going on. Linda always loved to watch their superb skills of handling knife and the style of food preparations.

The chef knew Linda because she had been there before many times with other friends. He smiled and asked, "How are you, Linda?"

"I am great. Tanaka, this is my fiancé, Pemba."

"Hi, Pemba, where are you from?"

"Nepal."

"You must be kidding. I was in Nepal: Kathmandu, Durbar Marga, in a Japanese restaurant on the second floor. Worked there about three years. I love Nepal; it is my pleasure to meet you." They both shook hands warmly.

For dinner, Pemba ordered *yakisoba* and Linda, *hibachi* shrimp. In the meantime, they observed the chef's entertaining presentation of a unique style of grilling and food preparation. Pemba thought Japan had unique verities of food, eye catching food color, and balanced calories—the reason the Japanese have the longest expectancy in life. Both of them had meals that were healthy as well as tasty.

Pemba was watching news on the television. Linda after freshening up in the rest room joined him in the living room.

"Pemba, my mother called again. She is saying Dad wants to talk with you, so be prepared. Amanda may also have the program this Friday, and we will be meeting for happy hour. I will confirm with her tomorrow, and then will be here to pick you up."

"I have a gift for Amanda. It is a black leather handbag with an *A* initialed in gold in the middle of the bag."

"Where is that? I can wrap it in a gift bag."

Pemba brought the bag and gave it to Linda.

"It is beautiful."

"Pemba, I do not want you to see the movie late night. Please join me after the news, okay?"

"Sure. I'll be there in no time."

The news came to an end at ten. The part of the news Pemba liked most was the weather forecast that was so accurate, precise, and vivid. Pemba entered the bedroom quietly and slept next to Linda, holding her from behind and giving her warm kisses and a passionate expression, holding her body toward him. Linda liked that gesture and submitted herself to his muscular and warm body. She felt his private part growing toward her butt, as if looking for a suitable place of entrance.

In the morning, Linda left for her office at seven. Pemba slept until eleven. He did not have an appetite for breakfast, so he had spaghetti for lunch and rested in the living room, watching several movies.

"Hello." Pemba picked up the phone when it rang.

"Hi, Pemba, Amanda confirmed we are going to meet tomorrow."

"Great. You will pick me up after work?"

"I will be home around six thirty." Linda replied.

Pemba prepared a dinner of spaghetti with small pieces of cooked chicken, along with creamy Italian alfredo sauce and fresh tomato sauce with parsley and other spices. The smell was good, and he was sure Linda would like it.

Linda walked in a nice pair of ash color official two-piece suit with a smoky silky scarf in the neck; she looked like an executive in the big corporate office.

She gave Pemba a big hug, who grabbed her hard and kissed her first on the mouth then on the neck and down to the breast. They stood outside for about a minutes in that position.

"Smells good. What have you cooked?"

"Wait until you see and eat."

"Let me change and I will be there; I am hungry."

Fresh inside and outside direct from the restroom, Linda jumped into kitchen. Pemba was not there. He came in with a French white wine in his hand.

"I had put this in the cooler this afternoon. Should I open it?"

"Of course, my darling."

They poured the drink in the wine glass; the taste was smooth, crispy, and mild.

"Dear, my dad may call you tonight—he is impatient to know you in person."

It was not her dad Linda was worried about. It was her mom, who was irritated by her daughter's marriage with an immigrant and a non-Christian. Linda felt she would keep nagging her until the last moment before their marriage. Moreover, her mom insisted on a church marriage in Ohio, but now Linda had her office colleagues and some friends in Los Angeles, and they might not have time to attend a ceremony in Ohio. She might have to have a simple reception in Los Angeles for the office as Mr. Smith had told her twice already. Besides, Pemba wished to perform a Sherpa marriage tradition at Dorje's monastery. She could visualize three ceremonies—one in the Ohio church, a monastery ceremony, and a reception in Los Angeles.

"Pemba, my parents are insisting on a church wedding in Ohio; we also a need a Sherpa tradition ceremony here at Dorje's place, and a reception for my office colleagues and friends in Los Angeles. Who do you want to be your best man? Aat least we need one for Ohio wedding."

"I would prefer Mihara, if he could."

The phone rang.

"Hello, this is Linda…Hi, Dad…We are fine, how about you and Mom? Okay, I will give the phone to Pemba.

"Hi, Pemba my boy, how are you?"

"I am fine, Sir; thank you" Pemba gave polite reply.

"You do not have to call me Sir? Just call me Dad."

"Yes, Dad."

"How you are getting along?"

"Fine, I presume."

"How do you like your new place?"

"Great, I love the weather."

"Do you feel you can be here for a long time?"

"I see no problem."

"That is good. Listen, I will be seeing you in Ohio soon."

"Thanks, Linda has told me."

Linda took the phone from Pemba. "Dad, could I talk with Mom? . . . Hi, Mom, we must have a date prior to the twentieth of June."

"I got it. I will check with the church and let you know."

"Of course, I need to have leave from work also."

"Thanks, I will call you next week."

"Good night, Mom."

It was Friday. Linda left for work and Pemba was still sleeping soundly. She did not disturb him while she pulled out the car slowly from the garage.

Pemba was ready for Linda to pick him up to see Amanda for the happy hour cocktails. Linda got there around six-twenty and they left for the bar. Pemba had no idea where they were going, but after nearly thirty-five minutes, they arrived at the bar.

The crowd was thin now. They approached the counter and got a gin and tonic for Linda and sea breeze cocktail for Pemba. The seat on the left corner of the hall was open, and they occupied the table.

"Amanda should be on the way; she is always late."

"No problem, we have nothing else to do but wait."

"What is meant by happy hour?'"

"That means they will provide drinks until eight in half price."

"What happens after eight?"

"The price will be regular."

"A nice business technique to draw a crowd. How many people will stay after eight?" Pemba was curious.

"Not many, maybe about ten percent."

"What does Amanda do?"

"She is a journalist."

"How long have you known her?"

"Over five years."

Pemba noticed a middle-height, short-haired, slightly long-nosed girl approach them.

"Hi, I am Amanda." She extended her hand toward Pemba.

"Hello." They shook hands.

"Are you going to get your drink?"

"Of course, Linda." Amanda replied.

Amanda penetrated the crowded bar area. Smoke clouds were rising, and Linda was not feeling good.

When Amanda brought the drinks, Linda asked, "What is that, Amanda?"

"It is a kosher pink wine called Hagafen."

Amanda faced Pemba and asked a question, "So, Pemba, how do you like Los Angeles?"

"Great, I love the weather."

"He manicured and landscaped all the garden and patio walkways," Linda said, showing her appreciation.

"Is that so, Pemba?"

"That is nothing, just a pastime for me."

"Oh, Amanda, do you also know any driving schools in our area?"

"Yes, is it for Pemba to learn?"

"Yes."

"In fact, there is one Korean driving school; they take good care to the learners. I have a girl who came from Israel go to that Korean school and she learned fast."

"Do you happen to have their phone number?" Linda asked.

"I think yes; let me check my notebook."

Luckily, Amanda found the number and gave it to Linda.

"Oh, here is your gift, Amanda" Pemba gave the gift.

When Amanda opened the wrapping paper, she just jumped from the chair and hugged Pemba. "It is so pretty. Thanks, Pemba."

"So when is the wedding?" Amanda asked.

"Before June twentieth." Linda replied.

"Are you serious that I should come to Ohio?" Amanda asked.

"Of course, you are my best friend."

"Listen, Linda, I am so busy with that special report, and Passover now is in my head. I have no idea; I may not be able to make it."

"Well, you have time to think about it. Please Amanda do your best."

"I thought you were going to invite Allure and Mihara." Amanda remarked.

"Yes, Allure cannot make it, so I dropped the idea of Mihara also. Maybe next time," Linda concluded.

It was now almost eight. The crowd, the loud murmuring, and the smoke clouds had become unbearable for Linda; she had smoke allergy. They decided to leave the place. Linda invited Amanda for supper at home. She declined because of her early meeting at work. So Linda and Pemba returned home.

"She is a nice person; I really like her," Pemba remarked about Amanda.

"Who, Amanda?"

"Yes."

"What are we going to eat?" Linda asked.

"There is some leftover spaghetti and I would like to cook some rice for me."

"That really sounds a good combination," Linda remarked.

For dinner they had a Bordeaux red wine that was very smooth, mild, and crispy.

"Pemba, dear, what would you like to do during your first weekend here in Los Angeles?"

"I would like to go to a movie and Disney World."

"Okay then, we will go to Disney World tomorrow and a movie on Sunday."

After dinner, Linda went to take a shower, and changed. She joined Pemba in the living room, who was watching the movie *The Sound of Music*. She really loved the movie; she did not know how many times she had watched it. The movie was normally played on regular TV on NBC around Good Fridays and Christmas for families. The movie finished; Pemba had never seen a movie more interesting than this one. Linda was sleeping next to him; he gently lifted her and carried her to the bedroom.

It was almost eight in the morning. Both the lovebirds were sleeping, as there was no alarm at six. Linda extended her hand. Pemba was next to her; she held him from behind and kept her body warm, holding her sweetheart tightly. They lay in that position for another forty minutes.

Linda gazed toward the table clock. It was almost nine. She needed to get up now if they were to avoid the big lines in Disneyland.

Normally, Disneyland was always crowded on Saturdays, and that day was not an exception. They spent a lot of time in lines going to each exhibit. Pemba enjoyed the rides, and all the attractions were completely new to him. They visited all the places and liked two teenagers' first time in love, holding hands and occasionally kissing and caressing each other. The day turned into night, and still they were not tired; they kept their passion and emotion fresh, still finding out new places.

"Pemba, darling, I am exhausted now. Let's have a quick dinner and head home."

They stood in the long line at McDonald's. After a long wait, Pemba ordered a Big Mac, big fries, and Coke. Linda had a garden salad, fish sandwich, and Coke, with no fries.

Somehow, for Pemba, the food in the fast food places tasted like cardboard to him. He never got good taste from processed food in fast food joint.

Before bed, they had some leftover red wine from the previous day and hit the sack. They slept a little apart from each other, without touching and caressing, as both were tired.

Sunday was a leisurely day-long sleep, warm tub bath, and brunch of their choice. They use mostly weekdays' leftover food that provided excellent taste with a mixture of various combination and flavors.

"Darling, what time would you like to go for a movie?"

"How about two thirty for the show at three?" Linda suggested.

"Great. We will be home early. IMAX may be a better choice; it will be new for you."

"What is IMAX?"

"A large screen where your entire vision from left to right is focused on the screen. In fact, it is a technique of wide screen cinematography that produces an image approximately ten times larger than standard thirty-five millimeter movies."

"That big?" Pemba was surprised.

"Yes, moreover, the sound and vivid pictures on the screen transfer you out of your imagination, providing the feelings that you are a part in the movie itself. Well, I do not need to explain. Let us go now, you will see yourself."

When they were inside the IMAX theater, Pemba's eyes widened, seeing the magnificent, large screen beyond one's expectation. When the pictures appeared on the screen, it was a helicopter hovering over Niagara. Pemba thought he was inside the helicopter going toward Niagara Falls. Actually, he had never experienced such a large dimension of screen—with crystal vivid pictures and the soundtrack that blew the mind. The picture was about the mighty Niagara Falls titled *Niagara Miracles*. It covered the entire falls' perception that could be viewed from naked human eyes in reality.

During the entire show, Pemba's vision was hypnotized with such an intense concentration on the screen. He almost forgot that Linda was with him. It was a mesmerizingly precious moment in his life. He thought of the new country, new people, new vision, and its roads, landscape, flowers, weather, and rule of law. The Americans were obsessed with cleanliness; there was not a piece of paper lying on the road. Footpaths around the houses impressed him a lot. Perhaps he might find a piece of paradise here on the other side of the earth.

***

CHAPTER THIRTEEN

May 1988

This was the second day Pemba was learning driving on the road. The previous day, he had had two hours, and for today he had a two hours' training schedule for him. The Korean trainer, Kim, was good and taught him well with patience and detail—how to stop at stop signs and techniques for merging onto and exiting the highway. He also taught Pemba about road signs and explained about highways in America—that even numbered highways always went from east to west and odd went north and south. On small roads, the speed limit was normally forty miles per hour and on highways, the maximum was sixty. The left lanes were for fast traffic and right ones for slow lanes in the highway. The HOV lane was meant for high occupancy vehicles during peak hours, for two or more people in a car only. You were not supposed to drive in that lane if you were driving by yourself.

He had been familiarized with stripes, straight line yellow, broken line yellow and white line, and procedures to take over on the two-lane road. In the class, they explained DUI (driving under the influence) procedures and law. Under this law there was a limit to how much alcohol was allowed in your system and what the punishments were if you ever drove under the influence of alcohol or drugs. Even driving was so complex here, for one had to pass the entire test, written and practical. In one way, it was much simple, and the other way, it could be complex because of so many regulations. But regulations and procedures were much simpler and easy to understand.

After a week, when Pemba improve driving skills on the roads dramatically, Kim took him for the final road test for driving licenses. A lady from the DMV sat next to him and instructed to go right and left on the road. He followed her instructions very well and up to her satisfaction; finally, she asked him to parallel park, which Pemba did without any problem. His photo was taken, and the DMV issued a driver's license after he paid the twenty-five-dollar fee. The license was good for ten years, and he was a happy camper. Now he was an independent person and could travel anywhere on his own.

Linda was also happy after Pemba got the license. They had a celebration with margaritas in one of the Mexican restaurants close to home. At their request, the mariachi band played a song in their honor. Pemba liked the Mexican food that was similar in taste to Nepali food. He particularly loved the dish known as chicken enchilada.

"Pemba, what kind of car would you like to have?"

"I prefer a pickup truck, not a car."

"Great, a pickup truck is good to carry household goods as well. We will go this weekend and buy the truck," Linda said.

"But, darling, I don't have the money to buy it now."

"Do not worry, I will be the sole co-signer for the loan."

"How much do I pay?"

"You build credit and may have to pay about two hundred and fifty dollars per month."

"That means I have to get a job soon."

"Well, take it easy. In the meantime, I will pay for you."

"Okay, whatever you say, I will do."

It looked like the margaritas had slightly intoxicated Linda. Pemba had the car key; so he sat on the driver's seat and proceeded homeward.

Linda kissed Pemba very smoothly and with lots of passion before leaving for the bathroom as she had works waiting for the following morning. Pemba sat in front of the TV in the living room and watched the news. He remembered the letter he had received from Dawa this afternoon. It was lying on the kitchen table. He opened it.

It was a long letter. First, Dawa had news of the office. Colonel Bradley had his daughter's marriage in London, so he had left for London for a month. Robert was in the hospital due to some problem in his heart. Office work was still hectic. Everyone was busy with groups, as it was the peak season. He also explained, the hotel situation in Kathmandu was getting tough, so some of the groups had moved to Pokhara without staying in the city. The tourists were arriving in large-scale groups and FIT. All the trekking companies were busy. He'd also gotten married and come back from Solukhumbu after three days together with his wife. His wife was planning to open a small carpet factory, and she had arranged a loan from the bank already. The family in Phaplu was in good shape, and everything was going along without any problems. That was the gist of the letter that took him a long time to read with intense interest.

Pemba remembered that he needed to write a long letter back to Dawa and send a beautiful wedding gift along with the letter. He prepared a lunch salad, sandwich, and lemonade. He finished the letter slowly with many details about his trip, starting with Thailand. He described Linda's house, her luxurious car, Los Angeles, Disneyland, and the IMAX, along with lots of appreciation for Linda. He also mentioned that he was going to buy a pickup truck this weekend. He explained about America in general and talked about the obsession with cleanliness along with the numerous roads and highways that existed in this country. He relayed to Dawa that he hardly saw people walking on the street. They all rode cars. Finally, he closed the letter by extending his invitation to Dawa and his wife to visit America as his guest sometime in future.

Pemba had a sound sleep and a powerful dream.

He had returned to Phaplu with two children and a lot of money after a twenty-five year stay in America with Linda. He started a very luxurious hotel for trekkers in Junbesi in collaboration with Marriott. They had built a nice bungalow on the top of the hill with lots of trees, waterfalls, a tennis court, cover-heated swimming pool, and jogging track. There was a beautiful swing set and play area for the children. In the hotel, he trained the Lamas to work in the hotel reception area, kitchen, and laundry, and set up a classroom equipped with all the audio-visual equipment. A documentary was produced about trekking in the Phaplu area and beyond for the trekkers before they trekked to the Mount Everest region. The hotel was equipped with short takeoff and landing airfields for small aircrafts, and next to the other corner, a helipad was built.

In his dream, many tourists were coming and leaving at the same time, and the hotel occupancy was over eighty percent from September to April. Linda took over the management of the hotel as per Marriott's policy and adopted their international marketing network. It had become one of the pioneer hotels in the Marriott network and provided quality international services. The hotel was able to get most of the groups that normally operated through Lukla to the basecamp trek. Besides, it had attracted FIT for easy trekking itinerary in Phaplu region only, for those who were unable to take high-elevation trek. The hotel had built up an excellent market through the pioneer tour operators in Germany, France, and America. Most of the Mountain Travel group now used their hotel for the basecamp trek through Phaplu.

His golden dream was spoiled by the piercing sound of the telephone. Pemba picked up the phone in his sleepy voice.

"Darling, are you still sleeping?"

"Yes, I was having a beautiful dream."

"Tell me about it."

"I will tell this evening. It was a long and sweet dream."

"Okay. I have kept sandwich and some salad in the fridge—please help yourself."

"Great. I'm hungry, so I will eat."

"I will see you around six thirty."

"Love you, bye now."

Normally, Saturdays were busy days in car dealers' place. Linda had appointment with Stacy in General Motor dealership in

Torrance. Most of the tables were occupied with the car-buying clients. The sales agents were busy making deals with them. The big hall was covered with cars inside the floor, and had occupied the space. Linda approached the reception area and inquired about Stacy, who worked in the accounts department. The receptionist called Stacy, who should be on the way out shortly.

"Hi, Linda, nice to see you after a long time."

They both hugged and looked at each other critically. Stacy was a medium-size lady with short blond hair, light makeup, in maroon-colored business suit and black shoes that matched her perfectly. She looked smart, a little mature, and poignant in her dealings and behavior.

"Hi, Stacy, this is Pemba, my fiancée."

Pemba shook the tiny and soft hand of Stacy.

"What can I do to help you, Linda?"

"He likes to buy a GMC pickup."

"Sure, let me get you a salesman."

Stacy led them to a corner table where a salesman was holding a phone but not chatting.

"Hi, Brandon, this is my friend Linda. If you have time, could you show them the GMC pickup?"

"Sure, Stacy, let me finish this call, and I will take care of them."

Stacy left them under the care of Brandon, who wrapped up the phone conversation quickly and asked Linda, "Hi, Linda, should we go to the pickup lot?"

They followed Brandon. In the lot, there were numerous pickups—all colors—shining and attracting new buyers.

"Any particular color you prefer?"

"Silver."

"Automatic or manual driver?"

Pemba did not understood the question Brandon put. He looked toward Linda.

"Automatic, Brandon," Linda made it easy for Pemba.

"Pemba, are you going to haul heavy stuff or light?"

Linda explained to Pemba about Brandon's question; again, this time also he was confused.

"Light stuff."

Out of twenty pickups, Brandon suggested silver 1987 B automatic truck. Since Pemba did not have insurance, Linda had to test-drive the truck. The truck was of middle size, very sleek, and drove smooth, like a boat. After the test-drive, Pemba made the decision to buy, and they went to Brandon's cubicle.

Brandon called Stacy and reported to her about the decision on the truck and gave the stock number to her for details. Stacy talked to the sales manager and called Brandon back.

"Brandon, waive dealership charge, reduce 10 percent on the cost, and make a final paper."

Since Pemba did not have any credit, the paper was made keeping Linda as a co-signer—who had good credit score. They got at 2 percent interest rate finance for sixty months, with no down payment, at $195 a month. When the deal was done and the paperwork was finished, Pemba got the key and got the truck. Linda asked Pemba to follow him and drive carefully.

Without any incident, they reached home. Pemba parked his truck behind Linda's car. Immediately, Linda called the car insurance agent at State Farm and enrolled Pemba for comprehensive vehicle insurance for $65 a month.

"Thanks, my dear, for the car and the insurance."

"Oh Pemba, do not be silly. If I do not help, who else will?"

"Are we doing anything else this afternoon?" Linda asked.

"Nothing particular. Why?" Pemba replied

"I was thinking of going to Home Depot for a job application," Pemba expressed his interest.

"Sure, let me go with you."

Pemba was eager to drive the pickup truck, and Linda sat on the passenger's seat.

"Please go and see the manager," Linda advised.

Pemba met a tall, short-bearded, rough-skinned, and rough-hand person with overall jeans who appeared to be a very active person.

"Hi, I am Peter. What can I do for you?"

"Hello, I am Pemba. I am looking for a job."

"Sure, Pemba. Get the application from my office, and return as soon as possible. I need someone immediately in my lumber department."

Pemba was happy to get the application form and reported to Linda about the brief talk with the store manager.

"In that case, please complete the form and give it back," Linda suggested

Pemba had not understood many aspects of the form. Linda helped him complete and dropped him back at the manager's office.

On the way home, they dropped by the grocery market and picked up their next week's provisions. Pemba picked up some goat meat, green vegetables, and lots of fruits, along with some wine and bourbon. On the way back home, Linda talked to Pemba about his personal matters.

"Darling, wouldn't you like to go to school?"

"Yes, I have a plan, not now, maybe later," Pemba replied.

"Sure, but schooling will help you land a good job, darling. By the way, Dorje from the monastery has invited us tomorrow. He wants to meet you."

"I would love to go there," Pemba replied.

"Also, we have to discuss our small marriage ceremony there," Linda suggested.

"Darling, I really love you a lot because you think of everything."

"You're welcome. Of course, we need to."

The following day, they went to Dorje's monastery to meet him.

"Hi, Linda, how are you?" Dorje hugged Linda after they had entered the monastery.

It looked as if the place was in a spring cleaning mood. All carpets were folded neatly and placed in one corner of the hall. The floors were mopped, window curtains taken off, and everything looked like a barren tree without leaves.

"Sorry for the mess. This is all for the Buddha Jayanti celebrations next month."

"Do not worry, I understand. By the way, this is Pemba, my fiancée."

Pemba was more than pleased to see Dorje and gave him a big smile and a warm handshake.

"I understand you are from the Phaplu area. I have a cousin in Junbesi monastery."

"Really?"

"Yes, he has been there for the last five years." Facing Linda, Dorje asked, "So when are you getting married?"

"June. We also need a small ceremony to observe Pemba's tradition here in the monastery."

"Do you have any particular day?"

"How about the last week of June, say, around the 28th?"

"Let me check our activities calendar for the month of June… Yes, Linda, that date is open, and we have no activities."

"Okay then, let's do a reservation."

"Done."

"How about the Lama who will supervise the ritual?"

"Do not worry about that, Pemba. I will settle everything."

Monday, Pemba woke up around ten. He prepared a light breakfast and enjoyed it. That day, he had an omelet, toast, apricot jam, and orange juice. He also had a leisurely bath. The phone rang. Pemba picked it up from the corridor wall.

"Hi, may I talk to Pemba?"

"Speaking."

"Hi, Pemba, this is Melinda from the human resources office of Home Depot."

"Yes, Melinda, how may I help you?"

"This is regarding your job application."

"Yes."

"We need your work permit or another document to work, or your visa status."

"I am on a fiancée visa that is stamped on the passport."

"Can you bring the passport to our office to make a copy?"

"Sure, can I come now?"

"Of course."

Without losing a minute, Pemba dressed up in jeans and a dark polo shirt and left for the Home Depot. He gave the passport to the office clerk, who made a copy and returned the passport to Pemba, requesting he wait for a call. Pemba returned home reluctantly; he had been hoping they would make the decision then and there, but it had not happened as expected. He had no choice but to wait for the phone call. The phone rang around three.

"Hello."

"Hi, darling, what are you doing?"

"Waiting for a phone call."

"How did you know I would be calling you?"

"I was waiting for a call from Home Depot." Pemba explained everything about the visit to them about two hours earlier.

"Don't worry, Pemba. They will call by the end of the day, or maybe tomorrow morning."

"Will they allow me to work on a fiancée visa?"

"Yes, they should. Sometime after we're married, they will send a residency card."

"Okay, hope for the best."

"Dear, I have to go. Will talk to you later."

It was almost quarter to five. The phone call from Home Depot had not come, and Pemba gave up hope for the day. *Well*, Pemba thought, *life goes on.* If Home Depot doesn't call, he might look for another job. Pemba had experienced lots of struggles in life. He had seen life's sweetness, bitterness, and ugliness. But somehow, he always followed the tracks that led him to success. A teacher's city life with low pay, life of Sherpa porter, cook, and guide with Mountain Travel, and now an immigrant to a promised land of millions.

Linda returned from work. She looked tired and had signs of fatigue on her beautiful face.

"Honey, I am home."

"What happened? You look tired today."

"Work, dear, and it has been increasing rapidly with my promotion recently. Hey, honey, everyone in the office wants to see you, including my boss, Mr. Smith."

"What was your answer?"

"They have to wait until our reception, nothing before that. Oh, did Home Depot call you?"

"No, they did not."

Linda got closer to Pemba and gave him a French kiss—warm, tantalizing, and alluring. "Do not worry, honey; they will call you tomorrow."

"Sweetie, let's have a unique and refreshing dinner tonight." Linda proposed.

"On one condition: you should also give me a unique lovemaking position," Pemba joked.

"Well, sweetie, if you want that prior to dinner, I am ready."

"Not now, silly, I smell bad. I must have a shower and only after dinner it will be proper."

They hugged each other, kissing and caressing all over their bodies, until Linda became flushed and felt Pemba's swollen middle part.

Linda whispered in a sexy voice, "Do you love my little sister?"

Pemba had hard time to understand. "What is that?"

She whispered again in his ear, "Silly, do you like my vagina?"

"My little brother likes it more than me."

"How about you?"

"I like your upper portion and boob."

"Okay then, I will seal my little sister."

It was good and at the same time silly, but both liked funny jokes. Linda especially preferred to talk dirty during their intercourse, but Pemba had to learn new words and American slang.

Linda went to take a shower. Pemba cooked goat meat in the pressure cooker with lots of spices. He preferred the really hot chilies they'd bought from a Mexican grocery shop, but Linda was not used to eating such spicy food. So he took a certain portion of the meat apart for Linda and added spices and hot chilies to the rest. He could smell the aromatic flavor coming out of the steam from the cooker. He thought it should be a good combination of food and exciting lovemaking this evening.

Linda came to the kitchen area after the shower. Pemba opened a chardonnay white wine and gave it to her. After a sip, Linda asked, "Oh my, which wine is this?"

"Spanish, why?"

"Outstanding taste and very smooth."

"Tell me honestly, is it better than me?" Pemba tried to be romantic, witty, and used his sense of humor at the same time.

Linda, who was sitting in another corner of the kitchen, raised her finger and indicated for Pemba to come closer, whispering in his ear with very warm breath and a husky voice, "Which do you want, a boy or a girl first?"

"What about you?" Pemba asked.

"I want to wait another five years." Linda replied.

"Why five-year wait? Any particular reason?" Pemba asked.

"Yes, my career is not yet in full swing."

"Honey, me too. I want to settle here first."

"That makes sense," Linda supported.

"Okay then, that is a deal."

"Deal." Both shook hands and exchanged a warm and passionate kiss.

"So what is for dinner?"

"It is me."

"Of course, I will have you, but a little later, okay?"

"I cooked goat meat. I do not know if you will like it or not, and special spaghetti for you."

"Pemba, I will not prefer meat. You may have it, but I love spaghetti."

Pemba loved his dinner that evening: meat, rice with some slightly sautéed vegetables and mango pickle.

The next day, around three in the afternoon, the phone rang. The manager of Home Depot was on the line. "Hi, Pemba, this is Peter from Home Depot."

"Yes, Sir, good afternoon."

"Congratulations, your job application is approved, and you are hired."

"Thank you, Sir."

"Hey, man, you do not have to address me as Sir. Just call me Peter."

"Okay, Peter."

"Listen, can you come now and complete the paperwork, and can you start Monday?"

"Sure, I can," Pemba replied promptly.

Pemba was not doing much except some small domestic chores. He rushed to Home Depot and completed all the paperwork. He was happy and excited to start the new work on Monday.

Monday, he reached work fifteen minutes earlier and reported to his immediate supervisor, who assigned him to the store's lumber department. Mostly his job was to help and assist contractors in choosing their construction supplies. He liked the job and was slowly getting used to his regular assignments and being familiar with the contractors.

Since Pemba had excellent public relations with his clients, the management and immediate supervisor were very happy with his performance. The first day of his job assignment, he met Peter and requested a six-week planned leave for his marriage and honeymoon trip to Europe from the middle part of June to the end of July. Peter congratulated him and filled out the vacation request. He would grant the leave but would be without pay as he had not completed ninety days' work schedule.

Since the store was busy on weekends, Pemba's off days were scheduled on Tuesdays and Wednesdays. Linda showed dislike of his off days. She had been looking forward to spending all weekends with Pemba and enjoying her off time with him. But they had no option at the moment—although it was gratifying that Pemba had been granted six weeks' vacation after working briefly in Home Depot. In the course of his regular contact with the contractors at the store, Pemba had become close to a small Japanese contractor Tanaka, who did construction work for the county.

They both liked each other. Tanaka was a middle-aged man, middle height, with a tough build, sharp, penetrating black eyes, a smiling face, and a totally pleasant personality. Tanaka had an accent when he talked, but his fluency and use of proper words in his dialogue were admirable. Tanaka lived near Pemba and Linda's residence and had an American wife and two doll-like children—a boy of ten and a girl age six. Pemba had been to his house a couple of times. His wife, Charlotte, had invited Linda and him for dinner, but somehow, Pemba had not yet been able to manage time. Charlotte was tall and slim, with blond hair and blue eyes. She was from a Midwestern small town somewhere in Wisconsin. She worked as a teacher in high school, teaching history.

Time flew. Linda could not believe it was already the second week of June, and they should be in Ohio in a couple of days.

Her wedding gown was not complete yet; she needed a final trial a day later. Her jewelry, makeup set, and other personal essentials were on the list but she needed to go to Macy's and select and finalize the next day. Her mother had set up wedding rehearsal in the church two days prior. Linda's mother had gone through the invitation list and made sure her school friends were all included. For the reception, a community hall with a capacity of one hundred and fifty people had been reserved. A tiny town with a population around fourteen thousand, Seven Hills did not have a large banquet hall in the big hotels like Hyatt or Marriott. Besides, this fit in their parents' budget.

Pemba also had a simple wedding preparation but not as elaborate as Linda's. He just needed a black tuxedo with matching shirt, tie, and shoes. Since Mihara could not attend the wedding in Ohio, they would find somebody else as his best friend in Seven Hills. Linda booked a flight with United on June 16th to Cleveland, and her parents' place was within a half-hour drive. The date for the ceremony was fixed on June 19th.

Immediately after the marriage ceremony, they would return to Los Angeles on the 22nd; the 28th would be the Sherpa traditional ceremony at the monastery, and on the 30th they had a small reception at the Marriott for the friends in Los Angeles. And they would leave for their honeymoon in Europe to London, Paris, Rome, and Greece on July 1st. Their schedule was not only tight but hectic. Obviously, the couple would not have complete rest until they were in Europe.

Well, this was life—sometimes hectic, sometimes restful, sometimes in between, and one cannot complain. It goes on like that until finally, you are no more to be seen after death, and you vanish beyond the horizon of the earth, the moon, and even Mars. Nobody knows where you come from and where you will be going; that is the reality of life. It is also true for Pemba, Linda, you and me, and for all living creatures.

Pemba's trend of thought was leading him to a new dimension. This kind serious, deep philosophical matter was a subject he would not like to think about at this moment—maybe later in life.

They arrived in Cleveland on the scheduled flight. Linda's parents, along with her sister, Samantha— looking cute like a Barbie doll in a red frock, red shoes, and small matching hat—were waiting at the baggage claim area.

"Oh my, you must be Pemba." Linda's dad hugged Pemba, and they both looked at each other critically but warmly.

Linda's mother scrutinized Pemba in a more filtering manner, analyzing Pemba's personality that might or might not fit with into their little conservative society in the small town. Linda knew her mother was the kind of lady who always believed in a little show-off among her friends and relatives. Linda was rather a pragmatic lady and did not believe in the artificial aspects of her society. She could not tolerate the character assassination, gossip, and false pretenders in the small town more. Pemba faced Samantha and hugged the little doll.

"How are you, Samantha, my dear cutie-pie?"

She expressed a very shy and not-so-warm reception. She replied in a low and shaky voice, "I am fine, thank you."

Pemba thought her behavior was shy because she had a new person in the family and she would adjust as time goes by.

In the meantime, Linda's mother asked Pemba, "Pemba, dear, how was the flight?"

"Good, very smooth."

"Did you like Los Angeles?"

"Yes. It is a big city, and I love Linda's house, which is really cozy," Pemba replied.

"Linda, rest today and tomorrow. The day after, at five in the evening, we have a wedding rehearsal at the church."

"Who else will be there for the rehearsal?" Linda asked.

"Our family, Aunt Elizabeth, some of my close friends, and Father Joseph, of course," Mother explained.

"How long will it last?" Linda was curious.

"Maybe over an hour." Mother replied promptly.

"Are my school friends invited?"

"Everyone on your list, except Wendy, who is out of town."

"I choose your close friend Marla for your best friend."

After a half an hour drive, they approached a driveway with lovely green lawns on both sides of the garage heading straight to a one-story house with red bricks, beautiful roof, red stone on the house all over, with white paint in the windows and door. The house was surrounded with tall trees, looked like a resort in the jungle, and was very quiet. In the backyard, there was a flower bed on the left side, and one part was filled with vegetables—red ripe tomatoes, Okura, cucumbers, and green lettuces for salads. They were grown in an organized manner, and someone had done fantastic profession-al-like work.

The house had three bedrooms of comfortable sizes, two and a half baths, and a large garage—which had a capacity of over two cars. The house was big, maybe more than 3,500 square feet, clean with shining wooden floor inside. The kitchen had up-to-date appliances.

Linda and Pemba were given separate rooms, as they were not supposed to be in the same room before the marriage—a tradition that still prevailed in the small town. This was the idea of Linda's mother, her parents had lots of argument in this subject. Finally, her mother had won the argument.

Linda tried to argue with her mother, "Mom, we have been sleeping together at my house."

"That is your house; you do whatever you like. But in this my house; my rules prevail."

Linda thought it was no use arguing with her mother as she would never concur with Linda's opinion.

The next day, it took only an hour to see all the interesting places in Seven Hills. There was not much to see or do. Pemba liked the small downtown area. It looked like some dramatic small city he had seen in Western movies that had unique culture, style, and magnetism. He loved this kind of small farmer's market that had a little resemblance to his *haat* bazaar in Sallaeri at Phaplu.

The wedding rehearsal was supervised smoothly and nicely by Father Joseph, and they all had to practice three times. Linda walked the aisle, holding her dad's hand; the flower girl walked slowly in her style, and they practiced a couple of times the way Linda and Pemba would be facing each other in proper gesture and pose while observing the "I do" solemnly in front of the crowd and Father Joseph.

On the wedding day, everything turned into a perfect order, and the formality was completed in a proper style and to the satisfaction of the church authority, parent, relatives, and friends.

In fact, the ceremony was simple but graceful and impressive. Linda's friends admired the function, and everyone commented on gorgeous looks of the couple. They mentioned that Pemba was an excessively handsome man and a suitable match for Linda, but there were a few in the corner who whispered in a different tone.

"She married a foreigner," a conservative redneck of the town said. Others nodded.

They arrived home a little tired with the formalities in Seven Hills. They had finished the family part, but here in Los Angeles, another show awaited to be performed. They had less than a week to make preparations. Thank God, both of them did not have to go to work until August.

When Linda played her messages on the phone, there was a message from Mr. Smith to drop by the office after she returned from Ohio. Linda had no idea about the reason of the call. Normally, the office would not call a staff when he or she was on vacation, unless something was important. It was already too late to call, as they had reached home just after eight thirty in the evening. She thought she would go to the office late the following morning with Pemba. But she immediately dropped the idea as she remembered that she would not expose Pemba until the reception. Let it be a mystery and curiosity until then.

The next morning, after finishing the usual chores and breakfast, Pemba, with working gloves and garden tools, wanted to use the morning in the garden that needed his attention badly. Linda advised him that she needed to go see her boss in the office as he'd left a voice mail on the phone.

Soon Linda was at the office.

"Congratulations!"

The moment Linda entered Smith's office, she was surprised by the excitement in his voice, and his body language expressed a kind of pleasant happiness.

"Thank you, Mr. Smith."

"Have a seat, my dear."

He picked up a white unusual-sized envelope from his right drawer and handed it over to her. "This is a gift from me and the office."

When Linda opened the envelope, it had a corporate check of $25,000 signed by Smith.

"This is too much, Mr. Smith."

"No way, this also includes some of your Europe honeymoon expenses."

"Thanks."

"Listen, Kathy already booked the banquet hall at the Marriott, and I think she's almost finalized the menu and beverages. Please look into it—you may add some items of your choice. Further, Linda, I am taking the privilege to invite our close clients, press, and TV stations on your wedding reception if it is OK with you."

"I have no objection, Mr. Smith."

"Great. Get busy and I'll see you at the reception and after your wonderful Europe tour at work."

"I am really obliged, Mr. Smith."

"You deserve it. Bye for now."

Linda left the office promptly without meeting anyone as she had to take care of lots of activities within a period of one week. She was pleased with the unusual and unexpected gift from the office. She should share the good news with Pemba first. She rushed home. Pemba was still in the garden, working.

"Sweetie, please wash your hands and come inside. I need to share a very good news with you."

Pemba seemed excited when she said very good news; he got closer to her.

"Okay, kiss me first; only then will I give you the news."

Pemba gave her a passionate French kiss, putting his warm and firm tongue inside her juicy mouth and keeping it there, holding each other in a firm grip. They had no control and moved to the bedroom in the middle of the day and made love like there was no tomorrow.

On Linda's suggestion, they were on the way to the Marriott Hotel to discuss the menu preparation and beverage selection for the banquet on June 29th.

"Hi, I am Linda. Could we see Anthony, the banquet manager, please?"

"Sure, just a minute."

They were waiting in the hotel lobby. A tall, overweight man in a dark suit with a salt-and-pepper beard and black eye appeared.

"Hi, Linda, this is Bob. I am the banquet manager."

"Oh, hi, I am Linda, and this is my husband, Pemba. I am here to talk about our wedding reception on the twenty-ninth."

"Oh, yes, I was talking with Kathy," Bob replied.

"Yes, she is from my office."

"What can I do for you?"

"We are expecting about one hundred and twenty-five guests. We have chosen Hawaii theme for our wedding reception."

"That sounds great."

"What can you do for us?"

"Well, Linda, that theme is nothing new for us. We have done it a number of times in the past."

"What are the things you will do for us?"

"Can we go to my office and discuss in detail?"

In the office, Bob ordered coffee, and they began a serious discussion.

"This is the brochure for our Hawaii wedding reception. You have hula singers, dancers, and Hawaii music. We prepare the aloha pig luau for the food and illuminate the premise with Hawaiian torches all around the garden. We include some typical juice, like coconut and pineapple, along with tropical exotic cocktails. To be short and precise, we will create a complete Hawaiian atmosphere in the garden. One more thing, your guests must come in Hawaiian outfits, shirts and skirts, with-printed outfits. No suit and business dresses are allowed."

"That is very interesting and exactly what I had in mind."

"Linda, do not worry; we will take care of everything as this kind of program is not new for us. You might be surprised when party ends."

Bob showed the menu they had agreed upon with Kathy, which looked just fine.

The next day, they visited the monastery and met Dorje. Linda left some money as advance for decorations and to purchase necessary things for the wedding ceremony on the 28th. Dorje planned to invite around fifty people from his community, and had arranged the catering from a local Tibetan restaurant. Both Linda and Pemba seemed happy with Dorje's preparations, and they hoped everything would run smoothly.

That day was the day for monastery marriage ceremony the 28th of June.

On the day, Dorje decorated the place with multi-color banners around the place of ceremony. He placed two decorated chairs for the couple in a slightly higher stage area with the floor cover with rich colorful Tibetan carpet. In front of the couple in the open space there were about sixty chairs for the guests arranged neatly. In the kitchen the caterer was preparing the food for guests. A monk in front of the couple was praying and reciting some mantras for blessing the couple. The empty chairs in front of the dash were filling fast with the guests. The atmosphere was jubilant. Guests, couple and people who were in charge of arrangements were all in happy mood.

"In Buddhist society," Dorje explained to Linda in a low murmuring voice "there is no spiritual ceremony of marriage. They are mostly concerned with experiencing enlightenment. However, the world is a place where we live and work on perfecting our awareness in that sense in which people are interested with the world. The core of Buddhism is freedom from attachment; the purpose of marriage ceremony seems to contradict the notion. But there is no paradox between practicing Buddhism and marriage. As in Christianity, Buddhism, has no set rules that a couple must be married to have sex. As per Buddhism philosophy two people could share a life together, love each other but be free of attachment. Marriage and attachment are not necessarily connected; love is love and attachment is attachment."

Dorje further continued, "The genealogy of the Sherpa still follows clans that descended through one's father. They still follow the tradition and accordingly, one is not allowed to marry within one's clan. But however, marriage with someone from one's mother's clan is permissible if they are not related within three generation. There are basically five stage of marriage in Sherpa society. *Sodena* is engagement, *Demchang* is the proper arrangement, *Trichang* is to fix month and the year, *Pechang* is to set the actual date and *Zendi*, the final ceremony when the woman comes to lives with man. Buddhist monks normally perform marriage ceremony and recite mantras or prayers to bless the couple and afterwards rest of the ceremony is handle by a judge who supervises the legal service."

Pemba was familiar with these procedures but Dorje explained them to Linda in a very precise manner.

After hearing about the Sherpa way of marriage from Dorje, Linda was curious and put a question, "But Dorje, since marriage is a celebration of love and close union of two people, they will naturally become attached within that relationship. How could they detach emotionally?"

"Linda, your question is logical, but remember the earth is a temporary shelter for our short life. If you get attached with it too intimately, you will not get the ultimate goal which is *nirvana* in Buddhism."

After some time the entire ceremony came to an end, guests congratulated the couple and blessed them. The gift which were brought by them were placed on the table right side of ceremony area. The pile looked colorful and bright in wrapping papers.

The Marriott provided complimentary honeymoon suits for the day of the party. Linda and Pemba checked into the hotel at around three in the afternoon. Around five, both Pemba and Linda strolled around the garden, where the party was being prepared for this evening. After critical observation, they were satisfied with the decoration, setting, and music setup with digital sound. It looked gorgeous. The torchlight created a different, magical Hawaiian environment.

In the distance, Kathy waved a hand toward Linda and came over slowly. Kathy looked gorgeous in a printed Hawaiian long gown that matched this evening's weather: around seventy, crisp and pleasant by all means.

"Hi, sweetie, I will take care of everything here. You go and dress up and get ready. Where is Pemba?"

"He was just here. Maybe he left to meet the beverage manager."

The gathering slowly started coming around seven. The guests were coming; gents were mostly in Hawaiian printed shirts and ladies in printed long evening gowns. Marriott had not left any effect to make the garden a piece of Waikiki setup except the beach.

The central large meadow with green grass felt like a soft woolen carpet, surrounded by lush green plants. A variety of flowers covered all around the light place in such a way that it did not hurt directly, and was conceived from eyesight but it created a wonderful impact in the garden. The light Hawaiian music floating in the background provided a soothing and relaxing atmosphere, trying to create replica of "hang loose" Hawaiian theme.

A little bit further left from the center, a stage was set for hula dancers and Hawaiian live musicians. Toward the right side of the lovely garden, a counter was set up for the cocktails; all sorts of Hawaiian cocktails and fruit drinks were displayed in a most articulate and attractive manner. Far in the southeast part of the garden, they prepared a luau pit for the pig meat cooked underground through the hot stone that transferred powerful taste of the meat more than a regular barbecue. It could be a great attraction for the guests.

The guests' presence was becoming denser each moment, and a crowd was gathering in a very unusual and in attractive environment. The highlight was the guests' casual dresses with Hawaiian outfits that provided free and friendly atmosphere.

Besides the other guests, Pemba had also invited some of his people, including Dorje and the Lama who performed their ceremony at the monastery.

Linda was wearing a turquoise blue long gown with a printed white orchid pattern. Pemba also had a similar Hawaiian shirt, and they just looked like an unusual couple from out of the world. All the office employees and Linda's other friends—including Amanda, Allure, and Mihara—seemed to be enjoying the party.

Linda noticed Mr. Smith slowly approaching the stage where the Hawaiian musicians were playing, and he approached the microphone that had been placed on the stage. Kathy signaled the musicians to stop the music, and Mr. Smith began to speak in a low, humming-like musical voice, "Good evening, ladies and gentlemen!"

The murmuring voices stopped; all around, guests were attracted toward the stage, and everyone stopped talking. They listened to Mr. Smith.

"Linda is in fact my employee, but I treat her like my own baby." There was a pause. "With you all, I am here to wish her the best in her future life."

Another long pause.

"I am also happy she chose somebody from the other side of the world as her partner. Let us welcome Pemba to America and to our society."

All the guests looked toward Pemba, who raised his right hand and slightly bowed his head toward the crowd.

"In my brief introduction, I found him a refined and articulate human being. Let us all wish a happy conjugal life to this dynamic couple, and let us enjoy the party. Thanks for coming, and make the evening a memorable one."

The party picked up to full swing after the short speech and lasted until just before midnight. Everyone enjoyed the music, hula dance, and luau dinner with a variety of cocktails. The guests left reluctantly as they needed to go long distances through the notorious Los Angeles traffic.

***

CHAPTER FOURTEEN

July 1988

London's political noise was still warm and fresh. The June 11 election results again gave Margaret Thatcher the mandate as the next prime ministers after the third consecutive election victory on the part of the Conservative Party. The Party campaign was based on a few basic foundations, such as strong economy, lower taxes, and a desirable level of unemployment and inflation. The Iron Lady, many world leaders believed, had made marvelous achievements. The media and the newspapers were still occupied with her news and political achievements.

The next day, the guided trip to London City was vibrant, entertaining, and enjoyable. The guide briefly explained that London was the world's finance capital—a historical place that spanned over two millenniums.

The city that was founded in first century by the Romans in the bank of Thames River had grown to a complex of multi-lingual, multi-ethnic combination from Europe, Africa, Middle East, and South Asia, and Commonwealth countries. Every race grew and thrived. It had developed as a center for trade, commerce, and banking. It grew with monasteries, hospitals, inns and hotels, and established theaters with interesting international-dimension themes and legends.

The tour was conducted on a luxurious, cozy coach. They traveled around Big Ben, Saint Paul's Cathedral, Parliament building, Westminster Abbey and West End. They also witnessed the fascinating Change of the Guards by brilliant pomp and pageantry of queen's foot guards as they marched in the most eye-catching way in red tunics and bearskin hats in Buckingham Palace.

Linda loved the garden in front of the palace just outside the front gate. The entire London City, Pemba found, was fascinating, well organized, and extremely attractive. He was impressed with people's manner, orderly fashion of transportations, two-story red buses, and underground movement of the city. It had some kind of sophistication and slightly eccentric, but it provided British charm.

Another magnificent highlight of London tour was the attractive night boat tour of *Harmony* that began from Embankment Pier of Central London on a magnificent glass-walled vessel dinner cruise for about three hours with four course meals on the River Thames. The luxurious boat swept the magnificent skyline view of the colorful London with astonishing spectacle of the Parliament House, which looked much different and more beautiful than daylight glowing with golden shine. South Bank reflected the modern museum; North Bank to the famous Saint Paul's Cathedral; and they appreciated the wonderful sight of Shakespeare's Globe, Big Ben, and remarkable close view of Tower Bridge illuminated in the dark London cloud at the background. The multicolored reflection on the water of Thames and the various rainbow colors, created a magical surrounding that impacted everyone's mind.

Linda and Pemba were not an exception. They had the most romantic rendezvous in such out-of-the-world experiences with live jazz music, cocktails of their choice together with typical British dinner of roasted breast of Sussex chicken, fondant potatoes, grilled mushrooms, shallot and springs greens, with strawberry *bavarois* as sweet dish. The night cruise experience provided one of the most remarkable impressions on the minds of our honeymooners.

Once, Ernst Hemingway described Paris appropriately as a city of "a moveable feast"—the Château, Gothic churches, medieval street, elegant wrought-iron balcony, stunning landscape, and architecture. Superb wine, perfection in culinary arts of centuries, paintings, literatures, and small boutiques, art gallery shops—all enticed the romantic young hearts from all over the world.

It might be for wedding, celebrations, anniversary, to propose, and honeymoon, or simply to enjoy sexy getaway—Paris was the ideal destination with unlimited amenities to romantic hearts. Both Pemba and Linda's heart thrived and became vivacious once they touched the ground of Paris. They had agreed to explore the icon of France, the Eiffel Tower, which the French called the "iron lady" with affection.

On their way up to the Eiffel Tower, a polite Danish-accent young man followed them and offered his service as a guide.

Linda had little resentment for his service as it was apparent he was not French, but Pemba liked the young man's approach and hired him.

"Hi, my name is Oliver. I have been a licensed tourist guide in the tower since last three years." The way Oliver spoke had strange accent of French, Danish, and English; it was different and pleasing to hear whenever he spoke.

The sight from the top of the Tower was fascinating as Oliver explained most of the highlights of Paris. On the way down, through the elevator, Linda requested Oliver to take them to the famous lock bridge for the lovers. The taxi passed through the shadow of Eiffel Tower and the bank of River Seine; they approached the famous lock bridge. Some years ago, a new trend had been started by the love-struck sweethearts: locking padlocks onto the chain in the bridge as a sign of their eternal devotion to each other. As per the tradition, Oliver gave the padlock and key to Linda and locked one more addition among thousands in the chain of the bridge and tossed the key to Seine River. On the suggestion from Oliver, they also held each other and kissed for a long time in the middle of the bridge, and Oliver took numerous photos of them kissing. It was the tradition that if you kiss on the bridge, your love life would be happy for a long time.

The next day, the tour company organized a special tour to Louvre Museum for the group members in order to cover the museum without being on the line and with an anthropologist and experienced guide employed by the museum. It was a comprehensive tour for about three hours that included three course luncheons at the end of the tour under the pyramid dome in a royal setting. The tour, as planned, began sharp at nine from the side 'employees only' entrance to avoid the large crowd. The museum guide Andre was on the gate to receive them and escort them to a small room. He briefed them about the tour in a precise manner and highlighted they were going to watch the masterpieces of Louvre—which was popular for the artists, commoners, dignitaries, celebrities, and world leaders.

There were some questions from the group about the museum, which Andre answered politely in heavy French accent; perhaps some of the people had hard time understanding him. But everything was spoken in simple English, as many in the group understood him in spite of his heavy accent.

Andre began, "It was in the sixteenth century that the museum was established as a private collection of King Francis in his residence, Louvre Palace. He had purchased the famous painting *Mona Lisa*. The collection grew slowly with precious arts and artifacts with generous donations and royal collection. During the French Revolution, in 1793, the Louvre became a national art museum and the precious royal private collection was opened to public."

After a pauses Andre continued, "This famous museum has a collection of over one million works of art, of which currently thirty-five thousand are on display, spread out over the three wings of this magnificent former palace."

Andre continued after a brief pause, "The museum has eight groups or departments and the collection covers from medieval time to 1848 including works from early civilization of the ancient world, and works of Islamic arts. The departments were shaped and defined by the intense activities of its curators, collectors, and donors.

Currently, under Paintings, we have 215 artworks, Egyptian Antiques have 207, Greek and Roman have 275, Near Eastern antiquities have 112, Sculptures have 83, Decorative Arts have 262, Islamic Arts have 11, and Prints and Drawing have 186 excellent artworks."

The tour had begun from the ground floor of Sully Wings with the famous statue of Aphrodite, which is known as *Venus de Milo*, from Greek collection department. The statue was discovered in 1820 in the island of Milo, was donated by Louis to Louvre, and became instant fame because of its beauty and exceptional artworks. It appeared the goddess originally wore metal jewelry, such as bracelet, headband, and earrings—of which the fixation holes remained.

The next visit was to the painting department. There were numerous exotic paintings of Blanchard that were dubbed in "French Titan," which had Venetian influence and color and his care in handling female beauty. One particular painting, Aphrodite, —goddess of beauty and love, sleeping with her son—along with three nymphs with glowing, voluptuous bodies counterpointed the velvet of improvised canopy above them. This, everyone thought, was a mythological mystery.

Linda watched that particular painting for a long time. It drew the attention of Pemba too, and he asked her about the specialty in the painting.

"It is something out of the world, the body sketches are so realist and have unusual attraction. I can hardly lift my eyes from them. It is just magnificent," Linda remarked.

They moved to further painting area, and Andre stood in front of a canvas life-size paintings and explained about the painting.

"*The Coronation of Emperor Napoleon* is a masterpiece of Jacques Louis David, who was commissioned by Napoleon himself to paint the grandeur of coronation and convey the political and symbolic message blended with art and history. In order to make the painting a reality, David created wax figures and wooden symbols around his studio and used rich pallet of colors to depict velvet, satins, furs. Various artistic designs and different realistic solutions were used to create this masterpiece. The congregation of royal family, the court, and the clergy dressed in ceremonial costume provided a total realistic appearance. All the eyes are fixed on the crown of Napoleon. His mother looked from the upper level VIP balcony area."

Linda moved closer to the canvas and realized she was also a part of the congregation and one of attendants in the ceremony.

The small group now moved to a large hall with high ceilings covered with walls without windows, and in the center of the wall, a small painting of about two feet in height and one foot in width was visible from almost all corners of the large room. The room had enormous crowd and close to the painting on the left area, there was a small, protected space where the crowds were not able to reach; this was the place the museum authority allocated for the special group to watch the world-famous painting, *Mona Lisa*.

The painting was created by Italian Renaissance man Leonardo da Vinci, who was multitalented in mathematics, writing, geology, music, engineering, and painting. He used new technique and improved color and method in the painting. The skin of *Mona Lisa* appeared to glow from layers of transparent oils. The mystery of *Mona Lisa*, actually—who sat for the pose and background landscape—is still unsolved; it is believed that she was an Italian lady, but it is more likely an imagination of Leonardo only. In 1935, during the Second World War, the painting disappeared in an ambulance due to fear of destruction or possibility of being stolen and went into hiding during the war period. Also, once, an employee stole the painting, considering that it belonged to Italy, and France did not deserve it. He tried to sell it to an Italian for money but was caught while making the transaction.

The *Mona Lisa* "smile" has become a trademark of Leonardo. For hundreds of years, the unique quality of the slight upturn on the left side of the mouth had provided her an enigmatic look that has fascinated the people of Europe. It became a fad some time in Europe, to smile like *Mona Lisa*—with upturn of the left side of the mouth. Husbands and lovers forced their wives and lovers to act in that manner. The small piece of art with two feet height and one feet width surpassed all popularity and imagination, and created a significant, powerful emotion throughout the world and occupied everyone's mind and uninterrupted attention in the museum with calmness and serenity.

The group was hustled to pyramid dome by Andre for a three-course gourmet French cuisine lunch and glasses of champagne. The restaurant was highly decorated with comfortable high chairs. The table had the most expensive utensils with cutlery, cut glasses, and cute gold-coated flower vases along with highly attractive fresh, colorful flowers. The spoon, knife, and fork appeared to be real heavy bright yellow gold.

For lunch, both Pemba and Linda chose seafood soup, salad *nicoise,* a traditional French salad with mixed green tossed potatoes, green beans, boiled eggs and olive topped with anchovies. The champagne they served was Le Blanc. Le Blanc was very smooth, fresh, and energetic. The food tasted Ambrosial and very fulfilling, and its nice taste lingered for a long time in the mouth. So far, it was the best lunch they had in Paris.

The ancient adage, 'All roads lead to Rome' seemed to be pertinent still in modern times. Rome had been seducing the visitors for its history, legend, and monuments along with interesting art, music, and religion. The Vatican was a sacred pilgrimage to millions of Christians and home of the Pope. Vatican Museums contained masterpieces of paintings, sculptures, and other works of art collected by the popes through the centuries. Saint Peter's Basilica was the most decorated and largest church in the world. Observe the ceiling of Sistine Chapel and walk in the footprint of Michelangelo, Bernini, and Raphael!

In order to really understand the culture and soul of Rome, one had to stand among its many wonderful trademarks and attractions, such as the grand Colosseum, a spectator's central oval arena; Roman Forum, an ancient central place for social and political activity; witness Trevi Fountain, a masterpiece of sculpture and architecture wonder; and throw a coin, as everyone else did, and remember the romantic movie *Three Coins and the Fountain.*"

It was a very soothing when Pemba and Linda arrived in the Eternal City. They were on the way to Westin Excelsior, one of the luxury hotels in Rome. The hotel occupied a large area in the center of the town surrounded by chaotic and unmanageable traffic; but once inside the hotel, the atmosphere was serene, quiet, and pleasing with rich decorations. Their room was one of the best rooms they had so far, better than in London and Paris: a large-size room with thick, mild yellow carpet printed with flower design. The wallpaper was of dark-maroon color with tiny flowers. The bed had luxurious design and was covered with pure white sheet, two yellow glittering similar chandeliers, one large, another slightly small, a covered bed, and the living area. The room had a few but gorgeous dark wood luxurious tables and chairs embroidered with golden borders. The color pattern and decoration was soothing and pleasing to most luxurious taste. Both of them had best night's sleep, which they spent embracing each other.

Sharp at nine in the morning, the luxurious tour bus left Westin with fifteen special groups from America for Saint Peter's Basilica, Sistine Chapel, and Vatican Museums for a three-hour walking tour. Their tour this morning was especially administered by a Vatican expert guide that arranged and skipped the line, avoiding general public tourist crowd in exclusive access through reserved entranceway to all the main event.

The tour company hired a guide that had good English and had special personalized commentary. The tour bus came to a stop in front of the gorgeous Saint Peter's Basilica. The large oval shaped Basilica was fairly large in size, and the top of the building was decorated with various saints. It gave an unusual impact in human mind. The square in itself provided life-size impact and created a wonderful feeling.

In the entrance of Basilica, a tall, sharp figure with dark jacket, dark-blue gin, and smoky shirt and a silk muffler around his neck provided an impressive personality typical of the Italian man. He approached the group and introduced himself, "Hi, my name is Avitus. I will be your guide for the walking tour of the Basilica, Sistine Chapel, and Vatican Museums this morning."

The group members also enthusiastically answered his hello and some shook hands with him. Avitus seemed to have good command in English but had heavy Italian accent.

The moment the exclusive group entered the church, everybody had the expression of ah . . . ouh.

In fact, the gorgeous size with out-of-the-world decorations transferred everyone to a fantasy land beyond one's comprehension.

The narration of Avitus began slowly with necessary pause, and it seemed he struggled to choose the appropriate words.

"This magnificent and the largest church in the world is 145 feet high and 614 feet long, and is the most famous Catholic church in the world. Its construction began in 1506 and was completed in 1626. This Basilica, now the pope's principal church, was built as per the tradition of the burial site of Saint Peter—one of the twelve disciples of Jesus and the first bishop of Rome. The church is admiring for its Renaissance sculptures, Baroque architectures, and decoration of Saint Peter's involving the greatest old masters of those days—including Bernini, Raphael, Alberti, and Michelangelo."

The tour took about an hour going through all the statues. On the right side, they observed the Michelangelo creation of Mary and her dead son in the lap. It provided intense emotions. At the end, on the left side, was a bronze creation of Saint Peter's statue, sitting in a chair, holding up the right hand slightly in an impressive gesture. People were sliding up to touch or kiss his outstretched foot; by now, one could notice it worn to shiny nub.

Saint Veronica's statue was holding the veil or handkerchief she used to wipe Jesus's face. It was said to have retained a miraculous imprint of Christ's face.

Finally, they were escorted by an elevator to watch Saint Peter's Square and surrounding area from the top. They also witnessed the dome prepared by Michelangelo—which was 450 feet from the ground and 139 feet in diameter. The top really offered a spectacular view, and it was amazing to be under the dome.

Now, everyone was eager to see the famous ceilings of Sistine Chapel, but prior to their entry to the chapel, Avitus warned that no one was allowed immodest dress, flash photography, and touching the work of arts. Moreover, photography and filming was forbidden in the Sistine Chapel.

The dramatic entrance to Sistine Chapel was stunning. The Chapel was most famous for the interior painting. The name 'Sistine' was derived from Pope Sixtus, who gave his name for the outstanding church. This Church was still used to elect the new pope, and the chimney in the roof indicated, by the color of smoke, whether a pope was elected or not. Black smoke indicated no unanimous decision, and white smoke indicated election of the Pope. The tradition still continued.

Earlier than 1508, the ceiling of the Church was painted blue and was covered with golden stars. In 1508, Pope Julius II hired Michelangelo to paint the ceiling of the chapel. Although Michelangelo considered himself as sculpture, his painting skills had not been recognized, and he was reluctant in taking the uncomfortable painting job in the ceiling. The reason why Pope Julius gave the lofty job was to instigate two artistic rivals, Raphael and Bramante, so that Michelangelo—who was less accustomed to painting—might grow so aggravated with Julius that he would want to depart from Rome altogether. Rather than falling on his face, however, Michelangelo rose on the task of masterpiece creation and surprised the Romans and produced one of the most memorable pieces of the world. The ceiling was painted on the basis of around several scenes of Old Testament, beginning with the creation of the world and ending at the story of Noah with the flood.

The paintings were oriented in such a way that to view them right side up, the viewer should be facing the altar wall. Above the altar, the sequence began with creation and progressed toward the entrance of the chapel. The most significant scenes on the ceilings were his frescoes of the creation of Adam and the fall of Adam and Eve and expulsion from Eden. It was emotional, and he had put such a vivid aspect that inspired most of the people to appreciate his paintings then and now.

After passing the courtyard, they moved through a less congested area, and arrived outside the Basilica to catch their bus again. As per the schedule, they were supposed to have lunch in the hotel and complete afternoon tour to Colosseum, Forum area, and Trevi Fountain at the end.

The bus halted at the Westin Hotel. Linda and Pemba followed the tour group to the dining area. The hotel had prepared typical Italian buffet lunch for them. The lunch buffet had chopped antipasti salad, garlicky white bean burger, spinach ricotta, creamy roasted pepper and tomato soup, farmer market minestrone, grilled pepper panzanella, grilled zucchini, farm salad with artichokes and summer green and rice soup. It seemed the luncheon had lots of salad, green vegetables, and fresh fruits. Linda chose garlicky white bean burger, tomato soup, and some farm salad. Pemba had green rice soup, grilled zucchini, green vegetables, and some fruits. The selections were fresh, and food was luscious.

After the food selection, both of them approached a corner table with food plates in their hands.

"Dear, what do you think of Saint Peter's Basilica Church and painting of Sistine Chapel ceilings?" Linda asked.

"To tell you the truth, darling, it was one of the most marvelous sights I had ever seen. I am not going to forget in life. The painting of Michelangelo was superb, and it touches human mind and imagination."

"I also have the same view," Linda supported Pemba. I understand the Trevi Fountain is very close to this hotel, and I would like to go in the nighttime after dinner. I was told it is one of the most fascinating romantic places here."

"Great, will go there after dinner," Pemba approved of the idea.

"How about we skip this afternoon visit to Trevi?"

"Okay, will go to Spanish steps then," Pemba floated an idea.

In the meantime, there was a signal to go into the bus for the next segment of tour.

The large block of ruins in the middle of the city was one of the most famous landmarks and tourist attractions of modern times. The Colosseum was a standing proof of grandeur and engineering marvel of Roman history. The arena held about fifty thousand spectators; its monumental size as well as practical, efficient organization and controlling large crowds with eighty entrances provided an easy access and exit. It was one of the famous amphitheaters that provided spectacular gladiators show, mock naval battles, and animals hunts held for public entertainments. For the dignitaries, marble slabs, and for commoners, wooden seats were arranged. The gladiator show was most popular; and in the name of sports elephants, lions, snakes, and panthers were massacred. In the modern context, it had become a challenge to archeologists and had become a popular place for events and shows among the Roman public and tourist as well.

The group spent about an hour strolling along the ruins, trying to revive the scenarios they had seen in the movie like *Ben Hur*, *Demetrius and the Gladiators*, *Cleopatra*, *Fall of Roman Empire*, and *Roman Holidays*. It provided a historical and vivid description of the ancient Rome and mighty Roman Empire that had established various reputations in the remains of triumphal arches, temples, and basilicas.

After the famous Forum visit, Pemba and Linda skipped the tour, took a cab and visited the famous Spanish Step.

Coming down from the top of the Spanish Steps toward right, they came to a small museum of romantic poet John Keats's house, who lived very short and died in 1821. In front, on the left side of the Steps, Linda noticed a tea room with elegant, rich decoration with a waiter in English attire, where tea and pastries were served. "Pemba, dear, let us have tea and some pastries," Linda proposed.

"Of course!" Pemba liked the idea.

Inside the room, almost all the tables were occupied—little right side, close to small window in the table of four, a British-looking person was having a pipe in his mouth.

"Do you mind?" Linda approached the gentleman with hesitation.

"Of course not, please join," the man replied in heavy Scottish accent.

"Hi, I am Linda, and this is my husband, Pemba," Linda introduced.

"Hello, I am Brad Campbell," he spoke again in heavy Scottish accent.

"Where are you from?"

"America."

"Nice to meet." They shook hands.

"Pemba, are you from Gorkha?"

"No, I am from Nepal," Pemba replied with a little confusion.

"No, I mean, are you a Gorkhali? I am a retired British army officer. I have met lot of Gorkhalis in the army," Brad explained.

"Oh, I understand what you mean," Pemba relieved himself with confusion.

"I had a very good friend, Tul Bahadur Tamang, in the army, a very brave, honest, and jolly fellow. Do you know him?"

"No."

"He is now retired in Pokhara," Brad continued.

In a while, they finished the English pastries and tea. They said good-bye to Brad, who was still enjoying the tea and view in the Spanish Steps area; they left and turned into a narrow alley. It seemed all the alleys were crowded with locals and tourists. They lost the way to their hotel. So, they took a cab, which dropped them at Westin for dinner.

Before venturing to Trevi Fountain on their own, they approached the reception for directions. The lady in the reception desk was pleasant and understood English language well and had good conversation command. She told them that it would take around ten minutes to reach the fountain by walk; she showed where the fountain was in the map and indicated the location of the hotel. They preferred to walk now and, if tired, they might take a cab.

The weather was nice to walk, pleasant with cold breeze in the air, making it very comfortable. Holding hands, they began to walk briskly toward the fountain as they were excited to see the place as soon as possible. Linda had more excitement in the fountain as she had seen it in the movie *Three Coins in the Fountain*, a 1954 fantastic love story seeking romance in Italy—which she had seen sometime in early eighties. She loved it and still remembered the fountain she had seen in the movie. From the fountain's perspective, the Trevi Fountain might not be the most beautiful fountain in the world, but it definitely was the most famous and most visited sites.

This impressive monument was situated in the small Trevi Square in Quirinale historical district of Rome surrounded by old houses of the residence area. The streets were narrow, and the place was crowded usually at night as the illumination brought unusual impact in human mind and spirit. This marvelous creation was the unique combination of outstanding Roman sculpture and architecture that had been refined in the marble monuments. It had become a very popular meeting or gathering place for the Romans and the visitors alike. The fountain was crowded with people from all over the world; there were Japanese, British, Canadian, American, and a few from Middle Eastern in their own attires—long white dress and black and white turban on their heads. Everyone was attracted to this fountain, where the central niche portrayed Neptune, the sea god, riding a winged chariot in the shape of the beautiful shell and driven by two attractive horses though the flowing water from the Acqua Vergine channel. The expression of the horses was reflected clearly—one showed calmness and obedience and the other one, restless. The artist had cleverly carried the impact of the horses with the sea during the stormy time and the other in the peaceful time. The water at the bottom of the fountain represented the sea.

According to legends, it was lucky to throw coins with one's right hand over one's right shoulder into the Trevi Fountain on the last day of the trip. As per the legend, throwing one coin would mean return to Rome; two coins, fall in love with a beautiful Italian girl or boy; and three coins, would mean marry that girl or boy. With this belief, both married and unmarried tourists were still throwing the coins, and the fountain was filled with coins. Even now, as Pemba and Linda approached closer to the fountain, there were people throwing coins.

The next day, the tour was scheduled for the most romantic, city of water and bridges, city of love and gondola. The city would amaze anyone in the arts, architectures, and culture. One could witness the famous Rialto Bridge that was the only bridge until nineteenth century and was mentioned by Shakespeare in *The Merchant of Venice*.

The tour operator had arranged special gondolas for sunset ride down the Grand Canal for the group besides being serenaded by the gondolier to all the lady friends. The tour had especially arranged a special serenade for the honeymoon couple as it was a tradition in Venice. Pemba and Linda had fun when everyone in the group wished for their happy conjugal life. At the end of the main market tour the following day, they would have a special traditional dinner at the best Venetian restaurant for seafood with fresh catch of the day. The most romantic city on earth, Venice, left a lasting impression in the life of the honeymooners.

Greece—an intoxication for the travelers, most popular destination in the planet with its alluring combination of history and hedonism, provided magnificent archeological sites, vibrant sparkling beaches, and quenched your hunger with things from ouzo to octopus. As the cradle of democracy, birthplace of scholars Socrates, Plato, Homer, Aristotle, land of God, inextricably interwoven with mythology, and unsurpassed in grace and harmony—a combination of unique blend—Greece one of the most coveted destinations for travelers from across the world.

Linda had special interest in Greek history, mythology, and arts as she had taken a few classes during her college days. Similarly, Pemba had enormous knowledge on Hellenic and Vedic similarity in mythology and religions. There was a distinctive similarity between Greek deities and Hindu gods and goddess. Greece had magical euphoria, distinct charm, authentic sophistication, and hypnotizing elements that attracted all human minds and spirits.

'*Myth*' is created out of Greek word *mythos* and is used to describe a story that explains events or objects that occurred in nature. Myths may also be stories about origin of customs and traditions. Greeks still believed in such myths and have strong faith in the gods that existed in Mount Olympus.

In earlier days, the extensive travel of early Greek culture helped explain why there were many different variations of each myth and why myths of different cultures often seemed very similar. The Greek people considered themselves as Hellenes' descendants, the legendary founder of Greek civilization. The word 'democracy' comes from the Greek word *democratia,* which means ruled by the *demos*, or the people. In 598 BC, Greece became the first world democracy, where free adult males were allowed to vote.

After almost the whole day watching outstanding sculptures, arts, paintings, and statues, Pemba and Linda felt that they had had enough for the day. After taking the guide's permission, they left for the hotel by a taxi.

"Pemba, darling, I really felt we need a rest. How about we have a swim in the terrace-covered swimming pool, have early dinner, and have a chat and discuss about the myths of Greek religion."

Pemba loved the idea as he was also eager to show the similarity and definite relationship between Hindu and Greek religions. After the swim, they came down to the dining hall, and since they would be talking about serious matter of myths and religions, they decided not to have a cocktail.

After they had ordered food, Pemba initiated the conversation.

"So tell me, what was your basic idea about the similarity between religions? It is believed in the Western world that everything worthwhile has its origin in Greece or Rome, but the Hindu religion has been around since prehistoric times. The creation of the *Vedas* around 1200 BC has established absolute knowledge and tradition in the religion."

"Being a Buddhist, how did you learn so much about the Hindu religion?" Linda questioned.

"Well, that's a good question. I learned about world religion during my college days as I had the passion to know about other religions. Indian contact with the Western world dates back to prehistoric time created through trade relations, migration, and established cultural relationship. Vedic literatures, *Jatakas*, Jewish chronicles, and the Greek accounts all suggest contact between India and the West. The famous Indian city Takshasila, now in Pakistan where the famous epic the *Mahabharata* was recited, is the place where the Buddha also studied." Pemba gave a brief description.

Pemba kept a small diary of his study and summary of world religion. He referred to the note from the diary whenever necessary and kept it in front of him.

"As you know, darling, the ancient cultures of Egypt, Mesopotamia, and Persia did not survive. But in India, the Hindus still seek inspiration from concepts advanced by their ancestors. Indian civilization is distinctive for its antiquity and continuity. Apart from its own vitality, the continuity of Indian civilization is largely due to its ability to adapt to alien ideas and harmonized contradictions, and the capacity to mold new thought patterns. Her constant contacts with the outside world also gave India the opportunity to contribute to other civilizations," Pemba explained.

"A question: how did the Indian religion and culture affect Nepal's religion?" Linda was curious.

"Both the civilizations came from the same origin. The script is also the same, with a slight difference in dialect. In both the countries, there is a remarkable tolerance and interrelation between Hinduism and Buddhism. Tell me, who is the main God in Greek mythology?" Pemba put a direct question to Linda.

"It is, of course, Zeus, god of weather, with lightning bolt as his weapon for justice and order. He lives in Mount Olympus," Linda answered.

"There is a similarity," Pemba said. "In Hinduism it is Indra, who is the king of gods in heaven, and creates the wind, rain, and storm and uses 'Vajra'—lightning bolt thunder—as his weapon."

"The Greeks have a god of death; can you name that god?" Pemba asked.

"Of course, he is called Hades," Linda replied without thinking. "He lives in the underworld, is greedy, and has vast mineral fields and precious stones. He's also the least liked god and the brother of Zeus."

Pemba replied forcefully, "Yama is the god of death in Hinduism. He also lives in the underworld and is hated by the people. He is able to bring death to anyone. He has the power to restrain human beings from immortality. Both Yama and Hades are associated with the planet Pluto. Name another god or goddess in Greek mythology; I will give you a Hindu comparison."

"How about Goddess Athena? Who is she similar to?" Linda challenged Pemba.

Pemba looked for more information. "Give me some of her descriptions and qualities first."

"She is the goddess of wisdom, courage, and protection. Her animal symbol is the owl, and she provided many olive trees to

Athens as her simple gift. She is considered the daughter of Zeus," Linda explained.

"Well, let me see. I strongly feel Athena can be compared with Goddess Sarashwati, who has all the knowledge and wisdom, along with courage and wit. She has a divine musical instrument and sits on the pure and virgin lotus flower. She is the cosmic musician that provides harmony and knowledge to the world."

After a convincing argument, Linda again questioned Pemba, "Let me see who you compare God Ares with. He was hated by his parents, Zeus and Hera. He has a destructive, furious nature, and acts like a wild bull, with a violent temper like a wildfire."

After a brief pause Pemba replied slowly choosing his words, "He could be compared with the most complex Hindu deity Shiva, who is both self-controlled and celibate and a lover of his spouse, Parbati, who is a symbol of power. Shiva is immensely powerful. Moreover, he is a destroyer. A thing that required to be destroyed, gets Shiva's touch. The destruction of power is generated both in positive and negative forms. Although his name indicates auspiciousness, his violent nature provides a destructive symbol, and he rides a bull, covering his body with tiger skin and a live serpent in his neck, indicating his power to control them in peace time."

"Well, that provides some kind of similarity, but what about the Goddess Hera? Hera is the wife of Zeus, respected to guard marriage law strictly in the society. She holds a position of privilege and power, affluence and fortune, and represents women and marriage," Linda said.

"She could be easily compared with Lakshmi, goddess of wealth, phenomenal side of existence. She is the wife of Lord Vishnu, who represents the beautiful and bountiful aspects of nature. Lakshmi and Hera immediately relate that both of them, as husband and wife, rule as God and Goddess together. Their power, wealth, and fortune and their divine femininity are grand."

"It seems Hera gets upset with Zeus often on his infidelity and sometimes becomes violent to keep him under control. Does Goddess Lakshmi do the same, sometimes?" Linda asked.

"No. It seems this is the only difference in their characters," Pemba replied.

"Pemba, dear, that was a very convincing comparison between two separate deities from distinguished cultures. What is the possibility of two myths, deities, and religions being so close?"

"In my opinion, those days, although travel, communications, and knowledge sources were limited, the people traveled a lot. Hindu religion is the oldest in the planet. Maybe the traders and some Greek scholars copied the tradition and culture."

"I understand, there are some examples in Homer and Plato supporting your claim," Linda reflected her opinion.

"Maybe, I am not aware. But about one thing I am certain: Hinduism has over 330 million pantheons and deities, but the Greeks have limited gods and goddesses, and perhaps the myth was created because of human needs," Pemba explained.

"Well, enough now about Greek gods and goddess. We need to talk about our future life."

Pemba had not expected that Linda would change the subject abruptly, but her usage of the phrase "our future life" drew his attention immediately.

"What about our future life?" Pemba asked.

"Well, nothing that serious. I was planning to leave my job and go to school for my master's and PhD, but Mr. Smith promoted me with a higher pay raise and told me that I have good potential to become a partner in the firm sometime in the future, which is an enormous offer, and it will boost my career. What do you think?"

"Well, what will PhD bring?" Pemba asked.

"A professor in the department of anthropology."

"What subject are you planning to study?" Pemba questioned again.

"Buddhist religion, of course." Linda replied.

"Comparatively, which one will have better financial benefit?"

"This job, but I may have respect in teaching." Linda compared the two jobs.

"You want respect or more money?" Pemba asked.

"I'd prefer both."

"But you may have to give up one." Pemba suggested.

"Let me have some time to think it over. From now on, Pemba, I may have to travel a lot in my work."

"Where, in or out of the country?" Pemba questioned.

"Inside, as our office is opening several branches in big cities and I am to assist with recruitment."

"Good for you." Pemba expressed his happiness.

"But you will be alone," Linda cautioned.

"You will not be gone for a long time," Pemba said.

"No. A few days a week and I will be home for weekends."

"But I will be working on weekends." Pemba said.

"Darn, I forgot about that. Pemba, do you think it might cause some distance in our relationship?"

"I don't think so. Why do you ask that?" Pemba reacted.

"Well, just my intuition," Linda consoled.

"Don't even think that. I may not survive without you," Pemba said, expressing his feelings.

"Pemba darling, you may have to change the job. Otherwise, what I am going to do on weekends?" Linda suggested again.

"Well, first I should have the green card in hand to search for other jobs," said Pemba, showing his difficulty.

"You will get that document in a few weeks, I guess," Linda assured him.

"I hope so," said Pemba, agreeing on what Linda said.

***

CHAPTER FIFTEEN

August–December, 1988

Both Linda and Pemba returned to their respective places of work and became very busy in their daily lives. The work had increased tremendously in Linda's office; one of her immediate assistants was on sick leave which caused another pressure at work. Besides, for the last few weeks, she had been constantly traveling to her branch offices. She had been to Chicago, Dallas, Boston, and Denver in the last four weeks. She'd left on Tuesday and returned home Friday afternoon. It made her body and mind totally exhausted, and Pemba realized she had also become short-tempered. They had not had quality time after coming back from the Europe trip.

In one weekend, the office hosted a grand picnic at Mountain View Park with barbecue, music, and lots of fun and fireworks toward the late evening. Pemba and all the employees had a great time and plenty of good food. Pemba was the main attraction for the office employees. All the time, people surrounded him, and Paul in particular had developed a special affinity with him. Pemba had an opportunity to build up a good rapport with Linda's office workers and some partners even. Most of the people who came in contact with Pemba had a good impression of his personality—tall, soft-spoken, a well-versed and cultured person. Linda brought him to her colleagues' birthdays, anniversaries, weddings, and all engagement parties, and he became an essential person in her friends and family circle.

Like Linda, Pemba also became a popular person in his department at work. Almost all the contractors looked for him and preferred his services. For working on weekends, he got off on Tuesdays and Wednesdays from the Home Depot. As per Tanaka's suggestion, he spent his two days off at construction site of Tanaka's project of building a new middle school for the county school district.

Tanaka gave him the responsibility of inspecting the construction site and watching his expense account, tallying the book once a week on Wednesday. Pemba had a very good family relationship with Tanaka; he treated him like his brother.

It was Friday, and Linda had come home from her trip to Cleveland. As usual, she was tired and had a slight headache also. When Pemba came home from work, she was having a nap after a shower. Pemba did not disturb her; he had brought a mango plant from Home Depot with him and was busy choosing the right spot in the garden. He prepared the ground for the plant and fixed it in south-eastern corner of the garden. It looked great, and the plant, being a hybrid, would bear its first fruit within less than eighteen months.

From the garden, Pemba heard music coming the bedroom after completing his garden work. He hopped to the bedroom, where Linda woke up and addressed him.

"Hello, darling. Sorry, I had a slight headache and slept when you came home."

"Never mind. I brought a mango plant and put in the garden."

"I was planning to have our date tonight, but could we change it to tomorrow?"

"Sure, why not? Let me take a shower. I am sweating."

When Pemba left, the tranquility returned again in the bedroom along with the soft music of Kenny Rogers. Linda loved his voice and country music; it helped relax her. She did not realize she slept again. The travel was drawing out energy from her body exhausted of travelling from one airport to another in a new environment—weather being cold in some place, hot in another one—taxis, new bed, new hotel, food in the restaurant in unfamiliar surroundings every week etc. Linda was not used to this kind of travel routine like a salesperson, going from one city to another to sell products. She would need to talk with Mr. Smith to slow down her travel routine.

Pemba came to check on her again in the bedroom after his brief shower. No surprise, she had again fallen back to sleep. He thought, *She must be really tired.* Without disturbing her, he left for the guest room just to relax and watch the television.

It was almost nine when Pemba woke up. Linda was in the kitchen, making some dinner for both of them.

"What's cooking, my dear?"

"Oh, finally. You must have been tired also."

"After the shower, I came to see you but noticed you had gone back to sleep."

"Darling, the week's travel really made me exhausted. I am going to talk with Mr. Smith Monday."

"I agree. They should give you some break from this routine," Pemba said in support.

"Honey, I am making some angel hair macaroni with lots of vegetables and boiled eggs."

"I love that macaroni." Pemba liked the idea.

"Could you pour me some chardonnay? It might relax my muscles."

"Of course, I will also keep you company. It has been a long time since we've had decent food together," Pemba complained

"Actually, your travel and my seven days' work are making us both tired."

"How are you doing with that Japanese man?"

"Pretty good; Charlotte has asked many times for dinner."

"You told me before, but you know, I do not feel like going anywhere after I get home."

"I told her you are busy and we will come one of these days."

Linda, immediately after the tasty, warm meal and couple glasses of chardonnay, felt sleepy and headed toward the bedroom.

"Good night, darling; you may sleep late tomorrow. I will leave around seven thirty for work."

It was too early to sleep after cleaning the kitchen. Pemba wanted to watch some Western movie on the television; so he proceeded toward the guest room. He slept around midnight after watching a good Kirk Douglas movie.

It had been a few weeks now. Pemba was used to sleeping in the guest room, and Linda, who always seemed tired, slept early on Fridays after coming home. Saturdays and Sundays when Pemba went to work, Linda still would be sleeping.

The phone rang. Linda, still in sleep, reluctantly picked up the phone.

"Darling, it is almost one, and you are still asleep."

"I'm sorry. I will get up now."

"What are you doing after lunch?"

"Oh, God, I am supposed to have lunch with Amanda today. Let me call her and postpone for tomorrow."

"Good, I called you on time." Pemba dropped the phone after saying bye.

Immediately after, Linda called Amanda. "Hi, my dear, where are you now?"

"Sorry, Linda, I am still at the office. About to leave now."

"Please, Amanda, we have to have lunch tomorrow because, guess what, I slept late again."

"Okay, never mind. Tomorrow, should we meet at the same place?"

"Yes. Sorry about today."

"Bye." Amanda hung up the phone.

Linda, after a shower and quick lunch, went to pick up some personal things from Macy's. She spent almost three hours in the departmental store; she also picked up a nice silk tie with a black background and white stars for Pemba.

"Darling, I am home."

Pemba was watching the early evening news on the television. "Welcome home," he said sarcastically.

"Oh, darling, I needed some undergarments badly, so I went to Macy's to pick them up," Linda explained. "What would you like to have for dinner?"

"I want you," Pemba joked.

"Don't be silly; we have a date today. I mean for food."

"Honestly, dear, I am craving for Thai food."

"Of course, let's have it then."

It seemed Pemba was an expert on Thai food. He ordered shrimp fried rice, some kind of chicken curry, one sauté vegetable, and Linda liked every item had mild spicy taste; it was different and had aromatic flavor.

Sunday, when Linda woke up, Pemba had already left for work. The day was bright and sunny, with a clear blue sky. The temperature was around seventy, very pleasant. This particular restaurant 'Aroma' was located in the Hollywood area. It was a cozy, sophisticated, and elegant restaurant normally used by Hollywood actors and actresses, top journalists, and fiction writers. Linda used the closest parking area to the main entrance. Normally, the restaurant was fairly busy and very popular for Sunday brunch. Amanda loved this particular restaurant and it was also a favorite place of Steven Spielberg. As usual, the place was crowded, but the waiter knew Linda as a frequent visitor in the past. He managed a small table for two towards the corner in the back, which was darker at this time of day. Linda had to wait for Amanda, which was normal—late was her trademark.

She ordered a pineapple drink. Before the drink arrived at her table, she noticed Amanda rushing inside the place and looking for her. Linda raised her hand to draw attention.

"Sorry . . ."

"Please, Amanda, I am used to it. You don't need to explain."

"So, how have you been? Tell what you want to discuss with me."

"Chill, just relax, and sit down. How is your boyfriend?"

"As usual, he has not changed, and I am having the same problem. David seems not interested every time we go to my religious ceremony in Synagogue."

"Don't blame him, that is not his religion. For God's sake, he is a Christian."

"Yes, but he could try. I really feel bad among my people." Amanda changed the subject. "How is Pemba?"

"Well, that is the serious problem, and I need your view. He works weekends, when I am off, and I travel Tuesdays through Fridays. When I come home, I am tired." Linda expressed her concerns as if she were talking to herself.

"So what is the problem? You have a conflict of work schedules?"

"I feel this schedule is pushing us apart."

"Hey, Linda, you both need to compromise to improve the relationship."

"Now, Pemba even works on his off days with some Japanese guy."

"So what will he do? Sit home without you on Tuesday and Wednesday?"

"It's not that, Amanda. I feel our love and whole relationship is affected badly."

"So what is the alternative? For God's sake, you are married to him," Amanda screamed.

"I understand, but due to our work schedule conflict, it is creating distance between us."

"Why don't you talk with him and see what else you guys could do to rekindle the relationship?"

"I am scared to talk with him; that might destroy our relationship further."

"Come on, Linda, whatever is coming your way, it is only the two of you that could solve it, nobody else."

"We had a wonderful time yesterday."

"Did you both enjoy it?"

"Of course."

"Then create that kind of situation again and again . . ."

"But in my mind, the way things are moving is not going to work between us."

"Come on, Linda, don't be stupid. Try hard. I am certain it will work, but you guys must talk to each other."

"Okay, my teacher. I will talk with him." Linda agreed with Amanda.

They had some kind of Jewish kosher sandwich, soup, and salad, and left the place after hugging each other.

When Linda came, home Pemba was still at work. Linda gave him a call.

It took long time for Pemba to come to the phone as he was busy at the store.

"Hi, darling, what time will you finish up?"

"As usual, my dear."

"I miss you, try to come as soon as possible."

"Great, dear! I will be there the moment I am off."

After about an hour, Pemba was at the door. "Honey, I am home."

Linda rushed to him and gave a passionate hug. She kissed him all over the face. They held each other for a long time, and slowly, they separated.

"Listen, dear. I do not feel like cooking tonight. I need to talk to you."

"About what, Linda?"

"It is regarding us."

"Okay."

"I am going to order pizza from Pizza Hut. Are you okay with that?"

"Oh, yummy. I love pizza."

"Darling, I am really sick of this regular travel. I do not feel like I'm living with you," Linda confessed.

"Could you perhaps talk with your boss? Maybe something will come out of it."

"Of course, I am going to talk with him tomorrow. Do you miss me when I am not here?"

"Of course, silly; I do very much."

"Also, do you have any idea how long you'll continue to work on weekends?" Linda asked Pemba.

"Dear, I have no idea how long I have to work in weekends."

"How about other jobs that you may not have to work on weekends?" Linda suggested.

"You know still waiting for the green card, I am not certain. Another place may not hire me without the document," Pemba explained.

"Do not worry, the green card will be mailed to you soon."

"Okay then, I will look around once I have the document." Pemba tried to convince Linda.

"You know I really feel lonely on weekends and would like to go out with you." Linda complained.

"I understand, darling."

"Tell me you love me like before."

"That is a silly question to ask. Obviously, you know I do."

As usual, Mondays were the worst days in the office. Things started with hectic schedules, meetings, deadlines, and conferences. The volume of business cases and new clients, including the Japanese association, had increased everyone's workload. Linda needed to go to Washington this week, and she looked for an opportunity to talk with Mr. Smith about her hectic travel routine. But he was also busy with clients, and there were some important cases in the court that needed lots of preparation that week.

Around three, the atmosphere cooled off in the office; Linda felt easy. Since Mr. Smith was alone in the office, Linda approached him and stood next to his large desk.

Smith asked, "Yes, Linda"

"Mr. Smith, if you do not mind, the regular travel has affected my health. If possible could you replace someone to take my travel job?" Mr. Smith just gazed at Linda and did not say anything. "If possible, can I train somebody to replace me?" Linda continued.

"Linda, I do not think anybody is else suitable for the job. What do you suggest?"

"Maybe we need to hire from outside," Linda suggested

"It will take time, Linda, so please continue for some time. I will talk with the board and try to solve the problem."

"Thank you, Mr. Smith."

"You're welcome."

Linda felt relaxed; her feelings were out, and Mr. Smith would do something as he knew the problem.

As assured by Mr. Smith, Linda may have to continue her weekly travel at least for some time. She had arranged for the flight and hotel to Washington for the following day.

When she arrived at the Delta check-in counter, there was a commotion. An employee informed, the flight was overbooked and they were looking for people to voluntarily withdraw in exchange for a two-hundred-dollar voucher for future travel. Linda could not withdraw as her hotel booking had already been confirmed. She held a good status due to her frequent miles; so they bumped her to first class. Next to her, she just could not believe, was Alex Ivanov—the most handsome young rising star of Hollywood—seated in the window seat. His recent movie, *Courage*, was sensational. People were talking about his outstanding performance in the movie that deserved an Oscar. A few weeks back, Linda had seen the popular movie with Amanda one weekend. "Hi, I am Alex Ivanov."

Linda suddenly lost her voice; she stammered and replied in a vague manner. "Hi, I am Linda."

In the meantime, an air hostess brought drinks, gave one to Linda and another to Alex. When the flight had reached above thirty-two thousand feet cruising height, the pilot turned off the seat belt sign.

"Do you like flying?" Alex asked.

"Not really." Linda gave a brief reply.

"How often do you fly?"

"Once a week."

"Always to Washington?"

"No, different cities."

"For work?"

"Yes."

"If you don't mind my asking, what kind of business are you in?"

"I work for a law firm."

"Are you a lawyer?"

"Nope." After a pause, she added "I work as a secretary."

"What is the firm's name?"

"Smith and Associates."

"Is that the one planning to open numerous offices nationwide?"

"Yes, how do you know?"

"Through television and newspaper."

"Do you get time for that?" Linda asked.

"I like your new movie, *Courage*," Linda continued.

"Thanks. A new one is coming out next year—I have a few shootings in New York."

"But this flight goes to Washington."

"Yes, I know. I have my family in DC. After two days, I will be in New York."

In the meantime, the stewardess interrupted and asked, "Sir, salmon or steak for lunch?"

"Salmon, please."

"What about you, madam?"

"Salmon also." Linda replied in a low voice.

No one talked during the meal. Just before landing, Alex made a request. "Linda, I will be back in Los Angeles after a week. Can I see you for lunch?" Linda did not expect such a request.

Linda hesitated for a moment. "Well, I have a friend who is your fan. Perhaps we could get together."

"Where?"

Linda did not like to meet with him alone.

"In Hollywood, there is a small joint named 'Aroma', but I will call you to confirm when I am back."

"Sure. I know that place. I will mention it to my friend. She will be excited." Linda concurred.

"Okay then, it's a deal."

"Sure."

Linda thought, *He did not even ask for my phone number*, and she was pretty sure he would not remember her after the flight. She was also going to forget him but needed to mention it to Amanda, who would become jealous.

Linda returned on Friday. Pemba was not home yet. She had a quick shower, fixed a gin and tonic, put on her Kenny Rogers tape, and relaxed on the La-Z-Boy. She had no idea when she fell asleep, or when Pemba came home. She heard a feeble television news voice from an anchor in the distance and realized Pemba must have come home. He did not wake her up and kept himself busy, watching the television. Linda moved towards his room. Pemba was watching the television placing his back toward the entrance door; she surprised him by holding him from behind.

"Darling, thanks for not waking me up. I was really tired." Pemba faced Linda and kissed her with emotion, holding her tight.

Linda made a request. "Can you give me a massage tonight?"

"After dinner or now?"

"After dinner. And will you please prepare meal tonight. I am like dead meat," Linda said, expressing her tiredness.

Linda slept until eleven in the morning. She had not been like this before; it was all because of her travel, which was getting to her system. When she was about to go to the bathroom for a shower, she heard the phone ring.

"Hello."

On the other line, Amanda was on the phone. "Hi, sweetie, how are you?"

"I am fine, how about you?"

"I have not so good news."

"What happened?"

"We are going to break off our relationship."

"What happened now?"

"No, it has been dragging for a long time. I feel David is not in love with me anymore."

"Is it your decision or his?"

"Both. We are not going to see each other from now on."

"How do you feel?"

"Well, good, in a way. He is not accepting my way of life. I have a hard time with him."

"Okay then. Maybe something better is in store for you."

"I hope so. From now on, I will seek a Jewish man perhaps."

"Hey, Amanda. I need to tell you something exciting."

"Really?"

"During my last trip to Washington, guess who was sitting next to my seat on the plane?"

"Tell me who it was?"

"Alex."

"Who is Alex?"

"Alex Ivanov, the handsomest and the best-looking rising Hollywood star of *Courage*."

"You are not serious." Amanda had hard time, trusting Linda.

"Swear to God, I am serious."

"What happened?"

"Nothing much. We had a small chat, and he promised to meet again. I suggested I would meet him with you."

"Where and when?"

"He mentioned Aroma, but he did not take my number."

"Does he know where you work?"

"Yes, let us wait and see. I will keep in touch if he calls."

"Thanks, dear. I have to go now; I have an important meeting at the office."

"Bye." Linda hung up the phone.

Monday morning again, as usual, was a very busy atmosphere in the office. Linda was used to this kind of situation and had adjusted well after coming back from her honeymoon trip. In the beginning, she had a hard time coping with the dramatic increase of work and still could not believe how so much change could take place within less than a month in the office. The other day, Kathy had been telling her that the law franchise project might take off much earlier than anticipated.

According to an office rumor, soon they were going to hire a few lawyers as junior partners, along with some more administrative employees. The firm was growing rapidly, and everyone was handling the pace with added responsibilities. Besides the one Japanese business they had last month, they had now added ten more large accounts from Japan. Besides, they had rapidly gained more local clients with important cases and a few clients with national reputation. Linda liked the improvements, and she was hoping that one day, Mr. Smith might take her as a partner in the firm. She could realize the potential of such benefits: a greater salary, bonuses, health insurance, transportation, and retirement benefits. Considering all these benefits and the possibility of a dramatic change in her lifestyle, she had slowly given up her idea for a master's degree and PhD.

Again, the next day, Linda had to travel to Minneapolis. It had become a routine.

Linda sensed there was a slight change in Pemba's behavior toward her. They talked to each other in the same words; everything was the same, but underneath, she was sure he was drifting away from her. She had no idea how long she had to keep up with this tedious travel. Perhaps Mr. Smith might do something soon, and she would have her life back.

Pemba made his breakfast and left home. Linda was still in the bedroom. He had a habit of not making noise and leaving the house quietly so that he would not disturb her. He had been sleeping in the guest room and Linda, in her bedroom. Their frequency of lovemaking had reduced dramatically. Pemba felt there was no much passion in their relationship now. Perhaps it was because of Linda's regular travel. He had noticed she had become short-tempered, whimsical, and unpredictable recently. He was doing his part honestly and went out of his way to maintain and improve their relationship, but Linda's behavior sometimes bewildered him. He tried to understand or even explore her reasons for being aloof and creating invisible demarcation in their relationship. He was also busy seven days a week between Home Depot and Tanaka's job that he had not spared much time to think. Pemba realized his weekend's work at Home Depot and Linda's free time as the main reason of the two falling apart. It also was taking away some meaningful activities they could be doing together on weekends.

For a working couple, weekends occupied an important role of revitalizing and rekindling their relationship to bring it to the next level. This was what was missing from the relationship, and Pemba knew that weekends were significant in American life. In fact, they lived for weekends. He could not leave work now. In fact, they had discussed this issue between themselves. In conclusion, there was no solution at the moment.

Pemba also was aware that Linda was trying to avoid so much traveling in her job; he knew she had initiated a talk with her boss, but she needed to wait for some time. Besides, on his last visit to Linda's family, he had noticed that her mother did not like Pemba, although her dad liked him.

Another weekend passed. Their life progressed normally without any excitement. Both of them were living under one roof but without much communication and without a meaningful relationship. He sometimes felt, although they were under one roof, their relationship was drifting apart further. Deep down in their hearts, both realized something was drastically wrong, but they were unable to improve their relationship. In fact, one time, Pemba discussed his situation with Tanaka, who made a strange remark.

"Pemba, since you are like my brother, let me tell you something about American ladies. They want glamour and excitement in life. Besides, for you guys, there is no common bond to hold the relationship."

"What do you mean?" Pemba question

"Pemba, normally children are sources of bond between husband and wife. Their mutual love towards their children helps keep their relation lasting."

Another week passed. Linda returned from her trip on Friday afternoon, tired and exhausted as usual. She had no energy to accomplish anything but sleep and relax.

Monday came again. The same routine in the office, but this week, Linda did not have to travel anywhere—an excellent and welcoming, wonderful break. But she had lots of work she needed to complete this week in the office. Besides, she was also one of the people chosen to conduct interviews of new hires. It would keep her week extremely busy, and then she also needed to prepare a report and make the list for selection final.

The week moved fast. Finally, Friday was a day later, a kind of relief for Linda. When she came back after lunch, there was a call-back note at her desk, which said "Please call Alex," and there was the number. She wondered how in the world Alex had traced her. Perhaps, she thought, through the phone book, as Smith and

Associates had a prominent page in the yellow pages. She called back the number as per the small pink call-back slip.

"May I talk to Alex?"

"May I ask who is calling?" the secretary asked her back.

"I am Linda."

After holding for almost a minute, a very distinctive husky, masculine, and familiar voice answered, "Hi, Linda, how are you?"

"I am fine."

"Remember my invitation? Could you come for lunch this Saturday?"

"Yes, of course. I am coming with my friend, Amanda. Is that okay?"

"Sure. You know the place Aroma?"

"Yes, I am familiar with it."

"Then I'll see you around one. Is that okay?"

"Fine, we will be there."

The next call Linda made was to Amanda. "Guess what, he called."

"Who?" Amanda was surprised.

"Alex. We have a lunch date this Saturday at one at Aroma."

"That is wonderful."

"Hey, Amanda, try not to be late this time, for God's sake."

"You'll see I will be earlier than you." Excitement was in her voice.

Saturday, Linda got up at ten. Pemba had left for work earlier. After a shower, she had a glass of orange juice and no breakfast. She spent nearly an hour picking the right, appropriate dress with matching handbag and shoes. She was not in favor of doing heavy makeup in the daytime; she just had base foundation, thin pink lipstick, and mascara.

It was a big surprise for Linda; Amanda was already waiting at Aroma.

"Amanda, I don't believe, for the first time in life you are early."

"Yes, that shows my excitement."

While the two old buddies were busy talking, a bright yellow-colored convertible Ferrari pulled inside the compound and gave the keys to an attendant for valet parking.

"Sorry, ladies, did I make you wait a long time?" Alex addressed them.

"Hi," Linda responded and introduced, "This is Amanda."

"Hello. Sorry I'm a few minutes late, traffic on Hollywood Boulevard."

"We understand."

"Mind a drink before the food?" Alex asked.

Linda ordered gin and tonic; Amanda, some Jewish drink; and Alex, a dry martini.

"May I ask what line of work Amanda is in?"

"I am a journalist. I work for a Jewish paper."

"Great. Are you Jewish, then?"

"Yes, how do you know?"

"Because of the drink," Alex guessed.

"Obviously," Amanda said. "Your acting in *Courage* was outstanding; people are talking about an Oscar."

"Oscar award, that is my dream. You know, the people in Oscar are highly unpredictable."

"What is your next movie about?" Linda asked.

"It is about immigration," Alex replied.

"What is the story?" Linda was curious.

"It is a strange and very complex story—immigration in our country acts in a weird way. It is about a love story between Greek mother and Russian father, which is actually based on my life story." Alex continued, "The producer found it fascinating and wanted to make a movie."

"How interesting. Based on your own life?" Amanda inquired.

"Yes, it has many twists and mystery in the story making worth for a movie," Alex said.

Linda was quiet most of the time, but she showed an unusual interest in their conversation and was carefully watching Alex, who was tall, gorgeous, and very pleasing.

"Hey, we're having a private screening of one of my movies that's going to be released around Thanksgiving. You interested?" Alex proposed.

"Yes, I would be glad, but when?"

"On October 15th. That is Thursday," Alex promptly replied.

"I might be travelling," Linda said doubtfully.

"No, I am sorry, I have to be in Synagogue that day. We have a religious congregation." Amanda declined the invitation.

"Oh well, I will find some other appropriate event to invite you guys," Alex consoled them.

They had lunch without much talking, but Alex and Linda's eyes were talking to each other. And they had done nothing but establish a rapport between themselves. In the meantime, a number of clients in the restaurant approached Alex and requested for his autograph. After lunch, Alex thanked them in a very courteous and respectful manner. "It was my pleasure to have you ladies for lunch. I enjoyed it and hope to see you soon."

It seemed Alex was very attracted to and interested in Linda. He showed understandable emotion and affection toward her. Linda also felt some kind of attachment to Alex. Time would tell what the future was holding. One thing they found out was that Alex was single.

"What do you think?" Linda put an unexpected question to Amanda after Alex left.

"About what? You mean Alex?"

"Yes."

"Do you want my sincere opinion?"

"Go ahead."

"I felt he likes you."

"What? I am a married woman!" Linda reacted showing anger on her face.

"It's up to you. This guy is a gem loaded with money and reputation."

"I agree. He is an unusually smart, talented, and handsome person."

"Do you know where he lives?" Amanda was curious.

"In Malibu. He has a large mansion next to Jack Nicholson."

"Oh, it looks like you did your homework." Amanda was in the mood to tease Linda. Linda did not feel like she needed to reply; she just smiled.

For Pemba, nowadays, every day was like the same day, one after another. He hardly had any reason to distinguish as he did the same things Monday through Sunday. Recently, he'd received a letter from his mother. Everybody was in good health, and things were normal. His uncle made frequent visits to his house and provided money on time. In the village, everyone was good. Pemba's nephew was going to Australia for higher education. It was rumored that Sir Hillary had arranged his education.

He felt that his relationship with Linda was not going well. There had been tense situations now and again. He thought his life was very sublime and pure; he was a happy-go-lucky person. But he had come to grips with this situation without knowing it, and had been entangled in a completely weird and new culture. He was doing his best to improve their relationship. In simple and plain terms, there was nothing wrong with their relationship; both were trying to improve their situation. But in reality, it was leading to a distressing situation. They talked nicely, behaved nicely, and shared their emotions normally, but they were turning into strangers living under one roof.

Linda, after meeting Alex, seemed like she was always daydreaming. She visualized a life with Alex and she also wanted to be an actress with his help. She had not shared her feelings with anybody just was keeping inside. But she was certain she needed support to change her lifestyle. She loved Pemba very much, but the current situation was forcefully pushing their lives in two directions. She had tried and was trying to bring them together, but the force of nature was trying to keep them apart. They had no choice but to continue their lifestyles in the same way and attempt to stay together.

On the other hand, Linda had a ray of hope to change her life with Alex, but she would not want this opportunity to destroy her faith and relationship with Pemba, which was still like a pure tie. But on the other hand, life was too short, and one needed to achieve their dream.

The previous week, Linda had a screen test in the same studio where Alex was shooting his new movie. The test was conducted by a prominent director on Alex's request. Linda has good mark in the test, her profile, her height, and beauty were suitable for an actress. She was very pleased with the outcome and she might get a significant role in the coming movie. Her life and new career was moving at a fast pace; she needed to have a serious discussion with Pemba. If the idea worked, she won't be able to work as a secretary any more. Linda needed to make her decisions fast.

Linda, very often, used Alex's guest house in weekend. Pemba was living in the house. Linda came only on weekdays because of her work.

One Saturday morning, Linda called Pemba in the house. Pemba sounded indisposed, and was in the house skipping his work.

"Hi Pemba, this is Linda. How are you?"

"I am not so well," Pemba replied in a weak voice.

"Are you able to go for lunch to day? I have an important matter to discus with you." Linda made a request.

"Sure; will try. What time?" Pemba asked.

"I will be home to pick you around noon."

"I will be waiting."

"Thanks, Pemba."

When Linda arrived in a long black limo, Pemba was ready.

"What kind of food you like Pemba?"

"Does not matter." Pemba was reluctant for the food.

"Why not we go to a Chinese?"

"That sound okay."

Linda chose that Chinese which might be crowded at this time of the day with luncheon gathering, but they had private rooms; so they could talk quietly. When they had settled in the private rooms on far left side of the entrance and ordered the food, Linda faced Pemba.

"So Pemba how are you?"

"You can see I am not in good shape."

"Are you unhappy I am not at home often?" Linda questioned.

"Of course Linda. Is not that obvious?" Pemba answered sarcastically.

"Pemba, as you know our conflicting schedule of work, my erratic traveling at office making me crazy to continue my life."

Pemba just nodded.

"I met Alex during one of my trips to Washington recently. He offered me a role in his new movie. I passed the screen test and I am taking a role in his coming movie," Linda continued.

"I am also quitting my job" Linda reinforced her decision.

"Linda, what has that got to do with me?" Pemba asked.

"Well, I will come to the point," Linda explained.

"Pemba, I know it will hurt you but I would like this glamour job." Linda finished in one breath. "This is once in a life time opportunity," she explained further.

"So what do you want me to do?" Pemba seemed irritated.

"Pemba, Alex also proposed me." Linda cleared her throat.

"You mean you are going to marry Alex?" Pemba seemed surprised.

"Eventually, but I cannot marry him unless I have divorced with you." Linda explained.

Pemba kept quiet. He did not talk for a long time. His face was dark and had a peculiar expression, mixed with anger and surprise.

"Linda, I came here just because of you and I do not know anybody else," Pemba explained.

"Pemba, I know that you may live in the house as long as you want. I will be helping you financially. Moreover, I will not stop sending money to your family immediately."

"Have you received the green card?" Linda asked.

"Yes, it came the other day," Pemba replied.

"Good, now you can go and find other jobs," Linda consoled him.

"Pemba, I have talked to a lawyer and he will send papers for you to sign," Linda informed.

"Linda, just like that," Pemba showed surprise in his voice.

"Please Pemba, this is for my new career and I expect you to help me out," Linda begged.

"So you also going to discard Buddhist religion?" Pemba was curious.

"Oh no Pemba, both Alex and I will be following it; Alex also is equally interested."

"Is that so?" Pemba did not believe.

"Yes Pemba, we might be going to Honorable Dalai Lama again after sometime." Linda surprised Pemba.

"Also I will visit Dorje's monastery whenever they will have programs," Linda assured Pemba.

"Well it is up to you," Pemba said half-heartedly.

"Pemba, I told the lawyer to send you five thousand dollars check with the paper. You can always call me if you need money any time."

"Linda, money is not an issue. I am depressed in life. I lost confidence." Pemba seemed desperate.

"Pemba, what happened? I did not anticipate this and I feel sad for us. For my sake, please compose yourself and be strong."

"It is easy for you to say that," Pemba pleaded.

After lunch, they hugged each other as if they were departing for the last time in life. Linda noticed Pemba's eyes were moist, and his face unusually hot, may be with the fever.

"Pemba I am not moving to join Alex now except on weekend and until I quit the job and resign from office also. It may take a month before everything is settled." Linda gave her last word.

***

CHAPTER SIXTEEN

1989

Linda and Alex met a couple of times in public and private. It enhanced their relationship to a desired level and soon they were going to marry after Linda's divorce with Pemba. Both had equal affection, fascination, and attraction.

At one point of time, a local magazine published a news about Linda in the tabloids, which indirectly indicated that Alex's new girlfriend was a married woman from Los Angeles. Pemba had not seen the article with the picture in the magazine. When he was at Tanaka's house, Charlotte showed him the article with a photo of Linda and the popular actor Alex. Pemba did not take it seriously.

It was Saturday. Pemba left for the office close to nine in the morning. As usual, Linda was still sleeping. He left home quietly. Although Pemba was not affected by the article and picture of Linda, psychologically, it impacted his work. He seemed lost in thought all the time, and he was losing concentration. This had been noticed by Pemba's boss and some of his colleagues at work. Pemba, who was always so eager to work, seemed to have lost interest, and he did not derive happiness from his work anymore.

Linda also noticed that Pemba was losing his sense of time, felt agitated, restless, and sometimes showed violent nature. It looked like he had lost some weight recently, and had trouble remembering things. The other day, he had been looking for the car key that was lying on the table.

Linda had a picnic type of lunch at Alex's mansion's swimming pool, where they expected around fifty people from the movie industry.

Linda did not arrive home until seven in the evening.

"Finally, you are here. Did you have a nice time?"

Both of them had stopped calling each other *dear*, *darling*, and *my love*—affectionate words—for some time.

"Yes. Alex had a wonderful pool party this afternoon." Linda explained her late arrival.

"Can I ask you about the article that had your picture with Alex?"

"That was nothing. They just want to destroy his image, and it was done out of jealousy."

"I understand that, but remember our own image is also involved in this issue." Pemba tried to clarify his point of view.

"I will make sure it does not happen in the future, not until our divorce is final," Linda assured him.

Pemba noticed that she was saying something that did not match her body language; obviously, she was trying to cover something up. Pemba understood basic human psychology, women's desire, and the nature of Linda's activities. He tried to compare Alex with himself. There was no comparison. Alex had everything—property, reputation, and dynamic image as an actor with great personality. Pemba had nothing—neither enough money nor even a good job. He was new in this country, and had virtually nothing except good character and ambition. Pemba doubted he would be able to compete with Alex, and he would not blame Linda if she picked him sooner or later.

It was around four thirty in the afternoon when the workload at Pemba's job cooled down. Somebody informed him the boss wanted to see him in his office.

"Have a seat, Pemba," the boss said.

His boss also had the same magazine and gave it to Pemba.

"Pemba, I like you very much and can understand your emotions and feelings." He continued, "I would also lose concentration and interest in life and work." The boss seemed sympathetic toward him. "I have noticed you are losing interest and concentration at work; there have been numerous complaints about you recently. Please put your life back on track; otherwise, you will have trouble. Please take this as a warning and improve yourself."

Pemba left the boss' office without showing any reaction. He understood a warning had been given to him, and the next step would be to fire him from the job if he failed to improve himself.

Pemba seemed frustrated and depressed, and he needed support to boost his morale and come out of the depression he'd been feeling recently. He returned home; Linda had not returned yet, and there was no message on the phone. He called Tanaka and drove toward his home. Tanaka's family were watching a movie, *The Last Emperor*.

Pemba sat with them, and Charlotte brought popcorn and beer. He found the movie interesting. It was about the Pu Yu, the last emperor of China in 1950: from his birth, to his brief reign in the Forbidden City—an object of worship of over half a billion Chinese people—through his renunciation, his decline and dissipated lifestyle exploited by invading Japanese, and finally, to his metamorphosis into an ordinary worker in the Peking Botanical Garden.

Pemba thought, although he was not an emperor, he had all the ambitions, desires, and motivations to be one in his life, but the current situation, especially Linda's detachment, was making him completely an ordinary, useless, and hopeless person.

Charlotte requested Pemba to have dinner with their family, which he accepted, as he had done in many occasions before. For the dinner, they had a combination of American and Japanese dishes. Pemba loved sushi, and he had some fried rice with eggs, tender ginger, and wasabi.

After dinner, Charlotte asked him about Linda. "How are you guys doing?"

"Not so good."

"Have you talked to each other seriously?"

"Yes, several times, but it seems Linda's priority has changed. Last Saturday she told me point blank she wants a divorce from me." Pemba expressed his opinion sorrowfully. In the meantime, Tanaka walked into the kitchen and asked his wife Charlotte "Darling, I am hungry, what is cooking?" He looked around the food, took plenty of sushi, and sat in the chair.

"So, Pemba, how is life?" he said.

"Turning from bad to worse."

"Never mind. This is America. Everything changes fast."

After the food, they moved to the living room and had brandy. The living room was almost L-shaped; the other end was connected to the kitchen furnished with comfortable leather sofa and lots of decoration with Japanese antiquities.

When Pemba came home, he did not see Linda. That meant, she had not come back yet. Normally, on Fridays, she was home early and tired. He checked the answering machine; there was a brief message, saying that she might be late. Pemba adopted the attitude that he did not care. *Why should I care?* He had really become indifferent towards her.

Saturday morning, when he checked Linda's room, she had not come home yet. He was wondering what happened to her. He did not care a bit, and left for work.

Saturday's workload was unusually high. The clients were coming regularly in the store; the employees were busy from ten to five. Sometimes he even could not get a decent time for lunch, and today was no different. He had prepared a number of delivery loads for contractors, made entry in the computer, and tallied a delivery of loads against the paid receipt. Pemba was exhausted and sweating for making frequent trips outside the store. There was a huge order for lumber that needed to be supplied to a construction site, and the store manager was personally supervising to make sure everything was properly loaded.

Finally, it was almost five, and on Saturdays, he could not leave unless he tallied each and every thing in the computer spreadsheet. He had not completed all his work; he still had a few things to take care of. When everything had been processed, the store looked empty— except that the manager was in his office, perhaps preparing the report of the day. Pemba did a good job despite his mental situation.

When he reached home after work, there was no sign of Linda. The phone had another brief message. She was out of town with Alex for the premiere of his new movie. This did not surprised Pemba; he knew things were moving at a fast pace between Alex and Linda.

He needed to think of alternatives in his life as well. He called Tanaka and discussed Linda being out of town with Alex on the weekend. Tanaka asked Pemba to come to his home so that he and Charlotte could give him some advice on his next move. He drove to Tanaka's residence; the children were in the video room. So, both of them were free to talk with Pemba.

"So it has gotten out of your hands," Charlotte commented.

"Yes, Charlotte! She told me her intention and asked divorce from me last Saturday."

"Now I have no idea. What should I do?" Pemba presented his problem.

"Well, stay in that house for some time until you will be served with a divorce paper," Tanaka suggested.

"I presume the papers are in process and will be delivered to you soon. California has no fault in divorce laws," Charlotte supported.

"I am totally lost. I am neither aware of the system nor the process here," Pemba said in a childlike, innocent manner.

"Do not worry. You will come and stay with us after divorce," Tanaka assured him again.

"I am losing sleep and concentration at work, and feel sluggish," Pemba complained.

"Pemba, it is nothing new. I can understand your feelings. Remember, I also had a divorce." Charlotte was trying to identify with him. "Did you have anything to eat?" Charlotte showed her concern.

"I'm not hungry," Pemba reply reluctantly.

"Try to eat something; you cannot go on like this," Tanaka said.

In the meantime, Charlotte brought some macaroni with teriyaki chicken and chowder soup with two bread rolls.

Pemba tried to eat the food, but it seemed he had no appetite and only took the bread and soup. The rest of the food, he did not touch. Just before he left, Charlotte brought an over-the-counter sleeping tablet and gave the entire bottle to him, asking him to take one just before bed.

Pemba left for home with a heavy mind. He could visualize a huge problem ahead of him. He was losing sleep, had no concentration at work, hardly had desire any for food, and had suicidal tendencies; he had no idea what had happened to him. As suggested by Charlotte, he took one sleeping tablet and tried to sleep.

He heard birds chirping in the garden outside. The sun was about to rise, and he realized it was already morning. He had no energy to go to work. He tried to sleep again. But he was not used to sleeping during the daytime. In fact, he had never slept in the daytime in his entire life. He had a hard time getting out of bed and had a headache and body pain. It also felt like he had fever. He forced himself and went to the bathroom to have a quick hot bath. Normally, he shaved prior to a bath, but he did not feel like doing it today.

Around one, he heard the postman drop a letter in the box. Normally, he did not worry about it. Usually, Linda took care of it, but since she was not here, he picked up the mail.

There were about seven normal-size business letters, a few papers with advertising mails and one large manila folder, which had his name printed on the front. He was curious and opened that large envelope out of curiosity. To his surprise, there were divorce papers from a lawyer. He had no knowledge how the divorce process worked in America and what he actually needed to do.

Since it was Saturday, Tanaka was at home. Pemba called him.

The older boy picked up the phone, "Hello!"

"Hey, Soma, may I talk with your dad?"

"He is out."

"Let me talk with your mother…Hi, Charlotte…Oh, Charlotte, how are you? Guess what, I think I got the divorce papers."

"You must be kidding."

"I am serious."

"It's sooner than expected."

"Charlotte, I have no idea how to process these papers. What time is Mr. Tanaka coming back?"

"He will be here soon. He just went to a nearby store to pick up bread and milk."

"Great, I will be there with the papers."

Pemba lost his way to Tanaka's despite several visits in the past. He realized something was wrong in his system. After driving nearly two hours, he reached Tanaka's house. Mr. Tanaka was at home already and looked like he was waiting for Pemba.

Tanaka embraced Pemba and dragged him upstairs to the den so the children would not disturb them. Pemba gave the papers to Tanaka. He realized his hands were shaking, and his whole body was shivering.

"Pemba, this kind of thing is common in America. I also divorced my first wife. You know, Pemba, it is a dangerous disease in America."

Tanaka went through the papers. It was a standard divorce agreement prepared by a lawyer and was not complicated because they did not have joint property or children. Linda's car was in her name and Pemba's in his, and they had no joint bank account even. Neither party was claiming any property, but Linda was generous to give Pemba five thousand dollars for signing. Linda had a separate clause in the divorce papers that she was not going to withdraw her guarantee on the car loan, which would remain as it was.

Tanaka explained the process to Pemba. If he signed the paper and sent it to the lawyer, that would be final, and he did not even need to go to court; it was that easy and simple. Tanaka suggested staying at their house for a few days and informing office that he was sick. Pemba had gotten lost on his way to Tanaka's. They realized he was not of proper mind and they needed to take care of him during such a delicate situation. People might commit suicide and take undesirable actions unknowingly, and in most cases, one would turn into hallucination and ruin life. Tanaka and Charlotte had enormous sympathy toward Pemba, who was a super simple guy, and this divorce was a creation of greed and only for glamour and materialistic accomplishment. Pemba did not have any fault. Tanaka tried to convince Pemba about American life—that it was mainly self-centered, independent, and 'me, mine, and myself' type.

He told Pemba, "Linda will get a lesson one day, when that guy divorces her and will realize how hard life would be after divorce." He told Pemba that this guy Alex, if he was smart enough, would have a pre-nuptial agreement with her, which would automatically deprive her of his property.

Pemba agreed to stay with Tanaka's family for a few days, which would divert his mind from the unbearable tension he was suffering at the moment. She had noticed signs of depression in his behavior. In fact, Pemba had not slept properly since last week, and last night, he did not have a minute of sleep the entire night, despite the fact that he took a sleeping tablet just before bedtime.

Somo, the elder son of Tanaka, brought a glass of milk to Pemba in his bedroom, which he kept next to his bed. Pemba also requested he bring two sleeping pills from his mother. He was sure he took two; one tablet had had no effect last night, and tonight he wanted to sleep. Perhaps two tablets might help.

He had a weird dream. He was asleep, but he was on a white flying horse that was taking him toward tall snowy mountains. There were beautiful blue lakes on the ground with lots of animals, which he could see on the ground grazing in the green pasture. Despite the snowy mountains, the air was not cold; rather, it was very pleasant and blowing on his face and all over his body mildly. After flying for almost another twenty minutes, the horse started a descent to a large beautiful meadow. Dense trees covered the entire meadow in a circular way. In the middle of the meadow, a large pond was situated, and in the center of the pond, a tall, white water fountain was spewing water. Around the water, one could see multi-color small rainbow signs in the background visible towards the sun rays. Deer, rabbits, and peacocks were chasing each other and running all over the beautiful green meadow. Far on the right side, near the trees, a white medium-sized marble pond with pure blue water was filled with lots of goldfish along with lotus flowers that were blooming attractively. A tall person—with a clean, shaved head, unusually bright face, sharp, black eyes, alluring smile, and wearing a white silk robe—was playing with the goldfish. He seemed talking with the fishes, which was inaudible, and the fishes were replying in some language that was hard to understand. That godlike, miraculous person approached Pemba with a smile.

"Pemba, you are a good person and are going through a difficult time in your life. For some time seek refuge; you go and stay with the Amish people."

The next moment, he heard a voice, "Uncle, tea."

When he opened his eyes slowly and with hard effort, he saw Somo standing with a cup in his hand.

"Thanks, Somo. Is your dad home?"

"No, he is on morning walk."

Pemba washed his face and finished his daily routine. He noticed that Charlotte was in the kitchen, cooking, maybe breakfast. He approached her.

"Morning, Charlotte."

"Oh, how are you, Pemba? Did you have a good night's sleep?"

"Oh, yes, indeed, very good. I also had a weird dream."

"That is good."

"Hi, Pemba," Tanaka addressed him while entering from the gate.

"Good morning, Sir."

"A very good morning. Did you have a good night's sleep?"

"Yes."

They all sat in the large family dining room and had breakfast together. Pemba liked Tanaka's children; they were very polite, well disciplined, and had great respect for their parents.

After the breakfast, Pemba requested Tanaka for some time to discuss his future plans. Tanaka observed Pemba closely, and he noticed that today his face was calm, not excited, and he seemed to be in normal condition.

"Yes, Pemba. What would you like to discuss?"

"Can you tell me what Amish is?"

"They are a special kind of people that came from Europe a long time back and settled in the back road of America as farmers and lived in primitive tradition way of life."

"Where do they live in America?"

"I do not know exactly, but in Midwest and more in Pennsylvania."

"What do you mean by primitive tradition?"

"I mean, they adopt lifestyle of two to three hundred years back, without car, electricity, television, computer, and even education."

"What on education? They do not go to school?"

"They allow their children up to eighth grade only, and they have a one-room private school in their community."

"Do you know anybody from their community?"

"No, I have hardly seen them in person I have seen them only on movies, documentaries and books."

"I had a weird dream last night, and a godlike figure asked me to go to Amish people and stay with them for some time."

"Do you believe in dreams?"

"Yes, I have had visions in the past through dreams."

"So what you want to do?"

"I want to go and live with them for some time."

"Look, Pemba. It is you who makes your own decision. I am not going to tell you to do this or do that, but in the first place, they will not accept you in the community, and in case they do, you will be losing your career and American dream."

"I lost faith in America and American people. I find them very selfish, self-centered, and extremely materialistic."

"Pemba, you are making a general observations based on Linda."

"Yes, America is a capitalist society," Tanaka added.

"Let me think for a day and will decide tomorrow."

"I suggest," Tanaka insisted, "take your time and come to right decision."

The next morning, the house was quiet. He realized it was Monday. Everybody was at their business. Tanaka and Charlotte were at work, and the children were in school, as usual. After taking a quick shower, he prepared to go out and came down. He noticed a handwritten note on the fridge door, which read, "Pemba, it is good you have had a great sleep. There is your breakfast on the table; please take it before you go out."

While taking a shower earlier, Pemba had decided to go to an Amish place and live there for some time. He needed to go to the bank to withdraw the money and give it to Tanaka to send to his family in Nepal. He had to submit a resignation at Home Depot, leave the truck at Tanaka's place, and go to Pennsylvania may be by bus the following day.

When Pemba finished all his chores, he also went to Linda's home to pick up some clothing. It was almost six in the evening. He came back to Tanaka's; only the children and Charlotte were at home.

"Hi, Charlotte!"

"Oh, Pemba, Tanaka told me about your yesterday talk. What have you decided?"

"It is painful, but I decided to go to the Amish people tomorrow."

"It is that what you want in life?"

"Yes, at the moment."

"Remember, Pemba, we both love you, and the children like you. We will not mind if you'd like to stay with us longer time until you find your own place."

"It is not that. Thanks for your generous offer, but I would like to leave this place for some time, get away from Linda's memory and explore in life something else."

"Well, it is entirely up to you. If you do not like at Amish, definitely come back."

When Tanaka arrived home, Pemba had an important chat.

"I have decided to go to Amish tomorrow. Here is about four thousand cash, and I would like to keep it in your account. Please send five hundred dollars every month to my family in Nepal. I will leave the truck with you; please take the necessary steps to dispose it, and I will sign all the papers. Here are the divorce papers; please send it to the lawyer."

Tanaka was hoping that Pemba would make the right decision, but this was not something he was expecting. He took the money, papers, and the documents from Pemba reluctantly. He was still hoping perhaps he would change his mind, but it looked like he was determined and noticed a strong confidence in his face. He felt he was making a big mistake in his life.

"One more thing! I will need a ride tomorrow to go to Greyhound bus stop."

Charlotte dropped him to the bus station on her way to work. Pemba took a bus to Lancaster in Pennsylvania, which left at quarter to nine.

When he arrived at his destination, Pemba hired a taxi and asked to be taken to the Amish community. The taxi stopped at a place as if nowhere in the middle of a rural half-dusty road. It was almost dark outside, so he asked the taxi driver to drop him at the nearby motel.

The next morning, he noticed it was a small village. There was nothing much around—a barber shop, a flower shop, a grocery store, and a couple of other business houses. He noticed a few people walking in the street in long coat, trousers supported by suspenders, and shirts, with hats and unmanaged beards. He had never seen people in such outfits. In front of the business places, a couple of buggies driven by horses had been parked. He walked inside the flower shop.

A man with the same kind of beard and trousers and suspenders asked Pemba, "What can I do for you?"

"Yes, I am looking for the Amish community."

"Well, you need to walk around two miles through the road and will reach the community and the church."

"Thanks."

After walking along a long distance, Pemba came to a farming community and walked to a large barn where some people were talking together.

"Excuse me; is this the Amish community?"

A mature person—with the same kind of beard but more on white hair and the outfits he had seen earlier—approached him.

"Yes. What can I do for you? We are Amish here, and this is our community."

"Hi, my name is Pemba. I came from Los Angeles. It will be my pleasure if you allow me to join your community."

The mature person was startled as no one before had come to join their community like this. In a way, it surprised him; he found it difficult to believer the offer.

"Son, normally we do not allow outsiders to join us, but the decision could be made by our bishop only." He looked closely and critically on Pemba's face and observed his personality.

"Peter, take him to the bishop," the old man asked a young lad who was standing nearby.

"Okay, Pa."

Pemba followed the young guy and came to a room furnished with the basic chair and table. A tall man with long white hair was sitting in the table and was reading something from a very old book.

When he saw a tall Mongolian-type person, he asked Peter, "Yes, Peter."

"This gentleman has come to join our community."

The bishop had hard time to believe what Peter was saying.

"Pa sent me this gentleman here. The man says, he would like to join our community."

He looked toward Pemba and asked him to sit on the chair, which looked like a naked wood without polish and was in rough shape.

"What is your name, and where do you come from?" the bishop asked.

"Pemba, and I came from Los Angeles."

"Why do you like to join our community?"

"I have heard about your community in my dream first time in my life."

"What happened in the dream?"

"A godlike person told me to join."

"Are you alone in your family?"

"Yes, divorced recently."

"What is your religion?"

"I am a born Buddhist."

"Will you accept our religion and way of life?"

"Yes."

"We do not allow outsiders in the community, but your intention seems sincere. We may take you on a provisional basis if it is approved by our senior committee members. They will conduct an interview, and if they approve unanimously, perhaps you may be allowed."

Pemba just nodded his head and did not say anything.

"Can you come tomorrow at eleven?"

"Yes."

"Where are you living now?"

"In a motel about two miles from here."

"Okay then, see you tomorrow."

The following day, when Pemba went to the community again, three elderly persons and the bishop were waiting for Pemba. He was asked to sit in a crude chair, facing everyone in the front. They asked several questions about his intention, origin, religion, family background, and education and specifically if he was willing to accept the religion, way of life, and regulations of *Ordnung*—a policy manual. He was given a one-page simple form asking his name, passport, and green card number along with some kind for emergency contact. They asked him to bring the form again the following day at eleven when the decision would be made by the committee.

The next day, Pemba filled out the form and was on time to hear their decision. Again, in the same room, the same people asked a few more questions on drug and drinking habit, which he needed to relinquish if he accepted to live in the community. It was a vigorous process they adopted in providing the membership. After nearly an hour, they put forward their conditions.

The bishop made the announcement.

"Well, Pemba, the committee has made a decision. We will provide you provisional membership for one year. If you break any of our rules, you will be asked to leave immediately. Do you accept the condition?"

"Yes, I will make sure I will not break any rules and will be a productive member of the community."

"Great, and welcome to our community. You may bring whatever belonging you have tomorrow, and we will assign you a family."

Pemba had been assigned with Mr. and Mrs. Michael Schmitz—elderly German couple without children. The man's age was about seventy, and his wife was sixty-five. Both looked tough and energetic. Normally, an Amish family had children from seven to ten. In some cases, the number could be higher. But this old German couple had lost all their children in various accidents, and they needed some support in this old age. They had a large field in front and back of the house. The house was nothing but a structure built of wood. It had two bedrooms, one small kitchen, a small pantry, a living room, and a dining room upstairs; and downstairs they had a large store room in one side, and next was the only bathroom in the house. Outside the house, the right area was covered with a medium-size barn where they had a couple of horses, cows, and a few chickens. There was one buggy in front of the house.

In an Amish country, no vehicle was allowed; they only allowed horse drawn carriages. As per the rules, for long distance travel to other communities, they only used charter bused and hardly traveled in public buses and taxis—the reason every house had a carriage.

Pemba was given a room upstairs, slightly smaller room than Michael's but it had a window and offered a great view of the fields. There was no fan, air-conditioning, television, radio, or any electronic gadgets in the kitchen. In fact, there was no provision of public electricity. There was a small gas stove for cooking. Outside in the barn corridor, he saw an ugly-looking, very old phone, and he had no idea whether that was working.

Pemba was now in the surroundings, like his village and everything was of almost three centuries back. The field was plowed with the help of horses, and no tractor was allowed.

Pemba did not have any knowledge of the Amish culture, life, history, or any other basic things. He needed lots of information and knowledge to survive in this new but peculiar society, which opposed all sorts of progress and lived almost three hundred years back compared to the current civilization in America, and led simple life.

Dinner was simple—homemade bread, chicken roast, mashed potatoes with creamed celery and pepper cabbage. It was simple and fresh, and for the first time in life, Pemba felt the taste of dinner so nice and fulfilling along with his new family.

After the dinner, in the small and shabby living room, Mr. Michael volunteered to tell Pemba about the Amish way of life in a brief way as advised by the bishop.

"Amish culture began in Europe, in Switzerland and Germany, around 1693. Amish came to America in two batches—one in 1700 and the other, in the first half of 1800 century, and my father came from Germany in 1880. He died in 1958. We bought this land of thirty acres in 1967 and have been working in the field since then. This property could be yours if you complete your provisional period of one year.

"Basically there are three other types of Amish communities besides us—they are Hutterites, Mennonites, and Brethren. We are from the old order and conservative among other groups. We are very careful in choosing and adopting a new system. During the latter part of nineteenth century, due to industrialization, science and technology, those who wanted to preserve old tradition have become old-order Amish. Although we look similar in our outfits of men and women dresses, our tradition prevails in different manner from one group to the other. Twentieth century is the most technologically advanced period in human progress, but our community not only survives without it, it also thrives. Actually, in every twenty years, our population doubles. The distinctive clothing women wear are head cover, bonnet, an apron, and three parts of dress fastened together with pin. The colors allowed are green, brown, and blue, and young children have no head cover. For men, a wide-brimmed hat, beard, black suit with hooks and no buttons make the outfit. Use of suspenders is allowed but no belts. Similarly, tailor-made suits and ties are forbidden. Jewelry, wedding rings, and facial makeup are prohibited.

"In education we allow one-room private school up to eighth grade that teaches reading, arithmetic, grammar, penmanship, geography, and history. The preferred class size is twenty-five to thirty-five students, and one teacher is responsible to teach all eight grades. We have normally a female teacher who draws twenty-five to thirty-five dollars a day, and our total annual expenses is $250 per student. We feel eighth grade of education is more than enough to work in fields and other small and cottage industries' work— the reason our community does not have physicians, engineers, nurses, and other high professional workers. Our educational aim is to prepare the youth for a meaningful life in the Amish society.

"Okay, Pemba, how about some more facts on Amish life tomorrow? I am feeling sleepy, and have a good night."

Pemba also went to sleep. He had a dream he was working in Ubon farm in Thailand. They were married and had two children, one boy and a girl, both very cute. They were both happy. He seems to be happy with Ubon and children. The farm provided all the food, vegetable and chicken meat for the family. When he woke up he found in the reality at the Amish community. Pemba send a post card to Ubon that day.

The next morning, after a very simple breakfast of corn bread, poach, and homemade peach juice and coffee, Mr. Michael took Pemba out to show him the boundary of his land and familiarize him with the local situation. The land was in oval shape. On the left side of the land, there was a small canal that followed to the south and, according to Michael, was the source of water for the fields.

"We do not use the regular commercial insecticides or fertilizers; we have our own compost system that works more effectively than the factory products. Normally, we have wheat, corn and potato. Did you see the back-side cover area behind the house? That is for kitchen garden.

"Our community allows owning private land, but in most of the other communities, private ownership is not allowed. We only use horse for plowing the land; tractors, and other equipment are not allowed. Our life is rooted in the soil; the land has nurtured our common and family life. We believe good soil provides good life, good church, and until the land provides, we can also work together, live together, and worship together.

"But as you can see, the cost of land is rising significantly. I told you we bought the land at $168 per acres; now it has gone up to $632. Suburbanization, tourism, growth of Amish population, all contributed in rise of farmland cost. Most Amish people are now diverting away from farming due to modern competition and government regulations to other small occupations working in cottage industry, factory employees, and constructions. As per the statistics, the farming occupation has dropped from 61 to 35 percent from 1970 to 1987. But as long as we have this fertile land with us and as long as it feeds us and our family, we are not going to abandon it. Whatever may come, we would face it."

While coming out of the land toward the southern part of road, they visited a flower shop owner, and Schmitz introduced Pemba as his adopted son who was a provisional community member for a year. The flower shop owner gave two roses free, one for Pemba and another for Mrs. Schmitz. After coming home, they had lunch, and Pemba came to know that he was going to a wedding in the afternoon. Since Pemba did not have the typical simple dress of Amish, Schultz gave him one of his dresses to try on. Everything—fit him perfect, except the fact that he looked odd in the arms.

The three of them used the horse-driven carriage, and Pemba asked to drive as a learner. After driving slowly for about twenty of rural blocks, they came to a large gathering; around one hundred people had assembled. Pemba was surprised there was no musical instruments, but people were in joyous mood and all were happy. Mr. Schmitz asked Pemba to sit with him as no one was familiar with him so far. Mr. Schmitz slowly narrated the wedding tradition in Amish community.

"Normally, wedding takes place on Tuesdays and Thursdays between late October to December. The festival starts in the morning after eight and lasts until midnight at the bride's home. Couples marry normally in their early twenties, and prior to marriage, they may date for one to two years. The vow is taken in the church, which is administered by a bishop where the couple can hold hands but no kiss. Marriage should last a lifetime; divorce is a taboo. As per the tradition, before marriage, the groom takes a letter signed by seniors of the church to the bride's family, which is a proof that the bridegroom has good standing in his home district. In the ceremony, no musical instruments, wedding rings, jewelry, and facial makeup are allowed."

Pemba noticed, during the dinner, that there was roasted chicken mixed with bread filling, mashed potatoes, and some kind of dark gravy, cabbage sausages, and other green vegetables—and for sweets, peaches, cookies, and pudding. He liked the simple but effective party where he had the opportunity to meet a couple of nice people from the community.

Since they had had the dinner, Schmitz asked for a cup of tea in the living room. Pemba brought it from the kitchen and began the next session on Amish life and culture. Schmitz was going to inform him about the religion.

"*Basically, we the Amish people see life as a preparation of eternal life, which is also the ultimate goal in Buddhism.* There are numerous similarities between the religions, as both believe in tolerance and forgiving. Our church district holds services every other Sunday, and our worship service at home reaffirms the moral order of the Amish life. Our baptism does not occur during childhood but when one is mature enough to understand religion—normally between the ages of sixteen to twenty-two—along with pledge, as per Amish theology, to uphold the *Ordnung* of the church for the rest of one's life."

Pemba also approved that religion was something not to be foisted at birth but should be a choice that was given in later part of life.

"During a congregation, normally, we adopt religion with singing, prayer, and two sermons that revolve without the aid of organs offering candles, flowers, crosses, robes. The members simply yield themselves to God in the spirit of humility. The punishment for a sin comes with confession and those who refuse to confess are sentenced to six-week probation. Those who are stubborn might face shunning—a cultural of solitary confinement."

"Our ways of life have been threatened by changes in technology and social change. Some progressive communities use common household items—such as, instant pudding, disposable diapers, ziplock bags, permanent pressed fabrics, gas appliances, and air power tools that are common. But the conservative community still uses outhouse and open area and does not have refrigerators, but as you have seen, we have one in the kitchen. Except for a few battery power gadgets, a home does not have electricity; it has no television, radio, computer, and private phones in the room. Similarly, electric dryer, air-conditioning, and microwaves are not found in the homes. We have washing machines, but they are powered by gasoline engines. Similarly, cooking and water are heated by gas, and homes are normally heated by wooden stoves, coal, or kerosene. Due to tremendous growth and development in technology and due to economic pressure and convenient way of life, there have been visible changes occurring recently. The use of instant coffee, gas grill, chainsaw, and plastic tricycles is not allowed. We tolerate some changes in the name of convenience as long as it does not threaten our existence, identity, and basic culture. The *Ordnung*'s old-order life is regulate. *Ordnung* is a German word and it means 'rules and disciplines.' Some groups have it in written form, others have them simply passed on understanding and oral tradition and practice. The things which are taboo in the *Ordnung* are hard to adopt, and it has embodied and regulated the use of technologies, worship practices, the methods to with outside world, dress codes, and gender roles.

"Pemba, there are hard works and inconveniences. We have strict restrictions in dress, individual freedom, convictions, education, occupation choice, friendship, marriage and mobility. Amish life provides basic human needs, caring, stability, identity, crimeless society and employment. moreover, it provides an emotional security. Besides, it is the only bestowed road to heaven—which is not super highway, though. It is an old, ancestral way that is prescribed by scriptures. Walk in the old road to know where one is going and why. It at least fills the human soul with true meaning. The basic reason of the growing of our community is living in nature and having simple, uncomplicated life and praying sincerely in the church. This is the only road to heaven."

***

CHAPTER SEVENTEEN

March 1990

By now, nearly after six months in Amish community—Pemba liked this simple, uncomplicated, and meaningful life. He had become very popular among the Community members. If someone was sick, he would go plow the fields. In holidays and wedding ceremonies, he would go to the member's houses and clean the place, removed the weeds, fix the pavements, and install the damaged barriers. He had earned great reputation from community, church and all seniors. Besides, he had become a favorite star among younger generation because of his skills in sportsmanship. He had been assigned the job of a substitute teacher, and if the regular teacher was unable to conduct the class due to sickness or any other reason, he handled it satisfactorily. All the students really liked him.

Pemba was so contented with the heavenly life that he made up his mind that after his sisters finished the local school, they might go to the third countries for higher study, and he would bring his mother here and keep her with him.

Out of emotions and during his depression because of the sudden separation with Linda about six months back, he burned his passport, green card, driver's licenses—all the papers he thought would be not necessary anymore. That time, he felt great relief in disposing them, which was like a curse in his life.

The way Linda behaved toward him was unimaginable and beyond his expectations. In fact, he did not have a grip of his new life in this country. He was shocked and totally bruised. He cried a lot in the first few days. Tanaka's family supported him during his fragile time and gave him moral support and courage to survive.

Pemba had seen horrible scenarios of America while traveling by bus to Pennsylvania. He saw the homeless people on the street, people going through garbage dumpsters for food, beggars asking for money—that had surprised him, and he thought, *how could this be possible in the land of plenty, the richest nation on earth that sends million dollars' aid to third countries in the world? Why were they not tackling such a horrible problem within the inner cities that had been marring the reputation of the nation on daily basis?*

On the other hand, he also witnessed millions of acres of unused land on both sides of roads that had not been cultivated and ranched for productive purpose. Those homeless people and beggars could have used their labor and made it productive like the Amish people were doing here. In the world, if one was not greedy, there were lots of food for all the population that had been given by God if they're determined to lead a simple life. Perhaps it was too early for him to understand the political system in America. Mr. Schmitz was also explaining him one day that America had a lot of welfare budget, and they had social security, unemployment benefits, Medicaid, and Medicare to support elderly and retired people. He said, the Amish people had fought against many regulations imposed by the government in education, farming, taxes, and they had won most of the cases through Supreme Court decision.

"We have our own faith, principles, and social fabrics that have preserved our society over three hundred years. Being in America, we are out of many government regulations. We do not believe in war; so we discard the draft system. Many Amish moved to Canada just to get away from American draft system. We do not participate in social security system, but we pay taxed, not get benefits. We are far from American political system. No Amish is allowed to affiliate and participate in the political process. We normally do not vote, but if an Amish goes to vote, we allow him or her. There is no penalty against it. Though we are in America, we have our systems and regulations. We avoid all the welfare benefits provided by the government, including Medicare and Medicaid."

Nearly about two weeks back, Pemba had come across the old address of Jack in Colorado and sent a simple postcard, telling him that he was in Amish country in Lancaster, Pennsylvania some six months back and was having a wonderful life. He was expecting a reply from him anytime; perhaps he might be happy for his new life in America. At home, Mr. Schmitz was normally healthy and energetic, but Mrs. Schmitz complained of abdominal pain occasionally. This morning after breakfast, she expressed sharp pain and told Pemba about it. Pemba asked her to go to the hospital with him immediately for check-up.

"You get ready; I am making the carriage ready for you, Mrs. Schmitz."

They went to the hospital as Mr. Schmitz was in the meeting at the church. The community hospital was of medium size, extremely clean, and equipped with all sorts of medical equipment—which Pemba had never seen before in his life. It took about an hour in the waiting room for the doctor to see Mrs. Schmitz. They took her X-ray, checked her blood and urine, and put her body inside a large white machine and scanned whole body. Pemba watched all the methods, which he had no knowledge of. All the examining procedures took another one hour, and finally, a doctor gave prescription to buy medicines and use for two weeks and come back again for follow-up. The pain in the stomach of Mrs. Schmitz was fading slowly, and it had become tolerable now.

Since both of them did not have the money to buy medicine, they needed to go to Mr. Schmitz and hand over the prescription. They drove to the meeting building in the inner part of the road, little far from main road.

"Mr. Schmitz, we went to the hospital because Mrs. Schmitz had acute pain in the stomach," Pemba reported.

"Yes, Pemba. How is she now? And what does the doctor say?"

With that question, Mr. Schmitz came out of the building and approached the buggy. "How is the pain?" he asked his wife.

"Better now."

"Okay, Pemba, take her home. I will bring the medicine."

Pemba helped Mrs. Schmitz to lie in the bed. He brought some hot water from the kitchen and put it next to Mrs. Schmitz's small stool.

Nearly after an hour, Mr. Schmitz brought the medicine and helped his wife take them. After the medication, she went to sleep. Pemba left for the barn to feed the animals and clean the area.

Pemba was like a breath of fresh air for the Schmitz family. He was taking care of the field, house, and barn very satisfactorily and took care of the family like his own. Mr. Schmitz and his wife expressed their happiness in having Pemba in their family and taking care of them. Mr. Schmitz loved him more than his own son.

During the Sunday school and fellowship get-together, in many occasions, Mr. Schmitz appreciated Pemba's contribution to his family in public, and his devotion to fields and animals. They were very fortunate to have him as their son and source of great help in family matters.

The next day morning was pleasant, as spring was approaching with calm and fresh air. Just before sunrise Pemba normally woke up with the sound of roosters and birds chirping from the nearby trees. This sound was very dear to him, which reminded him of his village life. Outside, the sky was blue; in fact, there was no sign of cloud patch in the sky, and he loved such weather and outdoor life. He had unusual affection toward the fields and the soil that provided nourishing life to mankind. Perhaps this hidden love for soil had drawn him to this unusual lifestyle. At the moment, he had not thought life beyond the Amish.

He knew his adopted parents loved him, although sometimes he remembered his father and his mother a lot. As for his sisters, he wanted to make them independent by providing higher education so that they could have enriched lives.

Normally, they had a nap in the house after the lunch for a short time in the afternoon too. But Pemba liked to go around and see the barn, check the animals, and supervise the source of water in the fields.

One day, while coming back from the field, he saw a fancy car in front of his house. He was curious to find out about the visitor. He approached the house slowly, and to his surprise, saw Jack in the living room, talking with Mr. Schmitz. "Jack, what a surprise?"

They hugged each other, and Mrs. Schmitz brought a cup of coffee for Jack.

After a small chat with the family, Jack suggested Pemba to go to his motel along with him for further talk. Mr. Schmitz allowed Pemba to go in his car as Jack promised to bring him back. Outside, when the car moved from the house, Jack began to talk after a long silence. "Pemba, I do not understand, what this nonsense is?"

Pemba did not answer, and remained mum for a long time.

"Jack, what am I supposed to do after the sudden divorce with Linda?" Pemba outburst.

"You could have written to me or informed me somehow," Jack argue.

"I was so depressed, I was not thinking straight and was losing my mind," Pemba explained.

"Look, Pemba; you saved my life, and you know I treat you like my brother."

"I am aware of that."

"So, how are you affiliated with Amish people?"

"Close." Pemba said.

"But, you do not belong here" Jack insisted.

"Now I do."

They reached the motel where Pemba also stayed before coming to the Amish community. They approached the restaurant and sat together on a table. Jack ordered some coffee and cakes for the snack.

"Pemba, what do you want to do now?" Jack put him a straight question.

"What do you mean?"

"I mean; do you want to stay with the Amish people or go with me?"

"Jack, it is not that easy to leave now." Pemba explained his problem.

"What is your obligation toward them?" Jack questioned.

"They treat me like a family," Pemba said.

"But they are not; your family is in Nepal," Jack argued again

"I understand."

"Don't you have your obligation toward your sisters and mother?" Jack challenged Pemba.

"I do. Someone in Los Angeles is sending money every month on my behalf."

"Pemba, money is not the only relationship toward your family.

Pemba paused and did not reply.

"How about your sisters? They need your support when they get married, and your mother needs your love and affection from her son."

"I understand," Pemba agreed.

"Look, Pemba! I do not have much time to spend here. I have my well-established business, and this is the high season I should be there."

Pemba nodded.

"I will provide you ten percent partnership without you putting money. Work with me." Pemba still nodded without reply.

"You do not have to worry about living place and car. For the time being, stay with me. I will soon get you an apartment, and you can use one of my company cars."

It seemed Pemba understood Jack's proposal, but he had not replied yet.

"Pemba you do not belong here. Tomorrow we will take a plane to Denver together."

Pemba had no words to express his feelings; he just said, "I cannot leave until the Amish community allows me." Pemba showed his inability.

"Do not worry about that. I will convince them today."

They drove back to the community at Mr. Schmitz's house and approached him.

"I need to take back Pemba with me to Denver due to some emergency in his family in Nepal," Jack approached Schmitz diplomatically.

Schmitz was bewildered with Jack's approach. Words could not come out from his mouth; he just gestured toward Jack with an amazed expression.

Jack explained, "Pemba once saved my life, and I consider him my only brother. It is my responsibility to help him out when his family needs him."

"You mean; you want to take Pemba away from us?" Schmitz stammered.

"Sorry, maybe temporarily. His mother is sick; he needs to go to Nepal immediately."

"I have no authority to let him go from the community. Go; talk with the bishop."

Pemba knew where the bishop's small office was. They drove there and requested the bishop to see them. The bishop asked them to come inside. The room was primitive with very old furniture. The bishop occupied a small table with old kind of leather-bound books spread around and asked them to sit in front the chair.

"What can I do for you?"

Jack explained to the bishop more or less what he told to Schmitz.

The bishop thought for a few moments and said, "How do you know Pemba?"

Jack narrated the life-saving effort by Pemba and explained how he considered him his own bother since then.

"How long will he be gone from here? the bishop asked.

"We have no idea, until his mother completely recovers," Jack pleaded.

"Let me give you this small form. Put an application. The seniors will have a meeting tomorrow and decide."

"I was planning to take him today." Jack was determined

"That is impossible; we must wait until tomorrow," the bishop replied.

Jack approved of it, reluctantly. He returned the simple half-page form after Pemba had his signature on it.

"Okay, thanks; we will be here tomorrow."

Jack asked Pemba to go with him but assured him that he would drop him back early in the night. Jack further convinced Pemba of all the benefits he would get in his life working as his partner so that Pemba would not change his mind later.

The next morning, around eleven, Jack arrived at the bishop's office, but he did not see Pemba. After some time, Schmitz brought Pemba in the old-style buggy. They waited outside almost ninety minutes until the meeting was over and the bishop asked them to come in.

"Well, it is good news. Pemba is allowed to leave the community—not in a temporary way as we do not have that kind of provision—but he may come back again whenever he liked. Because of his noble contribution to our community, he will be welcomed back anytime he wants."

That was a welcoming news for Jack; he had finally succeeded to pursue the Amish community to take Pemba away.

"I appreciate you for your efforts. On behalf of Pemba, I would like to thank you for your generous decision," Jack expressed his appreciation.

After the approval to leave the community, the emotional departure with Schmitz and other prominent community leaders, Pemba left with Jack by the car along with some basic belongings. They directly drove to the airport. Jack purchased a one-way ticket to Denver for Pemba, and the flight was at eight twenty. The flight arrived in Denver at around ten. Jack left his car in Denver Airport and picked it up from the parking area and drove to Boulder, Colorado.

Pemba slept in Jack's house in the guest room elaborately decorated and had all kind of luxury in the room with television and computer. It has a fancy bathroom with separate a blue glass, standing shower area, and large Jacuzzi bathtub. When he got up, no one was in the house; there was a note in the refrigerator about a prepared breakfast plate with omelet, sausage, and bread he needed to toast. When he was eating the breakfast, the phone rang.

"Hi, Pemba, this is Jack. I did not disturb you earlier. I am glad you woke up. Please be ready; I will come to pick you up after an hour."

"Great, I will be ready."

Jack took Pemba to his office that had a large space in the corner, a small cozy office with a secretary, and a receptionist in the front. The office was decorated with pleasing interior decoration with matching furniture, drapery, and carpet. It was an impressive office and occupied a whole building. "Pemba, this is going to be your office."

A midsize room with all kinds of amenities—a computer, phone, and large credenza for the files, and a big glass door store area attached to the wall. In the right-hand side, there was a large window reflecting a mountain and stream in the distance, which was clearly visible.

"Jack, I have a problem."

"What?"

"I destroyed all my documents—passport, green card, and driver's license when I was depressed"

Jack could not comprehend the reason for destroying such important documents, but he showed compassion rather than anger toward Pemba.

"Do not worry; we will go to social security office tomorrow and apply for a new one in replacement. Driver's licenses could be replaced also, but you need a Colorado State now. Regarding the passport, call your embassy in Washington. They will send you the form to fill out, and send them back with your pictures. You might receive it after nearly two months."

Pemba had no idea about the whole process, as explained by Jack. It seemed simple. he was thinking perhaps it might be very complicated and would be problematic.

Jack had come to his life as an angel, who provided all his dreams and wishes; but he needed to work hard in the company and be a productive member soon. The line of work he was going to adopt was not new; only it had a different scenario in the new country.

Jack handed over the rafting group files that were coming from April to December this year. When he observed the files, it seemed each month they had in the average of twenty groups, mostly from inside the country and a few from Spain, Australia, and Germany.

As explained by Jack, Pemba would get familiarized with the rafting procedures, river pattern, and some delicate matters that needed to be protected from insurance point. Jack also mentioned to him that there was a disease of suing in America. So they needed to be prepared from different potential litigation cases.

Pemba needed to learn many new systems and working procedures in America. Many things were simple, but legal matters were complicated and cumbersome. Pemba had confidence he could learn anything but needed time; anyway, Jack was there to help him achieve the goal.

He needed to call Tanaka and tell him about Jack and his life in Boulder with him. Both Tanaka and Charlotte would be extremely happy in his new adventure. They always had been a source of encouragement and provided all kinds of support, mental or otherwise. He would stay late in the office like in Mountain Travel and complete the files and make a plan to start the system in his way. Of course, he would consult Jack for all important actions, as he had very limited idea of the total operational process.

Jack asked Pemba to call so that someone would pick him up and asked him not to drive until he had license and insurance. It was already almost nine. He had only finished few files for follow-up and completed the procedures and saw that the rafting tour, which was within ninety days' full payment must be received from the clients. Pemba decided to call Tanaka, as it was only eight in Los Angeles.

"Hi, is this Somo?" Pemba asked.

"Yes, who do you want, please?"

"Hi, Somo, this is Pemba. May I talk to your dad?"

"Sure, hold on a moment."

"Hello, Pemba, my dear, how are you?"

"I am fine, Sir."

"So what is new?"

"Big news. I moved to Boulder, Colorado."

"Is that Amish community?"

"No, not with Amish, but with my friend Jack."

"Who is Jack? And how did you know him?"

"Long story. We met in Nepal long time back. He has well-established rafting company here."

"Will you work with him?" Tanaka asked.

"Yes, he took me as ten percent partner in the company."

"Pemba, that is a great news. I am really happy for you."

"I have a few letters for you, some are from home, a few local, and one from Linda's lawyer."

"Let me give you my address here. Please send me at your convenience." Pemba dictated the office address. "How is Charlotte?"

"She is great; I will tell her you called."

"Hey Pemba, do you know Linda has become a popular actress?"

"Good for her," Pemba made a short remark.

"Pemba, keep in touch. Now you have a telephone in the room, not in the barn."

"Sure, will be my pleasure."

Pemba felt relieved after talking to Tanaka. They had done enormous help; someday he would need to return the favors.

It was going to be almost ten. Pemba called Jack who promised him to send Tony, who lived close by to drop him to his place.

Nine months passed quickly, working with Jack. Pemba had his own apartment, not far from the workplace, a Toyota red pickup, and a decent bank balance in some savings. The company was doing very well. Income was great every month, and the profit margin was almost forty percent. This made their income in high bracket. Pemba's salary, bonus, and his income exceeded six figures per month. Besides, the company paid for his apartment and car. He just put the gasoline that cost around twenty dollars per week. Jack and Charlotte from Los Angeles always pushed him to get married soon. But he made a promise to himself, he would not marry anyone from here. He would go to Nepal and find a suitable wife later. Now he was too busy in the new very fulfilling and satisfying work situation. A month back, got the green card again, Colorado driver's license, and passport from the embassy. He could not believe he destroyed such important documents; he must have been partially crazy that time.

Pemba was in contact with a real estate agent Silvia, and was seriously contemplating to buy a house at least with three bedrooms, two bathrooms, and a garage in a nice locality. He would be going to see some coming weekend.

Jack assured Pemba, "Go ahead, and find something you like. If you do not have cash, I would manage for heavy down payment and co-sign the papers."

The real estate agent knocked at the door Saturday morning at around eleven. The agent was in his apartment, and they both left in the agent's car to see some houses.

The agent Silvia, asked him, "Do you have children? Do you want a house close to a school?"

"I do not have now, but maybe later, if I get married again." Pemba replied.

"It will be a good idea and also will be a good selling point to have a house close to a nice school."

"Yes, let us consider that option." Pemba suggested.

It was a middle-class locality primarily white-color workers in offices and schools. A few had their own small retail business. The area was open with neatly maintained landscapes, broad roads, and well-maintained houses that provided an impression about the neighborhood. The cars in the driveways were clean, bright, and almost looked new—most of them. Pemba liked the external look of the houses—mostly neutral of color, light brown and cream. All houses were of two stories with comfortable front yard and backyard.

Silvia stopped the car in front of a house that had light cream color paint, good proportionate front yard that had been manicured properly, and everything looked very clean and attractive.

"Here we are."

"Looks good, Silvia." Pemba liked.

"The house was built in 1983, has three bedrooms, two-car garages, and three baths. The living space is two thousand square feet and was announced for sale just last week."

"Do you have any idea why the owner is selling?" Pemba asked.

"Moving to Florida for retirement."

The house was even more impressive when they entered. Silvia took a key from a locked box and opened the main door. Immediately after the entrance was a cream-colored tiled passage, and there was a small closet on the right side of the room.

"This is for shoes," Silvia explained.

When Pemba looked inside, there were lots of shoe racks and were made to make family and its guests comfortable to store the shoes the moment they entered the house. All the shoes could be stored in the hidden closet, and no one would see them. Pemba thought it was a bright idea to store the shoe rack at the entrance of the main gate.

The living room was huge with high-vaulted white ceilings that had three golden chandeliers, a large one in the middle, and two small ones on the right and left. On the right side of the wall, it had wooden panel with matching color of dark wooden floor, shining and very impressive.

Toward the back green-grass yard was a large French window that commanded an excellent view of backyard with colorful flowers and two large trees—one on the right side and the next on the left—toward the back compound gate. The white fences were made of wooden panels and looked new. They added a spectacular view. The trees had green leaves that looked bright and shining and provided an impression. The dew was about to come out from each leaf. In the middle part of the backyard, there was a small marble fountain. Thin sprinkles were coming out from the beautiful jar, which was held by an angel. In closer approach, Pemba noticed that small goldfish were scattered in the pond of the fountain.

On the right side, there was a glass panel that reflected a private place for the kitchen that had fascinating new appliances—black stove, double-door white fridge, white countertop, built-in black microwave, small glass table with a television and a radio on the side, black dishwasher, four matching chairs, and a table for a sit-in place in the kitchen. The whole kitchen area was concealed from the living room and provided a private cooking area. There was a half-size window that provided a green view of the garden and the trees' leaves that touched the outside glass panel of the window.

On the back of the living room, there was a nice guest room, which had attached bath, and the large windows had commanding view of the pleasing backyard. Towards the front of the guest room was a staircase that would take them up to the second floor, which had a master bedroom and attached bath with large size Jacuzzi tub. Both the rooms and bath had very comfortable size and were pleasantly decorated with thick cream-colored carpet and matching drapery in the windows. It had the extremely soothing view of the properly manicured landscape and flower plants at the edge of the meadow. The family room was away further from master bedroom and also had a comfortable size with matching carpet and drapery in the widow. The full bath was also attached to the rooms. Pemba thought perhaps this room was suitable for children. Both the rooms had large panels of the windows tinted light-blue sky color, and it had soundproof and storm-impact glass windows.

Overall, Pemba liked the house setup, build, and living area—which was just perfect for his future family. It matched his lifestyle at the moment.

"What do you think?" Silvia looked at his face curiously.

"I like the house. How far is the school?"

"About two blocks down. I will show you on the way out."

"Is Jack's house close by?"

"It may take about ten minutes' drive," Sylvia explained.

"Silvia, I may not have good credit."

"Don't worry. Jack will co-sign, and also arrange your down payment."

"What is the bottom price?" Pemba asked.

"The owner is asking $265,000 but if you provide a reasonable price, I am sure he will accept."

"Okay. Please prepare the offer paper with $250,000," Pemba requested Silvia.

After three days, the owner approved of the price offer from Pemba at $250,000, after checking the credit report from the mortgage lender. Because of Pemba's credit report, Jack must sign in the loan guarantee agreement and must have twenty percent down in order to process the documents. Jack had agreed to all the terms of mortgage lender and signed the closing paper after one week.

After three days of closing the paper, Pemba moved to a new house and slowly began to furnish. It took him about three weeks to furnish the house to his liking. He also made a prayer room in one corner of the house where he assembled all the gods—Buddha, Jesus, Mohammed, Jewish replica of Torah, and Hindu god Shiva. With his experiences in life so far, he was of the opinion that all gods provide peace, guidance, and purpose in life; that was why he was going to adopt all gods equally without discrimination.

After about two weeks of his movement into the new house, Pemba began to feel lonely. So, he started seeking a companion. Tanaka suggested in his letter to marry a Japanese lady, which they could match-make for him, but he decided not to marry from other cultures after the bitter experiences with Linda. Linda had sent a five-thousand-dollar check as per her promise, and divorce was final now. Pemba thought perhaps he should seek the view of Jack as he knew almost everything about him.

One evening, after work, he suggested Jack for a drink and took him to a Boulder Nepali restaurant that provided all sorts of typical Nepali food. Pemba knew Jack would like that kind of food. The name of the Restaurant was Rodi Ghar, and the owner was from Khandbari area of Nepal. Pemba knew the owner casually. The decoration was basic with few antiquities from Nepal. A large sitting Buddha statue had been placed on the right side in the entrance. A few handicrafts were decorated in the wall, and they had a *sukul*—a floor mat—with some very odd-looking table. The paint decorations were bright yellow in one side, green in other, and dark-red portion in the remaining wall. It provided an unpleasant and cheap combination overall.

A waitress in Tibetan *bakkhu* approached with a menu in hand.

Jack ordered a beer, fried chicken, and one mixed soup with yellow saffron rice. Pemba order a beer, *momo*, a kind of fried wonton, and chicken chowmien.

"Jack, thanks for the house's down payment."

"Pemba, the down payment is only a loan; you will pay me back when you have enough money."

"I understand that. I want to get some advice on my personal matter, if you don't mind." Pemba looked with expectation toward Jack.

Jack was eager, and his body language was positive to solve Pemba's problem, whatever it may be.

"After the sudden and unexpected divorce from Linda, my life has been thrown into a sort of chaos."

"I can understand, Pemba! I also had a divorce in my life. It is a part of the American culture, and we do not have much control."

"I am not clear whether I should get married again. Now you provided me the house and a steady income, and brought me back from the Amish society." Pemba put his argument.

"Pemba, knowing you who you are, I can suggest you to get married again not from another culture but your own." Jack suggested.

"I am planning to go Nepal soon if you would let me and explore the possibility."

"By all means. Make a plan to go, and come back soon." Jack suggest

"You mean, should I go now?"

"Of course." Jack encourage him.

At dinnertime the restaurant was crowded. Jack understood, the people who had been to Nepal and were familiar with Nepalese food were its frequent visitors. An idea flashed in Jack's mind, which he would share with Pemba on the way to their home later. The food is delicious and also reasonable as compared to American restaurants' meal prices.

Since Jack picked up Pemba in his car earlier, he had to drop him back to his house.

"Pemba, I just have a vision. Can I share with you?"

"Sure." Pemba encouraged.

"How about opening a Nepali-Tibetan restaurant in Boulder close to our home?"

"It is a fascinating idea, but I have no knowledge how a restaurant runs." Pemba confessed.

"We will have an experienced manager." Jack cited the alternative.

"Let me come back from Nepal, and we will explore the possibility."

"That sounds good, Pemba. That way, your future wife might be a good asset to run it."

"I do not know about that; everyone does not have knowledge."

"Well, let us send the issue aside at the moment. Further, I have a friend in the department of anthropology at the University of Colorado, proposing me to organize a tour to Nepal," Jack said.

"That will be great idea, a tour company and a restaurant!" Pemba seemed excited with the thought.

After the permission from Jack, Pemba was determined, and made a plan to leave next week for Nepal. He called a Nepali who had a travel agency in Denver and booked the ticket.

As per the itinerary, he had to go to Los Angeles from Denver, and to Hong Kong and then to Kathmandu. He requested the agent to provide at least three days' stopover in Hong Kong so that he could buy some electronic goods and some clothes for his sisters and mother along with some gifts to his friends.

Pemba had stayed in Shangri-La Hotel in Hong Kong—which was so big it had a city inside the hotel with supermarket, department store, movie theater, and a number of restaurants. He could get everything inside the hotel, but Pemba knew that he could get bargain prices in Kowloon side, not in Hong Kong. He took the ferry that put him in no time to Kowloon. On both the sides of the street, he noticed shops everywhere. It went miles after miles. In fact, he had not seen so many shops of electronics goods, clothing, and gift articles standing together in a row. The market area was crowded; he saw nothing but people everywhere. Chinese and some foreigners, mainly tourists from different countries, were running from one place to another, looking for bargains. Pemba found Chinese retail shopkeepers mostly rude, as they behaved badly with the customers, though a few were exceptionally nice and polite.

Hong Kong, as Pemba found, was very fascinating. The British had really built it as best port for Duty Free shopping all the world over. About ten thousand people arrived every day and stayed an average of three to five days and spent minimum of five to ten thousand dollars on each shopping trip. Hong Kong was extremely fascinating in the night with numerous lights in the city. It illuminated like Christmas every day. The pick tram provided spectacular night scenery from the top, and Hong Kong looked like a bride decorated with glittering ornaments.

Pemba had all the necessary shopping and collected numerous bag, which were virtually impossible to carry by a ferryboat. So, he hired a taxi to go to the other side of Hong Kong.

***

CHAPTER EIGHTEEN

April 1990

The Nepal Airlines flight took a circle of the valley before landing at the airport. The flight was smooth, and inflight services and food were superb. Pemba liked the Asian service more than the American ones in flight services.

Although Pemba left from the same Kathmandu airport on his departure to America not long before, the airport looked clumsy, narrow, crowded, and not clean. The baggage reclaim area was congested and it took an extremely long time for the baggage to arrive. He seemed impatient due to long flight and not having proper sleep during his entire journey.

Pemba knew that his family had arrived from Phaplu the other day and was staying at Dorje Lapka's house in Boudha area. He had seen his distant uncle from his mother's side a couple of times in family gathering, but was not very close with them. They all must be outside the airport, waiting for him anxiously. Pemba was happy he had brought gifts for all of them, including his mother and sisters.

Pemba noticed that the luggage started arrive in the conveyor belt, but he had not seen any of his bags yet. He had put a red ribbon for the identification of his luggage, which should help him to pick it from the belt from among piles of luggage easily. He waited another half an hour, and eventually he saw some of his bags. He pulled them out one at a time and kept at one separate corner. Altogether, he had four luggage bags. A bag handler fortunately approached him to carry the luggage outside on the trolley.

He noticed a big crowd outside the custom area in the airport, and taxi vendors were howling at him. He politely refused them and moved to the area where his family was waiting.

His Uncle Dorje approached him and said, "Hi, Pemba, welcome to Nepal."

They embraced each other, and he paid respect to his mother and sisters. They approached him with affection. Everyone had a seat inside the Toyota Jeep. They had separated some space for the luggage.

The house where Pemba was taken had a large compound, and in the middle, a tall white marble Buddha statue stood under a Banyan tree that had thick leaves hanging all over the statue. In the front side of the statue, a very attractive pond with goldfish floating made the atmosphere peaceful. Surprisingly, lots of white pigeons were on the tree, and around the meadow, they were apparently searching for their feed.

Although the house had three stories beautifully built and was a nice house, the rooms were small—maybe because they liked to have more rooms in the house. It was a trend in this part of the city to provide each room on rent for two people or to a small family living as a unit. The house-owner usually lived in the third floor, and the entire first and second floors were rented away.

Although the first and second floor were narrow and congested, the third one—their living quarter—was bright, spacious, and much cleaner. Pemba liked his room that faced south, which was not only large, but also bright and airy. The room also offered a commanding view of the area, and the ground that occupied the house looked green.

Two children were trying to feed a baby deer that was a pet of the house.

Uncle Dorje entered Pemba's room asking, "Are you feeling well? Not tired with your trip?'

"Tired, but I can manage. I hope it will heal with time."

"Pemba, this is my niece Mona, who lives in Pokhara. She is smart, good-looking, and educated."

Dorje showed the photo of a fair-complex, large-eyed, and kind of sophisticated lady who was in jeans and beautiful red top. Pemba thought she had beautiful hair, and her styles of doing the hair were gorgeous.

"Pemba, I should be honest with you. Since I am handling the delicate matter of matchmaking between my two close families, I really deserve sincere and frank opinion from you."

"Uncle, trust me; I will deal sincerely with you in this matter."

Dorje said, "Let me ask you, how serious are you for the marriage?"

"You know, I am. I had divorce from Linda, and I am alone."

"How long will it take Mona to join you after the marriage?" Uncle asked.

"I have no idea. I could check with the embassy, but as per my information, it might take two years."

"That matter you need to decide between you two. Mona is an educated girl, who did her early schooling in Saint Mary's Kathmandu. At present, she is doing her higher study in Pokhara. She also manages a nice restaurant, International Fusion, in Pokhara at Lakeside, and she is fluent in English. If you like her, we have to go to see her in Pokhara and also meet her family."

Dorje asked immediately again, as though he had recalled an issue he had forgotten a while ago, "By the way, how long you are staying?"

"Maybe two or three weeks maximum."

"Do you feel all the process will be completed by that time frame?"

"I have no idea about paper and government formality, but I am willing to hire a lawyer to expedite the matter."

"Well, the first thing is, we need to make a plan to go to Pokhara immediately. You two have to like each other, and both the families should support the liking."

"I have nothing else to do here. I may be going to Pokhara day after tomorrow."

"Great! Pemba, I will make plans to go day after. How would you like to go: by plane or by car?"

"I think car will be better. I would like to take my sisters and mother along."

"That sounds good," said Dorje, supporting the idea.

He understood, in America, every second, marriage turned into divorce due to greed and attractive options in every step. His conclusion was that Linda's divorce was one-sided, and he was made a victim without any fault or ill cause on his side. So he had freed himself as a purified person and detached from her, even from her memory. If he was going to marry Mona, he needed to be detached from Linda's attachment in life. He needed to turn his attention towards Mona in totality now. The picture of Mona was appealing, and from American perspective, she would be a suitable person.

Pemba thought it would be an easy adjustment for her in the new country. She could mingle like water in the society, but he had fear in one corner of his heart whether she would like him or not. He had been told, she had some knowledge of the Western society and way of living. Besides, Saint Mary's was a British mission school that had tough discipline and was considered one of the best schools for girls. She must have achieved good education that could her life in a good course, and she might be a lasting life partner, and a wife. Moreover, she might be a loving mother to his future children, which was important in life. Love was a strong tie that held everyone in the family and was vital source of happiness. Other important part was perception between two unknown people which was necessary to develop a lasting relationship. Couple must have mutual respect and trust to make their relationship prosper in life. It was hard to predict about a person through a mere picture. Perhaps a conversation might throw some light. Pemba was not sure if her family would allow a meeting between them; he had to request Uncle Dorje.

All through the night, Pemba had many thoughts about his future life. Toward the morning, he composed some sleep, and when he woke up, he found his mind and body fresh.

They would be going to Pokhara soon. Uncle Dorje had a Toyota Jeep that would accommodate everyone and the luggage and would give them a comfortable journey. Pokhara trip always excited Pemba, but this time, he had double excitement, added by the prospect of meeting Mona. This time of the year, nature, flora, and absolutely green mountains all around the road and the lovely river on the right side enhanced the charm of their journey.

Their accommodation was in the Lakeside area, towards the end of Lake, close to a mountain at Tranquility Lodge that had spacious rooms, and magnificent lake view mountain view with beautiful swimming pool and a garden with lots of peacock, baby deer, and small cute white rabbits at the backyard of the resort. It really gave a true impact of tranquility. The name sounded appropriate and was attractive.

When he was unpacking his belongings, Pemba noticed his mother enter his room.

"Pemba, did you have enough sleep last night?"

"Oh, Mother, not enough, but just okay."

"May I ask you a question about Linda?"

"Sure, Mother."

"What went wrong with her? You divorced, or she divorced you?"

"Not me, Mother; she did."

"Was there a sufficient reason, or just like that?"

"I have no idea, Mother. She just left unexpectedly."

"Were you hurt?"

"A lot in the beginning, but not anymore," Pemba said.

"Is she likely to come back?" an innocent question was posed.

"No way, Mother. Once it is divorced by the court, it is over."

"So if you marry Mona, she will not make trouble," Mother wanted to be sure.

"No, Mother."

"I understand Mona is a good lady, and she does not have a boyfriend."

"Who knows! I will find out."

"Yes, Pemba. She is from a good family, and their restaurant is a popular place for tourists."

"What do my sisters think about her?" Pemba asked.

"They are also in favor now, but they were really surprised when Linda divorced you."

"Yes, Mother, it happens in America. That is a strange country."

"I would like you to think over about this relationship. Make sure it does not happen again."

"Sure, Mother. I will make it certain and be careful." Pemba assured his mother.

Mona's family invited Pemba for lunch in the International Fusion restaurant at one p.m. Dorje arranged a meeting with Mona at nine in the morning. Pemba was nervous, first time meeting Mona—whom he did not know at all. He had hard times deciding what to wear on his first date. He was supposed to pick Mona from the other side of the lake and go by a boat to her house. Uncle Dorje agreed to go by the same boat as Pemba had no clue of their house. Finally, Pemba picked dark-blue jeans, a charcoal shirt, and a thin, light-blue pullover as his dating outfit.

"Pemba, you're looking jazzy," his uncle complimented.

"Thanks, Uncle."

"Are you nervous?"

"A little."

"You should be. I was sweating in my first time meeting with your aunty."

Both laughed. The boat was a slow one. It used paddles as the local authority did not allow motorboat due to noise and water pollution they usually caused. In less than ten minutes, they reached the other side of the Lake.

Dorje led Pemba to Mona's house. The house had a large compound with tall trees around. The two-story house was in the middle of the compound, white washed with light blue color in the border, building up tremendous beauty and dynamic and majestic look.

When they approached the main gate, two large brown German Shepherds drew near them with loud and dangerous bark. A Sherpa boy came running after the dogs and controlled both the veracious dogs. Uncle Dorje seemed to be abnormally afraid with the dogs. Pemba took it easy. They were asked to wait, and after five minutes, a gorgeous-looking, tall, white-complexioned, dark-eyed lady approached them.

"Hi, I am Mona."

Pemba had the most amazing expression, but he tried to hide it unsuccessfully.

"Hello, Mona, this is Pemba," Uncle Dorje introduced. Pemba just uttered the word, "Hi."

They exchanged traditional greeting in Nepali "Namaste!

"Okay, you guys have about four hours; please get back for lunch in the restaurant on time," Uncle Dorje ordered.

"The Jeep is waiting on the other side, and you guys could go wherever you like. But come back on time. I will be at the restaurant."

Mona and Pemba exchanged a glace and were perhaps asking each other where to go. When they reached the Jeep, Pemba asked Mona, "Where would you love to go?"

"Sarangkot may be appropriate," Mona was very candid.

Pemba agreed with her. They sat on back side of the jeep as the driver was in the front. They had a decent space in between them so that perhaps they would avoid touching their bodies at this early stage and in front of the driver.

"I am sure you have been to Pokhara before. How many times?" Mona broke the ice.

"Maybe four or five times, I am not sure."

"What is the best part you like in Pokhara?"

"Obviously, as everyone else, beauty, mountains, and the lakes."

"How about people?" It was a teasing question from Mona.

Pemba did not answer immediately; he just paused and gave a mysterious smile.

"Perhaps people are not so beautiful." Mona had a provocative smile.

"I am forced to change my view after seeing your charming look."

"I am not so pretty; I consider myself an average person."

"Well, if you consider yourself average, what an average person is like will be a big question."

In the meantime, they reached nearly the top area of the mountain. Mona asked the driver to stop the car. The slope of the mountain area was exposed to red soil. The green meadow was missing. The slope looked challenging, and views down looked really attractive. In the distance, the lakes were glittering in the sun. Pokhara Valley looked magnificent with colorful dotted houses, tiny roads, and in the distance, the airport and some small planes in the airport looked like an artist's image—vivid, colorful, and lively.

"How do you like this view?"

"Gorgeous!" Pemba could not think of more appropriate word for the beauty's description.

"Well, I always love this place. You know, I love to fly in a large colorful balloon from here and reach slowly to my home on the shore of the Lake."

"You have a fantastic imagination."

Spending about a few more minutes watching the magnificent view down under the valley, the driver informed them they needed to walk for the top as the car would go no further.

It was a welcome notion for Mona; she was looking for adventure with Pemba to analyze his character and determination in life.

When they began to walk together alone, Mona asked a question, "I heard you were married to an American lady. Are you divorced now?"

"Yes, I was, and divorced now."

"Who divorced, you or her?" Mona asked.

"She did."

"Were you unhappy?"

"Yes, for a long time and was depressed."

"What guarantee do you have that you will not divorce *me*?" Mona gave expression to her suspicion.

"Look, Mona! Divorce is a matter between two people. From my perspective, I can guarantee ninety percent that from my side, I shall not tender you a divorce. The ten percent, I will leave on your part."

"I will use that ten percent if you stop loving me," Mona had a firm reply.

"Do you want children?" Mona's question was pertinent.

"Maybe two, one girl and a boy." There was calmness in Pemba's voice.

"How old are you?" Pemba asked again.

"I am not going to tell you that; ask to my parents," a weird answer.

"Do you have a boyfriend?"

"What kind of silly question? If I had one, I would marry him, not you." A candid reply from Mona.

"Well, it is hard to believe, not having a boyfriend in this modern time."

"You believe whatever you like. I gave you an honest answer." Mona replied.

"I understand; I will have to wait for the paper for over two years to go to America. Is that true?" Mona questioned Pemba.

"Unfortunately, it is true; they have visa-awaiting period."

"What will you do if I find a man and go with him within that long two-year period?" Mona joked.

Pemba did not have immediate answer to this highly unpredictable question. He kept quiet for some time and answered slowly, "I hope you will not do such a thing."

"Do you trust me?" Mona questioned.

"I have no option," Pemba answered.

Talking about personal matters mixed with a little romance, they reached the top of the place. The restaurant on the top had a balcony, a feast for the eye to observe the splendid view of the close-by mountains and Pokhara Valley down there. The view provided a magnificent look of Pokhara, which was such a commanding classic point. This place had inspired many romantic couples, poets, artists, and common people and tourists from all over the world.

"It will be better if they build a moving tower with an observatory on the mountain top." This was Mona's imagination.

"Tell me, what do you like best in America?" Mona questioned again.

"Sincerely, creativity and independence." Pemba gave an honest answer.

"I read lots about crimes, poverty, and broken family stories."

"Indeed, it is everywhere, but in America everything is open. The press has tremendous freedom; so you get the news out, but China and Russia are close countries, and they censor news. That does not mean they have no crimes." Pemba's explanation was convincing.

The waiter brought coffee and omelets ordered earlier. The coffee had strong, very soothing flavor, and they both enjoyed together. Pemba quietly checked the time; his watch indicated it was almost midday.

"Mona, we should be leaving now," Pemba suggested.

"Oh, so soon. What are we going to tell our family whether we like each other or not," Mona said.

"I may have to think it over," said Pemba, trying to play with Mona's emotions.

"Seriously?" Mona questioned again.

"No, I am joking. What do you think?"

"Honestly, so far, I like you. That's all," Mona expressed her feelings.

"So what is our conclusion?"

"Tell them we like each other; that is all they have to know now. Hey, Mona, tell me how come you have hardly any accent when you talk?"

"What do you mean by *accent*?"

"Normally, if you know other languages, they have accent. That is how people talk about in America"

"Silly, I had basic education from a convent, and our medium was English."

"You will be a great asset to the American society."

"I do not know about that until I reach America," Mona was honest.

"You will see when you come, maybe after two years."

"What do you mean by *maybe*?" Mona questioned Pemba.

"Well, visa is not in my hands; it is with the American Government." It was a provocative statement.

"Do not tease me. I am not coming if it is more than two years, by God." Obviously, Mona had a short temper.

"You know, you more beautiful when you are angry." Pemba whispered.

"May I kiss you?" Pemba asked.

"It is too early for that." Mona rejected the proposal.

"Well, will wait for that golden moment."

Pemba found Mona smart, intellectual, and articulate—both in her body language and style of conversation; she was going to be a great life partner.

Mona, on the other hand, liked Pemba on the face value, but she needed to find out lots of things about him, and she was very cautious on male characters that could be deceiving up front. But overall, Pemba seemed to have excellent morale character—along with his handling of the lady, which was polite and soft. He had some kind of hidden attraction in the personality.

The two families' lunch at the International restaurant was set on a large table in the northeast part of the corner. On one side, Dorje, Pemba, two sisters of Pemba, and his mother sat. On the other side in front, a mature man, a mature lady, two little girls, and a teenage boy sat. At the end, Mona occupied the table. When everyone had settled in the table, Dorje got up from his seat and introduced the first side of family members.

"Toward the end is Pemba's mother, these two cute young ladies, his sisters, and this is Pemba. In the head table is Mr. Kalden Sherpa; he is Mona's father. Next to him, her mother, these are his two younger sisters, and that young man is Mona's brother."

They exchanged traditional greetings among each other, and Mona's parents offered soft silk scarfs to Pemba, as an expression of respect from their side. It was because both the families were hopeful they might have good relationship in future.

Once they ordered traditional Sherpa drink *chhyang* for the men and soft drinks for the ladies, Dorje led the conversation in a very polite and soft manner.

"It seems the two of them have had a little chat. Pemba and Mona have consented that they are ready for the matrimonial relationship."

"Since we have only three weeks, as Pemba needs to leave, everything requires to be completed within this short period. So first we have to pick up the marriage date as soon as possible. Pemba needs to get some papers from the American Embassy, and we need to register the marriage at CDO office. The CDO office, needs at least two weeks to issue a marriage certificate. These official formalities are cumbersome and are essential processes in order to apply for US visa for Mona," Dorje explained.

In the meantime, the food began arriving on the table, and everyone's attention turned towards the cuisine.

"I will work closely with Kalden and will handle all the issues jointly and solve it pragmatically," Dorje seemed to conclude the meeting. "Finally, we would like to congratulate Pemba and Mona for their happy future life."

The next day, after a long and tedious discussion, Dorje and Kalden fixed the date for the marriage. They also mutually agreed on the venue; it would be in Pokhara. The date for the marriage was set after three days in a resort where Pemba's family was residing now, and the following day, Pemba would go to Kathmandu to get the documents from the American Embassy.

The marriage date arrived. Both the families were busy making all sorts of arrangements. Pemba invited Dawa and his wife. They could be great support during the main event.

The day was filled with commotion. Mona's family sent two helpers to provide support to Pemba's family for necessary arrangements. The whole colorful event that involved members from both the families and numerous helping hands completed the big ceremony as per the Sherpa tradition. Both the families jointly organized a grand dinner party for about three hundred people at Mona's house. The house was decorated with numerous colorful lights, and it looked like a small palace with bright white-color cover with many trees around. Both corners of the house were occupied with two large tents with huge dining tables placed in the middle. Guests talked about the taste of the food that was "ambrosial" and divine, as most people knew it was catered from Amber Restaurant of Pokhara that had outstanding reputation for more than a decade.

Around nine, it seemed the party was winding up. Most of the guests had left, but some close friends and families were still there. It seemed, they were enjoying the happy moment and finding it hard to leave. Most remaining guests were close friends and family clusters—either with Pemba or with Mona. The sequence of laughter, music, songs and jokes were shared among themselves as most children left for their bedrooms. Finally, the remaining guests and families too left around eleven thirty. It seemed, they were also tired and needed rest for the day.

The next day, Dorje, Pemba, and Mona left for Kathmandu to apply for marriage certificate, the presence of both was necessary to sign the petition. They left Pokhara at dawn so that they would have enough time to go to the concerned office for the petition.

Dorje had invited an ex-minister to help complete the office process on time. When they reached the office around two, the ex-minister and his helper were waiting for them. He took them to director's office and explained his reason of coming, indicating to Pemba and Mona. The director asked a section officer in the office to help them process the document soon as possible. Within less than an hour, the petition registration process was completed, and they were requested to come to the office after two weeks. It appeared they needed to investigate the legalization of marriage and complete the government procedures that required two weeks.

Now, it seemed the newly married couple had two-week honeymoon for themselves, and they requested Dorje to drop them at Hotel Shangri-La.

The last few days were real tiring for Pemba. He never realized that they had so much details. The old marriage tradition, in a way, was good in the sense that experience provided one lifetime event that would keep the marriage ties intact lifelong.

Mona wanted to go to her sister's house in the *Budhanilkantha* area, but Pemba suggested that it was their honeymoon period. Relatives' house would not be a suitable place for the same. He insisted that this time was important for them to know each other closely. Mona agreed, but when her sister called, it seemed they were not very happy for the hotel stay. Mona promised to come to their place for dinner one night.

It was hard to believe that the newly married young couple slept like a log soon after dinner. The whole night, they did not even touch each other due to extreme tiredness. When they woke up around noontime the next day, they just exchanged meaningful glances but had not talked until both took a bath and hit the bed.

First time, Pemba wanted to deal very delicately with Mona, as he knew ladies did not like rough and speedy behaviors while making love.

As they were sleeping naked, holding each other, Pemba whispered to Mona, "Have you had sex before?"

"Never."

"It is hard to believe a twenty-seven-year young lady has not had it yet. You know in America, young girls in high school are sexually active."

"Well, this is not America; you will have tough time to seduce me. Remember, this is my first time; you should be extremely gentle."

"Do not worry. I have lots of cream to apply on your private part so that it will be a gentle penetration."

"I am worried I might bleed. Let me see your thing, how large it is. As for mine, it is humongous. Let me see how it will go inside me."

"Darling, you are a grown-up lady. It should not be a problem."

"Will you promise you won't insert the whole of it?"

"I will be careful, and let me know immediately if it hurts you."

"But you might be enjoying. How can I stop?" Mona objected.

"I will; this is my promise." Pemba assured.

The couple had foreplay for about half an hour. Pemba tried to penetrate his penis inside of Mona— slowly, gently, and softly. She cried in the beginning, but it subsided and let Pemba move inside her delicately. It was really painful in the beginning when it penetrated her, but the moisture seemed to have comforted Mona. She held Pemba tight, and moaned joyfully. Mona had heard that sex was bad and it hurt, but the joy she had now proved that notion false. She began to like it, and wanted Pemba to move faster inside her.

When Pemba noticed that Mona was having pleasure, he thrust hard from the top into her vagina. When they reached climax, both moaned louder, and Pemba fell on her body, like a large tree coming down in the ground during a big storm.

They stayed in that position for nearly ten minutes. Nobody moved, talked, or felt uncomfortable. It was a moment of joy and pleasure; they had it first time in life. Mona was wondering how God had created such a thing between man and woman—man had a thing like a banana in the middle part of body, and woman had something closer to papaya. She shared with Pemba in a whispering voice, like a pillow talk, "I feel wet under my butt."

"Let's have a look."

Both noticed that the white bedcover sheet was red with blood.

"See, I told you. It means I was a virgin," Mona seemed happy.

Both laughed and, at the same time, felt uneasy in the stomach. It was apparent that they were hungry as the clock in the room struck had two. They were not in a position to go out and eat their lunch. So they opted for room service.

"Let them change the bed sheets also. Tell them you have monthly menstruation," Pemba suggested.

It took around two hours to complete lunch, and the maid change the bed sheets and fixed the bed. They had received a call earlier that agitation was going in the city and everything—all the transportation— was halted. They had no option but to stay inside the room and sleep, maybe make love again and again.

The two weeks really moved fast as they visited Phaplu. Mona liked the house and the surroundings in the Phaplu area. She met lots of Pemba's relatives and a few friends. They visited the school where Pemba studied. It was very clean, and now school was operated by a mature person from New Zealand working as its headmaster.

After a week, Mona and Pemba returned to Kathmandu; his mother and sisters were left back in the house. They really spent quality time with the family, and Mona liked a lot, Pemba's cute sister. She also showed loved to his mother, who was a very affectionate mother-in-law. Mona thought, although she liked Phaplu, it would be hard to spend time doing particularly nothing except a few household chores. They discussed the problem among themselves and came to the conclusion that Mona would stay in Pokhara but visit Phaplu during big festivals and stay as much as she liked there with the family.

In Pokhara, Mona had a meaningful job overlooking the International Fusion Restaurant that was virtually filled up during lunchtime, and in the dinnertime, the tourist had to wait for the table. Sometimes it exceeded an hour. But the restaurant was so popular, always overcrowded with international tourists. Most of the time, it was booked by large tourist companies in advance. The chef was from France and had now become an international celebrity because of his outstanding art in French cuisine. The groups insisted that the chef Andre visit their table just after dinner to say hello to them. Andre's pictures were published in some popular French tourist magazines, and recently, a popular French travel writer had published an article describing Andre's skills of some of the French dishes titled "Miracle on Food, Another Corner of the World." It had made Andre very popular of late.

Mona's skills in management were superb. She even hired Andre, who came as a tourist and had a dinner one time. Mona persuaded him to work as French chef and offered lodging, food, and a hefty salary. Andre could not refuse. Besides, his love for Pokhara as a tourist destination was overwhelming. Attractions of the place, Mona's art of persuasion, hefty salary, and lovely lodging bungalow were powerful combinations for Andre to accept the position. He had now realized that he was more popular here than in France where he used to be a chef in one of the restaurants in Pigalle, a red light area of Paris.

Mona and her entire family felt proud on her skills of managing the restaurant. Her extremely superb style of customer care, employee handling, and handling of vendors had earned the reputation of International Fusion in Pokhara and beyond. Most of the time, French diplomats and guests of French ambassador made a weekend visit just for the superb French cuisine they served. Mona noticed that a few German tourists were also beginning to like the food. She was now planning for an addition of German dishes and looking for a chef.

Mona's family members were worried that once she moved to States after her marriage, the restaurant would have a management crisis. So they put a young boy Manish, who was still at the college going for MBA course, to take over, and he soon started to work under Mona as a trainee.

Two weeks passed quickly. Pemba and Mona returned to Pokhara after collecting their marriage certificate from the CDO office. Pemba was leaving for States the day after.

There was a big farewell arranged for Pemba. Mona's family, Pokhara dignitaries and friends gathered at the restaurant. The whole place was crowded mainly with international tourists, and in a separate room, the Pokhara elites gathered. Everyone seemed to be in happy mood except for Mona. She knew this was going to be their last night until she was going to meet him again, which no one knew when.

Just before they left Kathmandu and went to the American Embassy to check probable time to process visa, they were not certain; but approximately, these kind of cases took two years. So both of them knew they had no option but to wait reluctantly.

The previous night, Mona cried; it was a natural human emotion to cry when they were about to be separated. Pemba had hard time consoling her with intimate efforts. He managed to control her nearly after two hours.

Pemba proposed Mona to visit Fish Tail Lodge after the party for their private time before the departure, maybe for two years. The bar in Fish Tail Lodge was simple and elegant, and provided a unique setting like living room of aristocratic Rana palace with a huge tiger skin hanging on the wall along with a bright and colorful golden chandelier in the middle, and extremely cozy fireplace in one corner of room. On the top of the fireplace, a number of large golden swords with protective shields that were used in the primitive wars were on display. The spotlight was placed over the area where the antiquity was displayed.

The room had a gallant look that provided boldness to the visitors in the bar and had a unique kind of style of conceived lighting that would not hurt the people sitting in the bar, no matter wherever you were located. The designer must have done elaborate work understanding human personality and infusing his vision and technique to assemble this extraordinary place. The bar was crowded, but Pemba picked a corner table next to a large window that provided partial view of the lake's dark water in the night.

Pemba ordered Scotch and soda for himself and for Mona, a glass of chardonnay wine.

"Are you going to come when the visa is ready?" Mona asked after they had settled in the cozy place.

"Of course, I will. It might be difficult if it is in peak business season, though."

"Do you feel I could come by myself?"

"Sure. You are not going to a jungle but to a civilized place. Where have you been in foreign countries?"

"Yes, India, Thailand, Hong Kong, and Japan."

"Is your passport valid?"

"I have no idea; I need to check." Mona answered.

"You better keep your passport up-to-date around the time when the visa arrives."

"Sure. Will you write me at least once a week?"

"Oh my God, you look so attractive. I would love to kiss you now."

"You are just half American; our culture does not permit such pranks in public. Honestly, I am going to miss you," Mona said with poignant emotions.

"What do you think I will do without you for two years?" Mona expressed sadness.

"Treasure our memory," Pemba suggested.

***

CHAPTER NINETEEN

January 2004

Boulder, for those who are from tropical climate, is not such a pleasant place if one does not like snow and cold. Danny and Monet were now used to winter climate, but Pemba and Mona still had hard times adjusting with chilly winter every year. In January, the temperature ranged between twenty-two to forty-seven Fahrenheit, and average snowfall was about eleven inches a month. During the whole year, it got around eighty-nine inches.

Pemba built the custom-made house in 1996, at the posh area of Boulder in Poplar Place, Foothill Community. Park was on northwest side, and North Wonderland was toward the north and Twenty-Eighth Street and Winding Trail Village toward the east—a charming location, extremely pleasant, unusually quiet, and suitable to raise a family.

The custom-made house cost around $975,000. They got around $7,640 monthly mortgages. The house was huge, around five thousand square feet, with four bedrooms, four baths, four-car garages, with solid granite counter, stone plus beautiful hardwood floor, occupying a big back patio covered with green vegetation and lots of trees. They installed a marble fountain with an angel dripping water from her beautiful finger, imported from Italy by a designer artist.

Danny, their son, turned twelve and went to the seventh grade. Monet, ten years, was in the fifth grade. Both the children were naughty and tough to control. The parents were facing hard times to monitor their school progress, track homework, and properly look after them as they were both extremely busy with their respective works.

Mona was busy in the restaurant Potala Palace—a Tibetan and international dishes specialized in French, Nepali, and continental cuisine—had turned into a popular place for the Boulder elites, well-to-do community. Rotary Club, Lions, and Jaycees all met there once a month on separate dates and times. Members and their families visited the Palace to celebrate birthdays, anniversaries and other special occasions. Besides, it was a favorite place for Colorado University faculty members and students.

In the high-tourist season, it was mainly occupied by tourists, both domestic and European. It was also a popular place for those who had visited Nepal.

Mona had hired two assistants, four chefs, and a number of waiters and waitresses from Nepali Community, who needed jobs desperately. The couple had recently moved to a larger and better location and hired a well-known interior designer to decorate the restaurant like a highly sophisticated place similar to a high-quality restaurant in New York, Chicago, and Denver. The decorator, as per the instruction theme, was base on Potala Palace of Tibet with lots of arts and antiquity brought from Nepal and England. The review of the restaurant by the critics was excellent, and most tourist magazines recommended it as a must-visit place for the tourists and visitors alike.

Popularity of the restaurant was at its peak. So was Mona's daily life. It was busy, and she hardly had time to take care of children. So far, they had grown up with the babysitters.

Similarly, Pemba never got home early in the evening. The workload at the office had grown so much that he normally left the office around nine thirty and shared the food Mona brought from restaurant at around ten. This was the only time they both could see each other, and children were already asleep. The babysitter would leave around nine thirty when Pemba got home.

That day, Pemba got a call from Danny's school to attend the Thursday's PTA meeting, and the class teacher should see both of them. In the past, they had not attended the PTA meetings; this time, the teacher kind of insisted as Danny's behaviors and his progress were not satisfactory.

"I am worried about Danny's behavior. He is becoming out of control," Mona raised her concern.

"I feel we need to arrange our schedule in such a way that one of us must be home early," Pemba agreed.

"I agree. At this age, we must give him proper attention and care."

"One of us also should help him with his homework."

"After school, he should go to the tutorials for reading and mathematics," Mona suggested.

"Jack recommends putting them in Kumon for math and reading," Pemba remembered.

"First, let's both make time to attend the PTA and see the class teacher," Mona proposed.

"We were not like him in our childhood," Mona raised here concern.

"Yes, but the education system is different here and is affected by peers," Pemba argued.

"I feel, education is making them independent and turning them into selfish people."

"I agree. People here are more on 'me, my, and myself' concept than at our place," Pemba observed, based on his experience so far. "Can you go to Kumon tomorrow and enroll them? I think it is on Fifteenth Street," he suggested.

"Okay, I will go tomorrow in the morning. Sometimes I feel like taking them back to Pokhara and placing them in a boarding school," Mona expressed her frustration.

"That sounds good, but then they will be growing without parents' love and care," Pemba continued.

"Besides, they may lose the accent and basic things for higher education," Pemba further argued.

"What would you like them to be in future?"

"You mean, their career?" Pemba asked

"Yes."

"Normally, an Asian parent would want his kids to be either doctors or engineers, but we should find out their interest and then only pursue it," Pemba gave his view.

"I have seen cases of suicide or rebellion when parents go against their children's choice."

"Okay then; one of us should be home when they come from school and help with homework. Also enroll them to Kumon."

Both agreed, and after dinner, they went to bed with heavy hearts.

It was really tough to manage time for both to them get back early in the evening which was usually their peak time. Especially for Mona, evening was the time she had to work more at the restaurant, making all arrangements for the dinner. But she had to manage time to go to Danny's school and see his class teacher that day.

Pemba was at the restaurant door. Mona noticed him coming through the front door. She delegated some work to cover for the dinner preparation to her assistant and left the work area to be with Pemba.

"Can you imagine, leaving one's work for some work just for a day is such a fiasco."

"I agree. It's same with me," Pemba seconded.

"Hi, nice to see you, Mr. and Mrs. Sherpa, and thanks for coming. Please have a seat." Mary, the class teacher, welcomed them to her office.

"How is Danny doing in the class?" Pemba showed his impatience.

"Well, let me be precise and to the point," Mary continued, "He never completes homework and his listening skills are dismally lacking."

Both nodded, and Mary continued.

"He needs everyday help to complete his homework and improve his reading and math," Mary briefed them further. "Although he is a very sharp boy and has basic knowledge of learning, he is currently not in par with his peers. If the current trend continues, he will not make it from the high school."

Both the parents realized that the situation was serious and needed improvement immediately.

"We are really grateful for your candid opinion on Danny. We will do our best to bring him in par with his peers soon."

With that remark, they left the school. Pemba, after dropping Mona at the restaurant, ran to his office to catch some urgent work that needed his attention. They exchanged thoughts about Danny's seriousness in the car, and both committed to give immediate attention toward this problem, and mutually agreed to concentrate on everything immediately. As planned, Mona would go to enroll him at Kumon the following day. She would also enroll Monet at the same time.

Kumon was at the Fifteenth Street corner of Elmwood Drive—not so large office, compact but cozy and apparently functional. The teacher—a tall Southern-accent lady with long skirt, white shirt, and black cardigan—approached her.

"Hi, my name is Melissa. How can I help you?"

"Hi, I am Mona. I am interested to enroll my children Danny and Monet to a tuition class."

They exchanged some information about the school, age, and grade and enrolled the kids with effective from that day itself. Melissa informed Mona that both of their schools dropped them at the tutorial's place after class. So Mona didn't need to worry for their transportation. However, she needed to pick them up around seven.

Mona left the tutorial place after taking a tour of the school, which provided an impression of the place and teachers.

Mona had immediate relief and felt that she had achieved something meaningful by admitting her children in the tutorial place. Pemba agreed to come home by seven on weekdays and help the children complete their homework every day, though Melissa informed

Mona that the coaching teachers would also help them to complete school homework on daily basis, especially on English and math.

Mona called Danny's class teacher, Melissa, after three months. She expressed complete satisfaction on his progress.

"Mona, I am so happy with his progress. You must have done something miraculous."

"Yes, and no. I put him in Kumon, and his dad helped him with his homework."

"That is wonderful, and thanks for calling," Melissa dropped the line.

Both the parents had noticed the dramatic change in Danny, especially in his behavior toward them. He dealt with them with respect, used polite words, and kept his room tidy and spent more time in study than on the TV and Nintendo. Similarly, Monet also improved her grades; now she had mostly A's in her work, except a C in history.

After dinner and just before bed, Pemba and Mona had pillow talk.

"I am really happy that we did an excellent plan on Danny," Mona started the conversation.

"Of course we did. Now he gives good respect toward us also."

"I called his teacher yesterday, and she is very happy on his progress."

"We have less worry in life now."

Both looked at each other with a pleasant smile.

"I had a letter from my dad today."

"What has he mentioned in the letter? Is it something good?"

"Yes, he is asking when you are going to build the house on my land in the other side of lake. He says the land price has skyrocketed now."

"Next month, I will visit there and build a small Spanish bungalow overlooking the lake," Pemba seemed excited.

"Okay, I will tell my father," Mona had relief.

After a long time, they had a sound sleep and an extremely most enjoyable lovemaking, which refreshed both.

During their pillow talk, Pemba asked, "Mona darling, our anniversary is coming soon. I would like to give you a nice gift"

"What do you have in mind?"

"A nice diamond ring, and I would like you to pick it."

"Where are we going?" Mona asked

"Precious gift, jewelry place in Denver."

"Why, do they have a nice collection?"

"Yes, they import from Belgium," Pemba answered.

"What is the name of the shop?"

"Exotic Collection."

"Okay, you decide when we will go," Mona told Pemba

"Maybe next Saturday, around eleven a.m."

Great. That sounds good."

Next morning, when they woke up, the weather was terrible. The snow was falling heavily, and the school was closed. Pemba phoned his office. Nobody was in the office. Mona phoned her restaurant; the phone rang, but nobody picked up even after a long ring. They decided to have a nice family breakfast as the school was closed, and the roads were really bad outside to drive. Pemba suggested a typical breakfast with fluffy pancakes, butter, and honey, and Mona started preparing spicy Spanish omelets. The children liked the idea. Monet helped her mother to crack the eggs and prepare some spices. Pemba's efforts for floppy, soft, and delicate pancake turned out as promised; they had butter and maple syrup along with the cakes. The breakfast idea was great, and everyone enjoyed the food. It was one of the best quality family time they had had together. It was all because of unusually heavy snow.

Mona phoned her babysitter and asked if she could get home before eleven. She assured her to try her best to reach before the time, depending on the road condition.

The restaurant business seemed to be slow for the dinnertime as light snow continued. Maybe the clients preferred not to drive on the sleek roads. Two employees also called in and said, they were sick. Mona was also not feeling well; the heavy snow on the road made her sick too. Mona's being home early was a surprise to the children.

They wanted to have some soup for the dinner, and Mona began to prepare the same for everyone. She phoned Pemba to join them for early dinner that if he had finished his work. Again, the dinner time turned into a quality time for family reunion. Everyone had fun with the soup and all-vegetable dinner with *momo*—a Nepali delicacy.

Finally, Saturday arrive. It was the day to pick up the ring in Denver. The couple left around eleven together.

Saturday mornings were always crowded at the jewelry shop. There were about a few people hovering over the counter; everyone was looking for a gift—either for birthday, wedding, engagement, or anniversary. Mona always liked the glittering stones. She noticed that her choices were good, and the ring looked expensive.

When the salesman approached, Mona indicated a ring that had white, green, and slightly pink color combination of diamond. It was splendid and very attractive.

"Oh, this an excellent choice. We had it from Belgium last week only, and it has nearly two carats. The cost is $8,995. The diamond is valued on cut, color, and clarity, and it has it all."

Mona tried the ring. It really suited her large, sharp, and attractive fingers. The color combination had strange bright sparkle when she moved the finger. It really generated dramatic sparks of light. They were engrossed in the ring. Suddenly, a shabby, bearded tall figure in dark pants, high tan boot, and black winter outwear with a checkered shirt and white glass entered the store and asked to see the manager.

A sharp, nice person in black business suit, white shirt, and blue white-dotted tie appeared and said, "May I help you? I am the manager of the store."

"Sir, I bought this diamond ring last week. But my fiancée broke the engagement, and I need to return this ring."

"Do you have a receipt?"

"Yes, I do." He took out the receipt and gave it to the manager.

After carefully examining the receipt, the manager said, "Okay, we will give you the store credit."

"Please, Sir. I am in a situation of serious cash shortage. I'll be much obliged if you refund the cash through your store check. As

I did not use my credit card, I paid you cash last week through my check."

Another lady from the store appeared. She was in long white-colored silk dress with simple but attractive jewelry and had a heavy makeup.

"Sir, we do not have eight-thousand-dollar cash at the store. Besides, we never refund the money but always provide store credit for future transaction."

"Well, you can return my check if you have not deposited it," The man with the beard requested.

"We have already deposited," the lady replied.

The lady signaled the security guard, who was standing close to front door. He grabbed the man's left arm and began to push him out of the store's front door. In the meantime, the angry man grabbed a gun with his right arm out of the guard's holster and aimed it to the manager.

"Give my money back, or I will kill not only you, but everyone over here," he roared.

The manager was shaken; his body shook, and he spoke in trembling voice, "We have no cash. We'll issue you store business check."

There were nearly six other clients in the store. When they heard the warning from this tall man with determined looks in his eyes, they began sweating. This included Pemba and Mona. Mona's eyes widened that had slanted upward and formulated wrinkles on her forehead. With her mouth slightly opened, she clenched Pemba in his left arm and hid behind him. They thought, they came to the store on a wrong day and time to witness such a fiasco. Pemba had seen such episodes on the TV many times, but Mona could not believe her eyes that such a thing could happen in America as well.

The manager issued a check, looking the receipt that the man gave him, and handed over the check. His hand trembled all through this process.

The man with the gun looked at the check critically, put it in his pocket, and asked that no one could move until he left. He further instructed the manager that he would mail the gun back to them after he cashed the check. He exited from the door slowly, calculatedly, looking at all the clients inside the store. There had been a pause in the store. After some time, all the clients slowly but deliberately left the store without making any purchase. The incident had scared all of them; Pemba and Mona were no exception.

Pemba reached Pokhara with an objective to build a small Spanish cottage on the other side of lake close to mountain and have full view of the lake from the land. Mona's father had given to his daughter the land as a wedding gift. The land was not that huge, but was enough to build a house with front ground area with lots of back area for kitchen garden, and they also could build animal shelter for chicken or similar kind of domestic pets along with a servant's quarter. The back portion of the land was very green, lucid, and had tall trees. The land was not so smooth and plain and needed some work from a landscape professional. Pemba brought the blueprint design prepared by a Boulder popular architect who was a close friend of Jack. The design was of two-story house with kitchen, large living room, and back area with built-in wooden patio—with a guestroom and attached bath. In the winter, the patio that faced south would have ample sunlight that penetrated inside some portion of living room as well. Upper portion would have three bedrooms, all with attached bath and large den on the south portion of the house. A huge balcony back of the den that would again provide ample sunlight had an extension from the room as well. The house would be equipped with all modern amenities, solar power for heating, internal intercom between rooms, and for bright light, sunlight in the roof that covered all upper-portion area. After the main entrance outside, toward the middle area, there was a provision for huge marble fountain that would be colorful during the night.

In totality, the design sounded very interesting, but it would be a challenge to find a contractor and skilled architect who could turn this dream into a reality. Pemba thought, if he was unable to find them in Pokhara, perhaps he would be required to hire a reputable contractor and architect from Kathmandu. He had first to research for one in Pokhara. Mona's father knew some contractors, and they were invited the next day to discuss the plan.

In the large living room, about ten contractors assembled, and they introduced themselves with their accomplishment of buildings in Pokhara area. Among all the contractors, he liked a young contractor with architectural degree he received from a Swiss university.

He asked that young fellow to wait outside, and when everyone else had left, Pemba had a very interesting conversation.

"I am sorry, what was your good name again?" Pemba asked.

"Yeshe, Sir," the name implied wise one.

"Please do not call me Sir. I am Pemba. Where did you get your degree on architecture?"

"In Switzerland."

"I mean, which city?" Pemba asked again.

"Geneva."

"How long did you study?"

"Almost seven years." Yeshe replied.

"What have you done in Pokhara so far?"

"Here is my binder that will provide all my information." Yeshe handed over a blue folder.

"That is nice. Let me go through it later. Can you leave with me?"

"Of course, yes."

"Let me show you the design I brought in from America." Pemba showed him the house design.

"Is this Spanish style?" Yeshe asked.

"Yes."

"The house will have about three thousand square feet inside living area. Itt will be a large house."

"Yes, it is." Pemba confirmed.

"You want to have all solar panels in the roof area?" Yeshe asked.

"What do you think about doing so?"

"Will be good; might be expensive." Yeshe gave his opinion.

"Don't worry about the expenses. I will take care of that portion. You need to build the house as per this design," Pemba insisted.

"Sometimes it is hard to get quality construction materials, and it may cause delay."

"How long will it take to complete?" Pemba was curious.

"If we get quality materials on time, it could be finished within two years."

"Why so long?" Pemba questioned.

"Transportation across the lake takes time; there are no easy roads."

"Can you give me the approximate cost, including, labor cost, materials, and your fee, complete with all finishing?" Pemba demanded.

"I could, but need to calculate. I can probably let you know by day after," was the professional reply from Yeshe.

"Okay. Take this design and give me the costing. Also bring your contractor with you."

"What time will be good for you, Sir?" Yeshe asked.

"Around eleven in the morning. Is that all right?" Pemba questioned back.

"Yes, that is a good time."

After the conversation, Pemba confronted his father-in-law, who asked, "Did you find someone dependable?"

"Yes, Dad, a young architect who had his degree from Switzerland." Pemba seemed happy.

"Good. There is similarity in landscape between the two countries."

"Besides, he had done lots of impressive works in Pokhara."

"Did he give you any idea about the cost?"

"Not yet. He will give me the day after and bring the contractor as well." Pemba told his father-in-law.

"Have you considered about earthquake factor while making the design?"

"Yes, Dad, the American architect knows this is an earthquake-prone area."

"When are they coming again?"

"The day after," Pemba repled.

"Great. Include me in the meeting. I may be able to do some bargainomg, as I have built three houses."

"Sure."

The house boy informed Pemba about a phone call that was waiting for him. He dashed to the phone area, and it was Mona on the line.

"Hi, darling, how is the progress?"

"It is good; I will know more details the day after. How is it with you?"

"Fine, except that Monet had some cold allergy and could not make it to school. She is at home with the babysitter."

"Does she have fever?'

"Not much, very low."

"How is the restaurant?"

"Extremely busy," Mona replied.

"Take care. I will call you back once I have the figures and approximate completion time."

"Sounds good." Mona is happy with the progress.

"Love you." Pemba expresses his emotions.

"Love you too."

Pemba liked to go to Begnas area for a change of scenario and have nature walk around the lake, but he needed company so that he could enjoy conversation. He knew a guy next-door, who lived in United Kingdom, and he was here on vacation. He sent the boy in the house to fetch him; surprisingly, he came together with the boy.

"Hi, Pemba, it is nice to see you after long time."

"Hello, you are Shyam, aren't you?" Pemba asked.

"Yes, man, how come you forgot me?"

"Not really. I was a little confused. Hey, Shyam, I have a Jeep, would you like to go to Begnash area?"

"Sure. I am not doing anything in the house. That will be fun."

Pemba drove the Jeep, and they were now outside Pokhara.

"How long you are staying this time?" Shyam asked Pemba.

"About two weeks. I came to build a house on Mona's land."

"Yes, her father was telling me last year, the land had been encroached slowly and need to have at least a compound wall," Shyam remarks.

"Yes, you know how people are here."

"Now I am here to take care of it. I already gave a contract for compound wall construction. They will initiate the work next week."

"Good. Is Mona still working in the restaurant?"

"Yes; we have our own restaurants now."

"Do you like America?"

"In the beginning, I had hard times adjusting immediately after the divorce, but now it is fantastic. How is England?" Pemba asked back.

"Well, I have my pension, and part-time work."

"Do you like it there?" Pemba asked.

"I have no option now. I am retired and cannot move to America. I have a small house in the northern part of England, and my two children go to school, the reason my wife could not come until the school is closed."

"Same with me. Tell, how is the schooling system in England?"

"Why, more or less same in both the countries."

"No, in America, it is different; they try to make the children independent."

"Is not that a good system?" Shyam asked.

"Yes, but they could be out of control sometimes."

Soon they reached the lake area on the top of the mountain. It had totally different view due to more vegetation than Phewa Lake.

"I really miss this part of paradise," Shyam echoed his voice, gazing toward the lake.

"Me too, but, Shyam, would it not be better if we have factories, mining, resources? People will have good job with good income. In that case, won't they be more than happy to stay in this country? Nobody needs to go out, neither you nor me." Pemba expressed his opinion.

"Nature has been generous to our country. Yes, I agree, we have no resources that could make us rich and happy," Shyam agreed with Pemba.

"I have excellent home. My children's future is bright. My and Mona's business is flourishing. We earn a lot of money, and people are decent. Now, perhaps, I am finding the other side of paradise in America."

"What is your definition of paradise?" Shyam asked him.

"Well, where people are happy, need not worry for tomorrow, have plenty of food, and nice place to live in." Pemba briefly explained.

"Pemba, that is your perception, and you are talking basically from a material point of view. How about spiritual blend in life? You are a Buddhist," Shyam continued, "you should have better awareness of the spiritual aspects than me."

"Yes, Shyam, I agree with you, but my concept of religion has changed now. I consider all the gods in the universe on equal footing. In other words, I respect and have faith in many religions. If you ever come to my place in Colorado, you will see that I have a separate room where I worship all the gods. I find peace and spiritual fulfillment."

"That means you gave up Buddhism?" Shyam was surprised.

"No, Shyam, I elevated Buddhism along with other religion."

"So your religious conviction has changed?" Shyam asks Pemba again.

"Somehow, yes. Now I believe religion should be given as a choice when a person matures," Pemba expressed his philosophy.

"What will you do when most people adopt it by birth and their faith is rooted in their life pattern?"

"Of course, one can adopt it at birth, but I feel it is forced on them when they are children and innocent," Pemba argued.

"Pemba, that is the tradition we all have."

"I am talking for those who would like to change their religion in later part of their life. If you have money, you would like to have best living place, best food, excellent transportation, and best clothing, etc., Why can you not be allowed to choose the religion of your choice?" Pemba seemed to be really passionate in the subject.

"You say when a person is mature, can you give me your definition of maturity?" Shyam asked.

"Shyam, maturity is an abstract term. A person of eighty years may not be mature, whereas an eighteen-year-old kid could be mature."

"Interesting concept. Could you elaborate?" Shyam seemed curious.

"In my view, maturity means the power to distinguish between right and wrong." Pemba gave his view.

"But how could an eighteen-year-old man or woman have that concept compared to forty-five years?"

"Indeed, the addition of age does not qualify to be mature but depends on his education and experience in life," Pemba explained.

"I am trying to see your perception. It is a very interesting concept, but I never thought that way. Still I strongly believe that religion should be adopted by birth and continue that way throughout life." Shyam liked Pemba's idea but was not convinced.

"Let me ask: what should religion provide in our life?"

"Peace, and guidance for a blissful life," Shyam answered precisely.

"Exactly All religions teaches more or less the same thing, but we do not derive peace and happiness from all. Some may consider that place is in the mosque; others consider church; others, synagogue; others, temple; and others, monastery. But I am adopting multiple religions and finding peace and bliss in life." Pemba seemed contented.

"Well, this is a never-ending argument," Shyam seemed to have grown monotonous with the subject.

"Let's enjoy this outstanding view."

After a good round-lake walk, they returned to the other the side of Phewa Lake and to their respective homes.

Yeshe was more or less on time for the meeting with Pemba on the scheduled day. He had a mature person with him, and Pemba figured out it must be the construction contractor. Pemba knocked at his father-in-law's room, and said, "They are here."

When his father-in-law came out of his room, he recognized the contractor.

"Oh, Surya, you are still active in the contracting job?"

"Yes, my son is in Australia, doing his course in engineering. When he comes back, I will hand it over to him, then I will retire."

"Great. Which son is in Australia, Surya?"

"The eldest one."

They used the dining table, and Yeshe slowly spread out his papers methodically and professionally.

"I have studied the design in detail. I have calculated the cost depending on present cost of the materials and considering about 10 percent inflation next year. This is the breakdown:

Material cost — 50 lakhs
Labor — 30 lakhs
Contractor — 10 lakhs
Architecture/engineering — 10 lakhs
Miscellaneous — 12 lakhs

"Total cost is in rupees one crore, twelve lakhs, and that is approximately is $135,000," Yeshe gave a clear-cut picture of the construction cost in local currency and converted it into dollars as per the latest dollar conversion rate.

Pemba studies the cost closely and critically, and after he was done, pushed the paper toward his father-in-law, who observed all the figures. He had a question on labor cost.

"I feel; the labor cost is too high."

"It looks that way after the government opened the Middle East labor job for Nepali people. We are facing acute shortage of labor, and we have hard times recruiting from the local market unless we pay higher wages. Further, there is shortage of skilled ones," Yeshe gave his argument.

"But the cost of construction materials too seems exuberant," Pemba's father-in-law argued again.

"Well, compared to last year's inflation, it jumped to 15 percent higher this year. Besides, Sir Pemba wants to use all high-quality materials," Yeshe further convinced.

"Finally, let me offer ninety-five lakhs for everything," Pemba's father-in-law gave his concluding view.

"In no case we can do it with less than one crore," Yeshe seemed determined.

Pemba looked toward his father-in-law for some kind of expression on his face; he had not noticed the resistance.

He spoke nearly after a five-minute pause, "Great. We will go for one crore local currency, but the choice of construction materials, cement, sand mixing and the interior should have an exact look as per the design." Pemba agreed the cost.

"Yes, we will follow the design procedures exactly," Yeshe seemed to agree.

So the deal was finalized and agreed upon.

"What will the time frame to complete the construction be?"

"Two years," Yeshe seemed to have a ready answer.

"Couldn't you do it within eighteen months?"

"We will try it, but we cannot guarantee."

"Great. My father-in-law will supervise the construction in my absence. He will pay you 33 percent now to initiate the work, 33 percent during middle of construction, and the remaining upon the completion of the task."

"In the middle of construction, pay us about 50 percent, and the rest at the end," Yeshe put a counter proposal.

Pemba looked toward his father-in-law for some expression; he had not observed anything.

"He will give you 50 percent toward the middle of construction. When can you start?"

"We will start immediately and complete the structure before the monsoon in July."

"That sounds good." Pemba seemed happy.

When that meeting came to an end, Yeshe and the contractor left after talking with Pemba's father-in-law about something in the local language. Pemba seemed to be happy with the outcome; he tried to compare it with the same-size house in the States that could have cost not less than half a million dollars.

Pemba was contented with his achievement in Nepal about the house construction and peaceful short stay in Pokhara. The only matter of regret on his part was his inability to meet his own family in Phaplu this time, as there were no air tickets available for whole month and the family could not come due to his sisters' school. Moreover, his stay was quite short this time.

Pemba left Pokhara with a heavy heart, and before his departure, he managed to send a letter to his family, together with sufficient expenses.

***

CHAPTER TWENTY

February 2015

Monet was selected for Pritzker School of Medicine through the University of Chicago, and the main campus was in Hyde Park area. Normally, the scholarship offered by the prestigious institution was only for a selective, high-ranking, and most promising students, and they must rank within 5 percent of the class. Monet had been recognized as valedictorian, being top of the class. Besides, she had great performances in sports and literally fields. This was her sophomore year in the medical school. She lived in the northern side of Chicago at Evanston area, as the city was demarcated from downtown area as North and South for whites and African Americans. Monet was proud to be associated with the school, which ranked among the top ten research universities in America. As per recently published data, about six thousand students applied for the medicine class of 2017. Only 604 were interviewed for the eighty-eight positions in the class. The applicants had medium 3.87 GPA and MCAT score of 37. This showed the rigid selective procedures of the school.

Monet had a boyfriend that was from Singapore. His name was Martin. Monet, who was very close to her mother Mona, had told her about her boyfriend. Monet and Mona did not look, behave, and treat like mother and daughter; but regarded each other as a friend first. Mona insisted on seeing Martin and asked Monet to bring him once she came next time. In fact, Monet already made a plan to go home during this spring break with Martin. She had already informed her mother about their visit in the later part of the month.

Pemba and Mona were very proud of their children. They had grown into wonderful persons both. Monet was beautiful, tall, talented, and had done exceptionally well in the academic field; and Daniel turned out to be an articulate personality that had done not so well in academics, but he had great skills in sports and was unusually smart in public relations and making friends.

In his school circle, he had more friends than anyone of his peers. His personality was dynamic. Tall, around six two, with dark, round and big eyes, wide forehead and beautiful nose—his entire facial features were proportionate and attractive. He was a popular leader in the school, who won numerous times in almost all students' body elections. He could charm ladies and had an outstanding quality of giving respect in the relationship. He had several girlfriends in the past, and now he was almost steady with Lena—a charming, sophisticated, very pretty, and respectable Swiss lady with adorable personality. She was in the same class with him. Daniel met Lena and visited Boulder together last summer but this summer, they were planning to go to Lena's hometown in Lucerne, Switzerland and also visit Nepal to stay in Lakeside Pokhara.

Daniel, who was in the Baylor University this year, would complete his internship from Baylor Scott and White Medical Center. Lena would be doing internship in the same center. Their schedules were erratic, and they still lived in a cozy one-bedroom apartment at Waco. They both commuted, but it took hardly ten minutes from the workplace to the apartment.

Both Daniel and Monet had full scholarships during their study, and they got $500 each month as pocket money from their parents and were prohibited to work until they finished studying. Both children had no complaint toward their parents; they had been provided with abundant love, care, and sincere efforts to make sure they had the best education and upbringing, and were kept happy by all means.

When Monet was driving around the Lakeshore, coming to campus, her mobile—which was connected through the Bluetooth—made an echo of a ring in the speaker. She answered hands-free through the speaker. "Monet, do you have your visit date fixed?" Mona was asking.

"Yes, Mum. The school closes on the twenty-fourth, and we will be there on the twenty-fifth of March."

"Great, you know, we have to make arrangements, and we both are crazy at work."

"Mum, we will not bother you. Mostly we will have outdoor activities during the day. Besides, Martin loves mountains, trekking, and hiking, and we have plenty of them."

"That sounds good. On the twenty-eighth, your dad has arranged a close friend's get-together to meet Martin."

"Where, Mum, at home?" Monet ask

"No, at the restaurant."

"That sounds wonderful, Mum."

"I have invited some of your school friends as well," Mona informed.

"I missed them a lot. Would love to see them over again."

"Monet, text me the flight details so that one of us will be at the airport."

"I will, Mum."

They hung up the phone.

Monet could not keep the information to herself; she needed to call Martin.

"Martin, I just talked to Mum."

"What did she say?"

"They are hosting a party on your arrival."

"That sounds interesting." Martin seemed happy. His voice depicted that.

"Did you book the ticket?" Monet asked.

"I will do on the web tonight."

"Are you excited to go?" Monet again

"You know, I love mountains."

"Is it more than me?" Monet teased.

"Don't be silly; you are a human. I love you more than the mountains."

"You know, my mum is dying to see and find out my choice." Martin expressed himself.

"My mum is also equally interested to meet you."

"Really?"

"She is. I am sure she will get jealous of your beauty."

"How can a mother-in-law get jealous? She will be proud of your choice, instead. Hey, Martin, I reached the campus and am late for the class, talk to you later."

"Bye for now." Monet dropped the phone.

***

Daniel and Lena worked for for different shifts, and sometimes they worked even seventy-two hours straight and slept at the hospital if they got time to sleep. They both were passing the hardest time in life without sleep and lots of pressure at work. Their life was abnormal in all the ways.

A typical day of an intern was spent around seventeen hours that began at five in the morning and ended at ten with fast-food while driving back home for a few hours' sleep. Although they lived together, they hardly had time to see each other. Most of the time, Daniel got home at around six a.m. after night duty, and Lena left home at four-thirty for work.

Today Lena had a meeting with the patient's family to discuss about the nutritional diets. She also had normal rounds, attending in emergency room, attend a presentation by a student on cancer research procedures, prepare report, log time sheet, supervise medical students, attend regular departmental meetings, and so on and so forth

Although, medical schools and residencies can feel frantic most of the time, many graduates describe the process as transformative.

Understanding what it is like to walk in an intern's shoe for a day is significant in making a decision on whether medicine is the best choice for you.

Lena knew she had a heart to serve mankind, and anything else might not be suitable for her.

Lena was eagerly looking forward to her dream vacation this summer with the man of her life to Lucerne and Nepal. Both had such a striking similarity in terms of geographical features, with lots of beautiful mountain peaks, flora, fountain, and heavenly outdoors—which she loved from her heart. She had treasured her dream since almost a year back, and the coming four-week summer would energize her and Daniel for the rest of their intern life, and this would definitely provide essential endurance. She remembered her childhood in Lucerne that had been spent mostly in outdoor hiking, trekking, mountain climbing, and skating on the ice. Although ice-skating was considered a winter sport, Lucerne had several indoor skating areas, which Lena enjoyed every other weekend with her father. Lena knew ice-skating helped to burn 250 calories in an hour—the reason she still looked skinny.

"Lena, could you provide the report of that ER alcoholic patient admitted this morning?" Matthew the senior doctor asked her. That woke her up from the dream her upcoming vacation this summer.

Lena, on her last visit to Daniel's family, loved his mum and dad. They had great personalities, and both treated her with respect during her stay in Boulder for two weeks. She loved the family and adored Daniel's sister Monet. She respected his parents and loved the house and rugged surrounding that created outstanding impression in her mind. When Lena's parents visited her in Texas last time, they observed Daniel analytically and gave blessings for their relationship, admiring Daniel's character and personality. In fact, her mother even admired Daniel's modesty and politeness and believed he must be from a respected family in Nepal.

***

Coming out from biology class, Monet received a call from Martin, even as she moved towards the cafeteria.

"Hi, Monet, darling; do you remember we have to go to a reception at Palmer House at six thirty?"

"Who has the reception?" Monet asked.

"Silly, you already forgot? It is given by Singapore Consulate." Martin freshened her memory.

"Great, I will be there by six forty-five."

"Whatever, please come as soon as you can."

The party was in one of the hotel's ballrooms, huge and spacious with lots of chandeliers. It was decorated in Singaporean style with oriental music. The arrangement was of buffet style; the food on the table looked attractive and tempting—a variety of delicacies brought by Singapore Airlines along with ten airlines hostesses at the reception area. As usual, Singapore had the best sarong hostess dress, and they all looked smart, articulate, and unusually attractive. Martin always admired the Singapore Airlines and in-flight services which he thought was the best in the world. He always used the airlines while traveling to his home. In fact, the airline's public relations manager Lee was his classmate in the school.

The room was slowly packed with airline's personnel, diplomats, politicians, press and media people etc. He looked around and could not locate Monet—who was, in fact, difficult to hide due to her height and dynamic personality. Martin sometimes got jealous with Monet as men gave her more attention than himself.

"Here is Martin." Lee approached him with Monet.

"Hi, Lee! Great party, as usual. You all have a style," Martin appreciated the party.

"This is us, my dear," Martin supported.

In the meantime, Monet hugged Martin and gave a loving kiss on the cheek.

"Monet, I need a dynamic personality like you for my partner," Martin suggested. Lee seemed jealous.

"Man, you have so many beautiful air hostesses. Pick one for yourself," Martin joked.

"Yes, Lee, you pick one up; they are all gorgeous," Monet supported Martin.

In the meantime, Singapore Consulate Mr. Huang appeared on the main stage and drew the attention of the people with an opening speech.

"Good evening, honorable diplomats, senators, congressmen, and my dear friends! I have the privilege to address you with few humble words during our fiftieth independence celebration on behalf of my tiny but dynamic country. It provided a fantastic glamour, overlooking from the rooftop pool deck of Marine Bay Sands Hotel, shopping at vibrant Haji Lane, or watching at the super trees in Garden by the Bay. It is almost impossible to imagine Singapore was little more than a fishing village just over a century ago. On the eve of its golden jubilee, there is no better time to discover the delight of the Lion City. Besides, Singapore has lowest crime and least unemployment rate in the whole world.

"As per World Bank, Singapore is the best city in the world for business. Recently, the Facebook co-founder Eduardo Saverin moved to Singapore, and we all welcomed him to our dynamic city. We have special tourism board promotional video presentations and hope you will all enjoy. Our sincere thanks for your attendance this evening and hope to see you all in Singapore soon."

Everyone seemed to enjoy the party with cocktails, wonderful oriental finger food, lavishes of lobsters, shrimps, and especially Singapore rice-chicken dinner.

Monet expressed an uneasy appearance through her eyes long after dinner.

"What's the matter, darling?" Martin asked.

"Dear, I have a test tomorrow, and I am due for a project research paper the day after. Do you mind if we leave?"

"Of course not, it is about time. Let me find Lee and say good-bye."

***

Mona's life had been much easy when they found a smart, active, and efficient manager for the restaurant—Peter Tamang, who came recently in Denver and arrived on Diversity Visa lottery. Someone referred to him to this restaurant for the job. He had worked as a manager in Yak & Yeti Restaurant for nearly ten years. Tamang was trustworthy, honest, and hardworking. Mona now didn't have to worry about the operation of the restaurant. Tamang consulted her only when they had a group and some important guests; otherwise, he was capable of handling everything on his own perfectly and efficiently.

Pemba's life also was turning easy. He was not required to take care of the paperwork so much now. He also found Dinesh Gurung, who too came from Nepal on Diversity lottery visa. Dinesh had worked with a growing trekking company in Nepal as office manager and had tremendous amount of knowledge on office operation.

It was not easy to get a first job in America, even if you had a green card. It was a situation, like, chicken or egg, which came first. Normally, no job was offered unless you had experiences in this country; no matter how much education or experience you have in other countries. On the other hand, if there were no job, there would be no experience. It was really hard to break the cycle for the newcomers. Both Tamang and Gurung were grateful to the Sherpa couple. Unless they found a much better offer and facilities, they were not going to move. Besides, they felt comfortable working with Nepali people as their boss—who, they were certain, unless anything so untoward happened. Otherwise, they were also familiar with hire-and-fire situation in all the levels of jobs in America.

After the "empty nest" situation in the house, both the parents felt that the situation was much different. Their affection, love, and closeness with the children were suddenly creating a big gap in their lives. As a result, Mona developed a sign of slight depression, and Pemba spent more hours in the prayer room every morning. Pemba found peace, blissfulness and strange tranquility through the meditation, and he had a feeling that all gods in the temple unanimously provided powerful emotions and strength in his life.

One evening, when they both were coming home early from work, Pemba initiated a discussion on the issue of empty nest and perhaps a suitable time for retirement. They were in their car.

"Mona, I feel we do not need this big house anymore as the children may soon have their families, and they may settle close to their workplace in a new city, wherever they get jobs."

"I was so depressed when they both left," Mona expressed her feeling.

"What do you think of retirement?"

"Well, it could be suitable time. You make the decisions. I have nothing to say."

"I want to move to Florida for warm weather."

"That is a good idea. I am also fed up with the snow and cold weather here."

In the meantime, Mona's cell phone rang.

"Hi, Alicia, how are you, my dear?" Mona answered.

Alicia's voice cracked through the Bluetooth speaker in the car.

"Mona, I am reminding you about our get-together tomorrow night for dinner."

"Oh my God, I almost forgot. My mind is not in place after the children left."

"I understand, we are also in the same situation," Alicia supported.

"We will be there definitely. Say my regards to Steve."

After Mona completed the phone conversation, she asked Pemba again, "Where do you want to retire in Florida?"

"Miami."

"My dear, I do not like the big city, you know that." Mona resisted.

"Actually, it is about forty minutes' drive away from Miami."

"I like that," Mona had a feeling of happiness reflected in her voice.

"Next week, we will go and see the place. As per the real estate agent, it is a small town and a cozy two-bedroom house."

"That sounds great."

When they reached home, both felt withdrawn from one another and slept after a light dinner of soup and salad with bread.

Alicia and Steve were excellent neighbors and had established a good relationship with Pemba's family. The children were also almost the same age and attended the same school. They helped each other in time of need and desperation as close family friends. Both families always went out of the way to help each other. Alicia was from Spain, and Steve's family came from South Africa. They were both exposed to international culture and food and liked diverse ethnicity and were also regular clients at Mona's restaurant.

Potable Palace had grown into a dynamic franchise restaurant, and it had almost 110 branches all over the country. They were also planning to open on in Spain, Japan, and Singapore soon. The success of the restaurant was because of international fusion of several foods—Tibetan, Italian, Japanese, and oriental blends. Jack handled the franchisee aspects, and Pemba supervised the management and training. Out of royalty fee, they did nationwide advertisement—along with Facebook, Twitter, and Instagram—quality control, turnkey basis management, training, and inventory supplies.

Pemba and Jack's rafting company had made tremendous progress; now they had at least fifteen to twenty tours in a month on low season. The amount tripled in the high season. Their anthropology tour to Nepal for Colorado University students was gaining popularity and had more than twenty tour groups in a year, which had about thirty students in each group. They also had prepared a thirty-minute promotional video on the tour to Nepal in collaboration with the Department of Nepal Tourism. It was an effective media to reach prospective students and motivate them to sign up for the tour. The operation of Nepal was the responsibility of Pemba, and Jack did all the marketing and promotion in the university. Jack was considering to float the tour idea to another university—such as, Berkley in California and University of Utah at Salt Lake City. They had also shown an interest after Jack's recent promotion with the video on Nepal. By all means, with the dedication, efforts, and approach to the right kind of market, it had produced excellent results, and credits went to both Jack and Pemba.

Within less than five minutes, they reached Alicia's house—which was on the middle of a large meadow, surrounded by tall pine trees—a huge building that occupied a large compound just beneath a tall mountain behind. It was always a pleasure to be in their house as they were very popular for unique, warm hospitality and respect they provided to the guests, along with enticing spicy food in Spanish flavor. There were about ten other guests in the house, who were from elite people of Boulder. Mona noticed a clergy, perhaps the father the church Alicia and Steve attended. The party atmosphere was subtle, peaceful, and charming at the same time. Mona normally preferred a quiet, disciplined party rather than a rowdy and a noisy one with loud music. In the background, a soft Kenny Rogers music was flowing in the air. That provided a unique pleasantness in the large and high-ceiling magnificent room with mellow golden lights emanating from several chandeliers and other lights, which were attractive and turned one's imagination a mellow and soft.

Everybody in the room was introduced. Mona and Pemba knew almost all the guests, except the clergy, who was introduced as Father Thomas.

Mona noticed that Father Thomas was very curious about them and was looking for the opportunity to get them close.

Finally, Father Thomas moved toward them and introduced himself again, "Hi, I am Father Thomas."

Pemba was not very close to Catholic religion in particular as compared to Mona, who had grown up in the Saint Mary Catholic School.

"Yes, Father, I am Mona, and this is my husband Pemba."

"Very pleased to meet you."

"We are also happy to know you, Father," Mona replied in a controlled, low, pleasant voice. It showed her real emotion of being happy.

"I am very curious with your culture, especially your arranged-marriage tradition. Could you please join me in that small table to eat together?"

"Of course, pleasure will be ours, Father," Mona replied with equal eagerness in her voice.

When all three of them settled in a small corner table with various food items and drink of their choices, Father Thomas broke the ice.

"I am not much aware of the cultural context of your society, but I am curious to know about your arranged-marriage system."

Father looked towards Mona with a feel of inquisition. He further continued with a question, "How can two people who barely know each other make such an important decision that will affect their joint future? And even more surprising, how can decisions made this way lead to positive outcome for so many couples with almost zero rate of divorce?"

Mona thought about the questions. There was a long pause as a reply to this question would not be easy, as the subject was quite complicated. Mona finally seemed to compose her thoughts, as this was an unexpected question from the clergy in such an abstract matter.

"Well, Father, in my opinion, if you have lower expectation out of a relationship, it normally leads to happiness and a lasting relation. So is our marriage," Mona explained in a very simple manner. "Besides, we have limited choices. In an arranged marriage, we trust the screening process of our elders, and importance is given toward compatibility and financial security over romantic love that will further contribute to restrained expectations. As research on satisfaction judgments shows, when expectations are low, they are more likely to be met or exceeded, leaving the newlywed highly satisfied. In a free-choice marriage, in contrast, high expectation often develops during an elaborate dating period, with the culture placing more emphasis on the romantic love ideal. This sets people up for a letdown after the honeymoon period is over."

Pemba was amazed and looked toward Mona, not believing her extraordinary knowledge on this abstract subject. Even Father Thomas seemed to be convinced by the argument put by Mona on arranged marriage.

"Mona, I am really impressed by your explanation. We in the church are looking at various systems that will curtail or prevent divorce. Do you have divorce in your law?"

"Of course, Father, we do, but the rate is absolutely less than a point. Besides, our social norms consider divorce a heinous crime."

"I am sure you are familiar with the rate of divorce at ours. In fact, fifty percent of our marriages end up in divorce. This, you know, will break the social structure, and as a result, we have so many stepchildren and broken homes."

"I am from Ireland," Father Thomas continued, "we did not have divorce there earlier, but now they changed the law, and the only country without divorce left is the Philippines."

Pemba was an observer until now. Finally, he expressed his idea to support Mona.

"Father, I believe human psychology does play a significant role in marriage. The concept of marriage is a dynamic process. What I believe now is my children may have a different perception, and they may not believe what we trust now."

"Pemba, the church tries to build a faith and conviction, and in reality, we are searching for the method to reduce the divorce in the society at the moment," Father reinforced his view and the current social prevailing problem.

Father gracefully and politely thanked the couple for the thought-provoking idea and recognized them with the remark, "Thanks, Mona and Pemba. I am sure you have a faith other than mine, but you are always welcome in my church if you like to drop by."

"Indeed, Father. I was born in a different faith, but now I embrace all the religion, and I have a blissful life." Pemba share.

"God bless you, my child."

Father, after saying good-bye to the host, left the party.

Mona was at the restaurant, and they had a big college reunion dinner; and she was very busy supervising all the arrangements so that she could maintain the quality of the food and provide excellent customer services. Tamang, who was now working as the manager in the restaurant, was an asset who had outstanding experience and superb job performance. He kept the restaurant under control and operated smoothly, like a tight ship. He kept his employees happy and got excellent job performance from them. Mona had no complaints from him.

"It is me," Pemba was on the other line.

"What happened? I am very busy."

"The real estate agent called me just now. He has fixed an appointment tomorrow to check the property in Florida and land for vineyard. Is it possible for you to go with me?"

"Perhaps not. I am too busy. Why don't you go by yourself and decide this time?" Mona suggested.

"Sure, we will go together after some time, when we have time. Tomorrow I will go and see. The agent says, it is a good deal," Pemba explained.

"Every salesman shows the urgency and scarcity of the commodity they are selling."

"I understand that notion," Pemba agreed with Mona.

"Where is the place in Florida, darling?"

"In a small agricultural city, Homestead, which is about forty-five miles southwest of Miami—an outstanding retirement place along with suitable land for vineyard."

"You are serious about the vineyard?" Mona showed curiosity.

"Of course. I have found an Italian partner who has all the technical knowledge."

"It is a new kind of business you are venturing into. Please make sure it is profitable," Mona raised her concern.

"Sweetheart, do not worry; we can afford it even it goes sour and not a big investment. Besides, it will be my pastime hobby. We are retiring after three years, not now," Pemba assured Mona.

"It is just a word of caution, and thanks for calling, I have to go now."

"Bye."

They both dropped the line.

When Pemba came back from Florida after two days, he was in cloud nine. He described the house compound area with lots of tropical fruits, extremely green area, quiet, peaceful, and in one word, a *paradise*. The description motivated Mona to see the paradise as soon as possible, but she was tied up to her work for a few days.

Pemba liked the house, garden, swimming pool, horse-riding track, and eighteen-hole golf course nearby. The house was equipped with sauna, pool table, Jacuzzi, and exercise room. He even allotted a cozy corner room for his prayer and meditation.

The house had only ground floor, but the spacious rooms were built in Bermuda style, with cross ventilation in 1998. It gave an airy and clear view, overlooking the lake with fountains that could be seen from the sitting area. The palm, papaya, guava, avocado, mango, and tangerine trees occupied a large portion of the backyard, along with vegetable kitchen garden that provided daily salad fresh bowl that looked tempting and offered impulsive and tantalizing effect on human mind. This had urged Pemba to retire immediately and enjoy this paradise with tropical climate in the sunshine state.

Besides, although he was not experienced in vineyard, the fifty-acre land looked just appropriate for producing red and green grapes that should provide a perfect wine.

By all means, Pemba was sold out on this idea and even paid a down payment both for the land and the vineyard. He was in contact with his partner on vineyard from Italy. Lucca had tremendous experience in winery as a grower of famous Malvisa and Trebbiano grapes that provided unique color and fragrance to his wine production plant in Tuscany. Lucca's father learned the art of wine making, working as chief foreman with Banfi winery that had produced the finest wine in the world. After working nearly for nine years, he established his own plant and cultivated quality on both red and green grapes in his own vineyard.

After Lucca's father passed away, within five years, Lucca established himself as a leading and quality wine producer in Italy. His plant won several prestigious wine quality awards in the international market; besides, he was the leading quality wine expert in Italy. He also earned several Italian Government awards in the last three years. He was looking into American market for his growth and expansion. He happened to meet Jack in California during the international wine exhibition last winter. When Pemba expressed his desire to manage a winery with vineyard in Florida during his retirement, that was how he got the contact of Lucca from Jack.

Lucca had shown tremendous interest to establish a vineyard in Florida with a production plant; he was happy to get a proposal from Pemba. On Lucca's invitation, Pemba will travel to Tuscany to see his vineyard and plant as house guest this summer. They had already signed MOU, and final documents would be signed after Pemba's Italy visit and Lucca's visit to Denver in the fall this year. They were both planning to survey the proposed vineyard and plant space in Florida at the same time.

Pemba had been spending his morning time longer in his prayer room that had been occupied by all the gods. After the empty-nest house, he found the place much quieter; and maybe because of the slight depression he had from the departure of his children, it provided time and concentration in his life more than before.

This morning was unusual. As he entered the prayer room, a different kind of sensation he had, a certain celestial feeling that all the gods he worshipped were present in the room. And in fact, the room looked much brighter than usual. He felt a phenomenal vision as if he was in Nepal at the Phaplu house, sitting in his room, and his children, Daniel and Monet, playing with Nintendo; and they were arguing on the game—Monet blaming Daniel for cheating in the game all the time. The house had been renovated with large playground in the backyard, and the front porch was covered now, which had decorated with multicolored flowers. The house had two indoor bathrooms, and the wooden floor was waxed and shined with bright space carpets here and there. As per the vision, both children lived in the same house and went to technical colleges that had been established with the help from the New Zealand Government. Now that the colleges and a university had been established in Phaplu itself, no children needed to go to Kathmandu and overseas for their higher education. The village had progressed a lot, and Pemba had retired.

Pemba could see Mona cooking in the well-equipped kitchen that had a gas burner. Everyone seemed content and had a smile on their faces. Pemba gave up the work at Mountain Travel; he had a small computer factory in the village that produced semiconductors and supplied to Intel, Microsoft, and Apple through a distributor in Hong Kong. Daniel was the manager of the computer company, and Monet was one of the distinguished architects in Nepal, who had several construction projects in Phaplu; she was working as the vice-president of a multinational company that had headquarters in Singapore.

When Pemba looked to a different part of the prayer room—which was darker and did not have that glow that he saw in the left part of room—it was darker and gloomier, and bore a peculiar sensation. He had the vision again: he felt sick with some kind of unknown disease. The medical professionals forbade him to work and carry heavy equipment and recommended him bed rest. Mona was nowhere to be seen in the house. It appeared he was alone, and no one was there to take care of him. His mother had died long time back. Both his children had left him. Daniel was working as a porter with Mountain Travel, and Mona lived with her husband in a small rented room in Kathmandu. They were suffering, as they were deprived of his income and hardly surviving on their own. He just came to know had Mona left him and picked another guy from his village for her new husband. He shivered with the fearful dream and found himself sweating and clenching both his fists tightly. Perhaps the later vision could have been true if he had not left the country and settled in America.

He woke up with strange feelings after the two contrasting visions. One consoled him, and the other was just too scary. Perhaps the gods gave him both the visions of his life that might or might not be true, but it appeared as if it had some kind of hidden meaning in his life—which was exposed as a vision and as something that could have happened if he had stayed in the country. The current phenomenal progress he had in his life could have been impossible in Nepal. The country was a paradise, but how can you enjoy the paradise without resources? This country gave him everything—a lot of money, reputation, flourishing business, and two beautiful children. In fact, Pemba changed and moved his generation to a much desirable life, and he was sure his future generation would flourish in a better way with competent education and better and prosperous life. He was contented, and thanked the gods for the good fortune, blissful life, and brilliant family. This newly adopted country had given him everything, and he had no regret coming here. In fact, this had proved a paradise for him in a genuine manner.

Mona and Pemba hardly had a quiet time for themselves. This evening, they were early from work. They were both in the den watching news channel, which normally carried nothing but murder, shooting, and robbery—all bad news. Pemba turned off the television.

"Are you happy now, Pemba?" Mona suddenly asked.

"What do you mean?"

"I mean, after the children left." Mona asked again.

"Not exactly, but they need independence and their own life."

"Guess so," Mona reflected her moods with a melancholic experience.

"You seem unhappier than me," Pemba said to Mona.

"Yes, I really miss them. Monet's images keep on coming around me."

"You are so close to her; I am sure she also misses you a lot." Pemba expressed his mind.

"She keeps calling me just to say, 'I miss you, Mum.' Well, now we are definite to retire after three years."

"Yes." Pemba supported Mona.

"What are we going to do this house?" Mona raised the curiosity.

"We'll, sell it. What else?"

"I have so many memories attached with it." Mona seemed unhappy.

"Do not worry, you will have new memories in the new house in the paradise," Pemba assured her.

"You keep on saying Florida is a paradise. Do you really feel that way?" Mona asked.

"You have to see it to believe it."

"When are you taking me?" Mona asked again.

"How about going this weekend?"

"That sounds good."

"Should I make the plan?" Pemba asked.

"Sure, I have less responsibility in the restaurant. The guy from Nepal is a soul."

"Okay then." Pemba supported.

"May I ask you a question?" Mona said again.

"Sure, go ahead."

"How much will it cost us to move along with vineyard?" Mona was curious.

"Nearly over two million dollars."

"How much do we get after we sell this house?" Monet put a question.

"Close to one and half million dollars."

"How much cash do we have in the bank at the moment?"

"Close to three million. Also we have bonds and stocks." Pemba answered.

"Tell me roughly how much we will have if converted in liquid cash?" Monet demanded to know.

"I figure, close to six million. We have regular income from the restaurant franchisee fee. Income also comes from the rafting company, and also some revenue from daily restaurant operation."

"Do you have a trust for the children and their expenses?" Mona was concerned.

"I do. We are sending five hundred dollars as pocket money each month, and I am going to raise it to a thousand from next month as Daniel keeps complaining. Also after our retirement, we will establish a trust for them," Pemba explained.

"Pokhara people inform me that we need some repairs in the house," Mona remembered to mention.

"Yes, I have already sent the money. They will repair after the rainy season."

"Do you feel we are going to be happy in Florida after retirement?"

"I see no reason not to be."

"You will be busy in the wine plant. What am I supposed to do?" Mona seemed frustrated.

"You will look after the vineyard, our front and back gardens."

"I would also love to volunteer for disabled rehabilitation for kids." Mona suggested.

"Of course, It is your time; do whatever you like best." Pemba aired his agreement.

The weekend for Florida visit was here. Mona seemed more excited than Pemba for the trip. They took a Friday flight to Miami from Denver and landed in Miami at around three in the afternoon. Mona could see the bright sunshine, blue sky up, and glittering dark-blue sea down just before landing.

They rented a car and drove to Homestead City, which took nearly an hour. On both sides of the roads, Mona could see green fields and meadow with a number water bodies scattered everywhere. It looked pleasant, soothing, and excellent. Lots of palm trees swaying slow and smooth to the blow of the wind provided tranquility and pleasantness. Besides, the bright sunlight, along with spotless cloudless blue sky cheered the human body and mind. In the gloomy and cloudy time, Mona always felt depressed, but this wonderful bright sunshine touched her heart deep inside. They were now in the country road—which was without traffic and pollution and was clean—and after driving for a few minutes out of the city, Pemba pointed toward a bright yellow house and said, "That is our home." It was slow and purposeful statement.

The house occupied a large compound covered with tall fence, a huge front paved driveway surrounded with multicolor flowers, and had a huge Spanish fountain in the middle. The house only had a ground floor; high ceiling led to a huge living room covered with black leather sofa and matching chairs, coffee table, and all the necessary furniture that was decorated in sophisticated Spanish style. The kitchen with all kinds of gadgets and appliances with television and radio, and the color combination was black and white with bright and shining countertop—a large kitchen with ample space. On the right side of the room, a corridor led to master bedroom on the far corner and guest bedroom, which was too far from the master room on the other side of the bend. The guest room was attached with a large bath and equipped with all usual gadgets and entertainment centers. The rooms' decoration and home design was of Bermuda style, open and spacious without walls in the middle.

The house looked airy and open, and grand in design. Mona fell in love with the house immediately. In the backyard, the house had a number of tropical fruit trees along with a big kitchen garden. Surrounding the house were lots of tall green palm trees that provided a dramatically unique atmosphere.

After the campground wall, there was a horse track, which was used by the members for horse ride. Further, after the horse track, a members-only private eighteen-hole golf course was clearly visible. In the backside of the house, another building stood inside the compound. This was a clubhouse equipped with a swimming pool, Jacuzzi, pool table, and table tennis on the other side.

After the house, they drove about ten minutes and arrived at large barren land, which was supposed to be developed for the vineyard. It was in a high place with slopes and provided open sky for the bright sunshine, which was essential for the grapes. As per the soil test, it had enough minerals and all elements to grow quality grapes that were essential for good wine production. The border of the land surrounding the vineyard was also covered with lots of palm and other trees. A pond was situated in the far corner on the left part of vineyard, which looked beautiful with Ibises and pink flamingoes. In the distance, Mona could see the small deer in a group running together under dense tree area.

After observing significantly all around—the green meadow, tall trees, and the glittering body of water in the distance—Mona had nothing to say but a word that came suddenly and spontaneously from her heart: *Paradise*! She heard the word escape her mouth again, "*Paradise*!"

***

